DISABILITY, CULTURE, AND

Alfredo J. Artiles, *Series*

C000160788

A World Away From IEPs

How Disabled Students Learn in Out-of-School Spaces

Erin McCloskey

TEACHERS COLLEGE PRESS

TEACHERS COLLEGE | COLUMBIA UNIVERSITY
NEW YORK AND LONDON

Published by Teachers College Press,® 1234 Amsterdam Avenue, New York, NY 10027

Library of Congress Cataloging-in-Publication Data
Names: McCloskey, Erin, author.
Title: A world away from IEPs : how disabled students learn in out-of-school spaces / Erin McCloskey.
Description: New York : Teachers College Press, 2022. | Series: Disability, culture, and equity series | Includes bibliographical references and index. | Summary: "Step outside of the IEPs and behavioral paperwork currently generated in schools, go where disabled people are thriving today, and see the results in learning, growth, and expression. This authoritative book offers readers alternative ways to think about learning and behavior in special education. Through illustrative case studies and a disability studies lens, author Erin McCloskey uses the voices of people with disabilities to show how these students progress creatively outside the classroom and school building-at the dojo, the riding arena, the theater stage, the music studio, and other community-centered spaces where disabled students can make choices about their learning, their bodies, and their goals. Balancing theory and practice, the book describes alternative learning spaces, demonstrates how disabled students learn there, and passes on the important lessons learned in each space. The ideas apply to students of all ages with a wide variety of disabilities. Book Features: Uses the voices of people with disabilities to promote alternative ways to think about learning and behavior in special education. Presents rich case studies and briefer interludes to illustrate how disabled students are learning and thriving in surprising ways outside of school where they have opportunities to explore. · Distills important key takeaways from each case study through chapter sections of "lessons learned." Promotes informed discussion of the concepts in the book with questions at the end of each chapter. Combines theory and practice to help readers put the concepts into action in a variety of settings with a variety of disabled students"—Provided by publisher.
Identifiers: LCCN 2021048648 (print) | LCCN 2021048649 (ebook) | ISBN 9780807766729 (paperback) | ISBN 9780807766736 (hardcover) | ISBN 9780807780916 (ebook)
Subjects: LCSH: Children with disabilities—Education. | People with disabilities—Education. | Experiential learning. | Non-formal education.
Classification: LCC LC4015 .M39 2022 (print) | LCC LC4015 (ebook) | DDC 371.9—dc23/eng/20211109
LC record available at https://lccn.loc.gov/2021048648
LC ebook record available at https://lccn.loc.gov/2021048649

ISBN 978-0-8077-6672-9 (paper)
ISBN 978-0-8077-6673-6 (hardcover)
ISBN 978-0-8077-8091-6 (ebook)

Printed on acid-free paper
Manufactured in the United States of America

Contents

Preface

Special education emerged as a part of the educational landscape when I started 1st grade in 1975. I did not know it then, but disability and ableism would shape the rest of my life.

I started my teaching life as a 20-year-old junior in art school. My mom was concerned about an artist's meager salary, so she encouraged me to consider art education. I started working with disabled youth at a city hospital, where my mentor encouraged me to pursue a master's degree in special education; it was in this graduate school experience that I felt a dissonance between my experiences as a teacher and being taught to be a teacher (for more on this, see McCloskey, 2021).

In this graduate program, my textbooks told me how to diagnose, teach, and remediate "special needs" students. However, my students at the hospital and later in special education schools, juvenile detention centers, high schools, middle schools, and elementary schools taught me differently. The textbooks did not mention the beauty, creativity, or humor that I saw in my students every day. The individualized education programs, or IEPs, were a world away from describing how my students learned and moved in daily life.

Most of my writing about special education has been critical, and while I note the positive aspects of special education in the first chapter of this book, I continue to critique how learning and behavior are structured in schools for disabled students through paperwork meant to describe how these students learn and behave. This critique is necessary, not because it is novel, but because the rest of the book challenges how special education structures our understanding of learning and behavior in schools. Learning and behaving cannot be reduced to goals and objectives on a piece of paper. Learning is a journey, and behavior is a form of communication.

In one of my earliest positions as a special education teacher a high school in Brooklyn, NY, I retaught or pretaught material in a resource room for half of the day and taught self-contained special education English classes for the second half. For the self-contained classes, I read through each student's IEP and discovered that some students were reading at grade level, some were below, some were new to the English language, and some had interrupted schooling that impacted their knowledge base in different ways. The goals on their IEPs were written the year before I met them. The students in these classes were diagnosed with disabilities, including learning disabilities, emotional/behavioral disabilities, speech and language impairments, and other health impairments.

I felt set up to fail. I soon realized that one student diagnosed with an emotional/behavioral disability seemed to have very little academic need for this self-contained special education English class. Another student, a 14-year-old recent arrival to the United States from Central America, had never learned how to read. Still other students struggled with literacy tasks but were so adept at knowing how to "do" school that they could fill in worksheets without reading them. These students deserved instruction that was engaging and meaningful to their lives, but it was difficult to transfer most of their IEP goals to meaningful instruction.

I sought out seasoned special education teachers for help, including my mentor, whose assistance was provided to new teachers by the New York City Board of Education. Some seasoned teachers told me to ignore the IEPs and design engaging lessons that would motivate my students to participate. Others told me to find packaged curriculum and assign different lessons to different students, and to walk around the classroom helping each child individually. Some said to give rewards when students completed the work assigned and to call home if "these kids" gave me any trouble. When I told my assigned mentor that one student threatened to throw a desk at me if I didn't give him an A, she told me to just give him the A because most likely he would just drop out anyway. Unfortunately, he did, and as I learned later, the dropout rates for disabled students then were about twice that of general education students (Hehir, 2005). Today, although there has been progress, the odds of disabled students graduating in some states lingers around 58 percent but in others the rates can be as high as 83 percent. It is worth noting that in every state, graduation rates for disabled students are lower than they are for their nondisabled peers (Johnson, Thurlow, Qiahn, & Anderson, 2019).

I moved around as a special education teacher, receiving and leaving tenured positions, hoping that the next school would be different. In my doctoral program, I began to understand that it was the system of special education, not the individual schools, that was causing my uneasiness. The system of special education had legal requirements that made it difficult to talk about learning in ways other than those structured by the IEP. I learned that special education was seen as a fix for students considered to have behavior problems, but rarely did or could these special education classrooms or schools fix the trauma these students had experienced. Sometimes these special education classrooms were a stop along the school-to-prison pipeline (Laura, 2014). My experiences only intensified when my first son was diagnosed as Autistic at the age of two.

As the mother of an Autistic son (who is now 17 years old and has given his permission for me to share this), one of the hardest parts of parenting was meeting with school officials about his educational, emotional, and behavioral needs. I was constantly pushing back against the medical model of disability and continually reminding myself that these professionals' predictions about him were just guesses. I tried to understand the intense complexities of these meetings by writing about them (e.g., McCloskey, 2013, 2019). Sometimes I needed to refuse therapy and placements I felt were harmful to his growth. I did not feel, then or now, that my son needed to be fixed, yet many interventions were designed to do just that. For example, my son's stimming behaviors, including rocking back and forth, help him regulate his body. Different therapists wanted to add IEP goals to stop this behavior. His pediatrician wanted to prescribe medicine. By thinking about disability as a medical condition, they were targeting aspects of his being that helped him, or they were trying to remediate a behavior they viewed as "abnormal" or distracting to his neurotypical peers. I needed to decide when I would push back against this ableist thinking at his school and doctor meetings. As he grew older, he could participate in making decisions, but while he was younger, it was my responsibility. The big and small decisions would structure his experiences and his identity as a disabled person. They would shape how he understood disability.

Parenting gave me an additional lens I did not have as a teacher. As I faced the many decisions about what was best for my own son, a constant tension existed between how special education structured his time in school versus experiences we had outside of school. The complexity of my son's personhood could never be accurately described in special education paperwork. Hearing and watching people view him in particular ways, in particular settings, was, at times, a lot, especially when they negated or dismissed *his* perspective.

Special education teachers often receive training about particular behavioral approaches, how to deliver individualized learning, and what it might be like to have students with certain disabilities in their classrooms. In the classroom detailed in Chapter 1, we see teachers delivering candy to students who complete a task as anticipated or respond to a question in the way the teacher wanted. In other learning spaces, outside of school, we witness students participating in learning events because of an internal desire to learn and be a part of the learning community, and because they feel control over the learning environment and their bodies in that learning environment.

In contrast to Chapter 1, Chapters 2, 3, 4, and 5 explore and celebrate the learning of disabled students outside of school to show how learning and behavior are nurtured when students are able to shed the paperwork written about them. Further, each chapter, written with the practitioner in mind, distills important concepts that can be brought into the classroom, although they are by no means exhaustive of all that there is to learn in these spaces. By looking outside of school, the reader gets insight into how teaching and learning happen in authentic and surprising ways, with seasoned practition-ers who view disability differently than the paperwork designed to regulate learning and behavior. We travel to the dojo, the riding arena, the theater stage, and the music studio where disabled students are learning and thriv-ing, where community is centered, and where disabled students get to make choices about their learning, their bodies, and their goals.

Between each of these substantial chapters are small interludes about other spaces where students are learning outside of school. These brief in-terludes are included to provide further portraits of the multitude of spaces outside of school where disabled children are learning. We look at pro-grams that are designed to include disabled students with their disabled and nondisabled peers, to develop literacy skills in a supportive and calm environment, to develop teamwork and collegiality, and to develop disabled students' math and business skills.

How I describe disability in this book has been informed by disabled people. I use identity-first language rather than person-first language. At first, it might be jarring for the reader to encounter the phrasing "disabled person" or "Autistic person" rather than "person with a disability" or "per-son on the spectrum" or "special needs." Identity-first language, as shared by Murray (2018), is used to express pride in one's identity as a disabled person and to express community in a culture. Disability is an integral part of people's identity and not an add-on to who they are as a person.

Finally, I share the beginnings of my own counterstory, offering the reader one version of how the ideas that are presented in the chapters might transfer to the classroom. I invite you to continue the story or create your own—and to help make the words on paper become real possibilities for transforming how we currently structure learning and behavior in special education.

Acknowledgments

I am forever changed by meeting the people who so graciously and enthusiastically participated in this project. Thank you for all the time you spent talking with me, for allowing me to linger in the corners, on the bleachers, in the wings, and all the other places where I could witness the incredible teaching and learning that were taking place. I am so grateful for our time together.

Thank you to my own educators, in and out of school, who have taught me that learning has no boundaries and happens everywhere, especially Bernarda Ghuneim-Jesinkey, whose lessons, love, and passion I miss every day.

To my family, biological and chosen, who continue to support and humor me, I extend my deepest love and gratitude.

Thank you to all of the past, present, and future scholars who locate their work in Disability Studies in Education for creating a research home.

I'm so grateful to work in the Education Department at Vassar College and to be surrounded by such fierce researchers and colleagues. I'm grateful to the Vassar College Research Committee for awarding me financial assistance through the Elinor N. Brink Fund. This support allowed me to work with Rose Ernst, whose editorial support was invaluable and helped make me a better writer. Thank you, Rose!

To my hearts, Chris, Wyatt, and Liam Sell, you all inspire me in different ways: Chris, your tenaciousness in the ways you love me; Wyatt, your incredible determination and pursuit for equity and to be included; Liam, your passion for creativity and joy. My unending love is always yours.

CHAPTER 1

A Special Education

It's winter and it's cold. I hurry into the school, The Special Center, that I am visiting today as the wind whips and the trees sway. Like most schools in the United States today, there are locked double doors, and I am not buzzed into the lobby of the school until I speak to a box on the outside wall to explain who I am and why I am here. I show the receptionist my driver's license through the glass window, and once she verifies that I have an appointment, a buzzer sounds and I pull the heavy door open. I enter the lobby where there are a few chairs, some children's books on the small side table, and a teacher chatting with the receptionist about a family party she attended over the weekend. I take a seat in one of the chairs while the receptionist calls the administrator, Ms. Martin, who I have an appointment with. Ms. Martin has offered to provide me with an introduction to the school and has created a schedule of classrooms I can visit today. I'll spend all day at the school and see many different classrooms and therapy rooms. The receptionist informs me that Ms. Martin is running a few minutes behind and will be with me shortly. I'm happy to sit in the lobby and wait.

It's about 9:20 in the morning and a few parents, all women, intermittently enter the school with their children in tow. The students are officially late to school, but no none mentions this. When the receptionist sees a student and a mother walking up the school, she immediately buzzes them in. The student and parent are greeted by the receptionist. The parent stays by their child's side until a teaching assistant from the child's classroom is called to come and retrieve the late student from their parent. Each time, the teaching assistant expresses joy at seeing the student. There is genuine warmth in this exchange. Some of the children seem to be a little anxious, but this seems to fade once the teaching assistant greets them. The children then seem to easily separate from their parent and walk with the teaching assistant to their classroom, sometimes holding hands, as the teaching assistant engages the child in casual conversation about the weather or what is for lunch.

The Special Center is a "special school" designed for students who are diagnosed with autism spectrum disorder, attention deficit hyperactivity disorder, and/or emotional or behavioral disorders. Every student in this school has an individualized education program (IEP), and the majority have a

1

behavior intervention plan (BIP). These two documents, which will be discussed in detail later in this chapter, describe the learning and behavior goals for individual students and guide teachers when they plan instruction and monitor classroom behavior.

I was told it would be best to arrive at about 9:15 because there are many buses that fill the parking lot before that. The Special Center, like many other special schools, enrolls students from across this county of approximately 180,000 people and occasionally from neighboring counties as well. Unlike neighborhood schools, students can travel from over an hour away to attend this school. Most arrive in small buses or vans, and at pickup and drop-off times, these vehicles snake almost completely around this one-story building. The child's home school district pays for transportation and for the children's attendance at this school, usually because the district does not offer a comparable program and the students' educational and/or behavioral needs are said to be too complex to be met by schools in their district. Most districts in this county transport their students with "substantial needs" to not-for-profit private schools because it is usually less costly to send a student out of the district rather than to create programming in the district. For the students, this means that if they started school in their home district, they are then removed and transported away from their neighborhood friends and from their siblings. It can also mean that the friends they make at The Special Center can live hours away, making it hard to get together outside of school. Parents are often faced with the very difficult decision of deciding whether to send their children away from their home district schools, where they can receive access to special education services and programs, or keeping them in their home district, where these services and programs may not be available. The children who attend The Special Center are anywhere from 4 years old to 12 years old, but separate special schools are available for disabled youth until they are 21 years old, at which point they age out of special education.

DECISION-MAKING AND SPECIAL EDUCATION

There are many decisions that need to be made once a parent/guardian enters the system of special education. These decisions can be life-changing for disabled children, and when they are young, it is difficult to include them in this decision-making. Parents can feel pressured by school officials, doctors, and other professionals to acquiesce to placements or services they are unsure about (McCloskey, 2010, 2012b).

Because special education was created as a parallel system and not as a part of general education, decisions about the "right" place for disabled youth entail discussions about how far removed they should be from general education (Connor & Ferri, 2007; Gartner & Lipsky, 1992). The Special

Center is an example of a placement where students are removed from general education completely, but there are many other options. However, special education is designed to be a set of services and not a placement, so deciding on placement can be complicated.

PLACEMENT

Deciding *where* a child might best benefit from special education services and programs happens in meetings where parents/guardians and school officials come together to form a committee on special education or an individualized education program (IEP) team. Where a student receives their special education services and program should be in the "least restrictive environment." Determining what constitutes the least restrictive environment happens through discussions at these IEP team meetings, where standardized test results are reviewed, teachers provide insight about the student's day-to-day learning in the classroom, and parents share what they observe in spaces outside of school. The law states "that to the maximum extent appropriate, children with disabilities . . . are educated with children who are nondisabled," "as close as possible to the child's home, "in the school he or she would attend if not disabled" (National Council on Disability, 2018, p. 18). When IEP teams decide that special schools are the least restrictive environment for disabled students, they are saying that the student's neighborhood school and the teachers inside that school cannot provide the support, accommodations, and academic instruction that the disabled student needs. Enrollment in a special school is the clearest demarcation of not belonging, as being too disabled, and for many students, the only place where this demarcation exists. Society in general does not have these boundaries. School is the only place where disabled youth experience special education and this level of separateness. Special education does not exist at the grocery store, movie theater, bowling alley, or religious services, and yet, disabled people are learning in all of these places, too.

Being removed from the general education classrooms has lifelong implications for disabled students and their peers. Even if disabled students are removed for a small portion of their day, say in a resource room within a general education school for 45 minutes a day, which is considered a less restrictive environment, all students learn that difference requires segregation. Strong messages about disability are sent to students, teachers, parents, and the community.

Learning or behavior needs are often the two most prominent reasons given for moving disabled youth to more restrictive settings. There are many research studies that investigate how decisions about the least restrictive environment are made in IEP team meetings (for example, Barnard-Brak & Lechtenberger, 2010; Fish, 2008; Wolfe & Durán, 2013; Zeitlin & Curcic,

2013). In the chapters that follow, we witness disabled people learning in different settings, outside of special education, where learning and behaviors are thought about differently. But first, let's turn to how learning is approached in special education.

LEARNING AND SPECIAL EDUCATION

When special education was created, it became important to detail how learning would look different for disabled students, and this has led to particular ways to describe and capture learning. In 1973, the Rehabilitation Act, and 2 years later, PL 94-142, the Education for All Handicapped Children Act, later renamed the Individuals with Disabilities Education Act, or IDEA, were created to ensure that all students who were determined to have a disability were guaranteed a legal right to a free and appropriate public education. This free and appropriate public education, oftentimes referred to as FAPE, would be detailed on the IEP, which is a legal document. This document is a written plan for each disabled student's "special education," detailing annual measurable goals for the student along with the services and accommodations the student will receive in their educational placement. Creating measurable annual goals once a year to comply with special education law meant that learning needed to be described in a certain way. A learning task needs to be isolated, an acceptable accuracy rate denotes that the skill has been learned, how this accuracy rate will be measured is described, and who will measure this learning is added. This four-part way of describing learning creates only certain kinds of learning opportunities. For example, here is a reading comprehension goal on the IEP of 9-year-old Patrick, who you will meet in Chapter 3. Patrick's mother related that he was diagnosed with a developmental disability and attention deficit hyperactivity disorder. This is the goal that is supposed to help Patrick strengthen his reading comprehension:

> Patrick will answer factual questions about reading (who, what, when, where, and how) 4 out of 5 times correctly, as measured by teacher checklists and worksheets, every marking period.

When I ask Patrick's mom about this goal, she mentions that Patrick does not like to read, probably because he has to complete a lot of worksheets. Then she continues, "But he does like when I read to him. He likes stories. I think he doesn't like worksheets because they're not interesting."

For students like Patrick, reading becomes an activity where he needs to answer certain questions with certain answers in order to be correct at least 4 out of 5 times. For many disabled youths, learning is structured to be the transmission of information from the teacher to the person and it measured in concrete ways, such as with worksheets. Freire (1968) referred to this style of teaching and learning as the banking model, where teachers transmit knowledge and students are viewed as empty receptacles to receive that knowledge. With IEP goals, each learning act must be measured according to how the teacher understands or interprets the disabled person's response. Of course, there are lots of placements that disabled youth can find themselves in at school: inclusive general education classrooms, integrated classrooms, small special education classes, or special schools like The Special Center. Still, the IEP structures learning experiences to unfold in a certain way, whether or not a teacher chooses to orchestrate the learning experience or measure it the way the IEP describes it. This creates tension for special education teachers, particularly if teachers want to design their instruction to include groups of children working and learning together. Furthermore, a transmission approach to teaching and learning focuses almost entirely on completion of the skill, and no attention is given to the path by which knowledge is developed. This can make it hard for special education teachers to develop a sense of a child's learning journey, and the focus becomes entirely devoted to results.

I've been thinking about the IEP for quite some time, over 30 years. There are parts of the IEP that I think are helpful—areas that detail a student's strengths, information added by parents, and summaries of the meetings had about the student. The IEP guarantees families legal rights to make sure that their disabled children receive services, accommodations, assistive technology, and more. School districts could easily say they are going to provide certain services and then decide not to. The IEP gives parents a written legal document of what their children are entitled to and holds school districts accountable for providing those services and accommodations. Before laws that guaranteed disabled students a free and appropriate public education, they were not only denied an education, but many were also shuttled off to institutions, taken away from their families, and all but warehoused in large industrial buildings with no educational programming. The IEP has substantial benefits.

The IEP also has, in my opinion, some serious drawbacks. Specifically, I have concerns about how learning and behavioral goals get translated to practice in classrooms. My goal in writing this book is to open up conversations about our understandings concerning how learning is framed in schools for disabled students. Learning, as described on the IEP, doesn't represent what I think of as real learning or real teaching—the sort of learning and teaching that are meaningful. This is not to say that special education teachers are not providing meaningful learning experiences for their students, but I believe that the way learning goals are structured on IEPs do not assist them in doing so. I contend that we can find this dynamic learning and teaching in out-of-school spaces when the IEP is not the center of the learning experience.

Learning goals on students' IEPs usually detail finite tasks to be completed, but there are also big consequences for students when it is believed that their learning must be individualized. For disabled students who are placed in general education settings, this individualization might have very little impact on their learning because they are part of a class where their classmates do not have this educational requirement for individualization. In these settings, disabled students may be included in reading and math groups, small- and large-group instruction, and project-based learning. But for disabled students in exclusively special education placements, like The Special Center, individualization can be costly to students' learning, social, and emotional needs.

INDIVIDUALIZED LEARNING

Students who attend The Special Center do so because it has been decided that this school is the least restrictive environment for them. The regular education, inclusive, and self-contained special education classrooms that were available in these students' districts were determined to not be conducive to their learning needs. The instruction at The Special Center is designed to be different, to offer a different experience for its disabled students and provide extra supports that might be needed, such as a sensory room and a break room that is padded for students who pose a risk to themselves or others. On my visit, this padded room remained empty. During my time as a special education teacher in both a special school for students with emotional/behavioral disabilities and at a juvenile detention center, I have witnessed students being taken to padded rooms, and for me, it is soul-crushing. Students at their most vulnerable are isolated, and many times their cries are ignored. Others have written elsewhere about the trauma of being sent to these padded rooms (see, for example, Aviv, 2018). I have talked with many parents who have refused to send their children to schools with these rooms, even though their districts recommend them. And yet, it is these sorts of arrangements that make these schools "special."

Because The Special Center is different from a traditional elementary school, learning and teaching will need to look different here, and indeed it does. During my tour, I see children working individually with teachers and staff, counting money, giving answers to flash cards, and filling in worksheets, and in one classroom, children as young as 5 are learning "life skills"—they are folding laundry and pouring water. I am told that each child's IEP dictates what they will learn in their classrooms and that there are two major divisions of classrooms: those that are academic in nature and those that will teach life skills.

It is at The Special Center where I witness how teaching devoted exclusively to IEP goals plays out, and this proves to be perhaps an extreme example. But in my own experience as a special education teacher and researcher, the IEP drives instruction, even in less restrictive settings such as resource room or inclusive classes, because special education teachers are responsible for evaluating whether or not IEP learning goals are met. They are also responsible for writing learning goals for IEPs, but this typically means that teachers choose from a bank of goals, and these are not specifically written for individual children. Most districts have IEP management software and teachers access this software and choose goals, and they are electronically added to the student's IEP. Importantly, because learning is often framed using the IEP, conversations with parents can be focused on goal completion. Rarely in these conversations is the student's perspective about learning activities present. As one parent interviewed for this research project stated, "My other daughter [nondisabled and in general education] wrote in journals and joined book clubs and did research projects and Charlie [her disabled son in a self-contained special education classroom] comes home with stacks of worksheets that couldn't be more boring."

There are also software and apps available to teachers and school districts to assess how students are progressing on their IEP goals. These different programs allow teachers to track learning by checking off when a goal has been reached. Because special education is grounded in legal proceedings, having proof of learning is tantamount. At The Special Center, all teachers keep multiple binders for each of their students, and they submit these binders to the administrators of the school at the end of the year. The school keeps these binders in case the state education authorities audit the school or they become involved in a lawsuit.

At The Special Center, there is one special education teacher and at least five teaching assistants, usually more, in each classroom of approximately eight children. The special education teacher is in charge of preparing the individualized learning for each child, and the assistants sit individually or sometimes, but less often, in pairs with the students to complete the tasks the teacher has determined will move them toward making progress their IEP goals. Each activity is a task for the student to complete and a form for the assistant to mark off if it was done correctly. For example, one students' goal was to correctly identify money. The child was asked, "What is this?" and he would need to respond "dime." The child was tasked with identifying both coins and bills. The students in this class stay with the teaching assistant until the teacher says it's time to move. The student I observed, Frankie, spent over 10 minutes identifying the same 4 coins and 4 bills. When he "lost focus," the teacher would cajole him into paying attention, usually by saying his name repeatedly until he looked at the money. The student started the activity knowing all eight coins and bills and proved it to the assistant over 20 times. After about 10 times, the assistant began giving the student candy to keep his interest, and she praised him repeatedly. After every set of coins, he received a small chocolate candy. It was the same for the bills. When the teacher announced it was time to switch, he moved to another teaching assistant and read words off flash cards for about 10 minutes. He also received candy for his correct answers. Then he was allowed some downtime but was told he needed to be sitting at his desk and doing something independently. There were not many toys or materials available, as a way to purposefully make sure that the classroom was not overstimulating for the students. The minimal decorations and materials in this classroom, and in every classroom I visited in this school, were by design to keep the atmosphere clear of anything that might distract students. One student put together an eight-piece puzzle again and again. The teaching assistant told me this was her favorite activity. Another student drew with pencil on a piece of lined paper. Another student flipped through a book about cars she had brought from home. Frankie decided to put his head down on the table and rest.

As I watched Frankie, I was struck by how different he was in this space as compared to the dojo, the out-of-school space I explore in Chapter 2. Here he was resigned, and in the dojo, he was just the opposite. Frankie attended the dojo sporadically, but I recognized him immediately. At the dojo, he was energetic, but here, he seemed so lethargic. In his classroom he is expected to sit and repeat information he knows and memorize new information so he can repeat it back to the teacher on another day. In the dojo, he worked with others and was a part of the group.

When learning is structured as the transmission of information from teacher to student, learning becomes unidirectional. When students are taught individually, they become isolated from their classmates. I actually witnessed teachers become fearful when students approached other students. In my observations of many different classrooms at The Special Center, there were no group lessons, not one. The teachers did not read children's books aloud to the class, and there were no class meetings where students gathered to talk about the day or share an experience from home. Of course, this should not be taken to mean that this doesn't happen at all in special education classrooms, but what I am suggesting here is that as students are placed in more restrictive placements, their learning situations also become more restrictive. The Special Center is among the most restrictive environments, barring a hospital or residential setting. The implementation of the IEP appears to drive all teaching decisions, and individualization is prioritized over building community.

It's understandable that learning might be restrictive when special educators are asked to design teaching and learning settings to include an array of students at different grade levels and with different strengths and needs. The structure of the IEP does not lend itself to thinking about instruction as a part of developing social, emotional, and behavioral skills. The restrictiveness of what constitutes a learning goal lends itself to learning that is cut-and-dried and assessment of that learning as either right or wrong.

Controlling learning so tightly can lead disabled students to disconnect from school, and they can communicate these feelings of disconnect in ways that are seen as inappropriate to school officials. Communication for many disabled youths, particularly for those who communicate in nonverbal ways, can be seen on one end of the spectrum as disruptive and on the other end as explosive. Stagnant learning environments dictated by such tightly worded learning goals lead to strong feelings. When disabled students express these feelings, they may appear different from how nondisabled people communicate strong feelings. The perspective of the disabled student might be overlooked, and the behavior is usually not viewed as a form of communication but rather as an outburst or problem to be dealt with. My observation of Paul, a student in a special education classroom within a general education school, provides an example of this.

BEHAVIOR AND SPECIAL EDUCATION

When Paul, an Autistic student, was in the 4th grade, he was in a classroom that used an approach that had all eight students in his class working in separate "offices." Few opportunities were available to socialize or interact with his peers in this classroom. This school, like many others I have worked in and visited, integrated its students in special education into "nonacademic" classes such as art, music, and gym. Recess was also an integrated environment. Paul was very interested in developing social bonds with his peers in general education. In his gym class, he reached out to a boy, a general education student, and tried to talk with him. The boy shut him down and called him an "idiot." This upset Paul so much that he sat down on the floor, cried, and refused to participate in any gym activities. Paul was so upset that he could not verbally communicate to the teacher what had happened. Paul sat cross-legged on the floor, hitting his head with his closed fists. The teacher had his hands full with a gym full of approximately 35 students, so he called the principal to have Paul removed from the gym. When the principal came into the gym and Paul saw him, he took off running. Once he was caught, Paul's mom was called to come and pick him up. The school was considering suspending him, but Paul's mom believed that Paul's disability was a major reason why he exhibited this behavior. At home, Paul told his mom what the boy said to him. To address Paul's inappropriate behavior, the school requested an outside agency to come and complete an assessment called a functional behavioral assessment (FBA). This assessment included observations of Paul in his classroom and discussions with Paul's classroom teacher and other teachers and assistants who interacted with Paul. When this assessment was completed, a behavior intervention plan (BIP) was written for Paul that described what behaviors needed to be fixed. When the behavior was correctly displayed, Paul would get a reward, and when Paul behaved incorrectly, there would be a consequence. This document structured behavior goals much like learning goals on the IEP in that Paul would exhibit the desired behavior or he would not. All the focus would be on Paul.

There were a lot of factors that led to Paul's behavior, and his general education classmate's too, that went unrecognized. Perhaps there were racial implications because Paul is African American and the general education student is White. Maybe because Paul's classroom was structured into individual learning spaces where little interaction occurred, he needed support to reach out and make friends. Maybe the general education student needed support to manage this interaction in an appropriate way. Still, the only factor that was addressed was Paul and his behavior, even though the general education classmate's response to his desire to play was both ableist and mean. There was never any context given to Paul's situation, and the price that Paul would pay for this would be extreme. The BIP would now play a large role in Paul's school day. For disabled youth, the more "severe" a child's behavior is determined to be, the more restrictive responses to behaviors become (Hart, Cramer, Harry, Klinger, & Sturges, 2010; Shyman, 2015). The BIP becomes the vehicle for this restrictiveness.

The reauthorization of IDEA in 2004 led to the creation of the BIP. While the IEP isolates learning goals, the BIP is written to isolate behavioral goals. Paul ended up with four behavioral goals on his BIP, two as a direct result of this incident. The behavior to be changed is described as "Inappropriate Social Boundaries." To change Paul's behavior, the alternative behavior that Paul should start exhibiting is:

> Increasing appropriate social interactions with others including peers—Asking peers to play and interact during leisure times in a socially appropriate way, accepting when peers do not want to play and making wants and needs known to staff in a socially appropriate way.

The other behavior to change from this incident was titled "Elopement," defined as "running away from activities which includes leaving the classroom or the immediate area." Here, the correct behavior to display is "Communicating wants and needs in a socially appropriate way which includes increasing appropriate social interactions with others including peers and indicating the need for 'help' or a 'break.'"

Although isolated from other students in his classroom and only given opportunities to socialize with peers during "nonacademic" time, in classes that use an entirely different approach to learning than his special education classroom, Paul, and only Paul, was what needed to be fixed. Paul's class was integrated into the general education gym class because there was no time in the day to have a separate special education gym class.

There was never any preparation work done, with either the general or special education students, to facilitate this. The gym teacher did not receive special training about how to work with this large integrated group. And yet the consequence for Paul, when he engages in one of these "inappropriate behaviors," ranges from reviewing rules with a teacher or assistant, being removed from the situation, or being blocked from leaving the situation. Glaringly missing is that these behaviors are driven by feelings and that staff are never instructed to try to *understand why* Paul reacted as he did. In fact, when Paul's mother later tried to explain to the principal what happened with his general education peer in gym class, the principal expressed skepticism that this incident occurred in the manner described by Paul.

Disabled people have voiced major concerns about this approach to behavior intervention. The Autistic Self Advocacy Network (ASAN) shares in their position statement that this sort of approach to behavior that provides rewards and punishments does not, "teach us the skills we actually need to navigate the world with our disabilities" and, importantly, "any therapy should help autistic people get what we want and need, not what other people think we need" (Autistic Self Advocacy Network, 2022). Controlling disabled students' bodies according to how nondisabled people understand behavior is a key component of the BIP.

All students' bodies are controlled in school to some degree. There is no arguing that permission must be granted for students to engage in a range of activities. Still, in special education, these actions are hyperscrutinized when students have BIPs because teachers and other school officials are tasked with monitoring behaviors and so they are constantly looking for behaviors that might go unnoticed in other contexts. In fact, assessment of the BIP is usually taken in the form of tally marks each time the behavior is noticed. These marks are then used to discuss, usually in meetings that exclude the disabled student, whether there is improvement. For example, if Paul were to ask a friend to play with him at recess and was told some form of no, it would be unacceptable for him to respond by showing sadness or anger. Paul is supposed to walk away and find someone else to ask. If any school personnel witnessed Paul crying about this event, they would report it as an instance of Paul showing the incorrect behavior. This would be officially noted, tallied, and shared. Yet these behaviors and responses happen for many children in school and go unreported. By virtue of having the paperwork, the disabled student becomes hypersurveilled.

My 30-year career teaching in, teaching about, and researching practices regarding special education has led me to wonder about the benefits and drawbacks of such scripted learning and behavior goals. Paperwork written about students leads to a transmission approach to learning and teaching, which so often creates tension for teachers. This research was designed to do something different. I want to highlight the engaged learning that disabled people are doing and celebrate the places that are rich learning communities.

My hope is that if we get a full picture of how disabled people engage in spaces outside of school, we can imagine ways to build community, create authentic learning experiences, and provide spaces for disabled people to engage creatively. My hope is also that we might view behavior differently, as a form of communication that needs to be understood from the perspective of the student. We also witness that behavior intervention becomes almost nonexistent when learning opportunities are rich and varied. I designed this research project around two central questions that would allow me to do this. The research project that is described in the chapters that follow investigates these research questions:

1. How do disabled students learn and behave in spaces outside of school when there is no paperwork to guide their learning and behavior?
2. What can we learn from the disabled people and those who teach in these spaces that can be brought back into the classroom?

Collecting data to inform these questions would be the next step, and equally important would be to design an approach that rethought learning in special education contexts, was built on a disability studies in education approach (DSE), and was grounded in case study research.

THEORY AND METHOD

The empirical research at the heart of this book is grounded in three theoretical and methodological approaches that are dependent on one another. First, I chose to define learning quite differently than how it is understood in special education. I view learning not as isolated tasks to complete but as complex pathways. Second, I chose to look *with* disabled people rather than *at* them. This distinction is hugely important because the majority of research done in special education is conducted by looking at disabled students without including them in the research. Third, I utilized qualitative case study methods and analysis to describe these complex learning pathways and highlight the contexts in which these learning opportunities are made possible.

Rethinking Learning in Special Education

Capturing the learning that participants in this space engaged in was informed by thinking about learning not as skills, goals, or objectives to be met, but as pathways that can "support a more nuanced account of learning—the settings in which it occurs, the time scales across which it occurs, and the dynamics of power as a key focus for analyzing how race, gender, language, disability, and other dynamics become consequential in learning setting and for learners" (Nasir, McKinney de Royston, Barron, Bell, Pea, Stevens, & Goldman, 2020).

Nasir et al. (2020) promote a new lens by which to view learning, one that is desperately needed in special education, that moves away from the transmission view of teaching and learning to one that weaves "together a number of complementary strands of research into the cognitive, physical, emotional and social dimensions of learning" (p. 10). Using the acronym RISE, McKinney de Royston, Lee, Nasir, & Pea (2020) suggest that we view learning as

- Rooted in our bodies and brains, which (according to a growing body of scientific evidence) can never be separated from our social and cultural practices.
- Integrated with every other aspect of human development, including emotion, cognition, and the formation of identity.
- Shaped through the culturally organized activities of everyday life, both in and out of school and across the life span.
- Experienced in our bodies and coordinated through social interactions with the world and others. (p. 10)

Using RISE principles, assessment then is not only the measurement of discrete tasks that are accomplished with a certain accuracy, but rather the noticing of development and growth along the way. Special education practice and policy need to take up McKinney de Royston et al.'s charge to rethink what it means to learn. When learning pathways are linked to other possible identities (being a judo player, an actor, a musician, and/or an equestrian), learning and an identity as a learner are both reinforced—the relationship is bidirectional (Nasir, 2002).

Thinking about learning in this manner corresponds nicely with a Disability Studies in Education (DSE) approach to conducting research with disabled people—an approach to research that is both theory and method. A DSE approach to looking at disability rejects a deficit model of disability and promotes full and meaningful access to educational opportunities.

Disability Studies in Education

A DSE approach to research that includes disabled people is dedicated to privileging the "interests, agendas, and voices of people labeled with disability/disabled people" (Valle & Connor, 2011, p. 32). In my own schooling to become a special educator, I was taught that special education was a rational system by which disabled students got the help they needed (Skrtic, 1992). I learned about policies such as IDEA and the right of disabled people to have an IEP, provided in the least restrictive environment. I was taught how to deliver standardized academic tests that would pinpoint the functioning of disabled students and then to create learning goals that were supposed to move them forward in their learning. As shared previously, what I learned in my classes was many times at odds with my ethics and teaching philosophy. When I started researching and writing about special education, I connected to people using a critical lens, and eventually found my way to a group of people who used disability studies as an entry to thinking about special education. Researchers using a DSE approach questioned the scientific knowledge base of special education (Gallagher, 1998), guided my understanding of how ideologies about disability negatively influenced dominant researchers' views on inclusion (Brantlinger, 1997), and helped me to critique the dual system of special and general education (Gartner & Lipsky, 1992). Ware (2001) also challenged me to bring disability as a topic into my own classrooms. My experiences very much mirror Connor's (2014) in that with DSE I too "immediately found a 'home' that reflected my long-held beliefs about human differences that were not represented within special education structures, schooling systems, and educational research" (para. 4).

While special education is a school structure, DSE casts a larger net. This is a simple but important concept that guides the chapters to come. I believe that special education asks disabled students to behave and learn differently than their peers. Inclusive classrooms are school structures that work to include disabled students, but they remain contrived, allowing only a certain number of disabled students or only students with certain "kinds" of disabilities or both. Disabled people are often asked to prove that they belong in inclusive or integrated settings by performing in certain ways, academically and behaviorally. And even in inclusive settings, as Watson (2017) details in her study of early childhood inclusive classrooms, "The discourses and practices of special education continue to separate and isolate *in* the classroom, and actively create a somewhere else for the marked to 'be', and potentially, to 'be cured'" (p. 13, emphasis in original).

Many scholars who apply a DSE approach to their research do so out of a concern for "issues and problems as defined by disabled people and as they related to social exclusions and oppression" (Gabel, 2005, p. 17). Using DSE as a theoretical standpoint, scholars have critiqued and celebrated theory, policy, and practice. Importantly, DSE has shaped the kinds of questions that guide research, and how the researcher chooses to look for answers to those questions. Here, Collins (2015) best describes my intent, as one to "recognize, include and learn from the experiences of people who have been positioned in special education categories or labeled as having a disability" (p. 219).

DSE allows for a jumping-off point to rethink how disabled students are engaging in learning environments, in school and outside. It influenced my research design because including disabled people became paramount, and understandings of what constituted learning need to be expanded. This influenced how I would collect data to inform the research questions I was interested in pursuing.

Qualitative Case Study Research

This book consists of four in-depth qualitative case studies, with smaller case study interludes. What makes these out-of-school spaces case studies is that they are intrinsically bound programs that cater to teaching distinct skills/topics to disabled and sometimes nondisabled people (Merriam & Tisdell, 2016). This research is best described as "multiple bounded systems (cases) over time, through detailed, in-depth data collection involved multiple sources of information" (Creswell, 2013, p. 97). The data I collected in each case were multiple and detailed observations (sometimes videotaped), multiple interviews in each setting, analyses of IEP and BIP documents when participants agreed to share them, and other documents shared by participants and the programs.

It is important when conducting case study research to draw boundaries so that the case is foregrounded "against a particular background or problem that animates the researcher to see boundaries of the case" (Dyson & Genishi, 2005, p. 43). For the cases described in this book, I am foregrounding the learning that happens in spaces outside of school to juxtapose how different they look in school. To gather data to do this, I started by talking with disabled people about spaces they learned in outside of school and that they found to be transformative. I chose transformative spaces to focus on because I was interested in highlighting successful learning spaces, and this sometimes meant rejecting spaces where it did not appear that the majority of people were engaged and feeling successful. For example, there was one space where I had initially started gathering data but realized that while some disabled people found the space transformative, others did not. The split was about 50%, and so I decided to abandon this research site.

I settled on four different sites: a program for learning judo, a horseback riding program, a music program, and a theater program. I spent many hours gathering data through interviews, many hours of observation, and document analysis of documents related to the space or the people in the space. These sites proved to be places where rich opportunities for learning, community, and engagement were made available to the people participating in these spaces.

I also explored other spaces, but less intensely, to provide smaller examples of still other spaces that disabled people described as transformative. These are presented as brief interludes between Chapters 2, 3, 4, and 5. I hope these small stops encourage readers to think about the many spaces in their own lives that include and celebrate the learning of disabled people.

Again, first and foremost in data collection was to prioritize the insights of disabled people. All communication regarding the research stated that

I was interested in centering disabled voices as the primary focus of this research. I understood voice to be movement, gesture, words (spoken, written, or pointed to), images shared (drawings, pointed to as communication), utterances, and a commitment to remain open to discovering other forms of voice I might not be privy to at the start of this research. All people who were interested in participating in the research signed consent and/or assent forms and were given access to the full document I submitted for research approval to conduct the research. A few participants chose to read and provide comments on how I analyzed the data. All identifying information has been assigned a pseudonym, including names, locations, and other details that would compromise anonymity. I am deeply grateful to all the participants, their families, instructors, and collaborators who allowed me to learn from them.

I've made many choices about the data and the sites I visited. This research, like all research, is filtered through my own perspective. I gathered data and analyzed them in a recursive manner. I used a researcher's journal to capture my reflections during the data-gathering process and also during the analysis, noting questions I wanted to pursue with participants, ideas that challenged my thinking, tentative themes, and things to look for in my next round of observations or interviews (Merriam & Tisdell, 2016, p. 35).

I wanted the reporting of this research to be as accessible as possible and for the reader to feel like they were sitting beside me at each site. My ultimate goal is for the reader to start to notice the learning happening in all spaces and to rethink the way learning and behavior are currently framed for disabled students in school. The questions at the end of each chapter are designed to start conversations and are in no way comprehensive of all the conversations that could be had. My hope is that the conversations never end.

So, join me. Let's push open the heavy doors of the schoolhouse and venture outside, where disabled students can shed the tests, scores, goals, and other people's desired behaviors to engage in learning that brings them joy and community.

CHAPTER 2

The Dojo

I'm in charge of warm-up. I am the leader.

—Cindy

Weaving through the streets of a small city, I find the two-story brick building that houses the dojo. It appears a bit run-down but also shows that someone has taken a recent interest in fixing it up. The building houses a few eclectic businesses. Besides the dojo, there is a dance studio, and what appears to be at least one woodworking shop. I climb the steep flight of stairs to the top floor, where double doors are splayed wide open, welcoming all who show up.

The room is not big. It's painted all white, with all but a few feet of the floor covered in a well-worn, taped-together white mat. Halfway up the sides of the front and back walls are more mats that protect the judo players should they hit the wall. On the side wall there are documents written in both Japanese and English—many of these are the official documents from Japan that signify that a judo player has achieved their black belt. There's one window that lets natural light into the space, and it's on the far wall. There is another wall, actually three-quarters of a wall, in front of that windowed wall which creates a small space for changing and a small bathroom, so really, only a portion of the only window is visible. Otherwise, the space is lit with fluorescent lights that are suspended from the ceiling and seem to be in desperate need of repair in some spots. An industrial heater also hangs from the ceiling, and when it runs, it's loud and blasts a hot stream of dry air through the dojo. On the other side of the room, about three-quarters up the wall, is a picture of Dr. Jigorō Kanō, the Japanese educator and founder of judo. On each side of Master Kanō's portrait is a flag—a U.S. flag on one side and a Japanese flag on the other. No one steps onto the mat without first bowing to Master Kanō's picture to pay respect and honor the work that will happen on the mat.

There are three chairs on each side of the doorway, lined up for spectators. Often there are more spectators than chairs, so people hang out just outside the doors or sit on the floor. Sometimes players are dropped off and then picked up at the end of class. Small cubbies for shoes are tucked into the front corners of the room in this small area. At about 9:45, Justin explodes into the room. He bellows, "I'm here!" and gets to business. Off come his shoes and they are pushed into a cubby. He throws his jacket down on an empty chair and bows to the picture of Master Kanō, and off he goes onto the mat. Justin has arrived in his *gi*, the white loose-fitting pants and jacket closed with his yellow belt. Justin squeals with delight as he runs the length of the mat.

Justin's mom Patty comes into the room, a little winded from the stairs. She steps into the room and sees Justin's coat on the chair. She picks it up, hangs it on the hooks above the chairs, and turns to say hello to Sensei Scott, the instructor of this class. Milling about with Sensei Scott are a few other people with black belts who attend this dojo and come to work out with the players in this class. Sensei Scott's adult son, Ned, and Ned's longtime friend Allen, both brown belts, are standing close-by to the other adults. Ned and Allen have been playing judo for about 20 years. Both are in their late twenties and are Autistic. Sensei Scott's other son— stepson, technically, but he never refers to him that way—is Kenny. He is 16, a white belt, and has been playing for about a year. Sensei Scott describes his participants as "playing" judo, which initially strikes me as odd. I later learn that the Japanese term for a judo player is a *judoka,* but I never hear that term in this dojo or used by Sensei Scott in our interviews. I had imagined judo as something more forceful and thought perhaps the participants were called fighters or something akin to that. Master Kanō (1986), in his book about judo, calls his players "students," and I learn that Master Kanō was a teacher for many years before and after he created judo. While I initially think of judo as a sport that might involve kicking and punching, I learn that none of this is true. There is no kicking and no punching. Judo involves throwing and balance and is described by Kanō as being founded on the concept of maximum efficiency. Also, there is an aesthetic experience that "is the beauty and delight of performing graceful, meaningful techniques and in seeing others perform them" (Kanō, 1986, p. 24).

People continue to enter the dojo, hang up their coats, and take off their shoes and socks. Many players head to the changing room to take off their street clothes and put on their *gis*. This allows for some unstructured time before class begins. Justin continues to roll around on the mat and repeat lines from some of his favorite TV shows and movies and Ned enjoys flipping through the calendar on the wall, while Allen enjoys engaging with the other adults, asking them how they are doing. When Allen is asked how he is doing, he responds enthusiastically, "I'm really good. Thanks so much for asking!" Kenny does not visibly interact with the other people in the dojo and stays to himself, although he does look around at others on occasion. He enjoys making sounds, looking closely at his fingernails, and sitting by himself. Today he is also making his hands into puppets, and one of his hands makes the sound of an owl. "Wooooo," Kenny repeats again and again. He will continue to make this sound throughout the class, and no one seems to mind except when it interferes with a move they are practicing. Then Kenny's partner might ask him to put the "puppets" away or move his hands to the place they need to be. Kenny's response might be to laugh or intertwine his fingers, but he does eventually move his hands to the place they need to be to execute the move. Sometimes Kenny says "home" to let Sensei Scott know that he would like to be at home with his things. Sensei Scott lets Kenny know that it will be a while before they get home. "Soon," he tells Kenny.

Sensei Scott's interest in teaching what he calls a special needs judo class started as a result of parenting Ned. Sensei and his former wife realized that Ned was not progressing like the other children they knew. Sensei shared that they wondered,

> Why wasn't he sitting up? Why wasn't he crawling or walking? Why weren't we hearing the words that other kids his age say? And we went on what we call "the quest." This was up and down the eastern seaboard of the United Sates. [We were] going from clinic to therapist to hospital to hospital. At the Yale [Child Study] Center they said, "I think your son has autism," and that was the first time I heard the word "autism."

At age 10, Ned attended a special school for children on the autism spectrum. At one of the meetings about Ned's progress, a therapist asked Scott if Ned spoke Japanese, and Sensei Scott smiled with appreciation that Ned had taken what he was learning in the dojo and shared it at school. Sensei explained that 4 or 5 years after Ned's diagnosis, he was helping his own sensei teach a kids' class at his dojo and he had Ned with him. While there, Ned showed some interest in participating. Sensei Scott related, "And he's rolling around on the floor and participating. The learning curve was very, very shallow but he enjoyed it and he kept participating and I kept bringing him." The school personnel at Ned's school thought this was great, and they asked Sensei and Ned if they would provide a special demonstration at the school. They did and it was enthusiastically received by the kids, teachers, parents, and adaptive physical education teacher. In 2002, they started their first class at this school, coming every Friday to work with children who were chosen by the teachers, staff, and therapists at the school. Ned, Allen, and Cindy were all in that first class of students and have been practicing judo ever since. Now Sensei, Ned, and Cindy still travel back to teach the class at the school, still on Friday. Allen can't make the Friday class because he works, but he joins them on Saturdays at the dojo. At the end of the school year, Sensei arranges a judo tournament at the school so his young players get the experience of participating in a judo match. Sensei extends an invitation to all who practice at the dojo, so the students at the school who have been involved in the Friday class get to try out the techniques they have been practicing on judo players of all ranks and ages. Family members and friends of the children come to cheer them on, videotape their performance, and celebrate the progress they have made in judo. Sensei Scott also believes it is important that the students at the school have the experience of practicing judo in the dojo, so he also arranges a field trip every year for the students at the school so that if they can't make the Saturday class, they can experience playing judo in the dojo at least once.

The Saturday class at the dojo was originally suggested by Cindy's father because he wanted his daughter to have the opportunity, outside of school, to continue her practice. Sensei Scott wasn't sure if there would be enough students to fill a class, but he decided he would give it a try and asked for other players to help out. Sensei advertised the Saturday class at the dojo as a special needs class, and currently most of the students, but not all, are Autistic. Some students come to this Saturday class because they also attend or attended the special school, and some hear about the class through word of mouth. Some students who attend this class also come to other kids' classes during the week, classes that are not designated as special needs, and are always welcome to do so. Some students travel a distance to attend judo classes, while others come from this neighborhood. One parent shares that this class has been helpful for her child, who has been diagnosed with attention deficit hyperactivity disorder and a learning disability, because he does not experience school as a successful environment. When asked why she wanted her son to attend this Saturday judo class, she responded, "School is so hard for Tim. He always feels like everyone is trying to fix him. I'm glad he has judo to feel successful and like he is okay, whole, not needing to be fixed."

Even though the Saturday class is listed as a special needs class, the practice of judo—the techniques, the sparring, and the mat work—is the same no matter who is playing. Sensei shares that even though Cindy is celebrated as one of the first special needs black belts in the United States, there is nothing "special" about the work she needed to do to earn it. He explains,

> Cindy works out four or five days a week. I think she's been doing it now for 16 years. In judo when you get promoted, it's very standardized, okay? A black belt in the United States is on par with black belts from Europe or Asia or the South Pacific, it doesn't matter. There's a standardization in the ranking system, in the knowledge system. And Cindy worked incredibly hard to make sure she had all of the knowledge down that she needed as well as performing the demonstrations that she would perform [to earn her black belt]. Some people work on it for several weeks; Cindy worked on it for several years, to make sure it was right.

It is 10:00 A.M. and class is ready to begin. Sensei asks participants to line up, and everyone works together to create a semistraight line. The line is fashioned by belt rank, with the black belts starting the line as it travels all the way to the white belts. Dotting the line are green, orange, and yellow belts. It takes a few moments for everyone to settle in. Sensei Scott waits. He knows that the line will straighten out and quiet down. He waits for the participants to kneel in their places and put their hands on the crease of where their legs meet their torso. He feels no need to talk. He waits with a smile on his face. Only if there happens to be a new player at the dojo will Sensei Scott narrate what the other players are doing as they line up. This allows the new player to follow along without feeling singled out. The highest-ranked player with a black belt at the front of the line asks in Japanese that all bow to and show respect for Master Kanō. Everyone in unison bows to the picture on the front wall. Next, the head black belt asks that everyone bow to Sensei and again, everyone does. Sensei waits and looks down the line. He looks serious, and it seems that each player falls under Sensei's gaze. Sometimes Sensei will share a message or make a comment about his hope for the day's practice. Sometimes, without comment, he stands, following the predictable pattern of tucking his toes, leading with his right leg and then his left, and he is quickly followed by the head black belt. Then, all are invited to stand up in the same way, and they mostly do, and find a space on the mat to begin to warm up.

There is something about this moment in the line that seems grounding for all players, an official start, a moment to join together as a community, and a moment to show their respect to their teacher. If by chance there is a player who is interested in being silly to get a reaction, the other players will just ignore this player until they come to understand what is required. Rarely does Sensei Scott need to address the behavior of players. Sensei Scott does not have an explicit list of "dojo rules" up on the wall. When new players join, they fall right into the rhythm of the dojo, learning from others in this space. Sometimes Sensei will narrate the routine of the dojo and sometimes he lets new players figure out for themselves how things are unfolding. One thing is clear: respect is expected. The opportunities to come together, to bow together, are tangible ways the players experience this.

Master Kanō (1986) has written that judo facilitates learning not only in the dojo, but also outside it. He outlines different maxims that he believes are important concepts in judo that players take out into the world with them. One maxim is "that one should pay close attention to the relationship between self and other" (p. 24). At first, it seems to me that the practice of judo is an individual endeavor and that the players in this Saturday class operate as individuals rather than as a team like in sports such as soccer or basketball. Quickly I observe differently, and I am reminded that I need to check my assumptions against my observations and interviews.

WARMING UP

Players run to different sections of the mat. They will usually check to make sure there is enough space between themselves and the next player, but if not, Sensei will ask the class to check their spacing. If a player is still too close to another, Sensei will go over and guide the player to where they need to be so they are safe. Cindy is in charge of warm-ups and will ask players to get started and give their attention to her so she can lead them through the warm-up routine. Cindy has a routine that she goes through, including jokes here and there, to keep players on target and interested.

It's clear from the many hours I spent in the dojo that each player has and shows respect for the other players, disabled and nondisabled. In fact, in reviewing the many hours of video taken for this book, I can't find one instance where a player disrespects another. That said, not everyone behaves perfectly. There are times when players get carried away: they might talk too much and do so during instruction, they may have been preoccupied when instructions were given and not know what to do next, but in this space, this is never viewed as disrespectful. Perfection is never the goal, but everyone needs to try and everyone needs to support each other.

Continuous support starts with Sensei Scott. I am struck by his ability to maintain safety and engagement when things get hard for students. During the warm-up, players might slack off while doing push-ups; sometimes they quit all together and just flop their bodies onto the mat. Push-ups are hard! Sensei Scott may gently assist, he may joke with students, he may see someone slacking one day and let it go. Another day, he reads his players and decides who to push. His ability to read students, carefully observing them both on and off the mat, and adjusting his instruction, is subtle but so very powerful. During one warm-up, students take turns practicing a hand movement used to get other players off-balance, called *kazuchi*. This movement mimics when the player has hold of another player's *gi* and pulls them closer so they lose their balance. As the players individually practice this movement over and over as a part of their warm-up routine, they take turns counting from one to ten aloud in Japanese. Players who are typically nonverbal participate. They count at all different speeds and varying degrees of audibility. Some players scream and others whisper under their breath. All ways are accepted by Sensei Scott and Cindy, which means that all ways are respected by the players in the room. If you are new to the dojo, you are encouraged to count, too, and using English is just fine. Soon, these new players will pick up how to count in Japanese by immersion. They learn by being present in the space. I do not witness any direct instruction about how to count in Japanese, and yet I witness new students quickly gaining this skill. Students are not told to go home and study Japanese counting, but sometimes they do so because they want to.

Cindy leads the group through an approximately 10-minute warm-up, which allows Sensei Scott to walk around the room and interact with players individually. Sensei Scott has supported Cindy's growth both in and outside the dojo. When Cindy reflects on the role judo has had in her life, she shares,

> I wasn't very sociable as a kid. Oftentimes I was afraid of being touched and I didn't like talking with strangers or anything. But judo has helped me overcome a lot of issues. Like, it's really helped me release pent-up energy. I'm much more relaxed. And it's also helped me socialize more with people. I've made a lot of friends in this.

This leadership position in the dojo is important for Cindy, but it's also important for the others who practice there. It allows all who are in the dojo—players, parents, caregivers, siblings, and other family members—to see an Autistic person as a leader. There are not many spaces where this is the case. Casey, the parent of an Autistic player named Alia who also attends the special school classes along with this Saturday class, highlights this importance to me. She says, "My daughter needs to see people with autism being leaders. She needs to see that they have agency and rights. My daughter doesn't see women with autism in leadership roles very often. I can't think of one other place now that I'm thinking about it, other than here." In fact, Casey shares that she believes it was Cindy's leadership at the special school that hooked Alia into being interested in judo at all. That Cindy herself was a student at the school means a lot to Alia. Casey shares that because Cindy has earned her black belt, she exists as a tangible example for Alia of how Autistic women can be powerful and successful. Alia shared with me that she would also like to get her black belt and also lead the warm-up, "just like Cindy." She shared, "Cindy is impressive." Cindy is also a powerful example of Autistic pride and self-advocacy for the neurotypical people who are in the dojo, as players or as spectators, as well.

Sensei Scott is crouched in the corner of the room while Cindy commands the space. She calls on people to count. She demonstrates warm-up moves so newer students can see what is expected of them. She doesn't miss a beat as Sensei Scott rises and interacts individually with players. He adjusts, compliments, cajoles a student to work harder, and does some stretching himself. When Cindy has cycled through all of the warm-up exercises, she lets Sensei know that she is finished. It is now time to move on to *uchikomi*, which is the practice of particular moves that are pre-organized by Sensei Scott. For this practice, students work in pairs. This allows them the opportunity to inhabit the roles of *uke* and *tori,* as discussed later in this chapter.

PRACTICE

Sensei Scott introduces the move they are going to work on for the day. Today, it's hand throws. Sensei levels the instruction by allowing players who have been playing longer and know more moves to choose which hand throw they would like to practice. For the newer players in the dojo, Sensei will direct them to which throw they should practice. Sensei demonstrates the moves with the assistance of another black belt and gives narration as he executes different moves. He also uses short phrases that seem designed to stick, such as "feet wide, to the side, and throw," after giving a fuller description on how one would move themselves and their partner to execute this move. As Sensei teaches and/or reviews these moves, the players sit against the wall. Interestingly, the players have many different ways of taking in the information that Sensei is sharing. Ned seems to look at his feet while Sensei is giving instructions until he gets to the shorter, more rhythmic phrases. Then he looks up to watch. Allen keeps his eyes on Sensei the entire time and engages vocally. When Sensei says, "My weight is fifty-fifty. It's split equally between my two feet, okay?," Allen responds, "Okay, Sensei." Cindy watches intently and quietly the entire time. Justin, who burst into the dojo at the beginning of this chapter, is a newer student to the Saturday class, 12 years old, and also attends the special education school where Sensei teaches on Fridays. As Sensei instructs the class, Justin looks to his right at the side wall. Only once during the approximately 2-minute demonstration does he look at what Sensei is doing, and he does so only momentarily. Kenny is making puppets with his hands and moving them in front of his face but is not making any vocalizations. Sensei is scanning the line and noticing each player. Sensei observes how everyone takes in information. No one is called out for not looking at him or for engaging in stimming. Sensei understands that learning can appear in all sorts of ways. I'm reminded of how important it is to presume competence, which Biklen and Burke (2006) contend is often missing when neurotypical people, particularly in schools, meet Autistic people. As Biklen and Burke explain,

> The notion of presuming competence implies that educators must assume students can and will change and, that through engagement with the world, will demonstrate complexities of thought and action that could not necessarily be anticipated. (p. 168)

Sensei has spoken to me about how some people don't believe that Autistic people can "manage" the physical intensity of judo. He has said that often people express fear that teaching disabled people judo will lead to them using it at inappropriate times. Sensei has not experienced this, although he is aware that at the special education school, students are chosen by teachers and therapists and so there may be instances where this is true.

I bring this up to Justin's mom Patty, and she believes the pressure of holds, when players put each other in positions and then hold them to try to prevent their escape, is actually part of why Justin connects to judo. As an Autistic person herself, she shares that she can relate to how her body feels more relaxed when she is experiencing deep pressure. As we talk a little longer, she reflects on Justin's special education classroom, where there is "fear when students touch each other." She tells me that students in Justin's class are taught to think of their bodies as being inside "bubbles," and that one person's bubble should not invade another's. "How sad," Patty continues, "to think that kids are taught that getting close to each other is wrong." Patty reflects on her own experiences learning in spaces outside of school. She tells me she found the pressure she needed through horseback riding and dance. Thinking back to her dancing days, she shared,

> I think that it all has something to do with the regulation and the sensory input of joint compression and the routine that allows the muscle memory to take over and let your brain relax. That's what I see and . . . feel in it. And I don't do it anymore and I'm not as regulated, I can tell.

Patty tells me that Justin's school accommodates his need for pressure through a weighted vest "for serious lessons." Patty says she regulates her own need for pressure by wearing "compression wear," which she can find pretty easily in clothing stores.

It's time to be paired with another player so that they can practice. Sensei will pair up students today, although sometimes he asks students to choose a partner. Sensei takes some time to think about who should be placed together. Sometimes Sensei will ask another black belt to stand with a particular pair to re-instruct or just monitor their practice. After a few minutes, the students are paired up and they find a spot on the mat where there is enough room to practice.

Uke/Tori

The room becomes busy and noisy with bodies in pairs grabbing *gis*. Justin is paired with Ned. This practice time requires that students engage in different roles. One will assume the role of *tori*, the person who is executing the move, and the other will be the *uke*, the person who adjusts their body to receive the move. Justin is *tori* first. He grabs onto Ned's sleeve and lapel and begins to execute the move. Justin is not using much force, so Ned moves his body so he can be successful. It's reminiscent of dance partners and the need for someone to take the lead. The *tori* should be leading the throw and the *uke* should be adjusting, but Justin's moves are so slight that Ned, as *uke*, is moving his body so that Justin appears to be leading. Slowly, Justin starts to take ownership over the *tori* role so that Ned, on repetition eight, is fully in the role of *uke*. Ned understands that he is the higher rank in this pairing, so he offers verbal tips to Justin as he works on his 10 repetitions. Ned's tips are often encouraging comments; he might move Justin's hand to the correct position, or he might give very brief verbal feedback like "move over." On number 10, the *tori* is supposed to throw the *uke*. When Justin finishes the move of number 10, Ned waits. Justin does not make a move to throw Ned and so Ned jumps in the air and throws himself. Justin smiles. Now Justin, still playing the role of *tori,* practices the same move but on the other side of this body. This time, Justin fully embraces the role of *tori* on the first repetition and on number 10, Ned does not have to jump. Justin throws Ned on his own, but Ned embellishes a bit just for good measure. When Ned hits the mat, he growls like he has just experienced a mammoth throw. Justin smiles, puts both hands in the air, and says, "Roarrrrrrr!"

Autistic people have been described as lacking "theory of mind," or the ability to understand the emotions, intents, and desires of others (Baron-Cohen, Leslie, & Frith, 1985), but Autistic self-advocates have decried this, to put it mildly, as inaccurate (see, for example, Yergeau, 2013). Watching all the judo players in the room adjust to each other, move their bodies in ways that support their partner, and encourage each other to try again or squeeze tighter makes it hard to believe that Autistic people do not understand the intentions of others. As Sensei Scott shares, "We see what we expect to see, and I expect to see judo players. That means cooperation on the mat." The practice of individual moves, where players inhabit the roles of *uke* and *tori,* provides the players in the dojo the opportunity to lead by example, cooperate for a common good, and do so while learning and practicing judo. Next, these players will take the moves they have practiced in isolation and incorporate them into the free play of judo, deciding what move to do and when to do it.

Randori

The free play of judo, or *randori,* is when players put into action the moves they have practiced as *uke* and *tori*. To the observer, this looks like a competition that will yield a winner and a loser, but being good at *randori* means that the judo player will be good at not only taking the lead, but also taking a good fall when their opponent throws them. So when a more experienced player is playing someone newer, they are engaging in this unstructured playing of judo, but they are also allowing the less experienced partner to make some moves and some throws. When partners are relatively equally matched, they try their hardest not be thrown and to throw their partner. Players are constantly adjusting their play according to who their partners are.

When it's time to play *randori,* three players line up on the mat, spaced as far apart as possible. They face the rest of the class, players waiting against the wall, to see who will choose them or be chosen by Sensei Scott. The players will have the opportunity to play many different people during this time, so if two or three players rush from the wall to play the same person, one will stay and two will have a chance in the upcoming rounds. When Sensei Scott chooses a player, it may be because he wants to match a more experienced player of a higher rank with a less experienced player. This is often the case for students who are just starting to play judo. In *randori,* students are using all the moves they know to freely compete against their partner. As Sensei reminds the group, it's important to take good falls. He says, "Take a good fall and live to fight another day." Learning to take a good fall is often the first skill that students learn. They learn how to break their fall by slapping their arm on the mat as they fall. No matter the level of one's opponent, if a player throws someone, they are responsible for holding the sleeve of the player they throw. Holding the sleeve with tension, almost keeping the person they throw off the floor a bit, helps to lessen the impact of the fall. Until a new student can show that they know how to fall well, they will play a more experienced player, or Sensei Scott will just ask them to observe during *randori* time.

Miles and Justin

Miles stands on the mat and waits for Sensei to pair him with someone. Sensei tells Justin to play Miles. Justin says, "Play Miles, okay," and he rises to meet Miles on the mat. Miles is a neurotypical 15-year-old player who wears a green belt. He attends this Saturday class with his father, a black belt. Miles moves slowly, waiting to see what Justin will do. Justin reaches his foot out and tries to sweep Miles's foot away from him so that he falls to the ground. His technique is not quite right, so Miles maneuvers slowly out of the move. It seems like these two are playing in slow motion. Miles says "almost" to Justin and Justin says in a loud, high-pitched voice, "Attack!" Miles smiles. Justin slowly tries the move again, this time improving his positioning. Miles could easily step over Justin, but he knows that as the higher-ranked belt, it's his responsibility to show Justin that with accurate positioning, making him fall is possible. Justin knew what he needed to do to fix his positioning, and Miles had just given him the chance to do so. Miles takes the fall. Justin stumbles back and looks around. He acts as though executing this move took all his strength; he stumbles a bit, playing up his brute force. Sensei chuckles and says, "You got him that time, Justin, but be careful, he'll want revenge." Both Miles and Justin smile. It seems to me that it is a privilege in many ways to have to adjust to a lower-ranked belt. As players improve and grow, they inevitably are in a position to monitor their strength against a lower-ranked player. Sensei is careful to make decisions about who to pair with whom based on whether the higher-ranked player is ready to take on this added responsibility. In my many hours of observation, I never witness a pair where anyone gets hurt. Sometimes Sensei will ask the higher-ranked player to "really hold onto that sleeve" as a reminder to the higher-ranked player that this new student will need their help. This match is over when Sensei yells, "*Mate*." All players stop and fix their *gis* by tightening their belts or straightening out their jackets. Sensei yells "Switch," and the players who were originally out on the floor take a spot against the wall while their opponents now wait to be matched with players. New partners are chosen, and *randori* begins again.

Three new matches begin. Allen (brown belt) is playing Cindy (black belt), again, both Autistic adults. Lance is also here. He is a 13-year-old neurotypical player who practices judo on Tuesdays and Thursdays but is also here on this Saturday to play in the same class as his Autistic brother, Wesley, a new player. Lance is playing with Oscar, also 13, a yellow belt and Autistic. Oscar comes on Tuesdays to play in that class and is friends with Lance. The last pair is Ned and Justin. Justin has been very vocal in this class as he loudly repeats lines from movies and TV shows that he likes. His mom isn't sure what the lines reference. She says that if he likes the sound of a line, he is likely to repeat it. Justin gets up from sitting by the wall and walks over to Ned. He screams, "Stop right now or you're fired!" He is smiling ear to ear. Many people in the dojo laugh, and Justin smiles along with them. That said, Justin responds easily to directions and encouragement, while also sharing his sense of humor with all who are in the dojo.

It's interesting to see the different types of play that take place. Let's zoom in on each pair and notice how this one space makes different types of play possible. The players who are spectators many times call out encouraging cheers or funny quips. Sensei Scott stands on the mat, walking around while observing all three pairs.

Allen and Cindy

Cindy chooses Allen for a match. She leaves the wall and comes over to face Allen on the mat. Allen fixes his belt while Cindy waits patiently. They start by bowing, and Allen makes the first move. He moves toward Cindy, but Cindy quickly brings Allen to the ground so that he is laying on his back. Allen is taller but weighs about the same as Cindy. Allen is laughing, and the sound is pure joy. A supervising black belt comes over from the wall to watch this match. He says, "Allen, get out of there." Allen laughs and repeats this phrase out loud. Cindy is laying on top of Allen and he pushes her to the side and lays on top of her. Allen says, "I got her." As soon as the phrase comes out of his mouth, Cindy flips him back over. Allen howls with laughter, and Cindy keeps her serious game face. Sensei Scott looks over from the other side of the mat and says, "Allen, you've been on the bottom pretty much this whole match. Why don't you get out of there?" Allen says, "I'm trying, Sensei!" Sensei Scott replies, "I think you're resting, Allen," and Allen laughs and says, "Resting? Nah, I'm not resting." He musters up his strength and flips Cindy over so that she is now on the mat while Allen holds her down with his body weight. Cindy smiles now and takes the move without much resistance. Someone compliments Allen on this move and he starts to say, "Thank you," but before he can finish, Cindy has flipped him over so that he now lays on the mat with her body weight on top of him. "Whoa!" says Allen, and then Sensei calls "Mate," and this match is now over. Allen repeats "Mate" and laughs and huffs and puffs. Without making eye contact, Cindy and Allen bow to each other. Allen stays out to wait for his next opponent, and Cindy goes back to the side and waits to watch the other matches or to be called to play again.

Lance and Oscar

Oscar waits on the mat to see if someone will choose him or if he will be assigned an opponent by Sensei Scott. While Lance doesn't typically attend the Saturday class, he has been coming to support his brother Wesley. Lance has been playing judo for several years, and only recently has Wesley agreed to try it. Lance is excited to see his friend Oscar, and he runs at the chance to play him. Sensei sees him move toward Oscar and nods his head yes. A big smile appears on both Lance's and Oscar's faces. Like Cindy and Allen, Oscar and Lance are pretty evenly matched, and neither one will have to consider the other's skill level in this round. Lance and Oscar are set to play *randori*. They bow to each other and they are off. Lance bobs and weaves while Oscar playfully walks toward him, perhaps imitating a zombie. Lance is inviting him to make the first move by motioning with his hands to come and get him. Sensei Scott is watching and says, "Go get him, Oscar." Both boys are smiling, and Oscar lunges in to grab Lance. They are playing competitively. They pull each other's *gis*, they try to sweep each other's feet out from under their bodies, and they work to execute moves they have practiced many times before. They both tumble to the ground. They look at each other and laugh, and then stand and start again. Oscar immediately sweeps Lance's foot out from under him, and Lance tumbles back and hits the mat. Lance says "Good one" to Oscar, and Oscar says thanks. Next, Lance makes a move. He sticks his foot out and seems to trip Oscar, and Oscar takes a good fall, being sure to slap the mat as he has been taught. Lance asks Oscar, "Are you okay?," and Oscar says, "Yeah, I'm good." They continue. Sensei is close by, watching. He doesn't say anything to the two boys while they practice, but he watches. Even though they are playing competitively, Lance, who is much slighter than Oscar, works hard to support the weight of Oscar by holding tightly to his sleeve when he falls. Oscar does the same for Lance, but it seems to take him less effort. Lance is moving around the mat, showboating a bit by jumping up in the air. Oscar sees his move, and as Lance's feet head back toward the mat, he sweeps them out from under him and Lance falls to the mat. Oscar has his sleeve, so he is protected. Sensei Scott sees this and enthusiastically says, "Nice job, Oscar! That's it, well done." Lance smiles. He too recognizes that this was a really good move. They play a little bit longer, and then Sensei calls *"Mate."* The boys bow and then chat, both smiling. They shake hands. Oscar walks to the side to sit and wait for his next match, and Lance takes on his next opponent.

Ned and Justin

Ned is told to go to the mat for *randori.* He turns to Justin and says, "Hey Justin, come play me." Ned really likes playing Justin, possibly because both love to laugh and they just seem to have a good time together. In fact, Justin looks like a smaller and younger version of Ned. Justin scoots on his butt toward Ned. He stands and says to Ned, "Let's go!" in what is supposed to pass as a menacing voice but only makes Ned giggle. Ned easily brings Justin down to the floor, being sure to still have a hold on his sleeve. Justin just lays on the mat. He makes a repetitive noise—not too loud, just for him and Ned to hear. Justin rolls back and forth on the mat while Ned looks on. Ned looks over to see his dad, Sensei Scott, looking over at him, and he says, "Come on Justin, wake up!" Justin just lays there. Sensei Scott yells, "Hey, Justin!" Ned says, "He's sleeping." Sensei Scott tells Justin that it's time to wake up and that he needs to go get Ned. Justin rises and yells "Aaaah!" in an animated way, as though he is imitating a superhero. Justin raises his arms to the height of his shoulders and zombie-walks over to Ned. Allen, watching from the sidelines, chimes in, "Come on, Justin, get him!" Justin, seemingly moving in slow motion, executes a move on Ned, grabbing Ned by the collar of his *gi* and sweeping his foot so that he knocks out Ned's foot so he will fall to the floor. Ned takes a glorious fall, pulling out all the stops of being slayed in battle. Ned exclaims, "Oh, man!" and lays on the floor.

Justin stands victorious, arms raised above this head. Ned pops up and sweeps Justin's foot and they both fall to the mat this time. They roll around on the floor until Justin stops and just lays on his back. Ned takes his hands and lightly drums on Justin's belly. Both laugh. Sensei Scott looks over and just smiles. He had, after all, instructed the group before the start of *randori* to "Remember, this is not the Olympics. We are here to practice judo and have fun." Mission accomplished, according to Ned and Justin. Allen says, "Oh, man," and shakes his head while others on the side also laugh. Sensei calls out *"Mate,"* and Ned and Justin find their way to their knees and then their feet. They face each other and bow.

Everyone in the class has had the opportunity to practice or play with each other. Sometimes they adjusted to players with less experience, and sometimes to players with more. Many of the players have rooted for each other from the sidelines, sometimes vocally or sometimes through jumping up and down with excitement. It's time to come together again, just like they did at the start, but this time to bring the class to a close.

Mokuso

Sensei asks the class to line up, and again, just like in the beginning of class, the players line up in belt order, from the highest rank to the lowest. Sensei sits and faces the line. He looks up and down the line, a small smile on his face. In Japanese he asks the line to *keiotsuke*, which roughly translates to come to "attention," and then to *mokuso*. When Sensei says *mokuso*, the players close their eyes, continue to look straight ahead as they sit up tall, and, as Sensei has explained before, "think about something that you learned today or just concentrate on your breathing."

These active, stimming bodies all settle in. As Sensei explains, he has seen players who have been described by others as struggling with impulse control learn to calm their own bodies down. He says, "They take this into other facets of their life." Patty tells me she will sometimes say *mokuso* to Justin outside the dojo as a way to connect him to his body. She then tells me in a small whisper that she sometimes says it silently to remind herself to do the same. Sensei aims to have the players sit still and breathe deeply for around 45 seconds. Occasionally it takes some time for players to settle in, so the players might be sitting with their eyes closed for 2 minutes until, at last, it seems that all are settled. It is not always super-quiet. Sometimes there is a little movement or some eyes open to look around. Often I witness players catching themselves and bringing themselves back to the stillness.

Then there is more bowing to Sensei and Master Kanō and, just as at the beginning of class, students make the mat their own, sometimes flipping and twirling, letting their voices fill the room. Those watching from the sidelines stand and stretch, chat, and call for their charges to get ready to leave. Coats and shoes are slipped on, and good-byes are exchanged. Players and their families head out to take on the rest of Saturday.

LESSONS LEARNED

It's amazing to watch the players progressing over the many months I spent with them inside the dojo. As Kanō promised, judo taught me many lessons that apply not only to the dojo but also to my everyday world. The dojo provides the space to think about how learning and teaching are continually cyclical processes. The importance of being both teacher and learner and inhabiting the roles of both *uke* and *tori,* resonates for me. When does the player/teacher push and when does the player/teacher stand back, step aside, and let the power of the push pass by?

Uke and *Tori*/Push and Pull

A powerful component of learning in the dojo is the utilization of the roles of *uke* and *tori*. Being able to inhabit the roles of the person who executes a move *(tori)* and the person who adjusts so that the *tori* can be successful *(uke)* allows for a robust understanding of what each task entails. And although judo roughly translates as "the gentle way," at the core of judo is the concept of maximum efficiency. Sensei Scott explains,

> If you take two people and each has ten units of strength and they push against each other and push against each other, nothing happens. But if one person turns to the side and pulls with two units of strength, that's an efficient use of the force. They'll take over control of that situation, and in a very basic way that's what judo is about. Okay? It's about giving way.

This balance of push and pull seems in direct contradiction to the way IEPs structure learning experiences. IEPs are almost always written from the perspective of neurotypical people, based on how learning looks according to them. On Justin's IEP, there is a goal under the heading of "Study Skills" that states: "Justin will attend to a task without distraction for 10 minutes during small group instruction." This is said to be evaluated "every marking period" using "recorded observations," and the measure to determine if the goal has been achieved is "9 out of 10 trails over 10 months." When I ask Patty about the goals on Justin's IEP, she says that they are always marked as "progressing satisfactorily" when they are evaluated. She says she never receives any indication if Justin successfully completed any of the trials or if they are actually even evaluating a goal that way. Rarely, she says, is a goal ever marked "completed." She says, "But of course it's not completed. Attending without distraction is just so silly. I've given up trying to reason with this paperwork and the goals. I just say, 'Sure, write what you want.' It [the IEP] comes in the mail and I stick it in a drawer." The IEP is all push, and Patty adjusts by stepping aside to let it pass by her, and housing it in a drawer. There is technically room for Patty to push back against the goals on this document, but the reality is, pushing back has been fruitless. She says, "At first I was like, 'Oh, let's put this and that,' but really, this paper is useless when it comes to teaching Justin. It's not for him." Patty is not alone in this view. Other parents concur that the IEP becomes useful for making sure certain things are in place, like assistive technology or certain related services like physical therapy, but for learning, it has little efficacy.

When it comes to regulating Autistic students' behaviors in schools, it is not uncommon for the neurotypical perspective to be centered, as is often done in the behavioral intervention plan (BIP). Returning to Justin, he has a BIP to address behaviors that get in the way of his learning. One of the behaviors to be addressed on his BIP is "Inappropriate Social Boundaries," which includes "invading someone's space." The use of "invading" here is very interesting in that it makes the assumption that Justin is actively and aggressively being an invader. I saw absolutely no evidence of this in the dojo. When I asked Patty about this, she said she also didn't see this but guesses that maybe since school is "so rigid," this is what it looks like to them when Justin engages his classmates. The dojo is a place where students are allowed to express themselves through vocalizations, stimming, closeness, and various movements as long as they are safe and respectful. I never witnessed anyone ask a player to change their behavior just because one person thought it should be changed. No one ever asked Kenny to stop making puppets with his hands just because they wanted him to stop. When the situation called for Kenny to play judo, he might be asked to move his hands to the proper positioning, but this was never about seeing his imaginative play as "wrong." In the dojo we witness people touching one another, an activity that is often frowned upon in schools, and for good reasons at times. But in the dojo, people are expected to get close to one another—it's expected and welcome to "invade" spaces.

What if teaching, learning, and behavior were seen as a balance between *uke* and *tori,* and what if each student were invited or taught how to inhabit each role? Behavior might be seen as a form of communication, and teachers would be encouraged to see behaviors as messages from their students rather than actions to change without consideration of why this behavior is occurring. The push might be the behavior, and the adjustment to the behavior might be seen as a shifting of intention. The teacher may need to see the intent of the behavior differently. The evaluation of learning might also be more long-term and would need to involve careful observations of interactions and outcomes. The goal might not be correctly completing 9 out of 10 trials, but the learning that happened along the way.

"The Path Is the Goal"

The dojo reminds me of young children before they enter "formal" schooling who crave learning, who want to read and write and learn willingly. I've watched preschoolers dive into writing because they want to share their experiences with the world, make people laugh, and connect with others

(McCloskey, 2012a). In formal schooling, the outcome, be it the grade or the score on a test, is often what is privileged over the path. For students with disabilities, we set the objectives and goals on their IEPs and BIPs and then measure them in ways that often emphasize only the outcome. "The path is the goal," writes Roosa (2016) in his book geared toward those who are interested in teaching judo. He reminds would-be instructors, "Perhaps the most valuable gift teaching judo provides is the constant learning and improving that accompanies instruction. Countless experiential lessons can keep you creative and motivated to improve not only your students but also yourself" (p. 77).

Judo, like learning, is a lifelong endeavor. While the belts change, Sensei Scott reminds players that it is the time spent in the dojo that matters. He shows this by sharing his long and extensive practice of judo. The players witness one another's growth when they watch players execute new moves, watch how players adjust to newer players, and move up in rank. Players also receive encouragement from black belts who are still practicing—doing the same warm-ups and practicing moves they were taught decades ago. Having other players witness your growth is powerful.

Sensei Scott is always teaching in the dojo, but he is not always talking. In fact, in an analysis of who was talking and when in the dojo, Sensei Scott's instructional talk is only about 5 percent of the total time. How is Sensei Scott supporting the learning of his players over time? Interestingly, Sensei Scott spends an incredible amount of time observing. He carefully walks around and watches. He also watches from many different parts of the room as his players interact with each other. When Sensei reflects on the learning that happens in the dojo, he says,

> They [the players] pick up techniques, they pick up on what they're supposed to be doing, on what they're not supposed to be doing, and it works. It's very effective. And the most important thing is that they're having fun. They're having a good time, they want to do this, and they do this willingly.

There are times when players focus on their next advancement and ask Sensei Scott about when they might get their next belt. Sensei Scott reminds them that belts are not bought, they are earned. It can take years to make an advancement, but when a student does advance, they know they have worked hard for it. There is a deep level of respect for oneself that develops because of this. It seems to me that playing judo is a natural way to apprentice students into a growth mindset. There is no judo IQ, no way to be naturally "smart" in judo, and resiliency is nurtured and develops as a by-product of being a participant. Everyone who sticks with judo grows in their judo skills. Everyone is welcome to participate as long as they care for each other.

Hold the Sleeve—Taking Care of Each Other

Embedded in this learning space is the notion that we take care of each other. This is taught directly and indirectly in each class. When I initially thought about looking at a space where a martial art was practiced, I expected to see an atmosphere built on competition. But in the dojo, competitiveness is focused on self, rather than what one can do to another. Pushing oneself to do better, to try harder, to be a good *uke* and take a good fall, become the important ideas that resonate throughout practice. I have witnessed players who have struggled with the feeling of "losing" come to terms with the reality that good judo requires not winning often, and that *through* the act of not winning, new insight is developed. Losing is never a complete loss; something can always be gained.

Apprenticeship into teaching requires the same level of care. In my classroom, I am the higher-ranked player, and this means I need to be guiding and modeling for my students. I need to show the strength and careful execution of learning strategies and hold students' sleeves as they embark on their own teaching. As a learning community, it is a must to hold each other's sleeves and push back against how education is often framed as a competitive act.

Disabled People, Front and Center

The Saturday class at the dojo shines a bright light on the success of its disabled participants. Disabled people are role models for each other, and for nondisabled people as well. Historically, disabled people have been hidden away in institutions, and in schools, special education classrooms were often located in the basements. Disabled people teach judo to newer players, taking on the role of more experienced player.

There are no other spaces that I know of that bring disabled adults, adolescents, and children together in a learning environment. This mix of disabled people allows glimpses of the present, the past, and the future. As Allen's mom shared with me, when Allen was younger, many professionals made predictions about what he would be capable of doing. She laughs at this now. Allen takes pride in his accomplishments in and outside the dojo. Other parents ask Allen's mom for advice or mention in casual conversation what teachers or therapists have shared about their children's future prospects. She is glad that Allen can debunk many of their fears by being a leader in the dojo.

Universal Acceptance as a Way to Build Community

No matter who you are or how you communicate, you are welcome in the dojo. Even if it has been a while since you last came, sometimes even years or decades, you are welcomed back, always. You will not be asked to change the behaviors that you find comforting. If you walk in with no experience playing judo or as a black belt, you are welcome. If you are neurotypical or neurodivergent, you are welcome. In my months of visiting, interviewing, filming, and just enjoying the dojo, I have never seen anyone turned away. If you are new, very likely multiple people will meet you at the door to introduce themselves. New students get an introduction from Sensei, usually multiple weeks in a row. After students finish bowing, Sensei might say, "If you weren't here last Saturday, you didn't meet Wesley. Wesley is at the end of the line. Be sure to introduce yourself and say hi to Wesley today."

Determining the placement for a student who is eligible for special education services must include a discussion about what setting is the least restrictive environment (LRE). The LRE for any student is the general education classroom, and any other setting is more restrictive (Rozalski, Stewart, & Miller, 2010). Sometimes practitioners wonder how they might educate students who have different learning needs in the same general education classrooms. I think the dojo shows us some possibilities in this regard. There are activities that take place during every practice session in which all students, from white belts to black belts, participate. Not everyone performs in the same manner, but each person warms up, practices old and new lessons, participates in different levels of instruction, and is responsible for learning and teaching others. Again, undergirding all these activities is a level of care and respect. There are people who assist when needed, much like how teaching assistants are available to students in schools. But this assistance is only given when it is needed.

The concept of Universal Design for Learning (UDL) contends that curriculum can be designed to address the learning needs of all students in the same classroom (CAST, 2018). Curriculum can be designed to take into account the learning needs of all students and to think about what motivates different students, how students need different ways to access materials, and how those materials might be differentiated to different needs. Critical to this curriculum design is the concept of universal acceptance. The special education system, by design, segregates students with disabilities through the addition of the word "special." Universal acceptance is the belief that all students belong in the classroom, without exception. Not every student, disabled or not, will earn a black belt. Cindy needed more time than the typical judo player to earn her black belt, but with practice, perseverance, and the universal acceptance from her fellow judo players, she sure did. Reflecting on this, Cindy shared with me,

> Earning each rank was not an easy task. I had to come to every class for a long time—work hard, and learn every bit of knowledge that I could. The black belt was the hardest part. But I'm happy to say that

I think it was a brilliant accomplishment. That I am very proud, to say that I, to know that I, worked hard for it.

I would love all my students—past, present, and future—to feel the way Cindy does about her time in the dojo and for them to see their time in my classroom as hard work but a brilliant accomplishment. "*Mokuso,*" I think to myself as I close my eyes and think about what I learned from all the players in the dojo.

REFLECTION QUESTIONS

1. How do you promote inclusivity and care in your classroom community? Are there aspects of judo class that are present in your classroom and others you might like to add?
2. What do your own observations about your students show? How do you use your observations to match students and/or push them ahead in their learning?
3. Autistic students are often taught to stop stimming or that their behaviors are "wrong." How does the dojo complicate this?
4. What outside learning spaces do your students participate in? How could you make space in your classroom for them to share these experiences?

INTERLUDE

THE FIELD

The town park is busy on this bright and warm Saturday. Children are everywhere—on the playground equipment, competing on the soccer field, and playing games of tag on the dark green lawn. Adults grasp cups of coffee and chat nonchalantly. I scan the park and eventually find the baseball field I am seeking. Parents and players are arriving for the game. Players are twirling, jumping in the air, whirling in their wheelchairs, and tossing balls back and forth.

I was invited to the game by Patricia, the mom of one of the players, Connor. Connor has a diagnosis of an intellectual disability. I spot Patricia and walk toward where she is standing and adjusting 12-year-old Connor's pants. She introduces me, and he thrusts out his hand, ready for a shake. While we shake, I ask him if he is excited about the game. He yells, "Yes, yes, yes, and my buddy, too." Connor will be assisted by a "buddy," who will provide him with the support he needs to participate in the game, but no more than that.

Patricia and I sit on the bench and wait for the game to begin. She says Connor looks forward to this extracurricular activity all week. He loves being a part of a team, he loves practice, he loves to compete (even though she says the games are not supposed to be competitive), and he loves baseball. She says, "There's no other place where the focus is a game, playing a game, not therapy and not fixing him, a game with friends." She continues, "And really, this is the place where he learned about the importance of being supportive, being a part of a team, why rules are needed, and to work hard and to keep trying." Patricia's voice trails off like she wants to say more, and she grimaces a little. I stay silent, waiting for her to finish. Finally, she says, "Sorry, I just really want him the chance to have fun with other kids."

Connor's buddy is Mr. Fent, the parent of another participant. Mr. Fent stands by as Connor grips the bat and moves to home plate. The coach places a ball on the tee for Connor and steps back, saying, "Have at it." Connor smiles, moves a little closer to the tee, looks out at the field, and swings his bat. He makes contact with the ball and celebrates by jumping in the air. "Run, Connor!" Mr. Fent screams. "That way [he points], to first base," and Connor takes off. He slows a little when he passes the bleachers to smile at his mom, and he keeps running, jumps with two feet on the base, and jabs his hand up in the air, with his pointer finger straight up. He shouts, "Did it!" Indeed, he has. The crowd goes wild.

Mr. Fent jogs to first base to high-five Connor. He points to the next base and tells Connor that is where he is headed. Mr. Fent steps back and watches the next batter come up to the plate.

Next up is Randall. Randall uses a motorized wheelchair and plays pretty much independently, as long as the path is smooth and unobstructed. Today, the baseball diamond is covered in dirt, so before the game started, parents and buddies made sure to kick rocks out of the way, ensuring that the path was clear, not just for Randall but for all the players. Randall has sturdy wheels on his chair, so it would take a lot to stop him once he takes off. Randall also uses the tee, but he uses it a little differently than Connor. The bat is tucked into Randall's chair so that it sticks out from the side of the chair. Randall stops about 2 feet away from the tee, and when it is time to swing, he zooms his chair forward so the bat hits the ball. The ball falls off the tee, and the only help Randall receives is that his buddy kicks the ball a bit further so it is in play and then removes the bat from the chair. Then, off Randall goes! The crowd cheers! He uses a joystick on his chair to rocket to first base. He gets to first and celebrates by moving his chair in a little victory circle. Then he looks at home plate to see who is hitting next to allow his advancement to second base.

It is Darla. Darla needs some encouragement to move toward home plate so she can bat. She moves her fingers in front of her face and squeals. It is hard to know if she wants to bat or if she wants to return to the dugout. A buddy holds out the bat and asks Darla, "Do you want this?" Darla moves a little closer to the bat, stops, and then moves closer again. The buddy holds the bat out, and Darla grabs it. She will not use the tee; she will wait for the coach to pitch her the ball underhand. Darla has been playing baseball for quite a long time, since she was eight. She is now 18. The coach says, "Here it comes," and pitches the ball to Darla. She swings and misses. The crowd encourages Darla with "you've got this" shouts. Darla drops the bat and moves her hands some more, and when she is ready, she picks it up. She moves closer to home plate, and her buddy encourages her to look at the pitcher. She does. The pitch comes, she swings, she connects, and it's going . . . going . . . gone! It's the first (and only) home run of the game. Darla stands at the base and jumps in the air. The buddy grabs Darla by the hand and says, "Let's run!" Together, Darla and her buddy run, skip, walk, and twirl around the bases.

In comes Connor, in comes Randall close on Connor's heels, and with what seems to me to be a "look at me" strut, in comes Darla. There are high-fives and woo-hoos, followed by water and orange slices. The coach comes over to Darla and holds out his hand as though he is waiting for a high-five. Darla takes his hand and holds it between her two hands. It is a beautiful day for a baseball game.

CHAPTER 3

The Arena

Give a squeeze, really make it happen. You need to do all the work. You're used to your leader being in control. Let's fix that.

—Gina

The drive to the stables is majestic—that's really the best word to describe it. It's a long dirt road, marked with potholes that make you drive carefully and slowly, it seems almost on purpose, so you can look around and see the large green fields off to the sides and the imposing trees that line portions of the road. Although it's beautiful, it also makes me feel out of place. This is like no other place I've been. It seems exclusive. I have no experience with horses or "horse people," as I have taken to calling them. I have chatted with horse people from three different stables and have visited all three stables. I have spent time watching all sorts of riders come and go. I have talked with instructors, assistants, volunteers, parents, and children. I'm excited to learn from the horse people and the horses. I am a blank slate, with no knowledge about riding, horses, the equipment, or how a horseback riding lesson unfolds. I'll start at the beginning.

I find myself sitting on the bleachers with my notebook in hand and holding my breath. There is a lot of movement in the stable as the next group of riders gets ready for their lesson. Some students come with their own riding equipment, while others borrow hats and other gear they might need. There's a lot of new sensory stimulation for me in the barn. The vastness of the space creates echoes. Because the barn is not heated, the weather fluctuates depending on the time of day and time of year. There are the smells of the horses, the hay, and the dirt. Gina is the instructor who will be teaching today's class. She has been a horse person for as long as she can remember. When I share with Gina my sensory experiences with being in the barn, she lets me know that I am missing out on the biggest one—the feeling of being on top of a horse. As Gina explains, some parents struggle with letting their children participate in this riding program. There is risk, big risks, should something go wrong. Gina states, "There is dignity in risk." This statement, according to Gina, is representative of her teaching philosophy.

THE REWARD OF RISK-TAKING

Are students with disabilities overly protected to the point that it inhibits their learning? Gina and I talk about this question during our first interview, and it comes up again and again in later ones as well. Gina is about five feet tall, in her mid-fifties, with short gray hair and piercing green eyes. Her voice bellows throughout the arena, and I'm struck by the volume and intensity of her voice the first time I hear it. Gina describes herself as a "no-nonsense" kind of person, and she does not feel the need to coddle riders. As Gina says, "I talk to my riders straight up. I don't sugarcoat things. I respect them too much for that." To say that Gina doesn't sugarcoat things seems like an understatement. She will tell an assistant to "back off" or that they are "not helping." I witness her directness one day with when a teenage rider arrives late for her class. All riders must arrive to the arena on time because they must mount their horses one after the other and proceed to the center of the arena, and then Gina officially starts class. One day while I am visiting, a student is late—not super-late, just a few minutes. Gina proceeds with the class as though this student will be absent, and just when all of the other riders gather at the center of the arena, this late rider comes rushing into the barn. Gina stops in midsentence and yells from her place in the center of the arena, "You are late. It's disrespectful to me and to the other students in the class to be late." Gina walks swiftly to where the rider has entered. Jenna, a rider with an intellectual disability, tries to blame her mom for getting her to the arena late. Not hearing any of it, Gina replies that it is up to the rider to let her mother know when it's time to leave so she will not be late. The rider looks a little embarrassed and her mother, who has rushed in after her daughter, even more so. Gina apologizes to the riders waiting in the center of the arena and continues swiftly to the side of the ring to assist Jenna so she can mount her horse. Gina bellows to an assistant who was just moving the horse back to the stable, "Turn that horse around. Jenna has decided to grace us with her presence," and a small smile creeps across Gina's face. Jenna smiles back. Gina narrows her eyes and commands, with just a hint of a smile at the corners of her mouth, "Don't be late again," and Jenna replies, "Never." I decide that I too will make it a point to never be late.

I had initially thought that these riding lessons would be more light-hearted. I am wrong. I also see over time that Gina, at first, can be super-intimidating but that this firm exterior cracks, especially when she is proud of what a rider accomplishes. Gina is genuine and will not offer her riders empty praise. As Jenna says later to me, "Gina don't play." Jenna's mom says that Gina holds very high expectations for Jenna, probably the highest of anyone she knows who works with her. "She might have an intellectual disability," says Jenna's mom, "but Gina doesn't cut her an inch of slack."

Gina is not alone with her riders in the arena. There are always assistants under her purview as well. They, too, come to understand that "Gina don't play."

GINA'S ASSISTANTS

There are so many volunteer assistants in the arena, always outnumbering the number of riders. Some assistants have been volunteering with Gina for many, many years and can anticipate what she is going to say before she says it. I talk to Mary, an assistant who has worked with Gina for over 5 years. Mary says that Gina's style in the ring is "down to business," but that she has a deep knowledge about each of her riders. The intake procedure for riding with Gina, or any instructor for that matter, requires that the instructor meet with the rider and their parent or caregiver before the class begins. Mary has participated in these meetings with Gina and shares that Gina always starts with the rider. Reflecting on her memories of these meetings, Mary explains that she has never seen Gina shy away from engaging a rider and will find ways to be sure each rider has some input into what happens in the classes. I ask for an example and Mary says,

> Okay, well, there was this one rider who had very complex medical needs. I don't know the whole diagnosis but it involved seizures and other physical limitations. The rider did not really talk, either. We weren't sure that riding was going to work for this kid. He was only about eight and had never rode. Anyway, Gina comes into the meeting, well, like Gina. There was no soft voice or gentle demeanor. She said something to the kid like, "Convince me that I should let you ride my horses," and the kid smiles. That smile was all Gina needed. I could see her developing a plan for that kid, and he did good. He did good.

Gina was not the only riding instructor who addressed how working with the volunteer assistants was a big part of their job. All of the instructors I talked with commented on how important it was to be in sync with the assistants. Gina was the only one who said that she often has to work with the volunteer assistants so that they understand that their role is not to minimize risk-taking, but to be there in case the horse needs additional input or students need immediate support. She believes her disabled riders are often shielded from risk and that this creates dangerous self-perceptions of what they are capable of accomplishing in the arena. Gina believes that the presence of the assistants helps to ease the concerns of parents and caregivers because they flank the horse and rider, but it's also a major part of Gina's teaching to "ensure the assistants are not overly 'helpful'" (using air quotes to emphasize the word "helpful"). Gina is the conductor in this space, and she is mindful that the assistants, the horses, and the riders must all understand with clarity the vision of her approach: to promote confidence and self-assurance in each of her riders by giving them just what they need, and never more.

Let's go back to the beginning and witness how a typical session unfolds. All four of today's riders arrive on time and begin by saying hello to Gina and meeting their assistants for the day. Some assistants already know the students, and some will meet for the first time, although Gina finds a few minutes between lessons to prep the assistants beforehand about the riders they are assisting. Once introductions are made, families move over to the bleachers, head outside to sit at a picnic table, or leave the stable and return when the session is over. The riders are ready. They wait in a single-file line to mount their horses, who are being brought into the arena from the stables next door.

MOUNTING—"ARE YOU READY?"

Mounting the horses is a very individual endeavor. I observed one class over 10 times before I realized that the riders are continually riding different horses. When I mentioned this to Gina, she replied, "Yeah, that's how the real world works. You don't get the same horse every time. You have to be flexible." Patrick rode a small brown horse in last session I observed, but for this one, he is given a large white one. When he sees the assistant bring the horse into the arena, Patrick says, "Whoa." Patrick seems really excited, but I imagine he is also cautious. Nope. Patrick runs up the steps of the platform and throws his leg over the horse rather quickly. The assistants move quickly to try to make sure he is safe. Patrick's mother previously shared with me that Patrick has been diagnosed with a developmental disability and attention deficit hyperactivity disorder, or ADHD, and he is nine years old. He has been riding for 2 years. Four people support Patrick as he mounts—there are two on the platform and two standing on each side of the horse on the ground. One assistant checks in with him once he is on top of the horse and asks if he is okay. Patrick smiles; takes both hands off the saddle, where he has been holding on; and gives a double thumbs-up. He sits tall in the saddle. Another assistant quickly adjusts the reins on the horse and helps Patrick with their proper positioning in his hands; she narrates what she is doing the entire time. When told to, and with an assistant on each side of him, Patrick squeezes the horse lightly with his legs and says, "Go!," and the horse walks slowly. Patrick's assistants tell him what to do so that he can guide his horse to the center of the ring to wait for the three other riders. Gina hears this and says, "Stop. He knows what to do." Once he arrives at the center of the ring, one assistant leaves his side and heads back to the mounting platform. While Patrick waits, he gets to know his horse. He pets the horse's head and laughs. He chats with the assistant as they wait for the others to arrive.

Marissa is next. She does not need the stairs and instead enters the ring, where she will mount her small brown horse. There is a conversation between Marissa and her assistant that seems to be about how she will mount. Marissa does not speak the entire time I observe her today. In the past she has spoken a few words, but today she communicates using facial gestures, nodding, and smiling. Marissa has experienced trauma in her short life, and because of this, she qualifies for special education under the category of an emotional disturbance. Marissa was adopted when she was 5 and is now 10. Marissa shakes her head to indicate to her assistant that she is ready to mount her horse. She stretches her foot up into the stirrup. As the assistant moves to give her a boost, Gina stops her by placing her hand on the assistant's shoulder. Gina says to Marissa, "Use your strength and pull yourself up and over the horse. You've got the strength. You can do this." Marissa does. The assistant learns what Marissa is capable of and seems to make a mental note of this when Gina gives her a look that seems to say, "See? She is capable." Gina says to Marissa, "I knew this would be a good horse for you today. Look at what you did!" Marissa smiles. Marissa and one assistant head to the center of the arena. Marissa's assistant says to her, "Look, Patrick is already here waiting for you." Patrick says hi to Marissa, and she smiles at him.

Next to mount is Karen. Karen is Autistic and has been working on modulating her voice in the arena. As Gina explains, Karen can sometimes be very loud, which can frighten the horses. Karen has learned to "use up her loud voice" before she mounts her horse. Gina tells me that sometimes before Karen enters the arena, she can hear her being loud outside, trying to get the loud out. Gina says, "It's important Karen learn to control the volume of her voice in this situation, not because it's not socially acceptable or anything like that, but because horses can be very sensitive to sound." When Karen's horse is small, she mounts from the ground, but because this is a large horse, Karen will climb the stairs to mount from there. An assistant asks Karen if she is ready. She nods yes. The assistant then asks if Karen would like to be held as she mounts, and Karen nods her head "yes" vigorously. With the assistant steadying her, Karen swings her leg over the horse and gently, slowly, slides onto the saddle. She sits still for a few seconds, and I wonder if she is okay. Then, as slowly as she slid into the saddle, a smile slides across her face. The assistants get to work; they are adjusting reins and setting the lengths of Karen's stirrups. They ask Karen which length of the stirrups feels better, higher or lower. Karen smiles. Gina comes over and taps Karen's leg higher and then lower. Gina asks, "Here or here?" Karen smiles again. Gina repeats her question and this time, Karen nods on the first "here." Karen adjusts her body in the saddle and the assistant gives her the reins. "No slumping," Gina says, and Karen sits up tall. She is ready to join the other two students in the center of the ring. Karen's horse moves very slowly, and Gina says to Karen that she will need to ask her horse to walk faster. Gina explains to Karen, but it seems to be to be for the benefit of the assistants, too, that it is hard for the horse to walk slowly and that it is more likely that the horse will trip when walking so slowly. Gina says to Karen, "Take a nice relaxing walk to the center, but not too slow. Squeeze a little." Karen squeezes the horse with her legs gently, and she and her two assistants head to the center of ring, walking briskly.

Our last rider today is Megan. Megan has cerebral palsy, a condition that impacts her core strength and muscle tone. Gina explains that she is working to help Megan improve her muscle coordination. Gina raves that horseback riding is excellent for this, and she goes on and on about it in every interview I conduct with her. Megan needs the most specialized help mounting her horse out of any of the students I observe in my time at the barn. Megan uses a walker to move around on the ground. She will climb the stairs of the mounting block, using the railing on both sides of the stairs to hold up her weight. An assistant is behind her as she climbs the stairs but does not assist. She is ready if Megan should lose her balance and need her. Two assistants wait on top of the mounting block as Megan climbs. When she gets to the top, they assist her by supporting her weight by grasping under her armpits and guiding her legs. They support her completely as they lift her up and onto the horse. Gina has worked with the assistants extensively so that they know how to support Megan. It's ideal if Megan can always have the same assistants, but this is not always possible. Today, Megan is assisted by one person who has worked with her before, and two who have not. Megan lands in the saddle, and her assistants do not let go of her until they are sure she has summoned the core strength she needs to hold herself upright on the horse. Megan does this, but she will need to go slow and have the support of the three assistants, one of each side of her and one guiding the horse by lead. Megan is on top of the horse and all of her equipment is adjusted. Because core strength is a workout for her, she always mounts her horse last. The assistant holding the lead asks if she is ready. Megan nods yes. "Then you know what to do!" the assistant says, and, undetectably to me, Megan squeezes the horse's sides. Slowly, Megan's body begins to fall into the rhythm of the horse's gait as they proceed to the center of the ring. Everyone is here in a circle, with Gina at the center. Like a conductor, Gina raises her hands and says to the group, "We shall begin!" The beginning of class is serious, solemn, and full of anticipation.

"TODAY, YOU ARE IN CHARGE"

Our four riders sit high atop their horses, assistants ranging in age from 15 to early 70s stand nearby, some holding equipment that is attached to the horse, some gently resting a hand on their rider's leg, some standing next to the horse and observing their rider. Gina sets the tone for the lesson. She says to the group, "Today you are in charge. We are going to work on controlling our horses as we become independent riders." She lets the riders know that they are going to begin walking briskly in a circle around the outside edge of the arena. Gina highlights that the students will need to keep proper spacing from one another and that they should adjust the pace of their horse according to where the person in front of them is located. Gina tells the riders they will need to communicate with their horses. She reminds her riders that they can do this in many different ways. They can squeeze their legs around the horses' belly, they can talk to the horse, they can use the reins in different ways, and they can adjust their body on the horse. She then adds, "Maybe you have another way that you communicate with your horse that I don't know about. That's good too, as long as it's kind." Gina tells the students that if they decide to squeeze their legs and their horses do not seem to get the message to move forward, the students should tap the horses with their heels. She adds, "This is not a kick because that wouldn't be right. When you use your legs effectively, your horse will do what you ask."

"Okay, Patrick, get going," Gina says. He starts nudging his horse toward the edge of the arena. When Gina thinks he has put enough distance between the group, she tells Marissa to follow Patrick, then Karen and finally Megan. All four students are now riding around the edge of the arena and have decent spacing. The assistants assigned to each rider walk swiftly to keep up.

As the students continue to walk in a circle. Gina turns her attention to the assistants, particularly the three assistants who are working with Megan. Gina instructs the riders to pull back on the reins so that their horses stop walking, and as they pull back, they can say "halt" or "whoa" if they like. After they fully stop, the riders should squeeze their legs so the horse starts walking again. Gina adds that if the rider would like, they can squeeze and say "go" at the same time. Megan is struggling to get her horse to stop walking, and her assistants seem unsure how to best help her. Gina instructs the assistants to be looking for when Megan pulls back on the reins. She tells the assistants, "She is doing her best, *you* have to adjust. We want the riders in control and she is doing it. Notice her pulling back. You also have to respond to the rider, it's not just the horse." Gina tells the assistants that when they see Megan pull on the reins, they need to stop walking. She says, "Stop, right then." The assistants focus their eyes on Megan and now expect to see her pull back on the reins. They look for the tiniest movement, and there it is! It seems that the movement is too slight for the horse to feel, but the assistants immediately stop walking and the horse then stops as well. Gina exclaims, "There it is, Megan. You did that. You did that. Okay, squeeze and get going again." When the assistants see Megan begin to squeeze, they walk forward and the horse follows. It seems to me that Megan sits up a little higher in her saddle.

Gina then instructs the group to sit "half-seat," which means to raise their bottom off the saddle and hover a bit. Some riders get individual help from their assistants. Patrick's one assistant says, "Rise up out of the saddle," and he does. Marissa needs no additional help, and her assistant just observes her complete this action. Karen's assistants repeat Gina's instructions and follow up with directions to "use your legs, raise your butt, make a space between the saddle and your butt," and Karen giggles and completes the action. The assistants on both sides of Megan physically assist her body and help to raise it off the saddle. Gina says, "Do just what is needed," as a reminder to give Megan some control of this movement. The students all sit back down in the saddle. Gina says, "Nice control, everyone."

Next, Gina tells her riders that they are going to reverse direction. She reminds them that she will give them the command "switch," and then they will reverse direction. She talks as the students continue riding in the same direction, waiting for instructions about how to change and the command. Gina explains, "Use your eyes, point your shoulders, but be relaxed in your arms. You have all done this. You've got it." Gina says, "Switch." Patrick is having a hard time making his horse turn around. His horse starts to saunter toward the center of the ring. Gina tells Patrick to get his horse back to the rail at the side of the arena. Patrick is trying, and his assistant is giving him the space to do so. Gina motions for the assistant to step back from Patrick and the horse. Gina tells Patrick to be bold. She says, "Your energy has to be bigger. If it didn't work the first time, ask again and more effectively. You tell your horse where to go." Patrick struggles a bit, and his assistant supports him by saying, "Look at the rail. Point your shoulders there. Pull the rein so the horse can feel it." Patrick gets his horse over to the rail and he is now riding in the unison with the other riders, in the opposite direction. Patrick has managed to get his horse to switch direction independently, and the other riders get the assistance they need to make this happen. For Karen and Marissa, this is verbal assistance with prompting about what to do. For Megan, her assistants gently tug the horse's lead and remind her to look where she wants to go. These different levels of assistance help each rider be successful.

The students walk and stop and walk again for a few more minutes. At one point Gina bellows, "Your horse is walking too slowly. You know who you are," and Marissa squeezes the horse with her legs so that it picks up the pace. Occasionally, Gina asks individual riders to take a half-seat. Gina notices that Megan seems to be leaning forward in her saddle. As Gina explained later, this is a sign that she is tired from the tremendous amount of effort she uses to keep her core upright. She adds to her instructions, "Only if you like, Megan. Let your assistants know. If you choose not to take a half-seat, work on sitting tall in the saddle," and Megan slightly shakes her head no and sits up a little taller.

Control at Trot

Gina says, "We are going to make sure we have control at trot. First we will walk to trot, and then we will trot to walk. You have to be in control." New to riding, I ask the spectator sitting next to me on the bleachers, "Do you know what that means?" I'm told that trotting is comparable to a light jog and that the riders will command their horses to pick up the pace from a walk to a trot. Then they will have to command the horse to stop trotting and walk again. It seems to me that the riders have all practiced this skill before, because only I need an explanation.

The students wait for Gina's command. Gina compliments the group by telling them they have nice spacing and that it is good they are not "crashing into each other." Gina asks Karen what she will do to begin to trot and Karen replies, "Sit trot." "Exactly," Gina replies. "Don't forget to lean forward and use the half-seat position," and then she tells them they are ready to begin.

One at a time, the students are called on to trot for a few paces while the others continue walking. Gina reminds the riders that they need to ask their horses with their bodies and/or their voices. Marissa is first. She starts to trot but doesn't stop squeezing her horse, and her horse veers into the center of the ring. Gina stops the horse and helps Marissa hand-over-hand, showing her how to move the reins so that her horse will go back to the rail. Gina asks another assistant who has been watching from the side of the arena to enter the ring to work with Marissa. Marissa knows this assistant and smiles. Gina says to Marissa, "You need to pull back. I know you can do that," and Marissa nods her head yes. Marissa successfully squeezes her horse, then stops squeezing and trots to the rail. She then pulls back on the reins and her horse begins to walk. A huge smile overtakes her face. Her assistant congratulates her and gently rubs her shin. "You didn't need me at all," the assistant adds.

Next it's Karen's turn. Gina asks an assistant to keep Karen's horse on lead. This means that an assistant will have hold of a rein that is connected under the horse's chin to the straps that wrap around the horse's head. After the riders leave, Gina explains to me that she was not sure that Karen could maintain complete control of her horse, and she had some concern that Karen might get scared and shriek, which could scare the horse. Gina says her concern was unfounded because Karen seemed to do just fine, and the assistant helped very little. Gina shared that she believes that Karen will be completely off-lead soon. Gina says she is a little disappointed in herself for not allowing Karen to try to trot independently. "Next time," she says mostly to herself.

Then it's Megan's turn. It seems that Megan uses her voice rather than squeezing the horse with her legs to get her horse to trot. The assistants on both sides of Megan start to quicken their pace, and the horse begins to move faster. Gina says, "Use that loud voice, Megan," and off she goes. "Yes, Megan, you have to mean it. That's it. You're doing it. That's gorgeous, and slow to walk." Megan does not trot as long or rise much out of the saddle when she trots, not like the other riders. The assistants are looking carefully at Megan to see when she pulls the reins so they can slow their pace. The assistants have learned to adjust. It seems they now understand that Megan is making the physical movements that Gina commands, and they have learned to notice them. The assistants move from a jog to a swift walk and finally to a more relaxed walk. They noticed Megan's movements and have responded accordingly. Gina seems pleased.

Patrick is the last rider to trot. He radiates excitement that his turn has come! Gina thanks him for waiting so patiently. She says, "Patrick, you did such a good job waiting for your turn. You must feel so proud of yourself." But it seems that Patrick just can't wait one second longer, and as Gina is talking he tells his horse to "Go!" His horse picks up speed and he suddenly seems a little nervous. His assistant runs to catch up to him. Gina tells Patrick, "Your body looks stuck." She illustrates what "stuck" looks like by holding her body rigid and then says, "You should be moving with your horse," and relaxes her body and moves rhythmically. With that, Patrick relaxes his body so that it can keep time with the movement of his horse, and Gina shouts, "That's it, Patrick!" On cue, Patrick pulls back on the reins and confidently says, "Whoa." His horse settles into a walk. All four students walk around the arena. Patrick's assistant looks happy that they are walking again.

Gina proclaims that it is now time to work as a group to trot and walk together. Not only do the students have to think about how to make their horse move differently, they must also consider the spacing of the other riders in the arena. I'm surprised that Gina does not give much instruction here. She says, "Is everyone ready to move as a group? If you're ready, nod your head yes." When Gina sees that all of her riders are ready, she says, "Okay, begin to trot." All of the students begin to independently squeeze their horses and lean forward. All are trotting. Gina says, "Everyone looks in control to me!" Some spacing issues develop, and Gina and her assistants help the riders adjust. They slow to walk, some saying "whoa" and others pulling back, and Marissa's assistant takes the lead connected to the horse. Gina looks satisfied. Her smile is reflected on all the riders, who look satisfied with their ability to walk and trot as well. Gina looks at each rider, nodding her head approvingly. She makes sure that each of her riders sees her approval. Then Gina says, "Now we are going to keep controlling our bodies and our horses outside. Let's take these horses outside and let's enjoy this beautiful day."

Outside the Arena

Gina tells me that when she can, she likes to take her riders outside the arena, where they can ride through the acres of the facility. There are trails carved into the wooded areas, and today our riders are headed off to ride on one of these trails. It's a beautiful day, the sun is shining, and it feels warmer outside the arena than inside. Gina comes over to tell me that they are going on "a real quiet, relaxed walk" and that I should step outside to watch but that I shouldn't follow the group. I watch the group of riders follow in a single line. In single file, with Gina at the head on her own horse now, the group disappears into the woods. I can no longer see them, but I hear a joyous howl from Karen. Then I wait in the sunshine, looking out over stretches of green grass that lead to the woods. About 15 minutes later, the students are back in view. As they reenter the ring I hear Gina say, "You were all off-lead and I wasn't scared. You were all in control."

With risk comes the prospect of control. For students whose behavior, bodies, and decisions are often controlled by the adults in their lives, these few moments of freedom seem like incredible gifts. Gina thinks it's important to ride outside the arena because the trails can be unpredictable. I mention that I heard someone laughing and she tells me a squirrel had darted across Karen's path. She describes Karen's reaction as a mixture of surprise and delight. She reflected on this as a moment of risk where the squirrel or Karen's shriek could have spooked the horse. "These moments can't be scripted, but they teach the students so much and give them opportunities to show initiative and control. This is how growth happens," Gina shares.

Karen's mom, Rachel, has joined me outside the arena to watch the group head into the woods. We chat about her experiences with Gina and riding in general. Rachel explains that Karen hadn't always enjoyed the riding experience. When they first started at the arena, Karen was overwhelmed by the vastness of the ring, how sound echoed in the ring, and the smell of horse droppings. She describes Karen as having many sensory needs that often overwhelm her, and she finds comfort in a few movement stims that help her regulate. Rachel describes Karen's friends at the ring as having disabilities that are different than her own, but she considers her fellow riders her friends. She has developed a social group of kids younger and older than herself, some who have ridden for many years and others who are relatively new to the program. Some students are very verbal and have physical limitations, some students are nonverbal but need no physical adaptations, and some students have many different modifications to help them ride, such as reins that are colored differently to help them differentiate between left and right and special saddles and stirrups. "Karen loves to talk about her friends at the arena and her classes when she is at home, and of course the horses," Rachel adds. Rachel smiles at me and adds, "I love that they go outside to ride in the woods. I love that Karen loves riding now."

Horses Don't Judge

The group is back in the arena again, gathered around Gina in the center of the ring. Gina smiles at each rider. She says, "You are all impressive. You continue to become riders who are in control of your horses. I will see you next lesson," and with this, she dismisses each rider to go to the area where they mounted to dismount their horses. Each rider, without being prompted, thanks their horse and pets their nose.

Patrick dismounts his horse and comes over to me and his mom. He is smiling as he prances to where we are sitting on the bleachers. His mom, Nan, asks Patrick if he had fun today, and Patrick jumps up and down, smiles, and says, "Fun, fun, fun!," each fun becoming a little louder than the previous one. Patrick does not share a lot verbally with me, but his actions can only be described as joyful—a wide smile fills his face, and it seems that his happiness is exploding from his body in the form of jumping, kinetic energy. Patrick wraps his arms around himself and spins. He says "horse" a few times. Nan wraps her arms around him and squeezes. Patrick squeals in delight. Pure joy. I comment to Nan about how happy Patrick is, and she tells me this is not unusual. She explains that unlike other sorts of therapy she's tried with Patrick, both outside and inside school, being at the arena brings a complete level of joy. Nan believes that this joy stems from the connection Patrick feels with the horse he rides. Nan says,

> It's hard to explain. It's just this deep connection to these really large animals that is very different than his interactions with our own pets at home. Maybe it's the size or the power, I don't know. Maybe it's the fact that Patrick can wrap his arms completely around the horse's neck and experience that love and respect, how the horse moves the way he asks. It's different, and it's powerful. It's taught Patrick a lot about his body, about balance and trust. Patrick can be who he is, and his being is perfect. Horses don't judge.

When I share these sentiments with Gina, she smiles. She says that Nan had told her recently that she had noticed a huge leap in Patrick's ability to follow directions. Gina states, "Once [Nan] mentioned it, I'm like, 'Yeah, me too!'" Gina pauses for a moment before she continues, "I just noticed his skill level in terms of being a rider, I wasn't thinking about his ability to follow through on directions." I'm struck by this statement. I have seen so many IEPs that have had "following directions" as the goal to be learned. How powerful it is for Patrick to have this skill taught in the context of learning to ride a horse.

During another lesson, I'm sitting on the bleachers with Nan when Catherine, Marissa's mom, joins us. We are watching the riders mount their horses and head into the middle of the ring. Catherine says to me, "There, did you see it?" I'm not sure what Catherine is referring to. I didn't see anything remarkable happen at all, so I say, "I don't think so. What did I miss?" Catherine instructs me to look carefully at Marissa. She points out that her shoulders have dropped and are no longer tensed up. "See how she just sighed and let out all the tension that she seems to be always holding onto?" Catherine says. I don't know Marissa well and have only been observing lessons for about a month, but now that Catherine mentions it, I do notice a certain lightness to Marissa that seemed to be absent when she was standing on the ground. Catherine begins to share a bit about the abuse Marissa suffered before she came to live with her, and she says that the first couple of years were a lot of therapy sessions, placements in special education classrooms, and dealing with many behavioral outbursts. "Things aren't perfect by a long shot," Catherine continues, "but riding is helping in a way that nothing else has. I almost don't want to say that out loud because I'm afraid I'll jinx it." Nan nods in agreement. "I think because it is not therapy. It is not special ed. It's not about changing her or talking about the past or anything like that. I think it's about having the chance to be in control." Nan wraps her arm around Catherine's shoulder and squeezes.

LESSONS LEARNED

On one visit, as I'm leaving the arena, I witness Marissa lingering next to her horse as she strokes his cheek, his neck, his chest. I have to stop to watch. I see the horse swing his head closer to hers, rubbing his face gently against Marissa's. Her assistants stand by and watch, each one smiling. Finally, one assistant grabs the reins and readies to walk the horse back to the stable. Marissa waves good-bye to her horse and walks to meet Catherine at the edge of the arena. Marissa grabs Catherine's hand and says, "I love that horse." As they approach me, I say good-bye and watch Marissa and Catherine walk out of the arena and get into their car. I wrote in my field notes, "It's like a beautiful ending to a movie. They both walk out into the sun, holding hands. It's so peaceful. I feel happy for them both that they are experiencing this moment together." I think about children leaving classrooms of all sorts, my own children walking out of math or social studies class, children I know leaving their special education classes for the day, my own students walking out of class thinking immediately about the next thing to do. I marvel at how this lesson in the arena leaves Marissa with what seems to me to be a deep sense of peace, and I think about how great that would be if we could all leave lessons feeling that way.

Building Caring Connections

There is a deep sense of care in this space. It's care for safety and for dignity, and also care for animals. The horses are nonverbal and hence communicate in different ways, and often it seems that the riders can really relate to this. Not only don't the horses judge the riders, they show up for them, and when asked to do something for their rider, they almost always do it. They are forgiving, too. If a rider squeezes too hard, or keeps squeezing, or pulls the reins a little too hard, it's often the instructor who will point this out to the rider. Never in the many hours that I visited did the horses react to the riders in any way that was scary. I was only clued into the fact that a student was squeezing their legs around the horse's midsection for too long because I heard Gina point this out to the riders. Often Gina noticed the horse veer slowly to the center of the ring and looked for small signs about what was happening. Gina directed her students' attention to the horses' movements and responses to the riders' actions, and she taught her students to read these signs as communication. I think because of the nuances of this relationship between rider and horse, a strong connection is built. This connection not only helps the rider learn to regulate their movement and behavior, but also underscores the need for care, compassion, and perspective. The riders are asked to think about how their actions might feel to the horses and consider how these actions have consequences that impact them.

The riders of course also connect to the people in the arena. Gina maintains strong connections with her riders starting from their first intake meeting. Gina centers the needs of each rider and is always thinking about how they are progressing physically, emotionally, and cognitively. She assesses her students in the moment, thinking about how to push them forward and how to keep them safe. Gina says that she believes her riders know she cares for them even though she can be "as tough as nails." What makes her time with her riders meaningful, according to Gina, is time. Gina is not relegated to accomplishing any one thing in a week, month, or year. Gina can take a long view about progress, and this, she believes, makes this time special. All the instructors I talk to, when I asked how their roles in the arena might be the same or different from teachers in a classroom, tell me that they are different from teachers because they don't have to be a "fixer" of kids. That is, they are not trying to fix children or cure them of anything; they are only trying to grow horseback riders. Often, as a result, other things happen to change as well. This is the basis for their relationship.

I spend some time talking to Alison, an instructor at a different stable in her mid-20s. Alison works with riders of all ages and tells me in her rapid-fire way of speaking, "Some are disabled, some have horrid experiences they are trying to live with, some have low self-esteem, some seem fine but what does that mean, some don't talk, you know, humans. What everyone shares when they come here," she continues, "is a desire for connection and control."

Body, Mind, and Soul

"Horses," Alison tells me, "are very, very intuitive. They pick up on energy and feelings intuitively because they are herd animals. That's a connection for a lot of our students." Alison tells me that she sees this with her riders who are experiencing post-traumatic stress syndrome, or PTSS. She believes that they, too, have developed an intuitive sense about their environments that makes them hyperaware and sometimes hypersensitive to things that the rest of us might not notice. Without sharing any details about her own childhood, she shares that she can very much relate to these feelings and, as a result, to horses. Alison started volunteering with a horseback riding program for disabled individuals as a teenager. She stated that her own riding experience was the impetus for volunteering. Her world seemed so out of her control as a teenager, and the only place she felt she truly had any semblance of control was the arena. She shared that she volunteered merely so she could have more time with the horses, but that she soon found herself connecting to the people at the arena as well. Alison began to notice herself, her struggles, and her victories in the riders she assisted. "This," she said, "came to me in a moment, a very powerful moment, that this would be what I would do. I knew it in my soul."

In schools, there can be very little space for students to have control over their minds and bodies, and little formal attention is paid to their souls in curriculum and required testing. In classrooms, students can be told to sit a certain way, not talk until they are given permission, what they will learn about, how they will walk in the halls, and when they can eat. And yet, Gina tells her riders what to do, how to do it, and when. What makes these two scenarios different? What can we take away from the arena that might add a new dimension to our classrooms?

I've come to see that the arena provides for integration of mind, body, and soul. Students are acutely aware that they must be thinking about how their thoughts and desires for action must be integrated with how their body moves, along with the care and concern for a living animal. In many ways, this is the polar opposite of what learning goals on IEPs and behavior goals on BIPs do. Rather than isolating ways to learn and behave, becoming a rider demands learning that engages a riders' whole being, not just one part. One way to think about this is that Gina is not just helping her riders to learn or act in a certain way; she is helping them to become.

Becoming

Although Gina tells students what, how, and when to do things, students are ultimately receptive to this instruction because it is meaningful. Gina doesn't ask students to complete a task just to complete it; it's a part of becoming a rider.

For many students who are placed in special education classrooms, the focus is on remediation and fixing, not on becoming. For a student's soul, this makes all the difference. If a student attends school, therapy, and counseling and in each session that teacher or therapist is trying to fix them, then that student is going to believe they are deficient. Gina does not try to fix her riders. She lets them know that to be successful riders, they need to think and act in certain ways.

What might this look like in the classroom? Teachers can design IEP goals, and hence instruction, to develop students' whole selves—to find ways to integrate the mind, body, and soul through the act of becoming. Rather than isolating learning into small bits of information, teachers could design instruction that is focused on helping students *become* scientists, mathematicians, writers, and thinkers. Flash cards and rote learning would play a very small role, rather than taking up the majority of instruction time. I believe that the difference between feeling broken and being told you need to be fixed versus an approach where you are becoming is life-changing.

Deciding to become is risky. It can take guts, and also trust.

Risk

The arena presents a physical risk to participants, and as Gina has shared, this is a very important part of the riding experience because the result of risk is dignity. There are many kinds of risk, and while schools may shy away from putting students, particularly disabled students, at physical risk, there are other risks they are sheltered from as well. How do we bring risk, and hence dignity, into the classroom? I imagine there are many ways.

In special education, paperwork about disabled children is rarely risky. For over 6 decades, disabled people and their allies have argued that risk-taking is essential for the development of self-esteem and dignity. Writing on this topic decades ago, Perske (1972) argued, "Overprotection endangers [the disabled] person's human dignity and tends to keep him from experiencing the normal taking of risks in life which is necessary for normal human growth and development" (p. 24).

There are many decisions that happen in schools that involve risk, although we might not see them this way. We choose or choose not to welcome disabled students into spaces that are understood to be for general education students, including classrooms and extracurricular activities. These decisions are often made by adults, not by disabled students. It can be risky to include disabled students in spaces that are not supportive of their needs, but as Gina proves, individual accommodations can be made and assistants can provide support while allowing students to take risks.

Not only do we need to provide physical risks, such as horseback riding, perhaps, but academic risks are equally important. Adults decide what disabled students are capable of accomplishing, as though we know! The paperwork created to describe what disabled students can learn, what track they should be placed in (academic or life skills), and who they can learn with contains only guesses. In my visits to The Special Center, described in Chapter 1, I witnessed children as young as five, in the "life skills" track, learning to pour water and fold clothes. There is no risk in these activities. As Gina shows us, we can promote risk while providing accommodations so that everyone gets what they need to participate.

Modification, Adjustment, and Accommodation

"If there was only one way to get on a horse, we'd be screwed," Gina says to me when I ask her about different mounting techniques used with her riders. I roll this line over in my head a few times. So much in the arena is changed for each rider that accommodation is the norm. Many times the modifications are made on the spot, in the moment, and in reaction to how her riders are understanding instructions. In fact, there is so much adjusting, modifying, and accommodating that it's hard to imagine the "norm" from which these adjustments occur.

Curriculum design often centers on developing a framework for instruction from which modification, adjustments, and accommodations are made. The aim is for the class to complete a learning assignment, and then adjustments are made for those who are disabled or learning English, especially if they have the legal paperwork that demands it. As I write this, in the time of COVID-19, when students are now receiving their educational experiences at home, I have witnessed teachers and parents adjust, accommodate, and modify like never before. They had to, just like Gina has to in the arena, to make sure every rider can mount their horse.

For my own children, learning in the time of COVID-19 has enabled them to see their teachers in a different way. They have watched them try new things, sometimes successfully, sometimes not so much. When things didn't work for their teachers, new technologies were difficult for them to operate, or assignments were too complicated for distance learning, they adjusted. More importantly, in many ways, their teachers have asked them about their minds, bodies, and souls. That's new. A pandemic does not bring a lot of positive outcomes, but as my children's teachers inquire about their mental states, ask them if they are getting outside and exercising, and have them reflect over videoconferencing about the amount and structure of their assignments, they are connecting with all parts of them—mind, body, and soul. Together they are becoming in this new world thrust upon them.

REFLECTION QUESTIONS

1. How do you understand risk and dignity in your own classroom and/or at home?
2. What is your own experience connecting mind, body, and soul? How have you witnessed this in learning environments both in and out of school? What would you like to see in these spaces?
3. Gina describes herself as "tough as nails." Why does this instructional style work for her?
4. What do you think of the idea of "becoming" in relation to learning and teaching?

INTERLUDE

THE LIBRARY

The staircase to the children's section of the library is a long, creaky climb. I grip the railing because the stairs are unusually steep. This library, established in 1899, services a small city of about 20,000 people. Taped to the walls on both side of the stairs are flyers offering classes to learn how to use technology, book clubs, and an array of programs geared toward children and teens.

When I reach the top of the stairs, there he is: serene, golden, laying on his side, but with his eyes fixed on the doorway. He picks his head up in anticipation when I enter the room. Of course, I immediately walk right over and give him my best puppy talk—a high-pitched "good boy" and "what a sweetie." Cookie's owner, Beth, comes over to shake my hand. She tells me a little about Cookie: he is 5 years old, and a rescue pup trained to become a therapy dog. It is then that I notice Cookie is wearing a distinctive orange scarf. Beth tells me that she volunteers here at the library a few times a month. Soon children will arrive for a chance to read a story to Cookie.

I grab a seat in the corner, and no more than 5 minutes later, I hear a loud pounding on the stairs. Someone is running upstairs at full speed, calling out "Coooookie." Into the room bounds Chivella, an 8-year-old girl with tight braids capped with multicolored beads. Chivella beelines for Cookie, and it is hard to tell who is happier. Beth stands nearby and watches with a big smile on her face. Chivella runs her hands through Cookie's fur, tousles his ears, and kisses him right between his eyes.

Chivella's mom, Monique, makes it up the stairs right as Chivella plants her kiss on Cookie. Monique shakes her head, indicating she is not a "dog person." Monique walks over to the duo, hands Chivella her book, and takes a seat at the side of the room.

In my conversations with Monique, I learn that Chivella receives special education services at school because she was diagnosed with a learning disability. "Chivella," she tells me, "hates to read. Like, hates it, always has struggled, always says she's stupid." Monique shakes her head a little bit like she cannot believe it, as if she is trying to reckon with how this bright child can call herself stupid.

Chivella says she knows she is not good at reading because "she's a level F" and that all the kids in her class read at higher levels. I am sad that Chivella understands herself, her whole literate being, as a "level F." She says, "I don't like reading because it's hard for me, and then I feel all scared if I have to read."

Book in hand, Chivella saunters toward Cookie and nuzzles right up to him. She uses her own singsong voice and says, "How about a fun story about a puppy for you, Cookie? I think you're going to like this one. I picked it just for you." She cracks open the book, sidles up to Cookie so they can both see the page, and begins. Chivella reads her heart out. She is animated and laughs at all the funny parts. She occasionally stops to see if Cookie is following and to give him a scratch if he needs to refocus. Chivella finishes up the book with a joyful, "That was a good book! Let's read another." As she peruses the library shelves, I whisper to Monique, "Well, she certainly doesn't look like a child who hates reading." Monique, with a smile starting to form at the edge of her lips, replies, "Mmmhmm. It's hard to believe that this is the same child who cries at the thought of having to read in her class." I shake my head up and down and think of all the kids I have known over the years who learned to hate reading.

Chivella settles on a new book and sits back down with Cookie. This time, she chooses a book she has not read before. "This one looks good, Cookie," she says as she reads the title and opens the book. Immediately Chivella says, "Oh, there's a lot of words in this book." She shrugs and begins. This is not a seamless read—not like the other book—but Chivella is not upset. She works through a few pages with her patient companion, who has begun to pant slightly. Chivella is working hard to keep up her pace so her story sounds good. She stops to sound out words now and again, sometimes successfully, and other times taking a guess and moving on. The point is not to focus on each word. The point is the story, her story to her friend who is so accepting of any version of the story; no judgment, no "that's not right," and no "go back and read that again." It is simply two friends enjoying a story.

Not too much later, two other children, siblings, come pounding up the stairs. When they see Chivella reading to Cookie, one turns to the other with a finger over her lips, saying, "Shhhhhh." They acknowledge the important moment unfolding. They tiptoe into the room, find a quiet corner, and wait their turn.

Seeing other children enter the room, Chivella looks at her mom, who shakes her head as though to say, "Wrap it up, and let's move on." Chivella says to Cookie, "Okay, one more page for you, and I'll read you the rest next time." Chivella checks this statement with her mom, and Monique nods in the affirmative. Chivella turns the page and continues until she reaches the bottom of the page. With a smile that spreads across her face, she says, "That's it for you today, good boy, Cookie. I'll see you soon." With this, Cookie pounds his tail on the floor a few times.

Chivella plants another kiss right in between Cookie's eyes and stands up. The two other children, patiently waiting their turn, begin to disagree about who will get to read to Cookie next.

CHAPTER 4

The Theater

Title: Affinity Spaces and the Theater

It's nice to be here with my people.

—Candee

ACT ONE

SCENE ONE: WARM-UP

A midsized metropolitan city. Traffic is fierce. The sounds of sirens and horns beeping.

I enter an unremarkable 12-story building, dodging the people rushing in and out. Though the building is unremarkable, I notice two ramps flanking the stairs in the middle of the lobby. I take the elevator to the 10th floor. The sign announcing the Abilities Theater Company (ATC) is posted on a door tucked away in a remote corner of the building. I push open the door and enter a large, airy white room with scattered multicolored chairs and plastic containers with props such as wigs and hats. A blackboard on wheels is pushed up against one wall, opposite windows overlooking the busy street below. Even on the 10th floor, I hear occasional sounds from the street. The linoleum floor is clean, although I imagine the scuff marks are the visible traces of past performances.

    I'm here before class starts to chat with ATC's founder, Melinda, and to observe the young disabled artists' class with children ages 8 through 14. ATC runs 15-week sessions where young artists socialize, play theater games, and create a production as their culminating activity. Though there is a definite age range for the class, this is flexible, much like the rest of the program. If Melinda believes a 16-year-old young artist will benefit from this class, she will enroll them; if students need extra instruction in an area, she will provide it; and if the final performance needs to be pushed back a week, she will reschedule it. Each class is about an hour, but as Melinda reminds me, that's "plus or minus depending on the mood and flow of the class."

Not only does Melinda seem to eat, sleep, and breathe the theater, she is also one of the most upbeat, enthusiastic people I have ever met. Standing at about 5 feet tall with bright orange hair, she exudes a boundless, infectious energy. Unsurprisingly, Melinda's twins in their late teens, Ivan and Illiad, also love theater and participate in the adult disabled artists' classes. Sometimes they come to the young disabled artists' class to visit or help out. Ivan and Illiad, like Melinda, proudly identify as disabled. Ivan tells me that he is Autistic, while Iliad shares that he has a disability. Melinda says she has been diagnosed with bipolar disorder.

Melinda started this theater program for disabled artists because she couldn't find any programming for Ivan and Illiad that embraced and celebrated disabled artists' identities. She shares that "there was always this vibe in classes I took them to, you know, like they were not true artists but they were disabled kids who needed help, and I'm like, 'What they need is to be seen as artists and creators.'" As a result, Melinda designed this space to celebrate disabled artists, evident in the photos hanging on the wall, depicting disabled people acting, painting, and playing music, as well as in her marketing materials that stress how the programming is designed to empower disabled artists. A small lobby space near the door houses chairs for spectators and a bookshelf lined with books written by disabled people or celebrating disabled artists.

I sit in this lobby space, awaiting the young artists' arrival. Finally the door squeaks open, and a face appears through the crack. Jamila is the first student to arrive. She bounces into the room and makes herself at home. Although this is a new session, Jamila is a returning student, demonstrated by how she owns the space: she hangs up her coat, looks over at me and smiles, and then struts into the space as though she is walking onto a Broadway stage. Jamila's dad follows behind, checking to make sure Jamila is settled. He waves to Melinda and leaves. More kids enter, some boldly and others with trepidation. The returning artists understand that they are free to explore the large containers of props, and soon the new students are trying on clown wigs and cowboy hats alongside them. When it is time to begin, Melinda announces, "Well, look at all these beautiful artists!"

Community-Building and Socializing

Melinda usually devotes the first few weeks to focusing on building community among her young artists. Melinda uses theater games to introduce students to each other, to create scenarios where the artists need to interact, and to find out more about the artists' interests.

The eight students in this session, ranging from age 8 to 14, are both returning and new students. Five have taken classes here before, but this is a new experience for three of them. Melinda says she focuses on observing the students during this early period, taking mental notes about activities and how students respond.

After Melinda welcomes her artists, she asks them to form a large circle. The returning students help the new ones by pointing to where they should stand or giving verbal instructions. Melinda reaches out her hands to show how each artist should have the ability to stretch their arms fully. Marvin, who uses canes, decides he needs more space so that he can extend his canes out as extensions of his arms. The circle adjusts to accommodate him.

"Now," Melinda says, "the first game we are going to play is to learn each other's names. Each person will share their name, and then they will pose in a way that feels good to them. Then the rest of the group will copy that pose and say or think about the person's name. Ready? I'll start." Melinda says her name and then poses with her hands over her head as though she is placing a crown on her head. She moves her body by sticking one leg out, her heel on the ground and her toes pointed up toward the ceiling. In this pose, she says "Melinda" again in a regal voice. The artists excitedly imitate her pose and say or think about her name. Melinda presents "thinking" as an option for students who are nonverbal or choose not to verbalize. There are various representations of Melinda's position and name.

Melinda looks around the circle at each person and smiles wide. Slowly, she nods her head up and down and says finally, "These are all perfect." Some students jump in the air and rock or move with Melinda's validation of their pose. The exercise works itself around the circle, from Brian to Candee, Marvin, Jamila, Chrissy, Florence, Malcolm, and finally Juan. The returning students—Brian, Candee, Marvin, Jamila, and Juan—move right into their positions, which I learn later are the positions they always use during this exercise. Florence, Chrissy, and Malcolm take a little longer, and their fellow artists cheer for them when they settle on a pose. Next week they will do the same exercise but add a small dance to the pose. The following week, they will add a noise or song.

As the group engages in other theater games, the young artists move around the room like their favorite animals, gesturing to each other to pass along pretend bolts of lightning and working together in groups to make shapes or tableaus. By the end of Week 3, the artists are independently socializing and connecting with one another. Brian does not use his voice to communicate, but he moves in ways that let his fellow artists know he is connecting. Brian stims by rocking back and forth. Brian walks over to Candee and stands next to her; he rocks back and forth. Candee turns to him and cheerfully says, "Hi, Brian!," and Brian jumps high in the air. Candee squeals and jumps, too, sharing this moment of connection with Brian. These artists have an array of disabilities: some are Autistic; some have trisomy 21; some have developmental disabilities, physical disabilities, and/or attention deficit hyperactivity disorder. Some tell me proudly about their disabilities, and others don't mention them at all.

Disability Pride

When Melinda is sure that her students have connected with one another and formed tight bonds, she introduces the group to disabled actors and artists. This creates a sense of disability pride and inspires students as they begin creating their own show. During each of the remaining weeks, Melinda spends about 5 minutes highlighting a disabled artist by rolling out a television as far as its cord will stretch. Some of the artists featured during this session are RJ Mitte, Keith Jones, Ali Stroker, Lauren Potter, and Alice Sheppard. The students watch, listen, and/or feel the performances. Some young artists stare at the screen, some move their body to the sound, and some move with the featured disabled artist, copying their mannerisms and movements. Melinda welcomes all responses. She chooses artists with disabilities that are similar to those the young artists may have, so they can see themselves in these professional artists.

Melinda uses the professional artists' performances to ask the class, "What did you learn from this artist? What does this artist want you to know about their disability, if anything?" Then she asks, "What do you want to share with the world about your experiences? About how you move? About what you feel? What should we make a show about?" Sometimes the students will answer Melinda's questions, and sometimes the questions just hang in the air while the artists think about them. As the session progresses, the questions become related to the show the young artists are designing. Melinda asks, "How did that disabled artist portray that they were sad? How can you do that in your show today?"

Melinda also guides the group of young artists to start thinking about their final performance. The artists get to work. They share their opinions, ideas, dances, songs, and jokes. Melinda notes these ideas on the blackboard and begins to help the group shape a show. She talks about skits and how one show can be made up of many different small shows or skits. With a sly grin on his face, Juan screams, "A skit show!," and the adults sitting in the lobby chairs burst out laughing, acknowledging how much "skit show" sounds like "shit show." Given this response from the adults, the young artists demand this be the title; some chant, "Skit show, skit show, skit show." Smiling, Melinda shakes her head, sighs, and, with an exaggerated air of resignation, says, "Well, if that's what the artists want, that's what we will do."

A Skit Show

Preparations for A Skit Show begin the following week. Melinda guides the group to think about how many skits they would like to create. They settle on two. As the group designs the first one, the young artists decide that they should all be in the skit and that it should involve all the things they love. Melinda tells the group, "What a fabulous idea for a skit!" Melinda goes around the room and asks the young artists to share something they love. The list includes dancing, trains, musicals, Pokémon, baseball, cookies, fairies, and Peppa Pig.

After some discussion about how these loved items can fit together, the artists decide the skit will take place on a train. "Well," Melinda asks, "what sorts of things can you envision happening on this train trip?" The young artists share things they want to see happening on the train, and Melinda guides them to think through how these different things might connect to make a fluid story. The young artists throw out ideas, looking to Melinda for confirmation. But Melinda tells them to talk to the other young artists. "This is your show, not mine. I'm just here to help make it happen," she says.

Some group members remain silent, while others take up a lot of space. Melinda reminds them that everyone must have input. Juan, who loves trains and has enthusiastically been sharing his vision, turns to Chrissy, who has been quiet. Chrissy loves Peppa Pig and says she would like to be Peppa Pig on the train. Candee, who has been active in the discussion, realizes that her friend Brian needs to be heard. Candee says she knows Brian loves musicals, and maybe he wants to sing a song. Brian's mom, Laila, who is sitting in the lobby space, shares that Brian has been enjoying a DVD of *The Music Man* (DaCosta, 1962) lately and that he gets noticeably excited when he hears the song "Seventy-Six Trombones." Laila starts to hum the song loudly, and Brian giggles a bit to himself and rocks in time to the humming, moving his head back and forth to the song. Melinda takes a mental note to find this song on YouTube for next week so that the class can listen to it. Other discussions ensue, and the excitement grows.

After 2 weeks, the idea of the skit is solidified. There are multiple discussions about how this skit will be a fluid story. Melinda shares video clips that highlight story arcs. When they arrive at a consensus on how to proceed, they start blocking out the final skit.

The skit starts when everyone marches onto the train to the tune of "Seventy-Six Trombones." Chairs are set up for each passenger, and the young artists decide where on the train they want to sit. Peppa Pig is a passenger, as is Pikachu from Pokémon. Suddenly the train breaks down, and the conductor, Brian, holds up a sign telling the group that the train is broken. Chrissy tells everyone that the train won't be able to move for hours.

One passenger, Marvin, wants to share his favorite cookies with the other passengers, but he is too tired and doesn't want to get out of his seat. Marvin delivers a short monologue about the joys of eating chocolate chip cookies. Luckily for the rest of the passengers, a dancer and a fairy agree to help pass out the cookies; by this time, all the passengers are very excited about the cookies. They show their excitement in many different ways: some stand and dance, others wiggle in their seats with big smiles, while others clap their hands. The dancer and the fairy twirl and jump their way around the train car, delivering the cookies and stopping to chat with each of the passengers. The fairy asks the last passenger to receive his cookie, Malcolm, who looks sullen, why he is not excited, and he remarks that he was going to a baseball game, but now that the train has stopped, he will miss the game. Malcolm takes his cookie and glumly takes a big bite.

The dancer suggests that they play a game of pretend baseball instead. The passengers move into position and play the game with an invisible ball. The conductor throws the ball out to the group, and they all move to catch it and throw it to another passenger. Sometimes they roll it, throw it high in the air, or throw it under their leg! Chrissy throws the ball to Marvin, and he bats it with one of his canes. The group watches the pretend ball fly high in the air and out of the train. They shield their eyes from the sun and open their mouths as they follow the pretend ball with their eyes. The passengers, now exhausted, all move back to their seats. They banter a bit more, and Candee cries out, "Oh, I think the train is moving." They begin approximating the movement of being on a train in their own ways. Peppa Pig has the last line in the skit: "You can always find friends and fun things to do if you try."

Watching this skit come together, from an idea to the final version, happens through weeks of hard work full of laughter and fun and, a few times, frustration. Each person is involved in every aspect of the skit, even if they are not the featured performer at a particular moment. Melinda promotes this through the concept of working as an ensemble.

Ensemble

When I talk with Malcolm about his experiences in the young disabled artists' program, he tells me that it is very different from his experiences in school. "School is a lot of sitting and waiting, and this is a lot of being [in] an ensemble where you are always doing something, so you don't get too bored," he says. I hear echoes of Melinda's lessons in this sentence. Since the beginning of the skit design process, she has reinforced the importance of being part of an ensemble. To substantiate her point that an ensemble must have all actors present, Melinda shows video clips of movies and asks the group to focus on what the background actors are doing. In one clip, the setting is a restaurant, and Melinda draws the group's focus to a table in the background. "Look," Melinda says. "See that woman right there? If she wasn't acting like a part of the ensemble, what might she be doing?" The group is silent. Melinda then breaks out in a wild dance, flailing her arms and legs around. "If she was doing this," she asks, "would you believe she was having a meal in a restaurant?" The group explodes in laughter. They add their own moves to show how ridiculous it would look to be dancing so wildly in a restaurant.

As the weeks progress, the young artists remind one another to be part of the ensemble. They learn that they are always acting, even if they are not center stage. They also learn how important background actors are to the performance. Interestingly, Melinda demands a full inclusion of their disabled minds and bodies in the ensemble. Melinda never asks her artists to appear more neurotypical or less disabled. She says to me that she never wants her artists to feel like they have to hide their disability while they are acting. She stresses to the group, "You don't have to stop movement that feels natural to you; you just need to incorporate it into the scene. Disabled people are everywhere in this world."

ACT TWO

SCENE ONE: THE SHOW

Inside the Abilities Theater Company.

It's show day! The performance is held outside class time, in the early evening when families and friends can attend. Chairs form a half-circle around the portion of the room that serves as the stage. The sets are minimal but effective in providing the audience with the information that the scene is set on a train. As the audience enters, they drop off plates of cookies, fruit, and chips for the group to enjoy at the reception after the performance. The young artists arrive a bit early and mill around in a back room, putting on their costumes and finding their props. An electric energy fills the back area, and Melinda's children, Ivan and Illiad, help the artists with everything from snaps on costumes to nerves. Ivan jokes with Candee about breaking a leg, and Candee jokes with Marvin about breaking a cane. The group runs some lines and gets together in a huddle before Melinda lowers the lights. Melinda asks the group if someone would like to offer a few words before the performance. Chrissy says, "We are all good people, and we make a good ensemble."

The group cheers.

The lights come on, and the audience erupts in applause. Brian jumps higher than I have ever seen. Juan introduces the first skit. He smiles as wide as his face will allow and shouts, "Welcome to *A Skit Show*! Our first skit is called 'The Train Trip.'" The recorded train sounds start, and the ensemble walks, runs, bounces, and skips onto the train.

The performance is funny, poignant, full of surprises, and, in a word, perfect. The young artists bow, some plugging their ears, as the audience gives them a standing ovation. The second skit, "A Funny Day at School," is just as amazing as the first. Malcolm thanks the audience for attending and waves to his family. The young artists receive a second standing ovation, and Malcolm, in his best sport's announcer voice, says, "The crowd goes wild!" There is laughter and bowing.

Melinda thanks the audience for coming and shares a few words. She lets the audience know that she finds such joy in working with the artists. She says, "These creative young minds inspire me each and every week."

Now it's time for snacks, and the young artists are off. The families socialize and congratulate the young artists. The performers greet siblings, grandparents, and friends who gush over their performances. Some artists are given flowers, and some are gifted trinkets. Juan gets a small train.

After an hour or so, the families start to say their good-byes. When everyone has left, Melinda turns to me and says, "Amazing, right?" "Indeed," I answer. "Every class, every young artist, that final performance, you," I add. She smiles and says, "And in two weeks, we start again. How lucky am I?"

Title: Inclusivity by Design

Out there, no one will say hi to me. In here, people can't stop talking to me.

—Xavier

ACT ONE

SCENE ONE: THE TOUR

A large, well-resourced high school in an upper-middle-class community outside a major metropolitan city.

I drive into the entrance of this large suburban high school on a Saturday morning, and I feel like I am on the set of a high school movie. The large, sprawling campus is littered with signs promoting different sports teams and activities. On the football field, suited-up teenagers practice while coaches shout at them to "hustle" and "block." Past the football field, I see a soccer field and a track encircling the field. I drive around the school a few times, looking for the entrance to the theater. After my third trip around the building, I admit to myself that I'm lost, and I have to call Maria, the parent in charge of letting me into the building. After she gives me some landmarks, I park and find the doors leading into the lobby.

Maria holds open the door open for me. I smile, remembering yet again that it's no longer possible to just arrive at a school; one must be let in, even on a Saturday. After we chat briefly, she introduces me to Karla, the director of this program, and Margie, her former student, who will give me a tour of this bustling space. I half-expected Karla to greet me in a sequin-covered chiffon dress emanating beams of light. In all my interviews, Karla is always described with long strings of superlatives. And yet, when I meet her in person, she is a mere mortal, busily running between set design, costume creation, and prop management. In my own conversations with Karla on the phone, I was admittedly taken with her philosophy of how theater can be a unifying, inclusive, and equitable context for bringing all students together.

As I haven't had the opportunity to talk with Margie yet, Karla starts to introduce us, but stops in midsentence and pivots to the small group of students next to us who are laying out costumes on the floor. Karla tells them that one actor's outfit they're planning is the wrong size and will not fit. She says, "You'll have to fix that." Then, picking up exactly where she left off, she finishes the introduction, telling me that although Margie has graduated, she occasionally returns on Saturdays to hang out and help. Karla says that I am in very good hands with Margie: "[She has] years of experience with the theater club and can answer any questions you have." Then she's off like a bolt of lightning. As I look at Margie, she says, "She's a very busy person."

I nod, affirming Margie's statement, and take the opportunity to survey the space around us. Gleaming framed posters of past productions hang from the walls, opposite a trophy case with awards the school has won for their productions and music program. I'm struck by the quality of the space; this isn't like the auditorium I remember from my own high school. This space actually looks like a professional theater. The high-ceilinged room's glass doors leading into the theater space are closed, since all the action this Saturday is happening backstage.

I tell Margie that my visit is to observe the theater club's weekly tech sessions, where students and occasionally family members gather to prepare the technical aspects of the play's production. Although the actors may participate (and indeed must do so for a few hours for each production), students gather on Saturdays to build the sets, design and sew costumes, construct and paint the sets, and gather props. Students help with hair and makeup design and sound design, design publicity materials, and reach out to local organizations for advertising support. On show nights, they take tickets, manage the concession stand, and serve as ushers. Saturdays are a time for students to socialize while also working on the production.

"Let's go!" says Margie, ready to begin our tour. As I catch up to her fast pace, she tells me that her best memories from her high school special education program called Horizons were after school and Saturdays at the theater club. According to a guidance counselor I spoke to, the Horizons program "mostly enrolls students with Down syndrome," and the students "have a separate classroom where they do a lot of their academics, and then they participate in some elective courses and wellness courses, physical education, cooking classes, things like that. They come into the general education classrooms for those electives." When I asked a student about Horizons, he shared, "Yeah, some students from Horizons came into my gym class, but I never really got to know them because you had to do what the teacher said to do. There wasn't time to hang out."

During our tour, Margie tells me she identifies as having Down syndrome, as a playwright, as an actor, and as someone who gets along with everyone. At one point during the very thorough tour, Margie smiles and points to a poster for a show that included a skit she had written and was performed by student actors. When she relates how funny it was and how the actors did a fabulous job, I recall what Karla had told me about Margie's foray into writing and directing her script. The student producer for the show came to Karla to share that the actors performing Margie's skit were "having a different experience than other groups." Margie had clear ideas about how she wanted her script performed and was not shy about directing the actors. Karla had let out a steady stream of air and responded, "Exactly! That's the shift, bringing everyone one in, I mean every single one, and not one person coming in and adapting to everyone else." Karla's initial exasperation was that the idea of a different experience was framed as a problem and this led to her decision to articulate her vision to the student director. Karla said, "I needed to say that out loud. She needed to hear that this space demands that we embrace disability and not couch it in 'different experiences.'"

In the back of the theater, students put large sheets of plywood onto the loading dock to go into storage. Other large pieces of wood are kept and are being repurposed for the next show. The head of the build group, Xavier, orchestrates this operation with his fellow students. Xavier's parents are here today, too, helping run some of the more dangerous equipment. Xavier's mother, Ingrid, stops me to say hi. We spoke on the phone about the theater program before my visit. She introduces me to Xavier's father, who is hauling a large piece of plywood out the door. Though I am excited to talk with Xavier about his experiences in the theater club, it's clear that I'll need to return when they're less busy. Margie takes me to the prop room to show me the baskets, candlesticks, bowls, and old-timey bicycle used in past theater productions. Margie shakes a maraca and does a little dance. "You're quite the performer," I tell her, and we laugh together. Margie puts down the maraca, turns on her heel, and walks rapidly from the room. I'm struggling to keep up with her when she stops abruptly, turns to me, and says, "You probably need to make a pit stop about now. The bathroom is right over here." She is absolutely right. When I return, she is waiting to take me back to Karla.

Margie returns me to Karla's charge and says, "I hope you enjoyed your tour." I tell her, "It was so thorough, Margie. Thanks so much. I appreciate your time." "No problem," she says, turning to chat with the students working on the costumes. A student named Hannah calls Margie over for her costume advice. Margie sits next to Hannah on the floor, and they chat about whether the costume is "flashy enough" to make an impact with audience members sitting in the back of the theater. Margie recommends more sequins, and Hannah says, "Yeah, I think you're right." They chatter away while Hannah sews on a few more sequins. After watching this scene, I turn to Karla, whose smile shows rather than tells how this after-school space provides multiple opportunities for all students (and alumni) to socialize and commit to completing a project.

I spoke with Karla a few times before coming to visit the theater club. She is very busy today—running between rooms, pushing students to solve programs, and referring students to other students to have their questions answered. I won't spend any time with Karla today, but she has arranged for me to speak to some students. Karla asks if there a certain place I would like to set up for my interviews with the students who volunteered to be interviewed. We settle on the back of the theater. I ready my recorder, use my phone as a backup recorder, and wait to see who will show up first. It's Xavier. He's 18 years old, so he signs his own consent papers as I explain the research project. He is ready to talk.

SCENE TWO: XAVIER

Truth be told, Xavier is the person I'm most excited to meet on this theater club visit. Before I arrived, Xavier's mom, Ingrid, told me over the phone about Xavier's disability, including his medical history, shared with his permission. Four days after his fourth birthday, Ingrid told me that Xavier "began to have seizures and . . . he really began to very rapidly go downhill, and so he was really ill from probably age four to age twelve." For many of these years, Xavier was in and out of hospitals while doctors provided "many scary diagnoses" in determining the type of epilepsy. Ingrid's voice slowed when she shared, "There was a point where they told us that he would die within the year"; the doctor added that "the likely trajectory was that he would become noncommunicative at some point and that he would likely need to be institutionalized." Ingrid sighed heavily as she recollected this conversation. Nevertheless, with brain surgery, Xavier improved and "surpassed these predictions." None of these experiences are apparent as Xavier strides toward me for our conversation. I'm reminded that predictions about children and their futures can be wildly inaccurate.

Xavier and I sit side by side at the back of the theater, surveying the stage as talkative students paint a piece of the set meant to mimic the grain of wood. We sit in the last row so no one can overhear our conversation. Xavier is a senior, feeling the pressures of graduation and his future. He is pensive and thoughtful as he begins to share his journey in the theater program.

His voice is so quiet that I push my recorder a little closer.

I lean in.

Xavier takes a moment to reflect on his classes and how his participation in the theater club has affected his school experience. I know that Xavier participates in both general and special education classes at this school. In almost a whisper, he answers, "If I am in the classroom setting, then I'm quiet—no one talks to me. I don't have friends or people I hang out with in classes . . . but in the [theater] club, I'm noticed. I'm spoken to like they're my friends." As the day at the theater progresses, I hear this sentiment again and again: the theater club provides a context for connection—a different kind of connection—that students just don't get anywhere else.

Xavier has participated in the theater club throughout high school, but this year he is a department head, a position one must apply for through a formal application process. Xavier explains the rewards and struggles of being a department head. The struggles include a seemingly never-ending list of problems to solve. Even when he is not at the club and working with his peers directly, he communicates with them online, "sending emails . . . checking due dates." Then he says, mimicking someone on his cellphone, "it's like, oh, by the way, the apocalypse just happened; we need some more stuff." Xavier smiles, shaking his head. He tells me about organizing groups of people to complete tasks, building platforms, and reworking sets. "Being a department head," Xavier continues, "actually means having to make a lot of tough calls and improvise on your own, where it feels a lot different. It feels a lot harder for me to do it if I have to communicate what I think about how to solve a problem alone. I'm more of a follower, and I do tasks if people believe I can. So that's what I'm worried about."

When I say that Karla must believe he can handle the position, since she offered him the job after receiving his application, Xavier replies, "I'm really grateful for the fact she gave me both the opportunity and she gave me enough confidence in myself to actually open up and express myself." He says this confidence has transferred over to music class, when he took the risk of sharing his music playlist with the class, something he would have never done before becoming the head of the build department.

Xavier's transformation is confirmed a few interviews later by a junior named Samantha who tells me about her relationship with Xavier—without prompting. When I ask Samantha why she wanted to talk, she says she wants to tell me how she found a home in the theater club. At the start of high school, she had just moved to the area from a different state; it was during this year that Xavier became her best friend. Samantha reminisces about when she first met Xavier: "Xavier was super-duper quiet, and I remember he was so quiet and we would just kind of sit next to each other, but we would work together, and he would be like, 'Okay now, it's time to move this.' We'd hang out . . . his whole family comes in to help, and they and Xavier are my best friends. He actually is saying my name now." When I ask Samantha what she believes led to Xavier opening up to her, she shares, "It's because of his leadership position." Samantha tells me she feels more connected to people in the theater club than anywhere else in or outside of school.

At the end of every school year, the theater club hosts a banquet for all those who participated, celebrating the many hours that students dedicated to the productions. Seniors receive individual attention, and the department heads have the opportunity to give a speech. Xavier shared with me what he described as an "early version" of the speech and asked me to keep it all a secret so I wouldn't spoil the surprise. The speech details Xavier's journey with the theater club and what he experienced during this time:

> I had been medically sick during elementary school and even had brain surgery, so I felt very different than everyone else. But then something peculiar happened, I was offered to be head of build. I thought about it for a good amount of time, and I was pretty sure if I accepted that role, nothing would change. I thought I would still be left out, not on purpose, of course, but still outside. But I said to myself, "Why not accept and see how this goes?" So I said yes to head of build. Almost instantly, I felt that was a change to how people would talk to me. What I realize now is that what changed was how I was talking to them. I let my guard down and let people get to know me. I started to tell my story to a few people on the crew as I grew to trust them, and I started to show people my strange dry sense of humor.

Unfortunately, COVID-19 prevented Xavier from giving his speech in person. The sets were ready, the costumes were made, the lines were memorized, but the performance was canceled. While that is a shame, I remind myself that in the more than 20 hours I spent talking to people about the theater club, no one discussed the importance of the final performance; everyone spoke about the journey—the hard work, the frustrations, the joys, and what they learned.

SCENE THREE: KARLA

Karla is clearly changing people's perceptions about what the theater can be and do: "It's really all wound up in Karla, and she is just truly unique. I have felt like Dominic's whole life . . . I just kept trying programs or organizations, activities for him, [I] just needed to find that one person who will have the patience and see what I see in him and have the patience to bring that out, and this is Karla," says Natasha. Her son was diagnosed with multiple disabilities, and school has been a very difficult space for him.

Funnily enough, however, *patience* is not the first word that comes to mind as I watch Karla in action. In the middle of our interview, while drilling down on what it takes to create an inclusive program, she notices Marcia painting a scene on a large piece of cardboard. Karla yells across the room, "Hey, Marcia, find a better background, please. Find a wall. Even this wall. Somethings that's not the ugly, crinkly, black-black, I don't know, anything else!" Marcia finds a sturdy, portable wall and asks, "Like this?" "Yes, thank you," says Karla, easily transitioning back to her thoughts on the importance of inclusivity in the theater.

Every participant and person affiliated with the theater club understands this extracurricular group to be a "different" kind of space. The school social worker put it this way: "High school, in general, is hard. It's even harder, I think, in a town like this. It's triply as hard when you don't align yourself with what other people deem important and have deemed important for the 12 years that they've been in the school system. So I've seen many, many kids be embraced [in the theater club] for their unique identities and for their unique skill sets, which then begets further confidence for their self-esteem. I've seen it really make a difference on a number of different platforms for a number of different kids." As I learn, Karla plays a huge role in this, and this inclusive environment is not by happenstance, it is by design. Karla implements her philosophy of inclusive spaces by providing structure so that "every single human" can be welcome and productive in this space.

ACT TWO

SCENE ONE: BELONGING BY DESIGN

Undercover Companions

Tiana, a senior with years of experience in the theater club, whispers to me that she has a secret she is not sure she should share with me. Finally, after hemming and hawing, she says, "Well, we have this whole system. It's called Undercover Companions." This is the first time anyone has, or will, mention this. Tiana describes Undercover Companions as a support system for all first-year students in the theater club, and for students in other grades, too, who might need some extra support. This structure is not shared widely with the theater club participants and Tiana says she was honored to be chosen by Karla to oversee this process. Tiana casually asks students who have been in the theater club before if they could make sure a fellow participant is feeling connected to others or helping them learn their lines. This casual "ask" by Tiana is a part of a structure developed by Karla. Karla and Tiana keep the Undercover Companion structure quiet because what typically happens is that this structure morphs into a friendship. By being asked to spend a little extra time helping out another person, the pair forms a bond and a true friendship.

The Undercover Companion helps their partner make social connections to other members and memorize their lines, and generally just makes them feel included and successful in the theater space. And Tiana explains that it is really not a huge responsibility, but it's the little things that I think make it so easy for *all* new students to be a part of the club. People have Undercover Companions and are Undercover Companions without knowledge of this structure.

I press Tiana further. "So, when you say that there are some kids that need 'a little more help,' are the kids you're referring to the disabled kids?" Tiana backs up in her chair and sits up a little taller. "No, when I said everyone, I meant everyone. It can be someone who is new to the school or is just struggling with fitting in. It really doesn't matter why you might need an Undercover Companion." Tiana says that Karla might suggest a student be paired with an Undercover Companion even if they are not a first-year student. "I don't know how Karla decides . . . Maybe counselors or parents ask, or maybe it's just what Karla observes." "So," I continue to prod, "all first-year students get an Undercover Companion no matter what, but if you're not a first-year student and it seems like having an Undercover Companion is a good idea, to just keep an eye out for you, then you can get one too?" Tiana laughs. I think she's amused that I'm having such a hard time with this concept. "It's pretty simple," she says.

No Cuts, Little Competition

The theater club is open to all, and many students comment on how different this structure is as opposed to other clubs or sports at the high school. As Karla explains, "If you want to be in the theater club, you are in the theater club." Karla has been welcoming all into the theater club for 3 years, as long as she has been director, and no one is turned away. Although the theater club has been around for decades, this inclusive structure is Karla's design. The previous director, Donna, describes how she used the buddy approach and asked nondisabled students to "bring the special needs kids in."

The guidance counselor and the school social worker often refer students to the club. Though this has fostered a culture of acceptance, it comes at a cost. Karla says, "The program has grown exponentially, and I think also word has gotten out that this is a welcoming, comforting place and that we will accommodate anything and anyone and we will figure it out. . . . This is the first year that I'm experiencing this tipping point of just numbers."

Although the idea is seemingly innocuous, the approach of accepting everyone contrasts with typical high school theater practices. As multiple students explain, high school theater is usually a competitive space, and competing for parts means making cuts, just like the sports teams at high schools. The tipping point that Karla describes means that as the numbers grow, she has less and less time to find and utilize the unique strengths that all students bring to the club. My interviews with Karla were full of examples of how her familiarity with individual students allowed her to invest in their strengths and interests. Students who could not carry a tune were amazing at applying makeup, shy students uninterested in stage roles created intricate props, and students excited about stage roles had multiple opportunities to shine through preshow announcements and other stage parts. But really getting to know students in this way takes time.

Though Karla is employed part-time by this school district, it's apparent that ensuring each student has an inclusive experience is a full-time job. I'm nervous for Karla because it's clear she will need more people and resources to thrive as more and more students flock to this space. Karla not only needs the support of the district; she also needs other adults who believe in her philosophy that the theater club should include all students. Karla's design has become a practice, but in order to reach all the students who want to be included, her approach will need support.

As I drive away from the high school, I notice the high school girls' soccer team practicing on the field. About 20 students are on the team. I wonder how many students tried out and were turned away.

LESSONS LEARNED

Purposeful Design

Karla and Melinda purposefully design their theater spaces to carry out their philosophies of how participation in theater programs can promote inclusivity. Karla believes that the theater is a space that can include anyone who wants to participate and that the space is richer when it is more diverse. Melinda believes that theater needs more inclusivity, too, but she focuses her intention on disabled artists. She provides this affinity space so that disability can be celebrated. Melinda highlights disabled artists to provide inspiration and role models for her young artists. These different approaches provide spaces akin to windows and mirrors–spaces for nondisabled and disabled people to see themselves in the theater, and to see others, too. This concept of windows and mirrors (Galda, 1998; Glazier & Seo, 2005) is often applied to the need to provide students with multicultural children's books, so they can see themselves in these books (mirrors) and also learn about cultures, identities, and experiences that are different from their own (windows). Books can be the vehicle for this validation of one's community or this new learning. This concept, pushed in a different direction, can be used to discuss spaces as well. Here, theater spaces provide doors to walk through to engage with others, and mirrors that are not flat, but convex.

Opening Doors

But for a few rare instances, the social spaces in Karla's school, outside of the theater program, are separate, with academic achievement and/or disability being the element that separates students. Multiple students expressed discontent not with how they were tracked in school, but with the lack of diversity in those tracks. When the students did mix in classes where multiple tracks came together, the teacher still orchestrated the classroom environment, so there was little time to get to know other students. After-school sports programming is competitive at this school, and so these spaces typically are available to only the students who had a deep history of playing a sport.

Karla's theater space breaks down these barriers, in part because it exists outside the school day. After-school spaces provide opportunities for students to work on a common goal while developing social connections. While the after-school instructor might have oversight of the space, the students are free to work on their part of the project independently from the instructor, allowing space and time for students to bond with one another and engage socially. In these scenarios, students aren't just looking through a window at one another, they are walking through a door to *be* with one another.

Grouping students by ability in high schools is often used to help teachers prepare them for assessments. Spaces like Karla's inclusive theater space prepare students for a diverse world where disability is part of the norm, not the exception.

Convex Mirrors

Melinda's theater space could be thought of as a mirror space where disabled artists are able to see themselves in the theater. Melinda's space does more than just present a flat mirror, however; she widens the view by creating an affinity space that provides examples of disabled artists in the world. She does this in explicit ways by sharing professional disabled artists' work, hanging posters of disabled artists around the theater space, and providing texts written by or highlighting disabled artists. These acts of sharing, displaying, and providing examples of disabled artists' work are rare in schools. Disability and disabled people are often not a part of the curriculum, and this space might be the only space where these young disabled artists can see others who look like them.

Melinda's goal to find disabled artists whose disabilities mirror the ones the young artists have is an intentional decision to show that the work they are doing in this space can be done outside this space, too. Adding this dimension is not difficult, but the power of widening the view, providing this convex mirror where the young artists can see themselves and also professional disabled artists engaged in this work, is important. Like the side mirror on a car, also a convex mirror, the message is that "objects in the mirror are closer than they appear."

Imagination and Social Engagement

Again, the paperwork that describes the learning and behavioral goals of disabled students in special education is often written as discrete learning tasks where students are expected to complete an academic task with a certain percentage of accuracy to show mastery. But what about creativity and imagination? How do we make sure that disabled students have opportunities to flex these muscles in ways that build agency and allow them to express their creativity? While disabled students are included in the arts programming at their schools, these classes often are predesigned spaces where an art activity or project is explained and then completed. The theater programs discussed in this chapter do much more. They invite participants to bring their imaginative selves to the space and create.

The opportunity to create is important, but the opportunity to create with others is what makes these theater spaces prime for exchange. The possibilities for the exchange of creative ideas, for expression and peer response, without the direct gaze of teachers, is powerful. Melinda and Karla both provided structures for their students to be creative, but they did not have a strict lesson plan about how the experience should unfold or strict learning goals that had to be met with a certain percentage of accuracy.

The creative space created in the theater is complemented by the social opportunities that open up. The act of sewing costumes together, or even just time before official class starts to play around with costumes, is time for participants to socialize in ways that are meaningful to them.

Leaders and Ensembles

In Karla's theater, the creation of department heads allows disabled people to hold leadership roles. In the high school where Karla's after-school and Saturday program takes place, different academic tracks run parallel to each other. Rarely do students in one track get to know the students in others, but if they do, disabled students are "added" to classes that are considered general education or mainstream classes. The opportunity for disabled people to take on leadership roles is significant because we see disabled people in charge, making decisions and coordinating tasks. There are not many spaces in school, and society, for disabled people to be leaders, and as Xavier shows, this opportunity allows him to not only show his peers how capable he is, but also helps to change the way he sees himself.

As important as leadership roles are for disabled people, it is equally as important for disabled people to be in community with one another. Melinda's theater space does not demand conformity, like many school spaces. In fact, Melinda makes it a point in almost every session to remind her young artists that they do not need to change their bodies or their movements to "be" actors or to be a certain way in this space; they should own acting principles in ways that honor their disability. For example, Melinda tells Brian, the conductor of the train for *The Skit Show*, that he does not need to use his voice. He can use signs that communicate to the audience, but he should act like a conductor. They look at photos of conductors, and she talks about how the conductor hangs out of the train door with their hand raised. Brian mimics this motion while holding his sign in the show. In one of my interviews with Brian, I notice how his energy level changes when we talk about Melinda and the other young actors. His mother interprets this as happiness and connection. Although Brian's communication is nonverbal, his pleasure in this group is apparent in other ways. As his mother notes, "It can be hard to get Brian excited about going to school, but that's never the case here [at the Abilities Theater Company]."

Karla and Melinda are intentional about disability in their theater design. In both of these spaces, learning is so much more than tasks to be completed, and the stage is open to people of all abilities. Bravo!

REFLECTION QUESTIONS

1. What spaces do you participate in that are designed to be inclusive? How might others become more inclusive?
2. Leadership positions in the theater club were available to disabled participants. Are you familiar with other places where this is true? How could leadership positions be expanded to disabled people in other contexts?
3. How are Karla and Melinda's teaching styles the same and different? Do you connect with one more than another?
4. How do you feel about after-school programs that make cuts?
5. How might disability pride become a part of your curriculum?
6. What are the benefits of affinity spaces for disabled people? How are these spaces be incorporated into schools or how could they be?

INTERLUDE

THE CAFÉ

"I love hanging out, and I wanted to be in a place where people could come hang out," Carrie explains. Her dad, Frank, stands behind her and nods. Carrie, who describes herself as "special needs," finished her school experience at 21 when she aged out of the special education program at her local high school. She says she did not want to go to another program, take another bus, or be in another class. With exasperation in her voice, she exclaims, "I just wanted to work at a job I liked!"

Carrie's café is beautiful. The large space with dark wood floors is filled with bright, multicolored couches and chairs to lounge upon, and orange plastic chairs and tables at which to sit and enjoy coffee, a sandwich, a salad, or the many specials of the day. Carrie invites me to sit with her on the couch, but first, we stop by the pastry display. I choose what proves to be the most decadent cinnamon roll I have ever eaten. Carrie brings me a hot cup of coffee, and we sit. Frank busies himself in the back of the café, wiping down counters and helping customers.

Carrie's dad secured this space for Carrie when she shared that she wanted to own a bakery. Carrie tells me that being a boss is fun but also sometimes hard. She appreciates her dad's help and says that while he helps her be a boss, she's not allowed to be *his* boss. Carrie throws back her head and laughs at this. Carrie and Frank are "bosses together." Her mom, Melissa, has a "regular job doing something in a court, I can't remember what," she adds. Carrie has a hand in all aspects of running the café: hiring, cooking, cleaning, customer service, ordering, designing the space, and anything else that arises. She hires "special needs" people first (her choice of language); right now, of the eight people working at the café, "six are special needs." Then Carrie notices a person waiting at the counter and leaves abruptly. I scoot back on the couch and observe.

I focus on Nick, who has been working at the cafe for only a week. His job is to clear the tables, take the dishes into the kitchen to be washed, and sweep the floors when he notices they are dirty. The café is not superbusy right now—only three of the 15 tables are occupied. Nick keeps busy, moving around the space and sweeping the floor when he notices a crumb. He notices a plate he believes is ready to be cleared and reaches for the plate. The customer lets him know that she wants to keep the plate. Nick lets out a squeal, and the customer sits back in her chair, startled. His hands flutter at his sides, and he walks over to Carrie and stands patiently by her side while she finishes up with her customer. Carrie says to Nick, "I know, let's go back together," and they return to the customer's table. Carrie introduces Nick to the customer, and the customer smiles. Carrie explains that Nick's job is to clear that tables, so the customer can just push her plate to the side when finished. Then Nick will know it is ready to be cleared. "Of course," the customer says, smiling. "Thank you!" Carrie responds in a singsong voice. She turns to Nick and says, "There. Now, do you want to sweep?" Nick heads to the corner to grab the broom. Nick moves his broom across the café with one eye on the customer's plate. Within 10 seconds of the customer moving the plate to the side, Nick zooms over and grabs the plate, placing it in the bin of dirty dishes. As he does, the customer says, "Thanks, Nick," and he giggles.

I notice Frank peering from the kitchen, watching this scene unfold. He does not move, watching Carrie handle it. I learn later that he has been supporting Carrie's "boss skills," as they call them, by giving her strategies to use. Frank tells me he suggested to Carrie that she tell her employees that if they are confused or do not know what to do, they should come over and stand next to her. Carrie adds, "Yeah, not everyone [who works here] talks."

As Carrie hears the door open, she says, "Welcome to my café. I'm Carrie." She heads toward the counter to take the order. When the customer asks Carrie for her recommended sweet treats, Carrie tells him about all her favorites: the cinnamon buns, the muffins, the scones, and today's special, cream-filled cupcakes. As she says the word "cupcakes," Carrie's eyes roll back in her head, and she licks her lips. Sold! The customer takes two cupcakes and an iced tea. Then he hands Carrie a 20-dollar bill, and Carrie calls, "Dad." Frank heads to the counter. He is working with Carrie to teach her how to make change. Carrie says to the customer, "He's the cash guy, and I'm the credit card girl," with a big smile that leads the customer to say, "Well, if I knew that, I would have used my credit card!"

The café hums along all day. Nick stays for 2 hours and then leaves—his shift is up. Carrie's friend from school, Jackie, works at the café, too, and arrives just as Nick is leaving. She will take over his jobs. Carrie introduces me, and I ask them how being together in the café is the same and different from being in school. Jackie grins and says, "I get paid!" Carrie giggles and says she also gets paid and does something she wants to do. Jackie adds, "I also get to meet cute boys," to which both girls break out in giggles.

I'll come back to this café often. Each time I visit, I witness Carrie being a boss, customers relaxing in comfy chairs to enjoy the day's treats, and café workers coming and going to work, picking up paychecks and enjoying their jobs.

CHAPTER 5

The Studio

My whole self is music, and here I get to be my whole self.

—Mark

Elena warns me that her studio is very small: "It's small but mighty!" I drive around this quaint rural community looking for the strip mall where Elena's studio is located, nestled between a post office and a small café. It's taken me a while to find a music studio that embraces disability and music-making. I was introduced to Elena through an acquaintance who is interested in disability studies and music. He shared, "Oh, you have to meet Elena. She is who you are looking for.

"She," he said, "breathes music."

When I reach out to Elena by phone, she shares that she has no diagnosed disability but suspects she is "on the spectrum." She elaborated, "I didn't bother getting a diagnosis. Why bother? But yes, I do imagine I am on the spectrum. I imagine my special interest is music. Really, though, what does it matter? Plus, they didn't really do that sort of thing when I was in school. I think they just thought I was quirky."

Elena also describes herself as very artsy and outgoing. When I ask her about the programs she offers, she talks for a full 5 minutes about her studio. Yet, I am still puzzled about the structure of her program. Sensing this, Elena tells me excitedly about all her students and how she combines students to create groups. "But," she says, "it's not really programs or classes—it's more about collaboration than about being in a class." Elena starts to tell me about the instruments in her studio when she interrupts herself in midsentence. "Erin, I think you need to just come to my studio and hang with us and see us in action."

The strip mall appears almost out of nowhere on this quiet road. I push open the door of Musicality, Elena's studio, and a small chime marks my entrance. The studio is larger than I imagined and is packed with a variety of instruments, from tiny harmonicas to enormous drum sets. Instruments adorn the walls, tables, and even the floor. Folding chairs are scattered around, along with a few beanbag chairs. Elena jets toward the front door and welcomes me with a "Hey, you're here!" She whisks around and starts walking away from me, and we are off to explore the space.

RHYTHM IN MY BONES

Elena started her business 2 years ago with the help of her parents' money to rent the space. Her greatest joy is filling the space with instruments, many of them donated or purchased from yard sales. She points out all sorts of instruments, noting their origins from around the world. When I remark on how many instruments there are to learn how to play, Elena says, "Oh no. You don't *have* to learn how to play every instrument, Erin. You have to be open to being called to an instrument and just trying it and experimenting. This is not about making classical musicians; it's about creating, feeling, doing.

"In this studio," Elena continues, "the goal is to help disabled people feel connected to music, although I will collaborate with nondisabled children, too, but honestly, it's the disabled musicians I enjoy the most." Elena says that parents often notice their disabled children's strong connection to music and, therefore, want to foster that connection. Elena carefully explains to parents that she will not start by teaching a student how to play a specific instrument but rather will follow the student's lead, encouraging them to experiment "with what speaks to them." When students want to learn more about an instrument, Elena then provides tailored instruction for each musician. When first meeting a new student, Elena describes her approach as being like a detective, searching for clues as to why her young musicians make certain choices about instruments. Gathering these clues includes how her musicians move about the studio, how long they engage with certain instruments, how they express their emotions, and how they decide what music they enjoy. "Once I have some clues," Elena says, "I begin to structure an experience."

In my over 20 hours of looking for innovative spaces that engage disabled people in music, I have talked with music therapists, music teachers, and professional musicians who identify as disabled. I wanted to find a space that did not use music to try to fix or provide therapy for disabled people, but, rather, engaged in the process of creative music-making. Elena's studio stands out as an empowering space that fosters so much more than only learning how to play music or engaging music as a form of therapy. Elena says that for as long as she can remember, "rhythm has been in my bones." In public school, which was her first contact with music lessons, she found the lessons to be boring and too much emphasis put on learning to be correct. In these spaces, music instruction felt very much the same as math instruction: it was all about learning notes and performing exactly as the teacher expected. Elena also notes that students in special education classes were rarely included in the school band. She continued, "I was different, maybe people saw me as weird, but I remember thinking that playing in the school band was torture. I couldn't stand having to sit a certain way or play the same song again and again. We didn't even get to pick the songs!"

At home, things were different. As a youngster, Elena spent much of her free time listening to music. Her parents always had music on in the house and took Elena to music stores to buy albums and cassettes. When she was older, Elena's parents would drop her off at the music store and return hours later to retrieve her. Elena describes this time as just magical: a time to peruse a range of albums and album art, to explore different musical styles, and to chat with the young people working at the store about which music they enjoyed. Elena laments the loss of this opportunity for young people, since most music is digital and bought online, so she tries to add that element into her studio—the opportunity to linger with music and be in conversation with others.

As a teenager, Elena began to experiment with musical instruments outside school. When I ask her if she had a favorite group or style, she says, "It never stops. I love something and then something else, and then something else." Elena describes her love for music as "always evolving."

While Elena took college classes to become a music teacher, she was dismayed that the classes always involved thinking about how to prepare young students to learn to play a particular instrument. Elena also "dallied in music therapy," but shares, "it wasn't for me." Elena knew exactly how she wanted to engage young disabled people in music; she just needed the financial support to open her studio. Her parents happily obliged and enjoy coming to the studio to visit. Elena shares that she is her parents' only child, and they have always been supportive of her love of music. Elena says, "Now, in my late twenties, I'm living my dream."

I am curious to watch Elena work with her musicians. She invites me to "be at ease" in the space. I find a cozy spot with a beanbag chair pushed into the corner of the room; in time, this becomes known as "Erin's spot." I sink into the chair and listen to Elena play a zither. Elena rocks along slowly to the music she makes.

SUZY

The door chime rings, and in comes Suzy and her aide, Bettina, who pushes Suzy's wheelchair over the door saddle. Elena is strumming the zither and looks up at the sound of the chime. She sees Suzy and exclaims, "My newest musician is here!" This is the first time they have met in person. Suzy's mom, Frances, spoke with Elena over the phone, explaining Suzy's deep love of music. Elena asked Frances to be put on speakerphone so that Suzy could also hear the conversation. Frances told me, "Right then, I knew we would be coming to Musicality. I knew that Elena got it, that she understood that even though Suzy can't communicate over the phone, her involvement in our conversation was important."

Suzy is 16 years old and has multiple disabilities, one of which is cerebral palsy. Suzy's movements are limited, and Bettina is there to assist only if needed. Her first session at Musicality is all about exploration. Elena says to Suzy, "You look at an instrument, and I'll go ahead and get it and bring it to you. If it's not the right one, tell me." I notice Suzy move her head a bit to her right. Frances had told Elena to look for this move as an indication of Suzy's affirmative response. Suzy's eyes seem to be scanning the floor, and then they stop. Elena watches Suzy intently. Elena starts to move along the wall until she reaches a small electronic drum pad. Elena stops and looks at Suzy. The slightest upturn of the right side of Suzy's mouth tells Elena this is the instrument. "This one?" Elena asks. Again, Suzy moves her head a bit to the right. Now I can see it, too. Elena takes the drum pad and asks Suzy if it is okay to place it on her lap. Suzy affirms, and Elena carefully balances the drum pad on Suzy's lap. Suzy slowly moves her hand closer to the pad. She rolls her hand on one of the four pads, and it makes a sound. Suzy makes a sound, and Elena tells Suzy, "Go ahead, have at it." The drum pad is sensitive, and a sound is made with each movement Suzy makes. Elena rejoices and says, "Dance party!" With that, Elena walks over to an electronic keyboard and starts to add a background beat with the occasional handclap. She dances and encourages Suzy, Bettina, and me to join in. Bettina says, "You go ahead," but I cannot pass up this opportunity to get up and move a little. It seems that Suzy is enjoying this.

Later, I learn from Elena that Frances shared the idea of a dance party with her because it is something they do at home. Elena lets Suzy continue, and when the drumbeats stop, Elena stops. Elena asks, "Time to move on?" Suzy seems to lift the right-hand side of her lip to indicate yes. Elena and Suzy explore a few more instruments. They look at a xylophone and then a cymbal. Suzy's gaze lingers on the cymbal, and Elena asks to strap a light wooden mallet to Suzy's wrist. Suzy agrees. Elena tucks the handle of the mallet into Suzy's fist. She holds the cymbal right above Suzy's lap, allowing her to move the mallet across the cymbal ever so slightly, making a delicate sound. When Suzy's hand drops, it is time to move on.

Elena excitedly says that she wants to show Suzy the mixing board. Elena pushes Suzy's wheelchair to the corner with a computer attached to a small mixing board. Elena spends a few minutes showing Suzy the mixing board and how to use it. She focuses solely on the slides and not the knobs, so Suzy can take control. Elena knows Suzy will have difficulty with the knobs, but the slides will be easier for her to manipulate with a stick. Still, the stick proves ineffective today, so Elena asks Suzy's consent to put Suzy's hand on top of hers. Elena asks once, and then again, to ensure Suzy is comfortable with this; Suzy nods her head ever so slightly, affirming each request.

As a beat echoes from the speakers, Elena and Suzy add different music tracks on top of the beat. Together, they slide and rotate the different controls to manipulate the sounds. Suzy squeals and smiles, which, in turn, makes Elena beam. Elena then begins to talk about emotions and changes the music to match. She says, "Okay, let's make a sad tune," and hand-over-hand, Elena and Suzy change the beat and the tempo. Elena fake-cries, and Suzy smiles, the widest smile yet. Next, they create an upbeat tune and then a tune that Elena describes as melancholy. Elena says, "I love how music can be a language. We can use it to communicate how we feel."

At the request of Frances, this is a short session of only about 30 minutes. Frances wanted to ensure that Suzy is not overwhelmed with the space and the task of music-making. Elena agreed that it was a great way to start and that they should have one session and see how things go. Elena ends the session by playing some music. She puts on the song "Look What You Made Me Do" by Taylor Swift. They listen to about half of the song, and then Elena asks Suzy if she can again attach the mallet back on her wrist. Suzy nods, and Elena places the strap around her wrist and the stick in her fist. She grabs a vertical sheet of paper with the numbers one through ten written in a large font and places it on a table in front of Suzy. She says she wants to learn about Suzy's taste in music. She instructs Suzy to move the stick to the lower end of the scale if she hates this song, the upper end if she loves it, or, if it is just okay, somewhere in the middle. Suzy guides the stick down carefully to about a three. "Ahhh," Elena says, "not a huge Taylor Swift fan. Good to know. Next week I think I'll try some metal and some hip-hop."

Suzy and Bettina leave the studio, entering the bright sunshine outside. Elena reflects on the session, telling me she feels good about how things went. She feels like Suzy had a nice combination of autonomy and instruction. "That balance," Elena says, "is not as easy to accomplish as it might look." Elena then turns to her journal and frantically writes down the clues she discovered about working with Suzy. I learn that on that same day, Elena talks with Frances, and they set up another session for the following week, this time for 45 minutes. When Elena tells me this, she grins.

JOSH AND ALLIE

Before Josh and Allie arrive at the studio, Elena tells me a bit about the siblings who have been coming to Musicality for about a year. She smiles wide and tells me that "Josh is five and Allie is six, and do they have energy to spare! I take some from them every time they come to the studio." Christa, Josh and Allie's mom, shares with me that "both children are diagnosed with ADHD, and Josh is also on the spectrum."

Because Elena expects the children soon, she puts on some mellow music so they will enter the space with music already playing. Soon enough, the chime rings, and Josh and Allie explode into the studio. Christa follows them, pushing a stroller with their younger sibling inside, fast asleep. Christa looks exhausted. She says "hi" to Elena and waves at me in my corner. She then nods to Elena and pushes the stroller out of the studio to go to the café next store.

Josh and Allie zoom around the space, picking up instruments, putting them down, picking up another and another for what feels like an eternity, though my watch tells me it was only 2 minutes. Elena just stands and watches. I am nervous that they will break something or crash into each other, but none of that happens. Elena explains later that this is their routine. She loves their excitement when they enter the space and does not want to squash it, so she lets them have this time to touch and explore. Then she grabs two small trampolines pushed up against the wall and brings them into the space. The trampolines have a railing the kids can hold onto while they jump, and Elena makes sure that they do just that. Elena says, "Freeze!" and the kids stop moving. "Are you ready to move your bodies to the music? Remember, there is no right or wrong way to do this. You get to decide how the music makes you feel." Elena changes the mellow music and puts on mariachi music. Josh bounces double-time to the beat, and his timing is perfect. Allie is enjoying jumping and making hand movements, experimenting with letting go of the railing, one hand at a time. Then Elena changes the music, and Josh adjusts his movement to keep time with the country music ballad. Allie pretends she is riding a horse and screams, "Yeehaw!" Elena says, "Your creativity is astounding, and you are moving your bodies the way you want to, just like musicians do when they play an instrument." Both kids smile and giggle.

Elena keeps things moving. She always has at least 10 different activities for the kids when they come to the studio. Next, she brings out some drums for them to play. They all sit on the floor with a bongo drum, and Elena instructs them to make a noise that sounds like sandpaper. Elena models this movement by rubbing the drum skin with the tips of her fingers. The kids watch and mimic her movement. Then they make thunder, rain, and a horse running; Elena asks them to call out what to make next. Josh and Allie have energy, and Elena harnesses that energy at every turn. When Josh gets up to run away from the drum-playing, Elena says, "Josh, it seems you want to move on. What's next?" Josh stops and turns to look at Elena. She gives Josh a choice of two activities, and he picks the one that involves dancing. He runs back and gets ready to move his body to the music that Elena will put on shortly.

Elena has a goal of helping Josh and Allie tune into their bodies. She describes vibration to them and demonstrates it with a guitar string, telling them to feel the vibrations in their bodies. She asks if they can feel the vibrations slowing down when she plays soft music. When I inquire why she uses this approach with Josh and Allie but not with the other students I have observed, she says that Josh and Allie experience many people telling them how to move, control, and quiet their bodies. The other students she works with will not necessarily have this experience. Josh and Allie are already being told in school to sit and act in certain ways. Elena believes that being diagnosed with ADHD as a child can have some damaging effects, the biggest being that it puts teachers in a position of power over the way students move and understand their bodies. Elena says, "I want them to develop a deep knowledge of how their bodies work, so they recognize that they have ownership over their bodies no matter what anyone says."

Josh is very interested in what I am doing in the corner, so he comes over every session to see what I am writing in my field notes. I ask Josh questions throughout my time in the studio rather than conducting one longer sit-down interview. This seems to work for Josh. One day, I ask him, "What are you learning today?" He responds, "I'm learning about me!" Over the course of our time together, I learn that Josh wants to be a musician, one who prefers to stand while playing instruments, and that the studio is his favorite place. "School," Josh tells me, "is just okay." When I ask Josh why school is "just okay," he spends 2 minutes describing how he must do things just the way the teacher wants. Josh takes me through his day, highlighting how he must sit in the morning circle, hold his pencil, stand in line, sit still, not jump off the swing at recess, and be "quiet, quiet, quiet." With this, Josh places his fingers over his lips and says, "Shhhhhhhhh." I reflect that Josh is only in kindergarten and has a long road ahead of him. Then he smiles and skips away from me, freeing his hand from his mouth to sing the lyrics of a song from the movie *Frozen*. "Let it goooo," bursts from his lips.

Allie decides she would like to participate in a short interview after her class at Musicality. Allie says she likes music and dancing. Being in the studio allows her to combine her two favorite things. I learn she has attended some dance classes, too, but that "you have to do it their way." Christa shares that Allie had difficulty keeping focus and following along for the hour-long dance class before finding Musicality. Allie would fidget and start to dance to the music in her head when she was supposed to be stand still and watch the teacher. The teacher told Christa she thought Allie was not mature enough to take the class yet but that she would be willing to let Allie try again next year. Christa's face drops as she describes how disappointed Allie was, because her friends from school were in the dance class. That is when Christa began searching for a program that would honor her kids' disabilities. "Here," Christa says, "Elena accepts my children for who they are and sees their 'immaturity' [Christa adds air quotes] as creative gifts."

Allie says she likes 1st grade and learning to read, "but sometimes it's hard to always be paying attention." Allie would like to be a dancer, an artist, or on TV when she grows up. Allie looks in the direction of her mother and lowers her voice. She tells me she wants to take a dance class again so she can be with her friends and still come to Musicality, too. "I want to do both, but I can't yet because the teacher didn't think I was behaving," Allie whispers.

Elena plays music and movement games with Allie and Josh as Christa reenters the studio with an unfinished cup of coffee in her hand. Elena glances at the clock and realizes it is time to wind things down. She puts on the song "Positive Vibration" by Bob Marley and the Wailers and cranks up the volume. Allie and Josh begin to move around the space to the music. Josh sidles up to a drum and keeps time with the song. Allie moves her body in time with the music, swaying her hips back and forth. After a few minutes, Elena lowers the volume, and the kids stop to look at her. She says, "Let's take these positive vibrations out into the world!" I learn that Elena always closes Josh and Allie's session with this song because it seems to bring a calming energy to the kids as they transition from her studio back to the care of their mother. Both kids run up to Elena and give her a quick hug good-bye. Christa waves from the door and says over her shoulder, "See ya next week," and they disappear.

JAM SESSION

It is Wednesday evening and Elena is expecting three young musicians to join her in the studio for at least an hour. She says that this group comes together to jam—to enjoy music together and create songs of their own. Mark, age 15, who identifies as "Autistic, a keyboard player, and a really nice guy," attends along with Simon, age 17, who identifies as "weird and passionate about percussion." Stella, age 18, a singer who identifies as "on the spectrum and as someone with perfect pitch," also joins them in the studio. Elena says this group is more about being in community with other musicians rather than about taking a class, which is why she calls it a jam session. The young musicians all started by taking individual lessons with Elena. Since she believed they would work well together, she suggested they collaborate as a group. They have been playing together for almost a year now.

Stella arrives first and says hi to Elena, who is already playing scales on her guitar. Although Stella is the resident vocalist, she also plays the ukulele as her instrument of choice. Mark and Simon arrive together, dropped off by Mark's parents. As the young musicians tear off their coats and hats, Simon says, "What's up, fam?" This is met by "What's up?" and a "Hey there" from Elena and Stella. Mark giggles and moves toward the keyboard that Elena has moved into the center of the room, next to the drum kit, so the group can all be situated in a semicircle. I abandon my beanbag chair and move a folding chair to the opening of the semicircle. I am the audience. Everyone takes a few minutes to noodle around on their instruments. It seems the musicians communicate in a way I don't recognize, because suddenly there is silence. Elena adjusts her guitar strings a bit, and when it is quiet again, Simon says, "Okay, let's go!" The improvisation begins.

Simon plays a steady beat on the drums. Soon the other musicians join in, not all at once, but when the music appears to move them, they join. Stella stops playing the ukulele and lets it hang by her side. She closes her eyes. After a few seconds of standing in silence, she adds some vocals. She intersperses humming and singing to mix in with the instruments. Stella does not seem worried about what she wants to add vocally; she has a few phrases figured out, and when she is unsure, she hums. Then she adds the ukulele to her vocals. Elena trades her guitar for a bass guitar, adding a steady low rhythm to the melody Stella creates with her voice. Mark plays the higher notes on his keyboard, adding his own melody that mixes so beautifully with Stella's voice. Simon keeps a steady beat. All the musicians' sounds converge, transcending their individuality. I realize I am staring at the group with my mouth wide open and hurriedly start adding field notes to my journal, trying to capture these moments where I transformed from researcher to admirer.

Suddenly Mark stops playing, and his arms hang at his side. He does not look at the other musicians; he just waits. Soon, Stella's voice gets quieter, she stops strumming her ukulele, and eventually she stops singing. Simon and Elena stop abruptly after Stella stops singing. Without talking, the group becomes quiet and just sits in silence for a few moments. Realizing how loud my pen is on the page, I stop writing.

The musicians are prompted to take an unannounced break when Stella walks over to her journal to add some thoughts and phrases from the last jam. Mark stretches his arms high above his head and leans his head back. Simon puts his drumsticks in his lap and cracks his knuckles. Stella rejoins the group, and somehow the group picks back up again—no instructions, no looking at one another—the music is their communication. The music is upbeat and jazzy. The group jams this way for 5 more minutes when Simon stops supplying the beat. The other musicians stop and are quiet, as though the moments they just shared are being integrated into their bodies.

Stella breaks the silence by asking if they want to play the song they have been practicing—a song for which Stella has written the lyrics and the musicians have supplied the music. No one uses sheet music. Stella wrote the words initially on paper and shared them with the group. Through practice over multiple weeks, the group has developed a somewhat regular rendition. Stella sings and the musicians start to fill in the music. They practice the song straight through, stumbling here and there but persevering to the end. Then they play it again, and this time, it is a little smoother. I notice the song changes in small ways, though I cannot quite identify what has changed. After the second time through, Elena asks the group if they would like to record this song. "We don't have to," she adds, "I figured I'd just throw it out there." The group looks at one another and agrees. Elena moves a table with a laptop a little closer to me and asks me to hit record. I do, and Mark shakes his hands in the air and says, "I'm nervous." Simon says, "We got this. Let's go." The group takes it from the top, but then they stumble and start again. Again, they start from the top and play through.

After the performance, the group listens to the recording and discusses improvements. Simon suggests they work on modulating the volume levels of different instruments because there are points where some instruments are too loud and it is hard to hear the lyrics. Everyone shakes their heads in agreement. Elena reminds them that this recording was just to get a sense of whether or not they wanted to make any changes to the song. It looks like Elena wants to say more, but she glances at the clock and lets the group know they need to wrap up. Elena asks Stella, "What should we do next?" Stella suggests that Elena email the audio file to the group members so that they can have time to relisten and return to the studio with other ideas. The group agrees this is a great next step. A car horn beeps outside, and Mark and Simon rush to put on their coats. Simon shouts over his shoulder, "See ya," to Elena and Stella. Stella, too, grabs her coat and heads outside. Elena looks at me and smiles. "I love that group," she says proudly.

After the session, Elena starts to return the instruments from the center of the room to their places along the wall. When I ask her to describe her goals for this group, she smiles and says, "My goals are their goals. These are three talented musicians who are learning to work together, to make and take suggestions. They want to create music, and I'm here to give them some structure, but to also to get out of the way so they can work together." I learn from all three students that, like many teenagers, they feel that they are often told what to do and when to do it. This, Stella shares with me, is even more pronounced because they are disabled. Stella believes that being on the spectrum means that people have a hard time letting her grow up. Stella is about to graduate high school and is involved in a school-to-work program. Stella does not enjoy this program or the workplace training she is receiving there. Stella says, "I get it. I need a job, but I want to find my own job. I don't always want to be told what to do. I think this might be the one place where I get to make the decisions that I want. And I get to create something."

Simon has a different reason for participating in the jam session: He enjoys the social aspect of this group. He likes to play percussion, but more than that, he likes to hang out with other kids around his age. He has an active video game group, which includes Mark, and they play online together often. But he also "likes to get out of the house and away from my family for a little . . . I like to be with other people, but I like to be doing things while I am with them. I don't just like to sit around, so making music while being with other people is perfect for me."

Mark and I communicate via email. Our exchange lasts months while I await a response. He never forgets to respond; he says he just needs time to consider what he wants to say. Mark writes that in school, he feels very isolated. He goes from class to class, some of them in general education and others in special education. He is shy and does not like to talk to people he has not known for some time. Though he likes being with people, it takes a lot of energy for him to engage. Music is important in his life, and his earliest memories involved music. "I think music is how I communicate best." What he likes best about participating in the jam sessions is how he contributes to the group project in a way that makes sense to him. "I don't have to try to have it make sense for people who don't understand my way. I spend a lot of time in school having to do that. Elena accepts the way I communicate through music, and I don't have to pretend to be a different way." In the studio, Mark feels like his authentic self, and in other places, he feels like he negotiates his self with what other people find acceptable.

MIRIAM

Elena is preparing for Miriam's guitar lesson. She tells me, "This is probably what you are used to thinking of when you think about a music lesson." Elena tidies the room so it is the way Miriam has experienced it in the past. Miriam has a visual impairment, and although she has some sight, it is dependent on many variables, including how the sunlight shines into the studio. If the space is always predictable, then Miriam can move around easily. Miriam is 12 and has been playing guitar for a few years. After asking for and receiving a guitar for her eighth birthday, she taught herself chords and songs by ear, as well as by watching YouTube videos. However, this took a lot of effort given her visual impairment. Miriam's mom, Corinne, describes how Miriam had to move her face close to the screen to discern how she should place her fingers; she also experienced frustration with having to rewind the videos multiple times. Though Miriam wanted to take lessons, it was challenging to find someone with whom she felt comfortable and could accommodate her visual impairment. Corinne discovered Elena's studio through the same contact I had. The family travels for over an hour once a week so Miriam can take lessons with Elena.

Elena says that teaching a young musician with a visual impairment involves more hand-over-hand work. "It's easier for me to position Miriam's fingers than to try to explain how she should move them." Because they sit close to each other, Elena makes sure to freshen up before each session with Miriam because she is aware of Miriam's heightened sense of smell. She does not use any products with perfumes or odors. This was not Miriam's request, but rather something Elena considered while preparing to work with Miriam. Elena researched what was involved when teaching students with visual impairments so she could learn some specific strategies and tips. Corinne explains this is why Elena is special and why she spends so much time traveling to these lessons. "You could see that she cared about how she would modify her instruction for Miriam. Other instructors were like, 'Oh yeah, no problem, I'll figure it out,' but Elena was like, 'Let me research best practices and get back to you.'" After starting her research, Elena shared what she learned with both Corinne and Miriam. Miriam adds, "It's like I was a whole person and not just this blind girl. She asked me for ideas, too. She cared about me. And I get to pick music I like, too."

Miriam arrives with her guitar in hand and turns to the general area where Elena is standing, sensing her presence. "Hey, Elena," she says and then moves her body to face me. Elena makes the introduction, and Miriam and I chat for a few moments. I learn that Miriam is enrolled in her neighborhood junior high school and has the assistance of a teacher for the blind and visually impaired. Miriam attends the special education resource room and receives help not only with ensuring that she has accessible materials but also additional assistance with math, which Miriam emphatically describes as torture. Miriam's parents insisted that she be included in her local public schools because they wanted Miriam to have friends in her community. They did not want her to travel outside her neighborhood for a school for the blind and visually impaired; the nearest such school was over 90 minutes away from their house. Miriam does not play music at school because she says she "doesn't care for school music." Miriam says she has a few close friends at school, and they hang out there and on the weekends too. She tells me excitedly that she is exploring adopting a service dog to help her manage navigation so she can be more independent. She does this little dance as she says this, showing me just how thrilled she is about this possibility. She adds, "I already have a few names picked out." I learn from Corinne that in addition to the teacher of the blind and visually impaired, she also has a teaching assistant with her to provide mobility support. Corinne tells me how this has been a difficult aspect of Miriam's school experience because the teaching assistant can sometimes do too much and interfere with Miriam's quest for independence. "It's a constant conversation," she tells me, "and I think the dog will help a lot with that."

Corinne smiles and says to us, "See you in an hour." Miriam replies, "Not if I don't see you first," and turns to me, laughing, and asks, "Get it?" I giggle, and Corinne shakes her head, pushing open the door to do some grocery shopping.

It is time for the lesson to begin. Elena sits across from Miriam and asks her to warm up her hands with some chords. Miriam expertly moves her hands up and down the neck of the guitar at an impressive speed. I learn that much of Miriam's playing is by memorization. She says she can hear a song on the radio and then translate that song to one she can play on the guitar. She also says that with the proper light and magnification, she can read music.

Miriam is learning to play the song "Shallow," sung by Lady Gaga and Bradley Cooper in the movie *A Star Is Born*. Miriam starts with the opening notes, but Elena wants to make a correction. Elena asks, "Miriam, I would like to help you make that stronger. Can I move your fingers?" Miriam nods, and Elena moves one finger just slightly, adjusting Miriam's hand. Miriam plays the opening again and nods in affirmation of the change. "That's it," Elena adds. Each time Elena wants to work hand-over-hand with Miriam, she asks for her consent. Each time, Miriam gives it.

After the opening notes are strong, Elena takes out the sheet music with an enlarged font, puts it on the music stand, and scoots to Miriam's side. She clips a bright light on the stand and asks Miriam to adjust it so it works best for her. Miriam moves the light around, experimenting, and finally finds an angle that works for her for now. The light will change in the room, and she will need to readjust. Elena asks, "Can I show you where I want you play?," and Miriam nods consent. Miriam releases her hand from the neck of her guitar, and Elena takes her outstretched finger, placing it on the section of sheet music on which she wants Miriam to focus. After scooting forward in her seat and looking closely at the sheet music, Miriam then slides back in her chair. She seems to be pondering something, looking up at the ceiling and then closing her eyes. Miriam strums the guitar to play the small section that Elena had pointed out. She opens her eyes and turns toward Elena. They fall into a rhythm, looking at the sheet music, working hand-over-hand, and then Elena picks up her guitar and demonstrates while Miriam puts her hands over Elena's. They also listen to a recording of the original song from the movie. Elena plays a section of the recording, and they discuss what they hear. Elena returns Miriam's focus to the sheet music, and Miriam adjusts the light and tilts her head to the side, so her stronger left eye is closest to the sheet music. Elena and Miriam's work is serious but jovial, and the hour passes quickly. Elena assigns Miriam some homework, sections of the song they worked on today, and also some scales.

Corinne returns and chats with Miriam and Elena about the session, commenting on how glad she is that Miriam is learning a new song because she (Corinne) was tired of the last one. Elena jokes sarcastically that Miriam should add practicing that song to her homework so her mom does not miss it too much. Corinne chuckles and hands Elena a check and Miriam a granola bar to eat during the long ride home. They open the door to leave Musicality, and Miriam calls over her shoulder, "Thanks, Elena. Bye, Erin. See ya, sort of, next time!" Elena and I laugh as the door swings shut, the chime marking their exit.

LESSONS LEARNED

It is March 2021 when I learn that Musicality is no more. Unable to keep her doors open due to COVID-19, Elena made the tough choice to sell some of her instruments on eBay, pack some away, and not renew her lease. When I contact Elena, there is such sadness in her voice that it is painful to talk to her. She says she tried to continue by offering her classes over Zoom, but it just was not working. "We need to share the space, share the experience of what it is to create together." Elena is hopeful that she may open her studio again someday, but for now, she is helping her family around the house and has a part-time job at a large commercial hardware store.

I ask Elena if she will talk with me about the lessons we both learned during our time at Musicality. Hope returns to her voice as we discuss our time in the studio and reminisce about the young musicians who taught us so much.

Aesthetic Experimentation

Elena's studio allows students to experiment with instruments and sound, providing a context for musicians to make choices about what appeals to them. The invitation to experiment is grounded in Elena's belief that it is important to build a strong connection to one's aesthetic stirrings. Elena's teaching promotes a level of connection that invites her musicians to make choices "that speak to them." By extending this invitation, Elena promotes a connection to an aesthetic self as a vital part of being a musician. As Elena describes, "School for me, and other disabled people, is often about fitting in, trying to appear normal, making choices that you think you should make." Elena teaches her musicians to think like artists, and to connect with their inner selves to make choices that work for them.

Creativity is a crucial element in Elena's studio, and so is the aesthetic experience—the feeling that one can experience through the act of creation. With musicians like Suzy, the first lesson is about finding that inner aesthetic voice. Elena asks Suzy to select instruments that speak to her, and this provides Suzy the opportunity to consider her aesthetic self. Elena does not need evidence that Suzy is exploring this self; she believes the invitation gives Suzy the go-ahead to tune into her feelings about which instruments are attractive. Elena supports this by looking very carefully at how Suzy moves her body, noticing small indications about which instruments interest her.

The structure Elena provides for Josh and Allie allows them to enjoy the space, explore music, and be creative, all the while incorporating movement. Josh and Allie are rarely still in the studio, and that is just fine. Elena harnesses their energy and incorporates it into their time, viewing their energy as a part of their aesthetic selves, not something that "interferes" with learning. She also teaches them how to monitor their own energy and feel the vibrations in their bodies. Elena believes that both kids have an aesthetic awareness connected to their disabilities, and she helps the children make this connection. Elena praises the children's energy levels and sees their movements as assets for music-making.

For the musicians in the jam sessions, Elena provides the context by which they can express their aesthetic selves. They have already learned how to tap into their artistic selves, so Elena provides the space of community where these individuals can come together in the spirit of community. Elena actively does not take control.

Aesthetic awareness is a large part of Elena's teaching, as her philosophy is grounded in finding aesthetic purpose and noticing how that feels in the body. Owning one's body provides her young musicians with the power to decide who does and does not get to touch their bodies.

Consent

Compliance with authority figures is not an uncommon trait fostered in children, but disabled youth are often raised in a *culture* of compliance (Smith & Harrell, 2013, emphasis mine). Ableism puts disabled children at a higher risk for abuse of all kinds. Ableist notions about disabled children "needing" their bodies to be controlled by nondisabled people can lead to disabled people feeling less in control of their own bodies. Elena says it was her own experience with sexual abuse as a teen that makes her vigilant about having her musicians understand their own bodies and having complete control over them.

Elena fosters a tangible connection between how music makes us feel inside and her musician's bodies. Allie and Josh, both of whom have ADHD, are often told how their bodies should be maintained and how they should not move. This can send the message that others have priority over how their bodies should move in spaces such as classrooms and that others regulate their bodies. Therefore, Elena changes the atmosphere of the studio—sometimes the music she plays or the activities she designs—and then guides Josh and Allie to notice how these changes resonate in their bodies, building connections between what is happening in the space and how that feels.

For Suzy, movement is slight, but Elena looks for the smallest moves that indicate how she feels in the moment. Movement and the sounds Suzy makes help Elena comprehend how Suzy is understanding her instruction. For both Miriam and Suzy, Elena headlines how she would like to adjust her musicians' hands and then asks for consent. Asking for consent requires that Miriam and Suzy must give consent each time for their hands to be adjusted. This allows both Miriam and Suzy to draw boundaries about what they consider to be an acceptable touch. Elena provides a model for both Miriam and Suzy about what should happen before anyone touches their bodies, and she hopes that these lessons carry beyond the studio.

Elena says that teaching at Musicality has taught her to slow down and think through her instruction. "I try very hard not to do something just instinctually, because I think my instincts have been shaped by an ableist society," Elena says as she looks up at the ceiling. We sit in silence for a few seconds, and she adds, "Being disabled in an ableist society is like always feeling like you don't fit and you have to try to. I feel blessed to have had the chance to create a space that asked people to just be who they are."

Music/Conversation

It is widely believed that music is a language and that through music, people communicate feelings, emotions, and meaning to one another. Elena also holds this to be true, but also builds on this to frame music as a conversation not only between people but also between sounds and the self. Elena asks her young musicians to consider music as a way to be in conversation with their own bodies, then, as in the case with the jam sessions, with one another.

This is highlighted when Elena starts working with Suzy. First, Elena asks Suzy to think about which instruments appeal to her. Suzy's connection with instruments is the underlying theory to Elena's approach. Suzy is not expected to stay with one instrument at all but, rather, to think about where she is in the studio at this one point and time, to tap into her own emotions and feelings, and to let those guide her instrument choices. Then Elena might connect Suzy's playing to other people in the studio and encourage a dance party that communicates joy and pleasure.

The jam sessions Elena organizes also create the space of communication and connection. The young musicians bring their individuality—ways of moving, being, and communicating—and then the differences between the musicians converge via the language of music. No one in the space tells another musician how to play. The young musicians share music, and they read the silences.

Elena also includes disability in the conversation by not addressing it. In the studio, disability *is* the norm. There is no expectation that a musician should operate in one particular way, and this allows all the young people to view themselves as musicians. Elena's love for music, alongside her belief that experimentation is an important part of music-making, allows disabled youth to engage without fear of making a mistake. There is no one way to play the electric drum pad; Josh might hit it with a stick, and Suzy might let her hand roll over the drum pad. Both ways create music.

Elena admits near the end of our conversation that she has experienced a bout of depression during the COVID-19 lockdown. "It's been hard not to be in community and playing music." Then a slight smile starts to creep across her face. "I think I can use this time to maybe plan a reopening of Musicality. Talking to you makes me realize how necessary this space is, not just for my students but for me. Yes, that's what I'll do." We end our conversation with this hope for the future.

REFLECTION QUESTIONS

1. In what spaces do you feel most in tune with your body? How do you help others find connections with their bodies?
2. How might you include the act of asking for consent more often in your classroom or family?
3. Do you think it's important for schools to support students' aesthetic growth? Why or why not?
4. Elena enlists Suzy's mom to understand how Suzy communicates her desires. How can teachers capitalize on parent/guardian knowledge about disabled students so that they can build connections between home and school and better understand styles of communication?
5. Think about the music programs at schools you know or attended. Were there disabled students in these programs? Did these programs make accommodations so these spaces were friendly to disabled youth?

CHAPTER 6

The Sinclair School: A Counterstory

When you push open the heavy door to enter The Sinclair School, formerly The Special Center, but now named after autism-rights activist Jim Sinclair, I'm standing right there and waiting for you. I am so glad you are here. We lock eyes, and then you look past me. I see you stop in your tracks, inhale deeply, and put your hand over your heart. You tell me that you immediately feel like you have entered a close friend's living room. You notice the lamps and a colorful carpet that bring warmth to the lobby. You notice that the students have been busy creating art that expresses their worlds, and it fills the lobby. Drawings, paintings, photographs, mosaics, and pottery are displayed with pride—each has a student artist's statement about the piece. Some are written by the student, some are transcribed, and some are a photograph of the artist looking at or creating the artwork. Colorful fish swim in a large tank in the lobby, facing large, comfortable chairs where students take some time, maybe with a weighted blanket, to watch the fish swim. You share that you've never been in a school lobby that felt so welcoming, and you try to find the words to express how you feel. I nod and watch you take a moment to collect yourself. It is stunning to be in a place that so joyfully and lovingly celebrates that you have arrived.

I am really excited that you have chosen to join me here at Sinclair, this exceptional neighborhood school where students of all races, cultures, religions, and abilities, ages 4 through 12, come to learn and grow together. Everyone who lives in this neighborhood is welcome in this school, a sentiment written into the mission statement. The school has multiage classrooms and more traditional grade-level classrooms, but there is no tracking. That is central to the school's mission statement, too. You are pleasantly surprised by how many other observers, volunteers, parents, and preservice teachers are also visiting the school today. There's a palpable energy in the air. School starts in a few minutes, but before we go to Clarissa and Juan's classroom to spend the day, I suggest we take a quick walk around the school.

You can't stop yourself from pointing out how accessible the space is; water fountains at different heights, desks that move up and down, posters and signs that include Braille and sign language, and tactile textures on the floor to indicate hallway intersections, stairs, and ramps. The contrasting colors that are used on the flooring and stairs are cheery and help those with low vision notice doors and the edges of steps. Your excitement is charming when you notice that the posters on the walls represent all kinds of students and families. When the principal happens to walk by, you share your appreciation for the space with her. She thanks you for noticing and remarks that it is continually a work in progress and is always changing based on the needs of her students. She smiles and rushes off.

"Look," you exclaim as you point to a group of older children reading to a group of younger children. These children have arrived at school early to eat breakfast, and now they are enjoying books together. The children are relaxing, connecting with one another, and sharing stories that seem to transfix them. "What a great way to start the day!" you exclaim, and I couldn't agree more. You start to move toward a room filled with different technological devices, but a bell rings and the lights flash, and we know we have seconds before the kids begin to arrive at Clarissa and Juan's door. We dash to the classroom.

Let's grab a seat at the back of the room and watch. Clarissa and Juan are co-teachers and seasoned professionals who welcome visitors in their classroom. Their only request is that you share feedback about what you notice so that they can learn from you. You take this request very seriously and commit to observing the nuances of the environment. You notice Clarissa and Juan standing near their classroom door greeting their students as they come into the room. Not only are the students being welcomed, but so are the many other adults, including different therapists and teachers whose specializations are needed by the students. Of course, these therapists and teachers will work with all the students in the class by integrating their therapies and services into what is happening in and outside the classroom. We will see this later during recess, when the physical therapist is working on gross motor skills with a student and his friends on the playground through a game of catch. In the classroom, we will observe the reading specialist working with a group of students to teach decoding strategies. The integration of specialized services limits the amount of time that students have to leave the classroom; in fact, at the end of the day we do not remember one student who left the classroom.

The students are drifting into the room, and while we are waiting for them to make their way to the carpet for their first activity, I share with you that the children in this school also have the opportunity to enjoy art, theater, and music. These instructors who teach these subjects will come into the classroom and also attend recess. During recess, the instructors keep things very informal by offering the children chalk to draw with, instruments to play, or music to dance to. All the adults at The Sinclair School realize the importance of understanding how students learn in multiple contexts, so they try to visit the many spaces the students inhabit. There are many opportunities for after-school instruction, too. Students can choose to join the theater club, the band, or the art club. The students can play sports, which change according to the season. No one is turned away from participating in any after-school activity, regardless of the level of expertise.

Students can also choose to participate in a few before-school activities, like the reading club we just saw. Another activity is to help run a small breakfast café. Students work with adults (both employees and volunteers) to create breakfast foods available for sale to the school and outside community. Students can learn how to bake, package, and market muffins and pastries. Proceeds from these sales support this endeavor. There is also before-school yoga and meditation for students.

"Sorry to chat your ear off," I remark. "I'll let you get back to observing."

Clarissa asks her students finish their transition to the carpet area so they can connect. Clarissa remarks to the class, "I can't wait for you to make it to the carpet so I can hear about how you all are doing," and I notice that you write this down in your notebook. Juan helps one student organize his materials and invites him to the carpet. Clarissa and Juan work to make the students comfortable. Some students sit on bouncy balls, and some decide they do not want to sit on the floor and sit at their desks instead— the students choose the seating best for them. Melanie, who uses crutches, wants to sit on the floor. Juan asks Melanie's consent to put his arms under her armpits to transition her to the floor. Melanie gives her consent, and Juan carefully moves Melanie to the floor and settles her in. Melanie smiles. Clarissa asks the group, "Who would like to share with the group how they are doing today?" Using his electric device to speak, a student says, "I had my favorite cereal for breakfast." The students start to chat about their own breakfasts. Clarissa asks them to bunch up in groups of four to share with one another. Clarissa and Juan each join a group. During these 15 minutes of connecting, the children share in multiple small groups and as a large group. The children discuss topics such as their moods, last night's activities, and what they are excited for today. Clarissa and Juan point out connections among the students but also how their preferences are different. Clarissa wraps up the check-in by saying that it is important to care for all the people in their community, and Juan shares how much he enjoys hearing from each person. Clarissa headlines the activities of the day so the students will know what to expect; they move into the first content area of the day, Science.

The students in this class are exploring different career opportunities in Science, Technology, Engineering, and Mathematics (STEM) fields. They have had guest speakers who have shared their work, and students have read, viewed, and listened to different scientists, engineers, and mathematicians talk about their work. Today, the class is talking about software engineer Farida Bedwei, born in Nigeria and diagnosed with cerebral palsy when she was an infant ("African Voices Features Nigerian Female Technologist," 2015). In addition to being an innovative software technologist and entrepreneur, Bedwei is also the author of a graphic novel about a young female

African girl superhero with cerebral palsy (Bedwei, 2019). These intersecting identities are explored in class, and Clarissa reminds the students that during language arts time the students will have the opportunity to create their own superhero graphic novels incorporating their own identities. When she says this, you look over at me with such excitement that I let out a chuckle. Clarissa looks over in our direction and gives us a sly smile. We learn that Clarissa has designed this lesson so that students can participate in the ways that work for them. She will encourage her students to try out new ways of expressing themselves, too. Clarissa tells the class that they will have the chance to write, draw, dictate, and drag and drop images to create pages. Clarissa adds, "There is no one way to create a graphic novel. I can't wait to see how creative and unique your graphic novels will be."

And the day moves on. Clarissa and Juan are purposeful in their classroom and lesson design. They continually return to their ideals of what makes a productive learning community to ensure that their lessons and behavioral strategies match. The school's mission statement calls for a learning environment that supports universal human rights and the mandate that all people should be treated fairly. Clarissa and Juan base their behavioral approaches on these concepts. If someone's human rights are violated, perhaps because they were called a derogatory name, Clarissa and Juan invite social action that leads to change. This might be fostering a conversation and connection between two individuals or asking the class to brainstorm ways to strengthen their classroom community. Clarissa and Juan both understand that this work is constant and ongoing. They must continually design their lessons and behavioral approaches to meet the needs of their students and the situations that arise in their classroom. Clarissa and Juan both believe that it is critical for students to tune into their minds and bodies; they include direct instruction in these areas by teaching students about how to listen to their bodies and ways to calm their bodies by modulating their breathing. If they witness a student becoming upset, they ask the students to share their feelings. Behavior is seen as an indicator that something in the environment is upsetting for the student.

We see an example of this when Patrick, a student you might remember from Chapter 1, gets upset when he is creating his graphic novel. Patrick is working on the computer and is importing pictures to the program he is using to make a graphic novel. His workstation is very close to his neighbor's, and while Patrick works the mouse with his left hand, his neighbor is using his right hand to manipulate the mouse. We both notice how their elbows hit as they work, but they seem to be managing. Then, suddenly, Patrick explodes. He jumps out of his seat and screams. Juan appears in a flash by his side. We watch as Juan comforts Patrick and gathers information about what has occurred. Juan says to Patrick, "Show me what happened," and Patrick shows how he tried to drag a picture into his book. Patrick points to his neighbor's elbow. Juan figures out that Patrick lost the picture he was dragging with his mouse when his elbow hit his neighbor's. He says to Patrick, "We can solve this. Watch," and he swaps the desks so the students' elbows will not bump. Juan encourages Patrick to take a few deep breaths and asks him to focus on calming down his body. Patrick settles down. We both marvel at how Juan has used the information he has gathered about Patrick to solve this situation, including the fact that Patrick shared he did not sleep well last night; his low tolerance for frustration, which they are working on; and Patrick's inability to verbally express himself when he is upset. All of this knowledge has gone into managing this situation. You look at me and mouth, "Wow."

Next we watch a math lesson. In Clarissa and Juan's math instruction, they design their lessons with an emphasis on how their students are becoming mathematicians—apprenticing them into the work that mathematicians do. This is much more than completing worksheets or memorizing facts. Clarissa and Juan are both well aware of the research that shows that "the development of identity, or the process of identification, is linked to learning, in that learning is about becoming as well as knowing" (Nasir, 2002, p. 219). Students work individually and in groups to solve mathematical problems that they encounter in their everyday worlds and then learn about how these ideas are represented in mathematical formulas. Like all other subjects that are taught, there is the overarching belief that learning is life-long and that each day is a walk down this path.

While the students head off to lunch, we sit and chat with Clarissa and Juan, who are eager to hear about what we have observed. You say, "In all academic and social situations, you both actively seek to assess, adjust, and modify. This seems to be the rule and not the exception: It applies to how directions are given, the tools students use to show what they are learning, the playground equipment, making friends, and so much more." Clarissa smiles and shares that is always the goal, but they are not perfect. She says, "We make mistakes, we miss things, but we have each other for support and reflection." I say that reminds me a lot of the writing by Dolmage (2017), in that designing a classroom for *all* students is an act that is never finished. "Yes," Juan starts, "and it's important to reflect that approach to learning in all aspects of our students' education, including the IEP and objectives for our students entitled to receive special education services." Juan shares an example using Patrick, who is working on developing his reading comprehension skills. Juan states, "His IEP goal, designed just for him, states that Patrick will participate in book group discussions twice a week and share his understanding of the text with his peers at least once in every discussion. These insights will be transcribed into Patrick's learning journey evaluation notebook, and the teacher will reflect on Patrick's growth every marking period in narrative form that is shared with his parents." Later, I'll ask Patrick's mom about this goal, and she mentions that Patrick loves to read and participate in these discussion groups. She notes that she has seen

Patrick's contributions grow over time and has noticed that he has learned to build on the discussion points brought up by other students. Patrick's mom adds that he asks to go to their public library so that he can read to the dog that visits on Saturday. "It's so different from when this school was The Special Center," she adds.

The school day is half over. There are many, many other content, aesthetic, social, and physical activities still to come, but I've got to run. You should stay and observe. I can only imagine all the innovative approaches you are yet to witness in this school where disability is a natural part of the classroom and school environment. My hunch is that you are going to notice amazing things.

References

African voices features Nigerian female technologist. (2015, February 9). allAfrica .com. https://link.gale.com/apps/doc/A400758377/ITOF?u=nysl_se_vassar&sid =summon&xid=102790ce

Autistic Self Advocacy Network. (2022). *Autism research and therapies.* https:// autisticadvocacy.org/about-asan/position-statements/

Aviv, R. (2018, September 28). Georgia's separate and unequal special edcuation system. *The New Yorker.*

Barnard-Brak, L., & Lechtenberger, D. (2010). Student IEP participation and academic achievement across time. *Remedial and Special Education, 31*(5), 343–349. https://doi.org/10.1177/0741932509338382

Baron-Cohen, S., Leslie, A. M., & Frith, U. (1985). Does the autistic child have a "theory of mind"? *Cognition, 21*(1), 37–46. https://doi.org/10.1016/0010-0277 (85)90022-8

Bedwei, F. (2019). *Karmzah: The unleashing.* Leti Arts.

Biklen, D., & Burke, J. (2006). Presuming competence. *Equity & Excellence in Education, 39*, 166–175. https://doi.org10.1080/10665680500540376

Brantlinger, E. (1997). Using ideology: Case of nonrecognition of the politics of research and practice in special education. *Review of Educational Research, 67*(4), 425–459.

CAST. (2018). *UDL and the learning brain.* Retrieved from http://www.cast.org/our -work/publications/2018/udl-learning-brain-neuroscience.html

Collins, K. (2015). A disability studies in education analysis of corporate-based educational reform: Lessons from New Orleans. In D. J. Connor, J. W. Valle, & C. Hale (Eds.), *Practicing disability studies in education: Acting toward social change* (pp. 217–233). Peter Lang.

Connor, D. J. (2014). The Disability Studies in Education annual conference: Explorations of working within, and against, special education. *Disability Studies Quarterly, 34*(2). https://dsq-sds.org/article/view/4257/3597

Connor, D. J., & Ferri, B. A. (2007). The conflict within: Resistance to inclusion and other paradoxes in special education. *Disability & Society, 22*(1), 63–77. https://doi.org/10.1080/09687590601056717

Creswell, J. W. (2013). *Qualitative inquiry & research design* (3rd ed.). Sage.

DaCosta, M. (Director). (1962). *The music man* [Film]. Warner Bros.

Dolmage, J. T. (2017). *Academic ableism: Disability and higher education.* University of Michigan Press. https://doi.org/https://doi.org/10.3998/mpub.9708722

Dyson, A. H., & Genishi, C. (2005). *On the case: Approaches to language and literacy research.* Teachers College Press.

Fish, W. W. (2008, Fall). The IEP meeting: Perceptions of parents of students who receive special education services. *Preventing School Failure, 53*(1), 8–14.

Freire, P. (1968). *Pedagogy of the oppressed.* Seabury Press.

Gabel, S. L. (2005). Introduction: Disability studies in education. In S. L. Gabel (Ed.), *Disability studies in education: Readings in theory and method* (pp. 1–20). Peter Lang.

Galda, L. (1998). Mirrors and windows: Reading as transformation. In T. E. Raphael & K. H. Au (Eds.), *Literature-based instruction: Reshaping the curriculum.* (pp. 1–11). Christopher-Gordon.

Gallagher, D. J. (1998). The scientific knowledge base of special education: Do we know what we think we know? *Exceptional Children, 64*(4), 493–502.

Gartner, A., & Lipsky, D. L. (1992). Beyond special education: Toward a quality system for all students. In T. Hehir & T. Latus (Eds.), *Special education at the century's end: Evolution and practice since 1970* (pp. 123–157). Harvard Education Press.

Glazier, J., & Seo, J.-A. (2005). Multicultural literature and discussion as mirror and window? *Journal of Adolescent & Adult Literacy, 48*(8), 686–700. https://doi.org/10.1598/JAAL.48.8.6

Hart, J. E., Cramer, E. D., Harry, B., Klinger, J. K., & Sturges, K. M. (2010). The continuum of "troubling" to "troubled" behavior: Exploratory case studies of African American students in programs for emotional disturbance. *Remedial and Special Education, 31*(3), 148–162. https://doi.org/10.1177/0741932508327468

Hehir, T. (2005). *New directions in special education: Eliminating ableism in policy and practice.* Harvard Education Press.

Johnson, D. R., Thurlow, M. L., Qiahn, X., & Anderson, L. (2019). *Diploma options, graduation requirements, and exit exams for youth with disabilities: 2017 national study (NCEO Report 409).* https://nceo.info/Resources/publications/OnlinePubs/report409/default.html

Kanō, J. (1986). *Kodokan Judo.* Kodansha USA, Incorporated.

Laura, C. T. (2014). *Being bad: My baby brother and the school-to-prison pipeline.* Teachers College Press.

McCloskey, E. (2010). What do I know? Parental positioning in special education. *International Journal of Special Education, 25*(1), 162–170.

McCloskey, E. (2012a). Conversations about jail: Inclusive settings for critical literacy. *Early Childhood Education Journal, 40*(9), 1–9. https://doi.org/10.1007/s10643-012-0528-7

McCloskey, E. (2012b). *Taking on a learning disability: At the crossroads of special education and adolescent literacy learning.* Information Age Publishing.

McCloskey, E. (2013). An open letter to Wyatt. In P. Smith (Ed.), *Both sides of the table: Autoethnographies of educators learning and teaching with/in [dis]ability* (pp. 185–198). Peter Lang.

McCloskey, E. (2019). Selves-advocacy and the meeting space. In P. Lalvani (Ed.), *Constructing the (m)other: Narratives of disability, motherhood, and the politics of normal* (pp. 51–65). Peter Lang.

McCloskey, E. (2021). Paintings on clear plastic that hang from the ceiling. In D. J. Connor & B. A. Ferri (Eds.), *How teaching shapes our thinking about disabilities: Stories from the field* (pp. 105–117). Peter Lang.

McKinney de Royston, M., Lee, C., Nasir, N. S., & Pea, R. (2020). Rethinking schools, rethinking learning. *Phi Delta Kappan, 102*(3), 8–13.

Merriam, S. B., & Tisdell, E. J. (2016). *Qualitative research: A guide to design and implementation* (4th ed.). Jossey-Bass.

Murray, A. (2018, October 15). Why I support identity-first language as a proud deaf autistic. *The Mighty.* https://themighty.com/2018/10/using-identity-first -language-disability/

Nasir, N. S. (2002). Identity, goals, and learning: Mathematics in cultural practice. *Mathematical Thinking and Learning, 4*(2–3), 213–247.

Nasir, N. S., McKinney de Royston, M., Barron, B., Bell, P., Pea, R., Stevens, R., & Goldman, S. (2020). Learning pathways: How learning is culturally organized. In N. S. Nasir, C. D. Lee, R. Pea, & M. McKinney de Royston (Eds.), *Handbook of the cultural foundations of learning* (pp. 195–211). Routledge.

National Council on Disability. (2018). *IDEA series: The segregation of students with disabilities.* https://www.ncd.gov/sites/default/files/NCD_Segregation-SWD _508.pdf

Perske, R. (1972). The dignity of risk and the mentally retarded. *Mental Retardation, 10*(1), 24–27.

Roosa, M. E. (2016). *The teaching of judo.* Wheatmark.

Rozalski, M., Stewart, A., & Miller, J. (2010). How to determine the least restrictive environment for students with disabilities. *Exceptionality, 18*(3), 151–163.

Shyman, E. (2015). *Besieged by behavior analysis for autism spectrum disorder: A treatise for comprehensive educational approaches.* Lexington Books.

Skrtic, T. M. (1992). The special education paradox: Equity as the way to excellence. In T. Hehir & T. Latus (Eds.), *Special education at the century's end: Evolution of theory and practice since 1970* (pp. 203–272). Harvard Education Press.

Smith, N., & Harrell, S. (2013). *Sexual abuse of children with disabilities: A national snapshot.* Vera Institute of Justice.

Valle, J. W., & Connor, D. J. (2011). *Rethinking disability: A disability studies approach to inclusive practices.* McGraw-Hill.

Ware, L. (2001). Writing, identity, and the other: Dare we do disability studies? *Journal of Teacher Education, 52*(2), 107–123.

Watson, K. (2017). *Inside the "inclusive" early childhood classroom: The power of the "normal"* (Vol. 5). Peter Lang.

Wolfe, K., & Durán, L. K. (2013). Culturally and linguistically diverse parents' perceptions of the IEP process: A review of current research. *Multiple Voices for Ethically Diverse Exceptional Learners, 13*(2), 4–18.

Yergeau, M. (2013). Clinically significant disturbance: On theorists who theorize theory of mind. *Disability Studies Quarterly, 33*(4). http://dx.doi.org/10.18061 /dsq.v33i4.3876

Zeitlin, V. M., & Curcic, S. (2013). Parental voices on individualized education programs: "Oh, IEP meeting tomorrow? Rum tonight!" *Disability & Society, 29*(3), 373–387. https://doi.org/10.1080/09687599.2013.776493

Index

About the Author

Erin McCloskey is an associate professor of education at Vassar College. Prior to teaching at the college level, Erin taught art, special education, and literacy in K–12 schools, a hospital, and a juvenile detention center. Currently, she collaborates with community youth organizations, reentry organizations, and correctional facilities and holds her college classes at these sites, creating expansive learning communities where college credit is available to all. Erin's research interests focus on educational injustices as they relate to disabled people and literacy instruction. She is the author of the book *Taking on a Learning Disability: At the Crossroads of Special Education and Adolescent Literacy Learning* (Information Age Press, 2012), and her research has been published in *Disability & Society,* the *International Journal of Inclusive Education,* and *Race Ethnicity and Education,* among others.

UNEXPLAINED MYSTERIES OF WORLD WAR II

First published 2014

The History Press
The Mill, Brimscombe Port
Stroud, Gloucestershire, GL5 2QG
www.thehistorypress.co.uk

British Library Cataloguing in Publication Data.
A catalogue record for this book is available from the British Library.

ISBN 978 0 7509 6011 3

Produced by arrangement with Quantum Publishing
Quantum Publishing
6 Blundell Street
London
N7 9BH

Printed in China

UNEXPLAINED MYSTERIES OF WORLD WAR II

Jeremy Harwood

The History Press

Contents

Introduction

Some mysteries are big, some small. Some affect the lives of millions, others only the people immediately involved with them. World War II is replete with mysteries of both kinds. Though the number diminished as time went by, there are enough that remain unexplained and unresolved to make investigating them interesting and well worthwhile.

An example or two of the bigger mysteries is sufficient to provide a taste of what follows in the main part of this book. One of the greatest riddles of the war's opening phase, for instance, is why, when Hitler launched his Blitzkrieg in the West in May 1940, the French armies facing the Wehrmacht collapsed so spectacularly, enabling the Germans to win a crushing victory and force the capitulation of France in record time?

INCOMPETENCE AT THE TOP

For years, the received wisdom was that the Wehrmacht's military superiority was such that its success in the West was inevitable. This, in fact, was not the case. On the ground – if not in the skies, where the Luftwaffe undoubtedly enjoyed aerial superiority—the balance of forces was roughly equal. Indeed,

the Allies between them possessed more and, in some cases, better modern tanks than did Hitler's vaunted panzer divisions.

What the French generals disastrously lacked, as events immediately showed, was the ability to react quickly and decisively when the Wehrmacht finally struck. Field Marshal Gerd von Rundstedt, in command of Army Group A, which was charged with making the crucial breakthrough in the Ardennes, certainly lived in fear of a speedy, bold French reaction. According to General Gunther von Blumentritt, his Chief of Operations, he expected 'a great, surprise counteroffensive by strong French forces from the Verdun and Chalons-sur-Marne area, northwards towards Sedan and Mezieres.'

No such attack ever materialised. Within ten days of the start of the offensive, the Germans had advanced 150 miles and reached the Channel coast. The Allied armies had been cut in two. On 14 June, the same day that the Maginot Line was penetrated south of Saarbrucken, the Germans entered Paris. Three days later, Marshal Petain's new French government sued for peace.

Even Hitler was surprised by the speed and extent of the success, which may explain why he ordered his panzers to halt rather than pursue the retreating British into Dunkirk. General Franz Halder, the Army Chief of Staff, noted in his diary: 'Frightened by his own success, he is afraid to take any chances and so would rather pull the plug on us.'

Many still believe that this was the Fuehrer's first and most significant military mistake. This is not the case. Hitler did not act unprompted. Despite what they said and wrote after the war, Rundstedt and other leading generals argued for the pause first. They then got Hitler to agree to it. By the time he rescinded the order, it was too late to stop the evacuation. More than 300,000 British and French troops got away to fight another day.

A 'SPECIAL RELATIONSHIP'

Dunkirk certainly was not a victory. As Churchill, Britain's newly appointed successor to Neville Chamberlain as Prime Minister, told the House of Commons, 'wars are not won by evacuations.' In any event, Churchill's hold on power was shaky. Regarded as reckless, untrustworthy and opportunistic by many of his fellow Conservatives, his opportunity had arisen as a result of the fiasco of the Norwegian campaign for which he, in fact, was chiefly responsible. When it became clear to even Chamberlain that he must go, George VI, most of the press, the Conservatives, big business, the top civil servants and the Labour leaders initially would have preferred Lord Halifax, the Foreign Secretary, as the new Prime Minister.

Across the Atlantic in Washington, Churchill was also regarded as a suspect character. Harold Ickes, the Secretary of the Interior, recorded Roosevelt's verdict when he heard of the appointment, 'I suppose he is the best man England has even if he is drunk half of his time.' As well as suspecting him of being an unreliable alcoholic, the President also harboured a personal distaste for the man. He told Joseph Kennedy, the American Ambassador to Britain, 'I have always disliked him since the time I went to Britain in 1918.' Roosevelt was recalling his one and only face-to-face meeting with Churchill when, as Under-Secretary for the Navy and before he was crippled, he had given a speech in London at Gray's Inn. Churchill had been in the audience. He behaved, Roosevelt later remarked, 'like a stinker...lording it over all of us.'

Only one thing united the two men— their hatred of every aspect of Nazism. They both understood that Hitler epitomised a new and terrible force with which any sort of peaceful co-existence would prove impossible. Roosevelt, however, was a long way from actively resisting Hitler, as Churchill was soon to discover. When he told his son Randolph that his intention was to 'drag the United States in,' Roosevelt was equally determined to avoid such an entanglement.

Even when he finally agreed to a desperate British request to supply them with 50 old destroyers, the President went to great pains to assure Massachusetts Senator David I. Walsh, a leading Democratic isolationist, that he was 'absolutely certain that this particular deal will not get us into war and, incidentally, that we are not going to war anyway unless Germany wishes to attack us.'

What Churchill failed to understand was that nothing Roosevelt said necessarily could be taken at face value. He was an impossible man to pin down. Eleanor Roosevelt herself recognised this fact. Later, she would warn the premier: 'When Franklin says "yes, yes, yes", it doesn't mean he's agreeing, it means that he's listening.' Even when the Lend-Lease Bill was finally passed by the US Senate by 60 votes to 31 on 8 March 1941, it did not mean that the British had been given the blank cheque they believed they had been granted. In Berlin, Joseph Goebbels noted: 'Roosevelt wants to encourage England to a prolonged resistance, so that afterwards it will be easier for him to inherit everything that's left. Now in London they'll once again forget all the defeats and setbacks and cheer on Washington. But how long will it last?'

THE ENIGMA OF STALIN

Churchill, Hitler and Roosevelt were three of the warlords. Stalin was the fourth. In many ways, he was the most enigmatic of the four. This book focuses on what is probably one of the greatest unexplained mysteries of the entire war—why, despite all the warnings he received, the Soviet dictator was taken totally unawares when Hitler struck at Russia in June 1941.

It was certainly not the case that Stalin blindly trusted Hitler to abide by the terms of the Nazi-Soviet Non-Aggression Pact, which, to the world's astonishment, the two dictators had hastily concluded in August 1939. A British Foreign Office spokesman summed up the revolutionary volte-face in the pithy phrase 'all the isms are wasms.' By November 1940, however, it was clear to Stalin that the two sides were drifting apart. 'Hitler is playing a double game,' he pronounced to Vyacheslav Molotov, the Soviet Foreign Minister after the latter's fruitless visit to the Fuehrer.

Stalin, however, believed that time was on his side. In early December, he told his generals: 'We know that Hitler is intoxicated by his victories and believes that the Red Army will need at least four years to prepare for war. Obviously, four years would be more than enough for us. But we must be ready much earlier. We will try to delay the war for another two years.'

For once, Stalin miscalculated. Hitler was busy planning with his generals for the attack. Reports started to flood into the Kremlin about the German build-up on the Soviet western frontier. Stalin refused to be alarmed. He told Marshal Zhukov, the Soviet Army's newly-appointed Chief of Staff, to prepare to speed up Russian mobilisation if and when it was authorised, but, at the same time, to avoid 'wild unrealistic plans for which Russia lacked the means.' As for the German troop concentrations in Poland, he assured his worried generals, the troops were there simply for training exercises.

The warnings mounted. Advised by his Bletchley Park cryptologists that the attack was imminent, Churchill wrote personally to Stalin to warn him of the impending assault. Stalin dismissed the warning as a 'provocation.' If the Soviets acted on it, he reasoned, 'Hitler would have a direct and fair reason to launch a preventive crusade against the Soviet Union.' On 12 May, he similarly failed to react to Marshal Semyon Timoshenko's report of the increasing number of Luftwaffe reconnaissance flights over Russian territory. 'I'm not sure Hitler knows about these flights,' he replied. In Berlin, it was generally believed that the Soviet leader was determined to avoid war at all costs. Stalin 'stares like a rabbit with a snake,' Goebbels noted in his diary.

Stalin simply scoffed at all the predictions he was receiving that weren't from his own intelligence service as to what the date of the attack might be. On 5 June, he told the Central Committee of the Communist Party: 'At first, our intelligence gave 14, 15, 20 May as possible dates of the attack. Now they claim it's going to be either 15 or 22 June. Apparently, these dates could also be wrong. Let's instead cherish the hope that 1941 will remain peaceful.' On 12 June, ten days before Operation Barbarossa was finally launched, he assured his generals: 'I am certain that Hitler will not risk creating a second front by attacking the Soviet Union. Hitler is not such an idiot.'

We can only guess at what exactly Stalin felt when he received the news of the German attack. Certainly, as the tales of disaster poured in, we know that he fell into a deep depression. On 10 July, by which time the Germans had penetrated more than 300 miles into Russian territory, he stirred himself to issue a peremptory order to his commanders on the northwestern front. 'Officers who do not carry out orders, abandoning their positions like traitors and leaving the defensive ridge without orders have not yet been punished,' he declared. 'It is time to put a stop to this shameful state of affairs.'

Soon, several high-ranking Soviet commanders were standing in the dock before Vasili Ulrikh, the corpulent, vicious President of the Military Collegium of the Supreme Court of the USSR, accused of 'betraying the interests of the Motherland, violating the oath of office and damaging the combat power of the Red Army.' They were Stalin's scapegoats. Among them was General Dimitry Korobkov, the luckless commander of the troops in the west whose forces had buckled at Minsk in the face of the Nazi onslaught. He, together with seven other senior army and air force generals, was shot.

GLOBAL WAR

Thousands of miles away, a new theatre of war was about to open. Some months previously, the USA had imposed an embargo on exports of oil to Japan. The Japanese response was immediate. They began preparing for war.

Where the Japanese might strike was a mystery. Perhaps they might pull back from the brink at the last minute after all. Certainly, Roosevelt thought this was at least a possibility. 'I wish I knew whether Japan was playing poker or not,' he confided to Secretary of the Interior Harold Ickes. One thing seemed clear. The consensus was that the Japanese might attack the Philippines, or possibly British possessions in the Far East. No one dreamed that such an attack would be directed against the USA itself. After a cabinet meeting on 25 November, Secretary of War Henry Stimson noted: 'The question was how we should manoeuvre them (the Japanese) into the position of firing the first shot without allowing too much danger to ourselves.'

Roosevelt left Washington for a short Thanksgiving break. On his return, he was handed four intercepts of decoded messages sent from Tokyo to the Japanese embassy in Berlin. One of them was from General Hideki Tojo, the Japanese Prime Minister, to the Ambassador in person. 'Say very secretly to them (the Germans,' Tojo instructed, 'there is extreme danger that war may suddenly break out between the Anglo-Saxon nations and Japan through some clash of arms. This may come sooner than anyone dreams.'

The President and Cordell Hull, the Secretary of State, conferred. 'We both agreed,' Hull later recollected, 'that from all the indications a Japanese attack was in the imminent offing.' Roosevelt decided to send a last-minute message personally to the Japanese Emperor. It was to be a plea to preserve peace.

Before the message could be sent, however, events intervened. On the evening of 6 December, Roosevelt received another decrypt. This time, it was part of a long message sent by Tokyo to the Japanese Ambassador in Washington. Roosevelt read it and then handed it to Harry Hopkins, one of his closest associates. 'This means war,' the President told him. Hopkins replied that it was 'too bad we could not strike the first blow.' Roosevelt apparently nodded. 'We can't do that,' he said. 'We are a democracy and a peaceful people.'

The next day, at 10.00am, Roosevelt received the last part of the decoded message. It read simply: 'The earnest hope of the Japanese government to adjust Japanese-American relations and to preserve and promote the peace of the Pacific through cooperation with the American government has been lost.' At 1.40pm, while he and Hopkins were eating lunch together, the telephone in the Oval Office rang. It was Secretary of the Navy Frank Knox. He reported that Pearl Harbor had signalled it was being bombed by the Japanese. In the words of the signal, 'this is not a drill.'

Why Pearl Harbor was not at least on alert to the possibility of such an attack has never been totally explained. The evening before, having read the first part of the Japanese message, Roosevelt had tried to contact Admiral Harold Stark, the head of the US Navy, but was told he had gone to the theatre and was unavailable. He got the same response when he called General George Marshall, the Chief of Staff, the next morning. Marshall had gone for his customary Sunday morning horseback ride.

Some attempt was made to warn Pearl Harbor directly. Radio communications, however, were apparently out of order. Instead, a Western Union telegram was despatched. It did not reach its destination until after the attack.

Not all this book is concerned with great events, like the ones cited here. The events leading up to Pearl Harbor, indeed, are well documented; it is certainly incorrect to argue, as some have tried to do, that Roosevelt deliberately failed to put the naval base there on high alert and provoked the Japanese into launching their attack. What this book does show, however, is that there is much about the Second World War that still remains unexplained, and that various incidents that took place during it still demand historical probing. It is a certainty there are still secrets to be revealed.

Bomb in a Beer Cellar

On 8 November 1939, Adolf Hitler narrowly escaped death when a massive bomb planted in a Munich beer cellar exploded only minutes after the Fuehrer had left the building. Who was ultimately responsible for the bombing remains a mystery. Was it the work of a lone conspirator? As the Gestapo steadfastly maintained, was the British Secret Service behind the plot? Or was it a put-up job, stage-managed by the Nazis themselves?

It was one of the few events Hitler never missed. Every year since his coming to power in 1933, the Fuehrer had visited Munich on 8 November to mark the anniversary of the 1923 Beer Hall Putsch by delivering a rousing speech to a handpicked audience of Gauleiters and other Nazi veterans in the Buergerbraukeller, where the attempted Putsch had begun. This year, however, the arrangements differed slightly from normal.

Hitler usually began to speak at around 8.30pm, finishing at 10.00pm precisely. This year,

he started and ended slightly earlier at 8.10pm and 9.07pm respectively. Usually, too, it was his habit to spend half an hour or so chatting with the 'Old Fighters' from the time of the 'struggle for power' once he had finished speaking, but this time he left immediately he had concluded. The reason for this departure from custom remains unclear. Some say that Hitler was anxious not to run the risk of being caught in a British air raid. Others argue that bad weather forced the change of plan. Hitler's initial intention had

been to fly back to Berlin for an important meeting at the Reich Chancellery the next morning, but Munich's airport was fog-bound and his aircraft was grounded. He decided to take the train instead. This snap decision almost certainly saved his life.

Above: *Hitler greets Paul von Hindenburg, President of Germany until his death in 1934. The aged Field Marshal was the last barrier between the Fuehrer and supreme power.*

Opposite: *Hitler is photographed with Brownshirts and Nazi supporters in the Munich beer cellar where he launched his failed putsch against the Bavarian government in 1923.*

THE BOMB EXPLODES

In the beer cellar, the 'Old Fighters' milled around, many disappointed that the Fuehrer had left so abruptly. Most of them slowly started to drift away, leaving the hundred or so staff to clear up after them. At 9.20pm, less than half an hour after Hitler's departure, a massive explosion ripped through the hall. The gallery and roof fell in and the blast blew out the windows and doors. An eyewitness gave an account of what had happened in a radio broadcast two days later.

'About a hundred "Old Fighters" were in the hall and I myself was about a yard from the door. Suddenly there was a flash overhead and a sudden pressure forced me out of the door. Almost immediately afterwards came a thunderous sound and then everything was over before we could think what had happened. The air was full of dust, we could neither see nor breathe. We held our handkerchiefs over our mouths and got into fresh air. When the dust settled, we went back and found that the ceiling

Right: *Hitler captured in a characteristic pose, saluting his followers at a rally held shortly after his assumption of power in 1933.*

Below: *Troops and police comb the wreckage of the beer cellar for survivors after the deadly bomb blast. Had Hitler not left earlier than anticipated, he almost certainly would have perished in the explosion.*

had fallen in. There were about fifty "Old Fighters" in the hall uninjured and we set about rescue work. It was dangerous because at any minute more of the ceiling might have fallen in. We worked for some time getting out the injured and the dead.'

In all, three of the bomb's victims were killed outright, five died of their injuries later and 62 more were wounded, some seriously. Among the latter was Fritz Braun, a 60-year-old schoolteacher who was the father of Eva Braun, Hitler's mistress. Many of the people who managed to struggle out of the wreckage— choking, coughing, bleeding and covered in dust—assumed that they had been the victims of a British air raid. Only gradually did they realise that the explosion had been caused by a bomb deliberately concealed in one of the beer cellar's central pillars.

Hitler got the news of the explosion when the Berlin express stopped briefly at Nuremberg. At first, he thought it must be a joke, but his entourage immediately disillusioned him. It swiftly became clear that the Fuehrer had escaped death by a whisker, saved by providence, as he said to his companions, so that he could carry on with his divinely-appointed mission.

From his viewpoint, Hitler told Heinrich Himmler, the Reichsfuehrer SS who was travelling with him on the train, the immediate priority was not just to catch whoever had planted the bomb, but also to establish whether the bomber had been acting alone or was part of a deeper conspiracy. The Fuehrer himself had no doubt that the latter was the case. He was sure that the British Secret Service had masterminded the assassination attempt. Himmler agreed with his master. He also told him that he would take immediate action to bring the likely culprits to book.

THE VENLO INCIDENT

For some months, Dr Franz Fischer, a German spy posing as a political refugee in neutral Holland, had been in contact with Captain Sigismund Payne Best and Major Richard Stevens, two leading British intelligence agents there. Fischer purported to have links to a dissident group of high-ranking officers, who were plotting Hitler's overthrow. Walther Schellenberg, an ambitious young SS Sturmbanfuehrer who was rising swiftly to the top in SS counterintelligence, had crossed the border himself to meet with Best and Stevens and convinced them of his bona fides as an army captain representing an influential German general who was leading the opposition within the Wehrmacht to the Nazi regime. In his memoirs, Schellenberg recorded how he was about to

meet the British again—this time complete with a fake 'general'— when the assassination attempt forced a dramatic change of plan.

'I had taken a sleeping pill to ensure myself against another sleepless night and had sunk into a deep sleep when the insistent buzzing of the telephone awoke me,' Schellenberg wrote. 'It was the direct line to Berlin. Drugged with sleep, I groped for the receiver and reluctantly grunted "Hello." At the other end, I heard a deep, rather excited voice: "What did you say?" "Nothing so far," I replied. "Whom am I speaking to?" The reply came sharply, "This is the Reichsfuehrer SS Heinrich Himmler. Are you there at last?"'

"My consternation struggling with my sleepiness,' Schellenberg recalled, 'I replied with my habitual, "Yes sir." "Listen carefully," Himmler continued: "Do you know what has happened?" "No sir," I said, "I know nothing." "Well, this evening, just after the Fuehrer's speech in the beer cellar, an attempt was made to assassinate him! A bomb went off. Luckily, he'd left the cellar a few minutes before. Several old Party comrades have been killed and the damage is pretty considerable. There's no doubt that the British Secret Service is behind it all. The

Fuehrer and I were already on his train to Berlin when we got the news. He now says—and this is an order—when you meet the British agents for your conference tomorrow, you are to arrest them immediately and bring them to Germany. This may mean a violation of the Dutch frontier, but the Fuehrer says that's of no consequence. The SS detachment that's been assigned to protect you…is to help you to carry out your mission. Do you understand everything?" "Yes, Reichsfuehrer, But…" "There's no "but'," Himmler said sharply. "There's only the Fuehrer's order—which you will carry out. Do you now understand?" I could only reply, "Yes, sir." I realised it would be quite senseless to try to argue at this point.'

KIDNAPPED AT GUN-POINT

Schellenberg obeyed. In a book published in 1950, Best described what happened as he and his companions waited for the Germans outside a cafe just across the frontier at Venlo.

'Somehow or other, it seemed to me that things looked different from what they had on the previous days,' Payne Best wrote. 'Then I noticed that the German barrier across the road which had always been closed was now

Above: *Hitler and Mussolini, the leader of Fascist Italy, review a Munich parade during the Duce's 1937 state visit to the Reich. The two dictators had met first three years earlier in Venice.*

lifted; there seemed to be nothing between us and the enemy. My feeling of impending danger was very strong. Yet the scene was peaceful enough. No one was in sight except a German customs officer in uniform lounging along the road towards us and a little girl who was playing at ball with a big black dog in the middle of the road before the cafe.

'I must have rather checked my speed, for Klop (the Dutch General Staff officer accompanying the British agents) called out, "Go ahead, everything is quite all right." I felt rather a fool to be so nervous. I let the car drift slowly along to the front of the cafe on my left and then reversed into the car park on the side of the building farthest from the frontier. Schaemmel (Schellenberg's alias) was standing on the veranda at the corner and made a sign which I took to mean that our bird was inside. I stopped the engine and Stevens got out on the right. My car had left-hand drive.

'I had just wriggled clear of the wheel and was following him out when there was a sudden noise of shouting and shooting. I looked up, and through the windscreen saw a large open car drive up round the corner till our bumpers were touching. It seemed to be packed to overflowing with rough-looking men. Two were perched on top of the hood and were firing over our heads from sub-machine guns, others were standing up in the car and on the running boards; all shouting and waving pistols. Four men jumped off almost before their car had stopped and rushed towards us shouting: "Hands up!"

'I don't remember actually getting out of the car, but by the time the men reached us, I was certainly standing next to Stevens, on his left. I heard him say: "Our number is up, Best." The last words we were to exchange for over five years. Then we were seized. Two men pointed their guns at our heads, the other two quickly handcuffed us.

'I heard shots behind me on my right. I looked round and saw Klop. He must have crept out behind us under cover of the car door which had been left open. He was running diagonally away from us towards the road; running sideways in big bounds, firing at our captors as he ran. He looked graceful, with both arms outstretched – almost like a ballet dancer. I saw the windscreen of the German car splinter into a star, and then the four men standing in front of us

started shooting and after a few more steps Klop just seemed to crumple and collapse into a dark heap of clothes on the grass.

'"Now, march!" shouted our captors, and prodding us in the small of our backs with their guns, they hurried us, with cries of "Hup! Hup! Hup!" along the road towards the frontier. As we passed the front

Above: *Georg Elser, the carpenter behind the beer cellar bomb, photographed in Gestapo custody. Though he worked alone, Hitler and other Nazis claimed the British Secret Service was behind the plot.*

Opposite: *A packed audience in the beer cellar awaits the arrival of their Führer. Even at the height of the war, the meeting to commemorate the 1923 putsch was one of the few occasions Hitler always attended.*

of the cafe I saw my poor Jan held by the arms by two men who were frog-marching him along. It seemed to me that his chin was reddened as from a blow. Then we were across the border. The black and white barrier closed behind us. We were in Nazi Germany.'

CATCHING THE CULPRIT

Even before Himmler contacted Schellenberg, the actual perpetrator of the assassination attempt had been arrested. Georg Elser, a quietly-spoken 36-year-old carpenter, was detained by a border patrol while attempting to cross the Swiss frontier illegally earlier that evening. In his knapsack, the police found a sketch of what looked like a bomb mechanism, bits of a fuse, a Communist Party membership card and a picture postcard of the beer cellar itself. These would have been incriminating enough at the best of times; now, they were to prove fatal. While Elser was being questioned, an urgent message arrived. It warned all border posts to be on the look-out for the beer-cellar bomber.

Elser was handed over to the local Gestapo and then taken back to Munich, where he was interrogated by Heinrich Mueller, the head of the Gestapo, and then by Himmler himself. At first, none

of Elser's interrogators believed that he could have possibly acted on his own, even though he stubbornly insisted that he had acted entirely on his own initiative. He explained how, as a former member of the Communist Party's Red Front Fighter's League, he had come to loathe the Nazis and all that they stood for and eventually decided to make his assassination attempt. He described in detail the months of patient work it had taken him to plan, build and install the bomb. He even built another one in a workshop the Gestapo put at his disposal.

However, Mueller failed in his main aim, which was to force Elser to admit that he had been part of a wider conspiracy masterminded by Best and Stevens. 'I haven't been able to get anything out of him on that point,' the Gestapo chief told Schellenberg. 'He either refuses to say anything or else tells stupid lies. In the end, he always goes back to his original story: he hates Hitler because one of his brothers who had been a Communist sympathiser was arrested and put into a concentration camp. He liked tinkering with the complicated mechanism of the bomb and he liked the thought of Hitler's body been torn to pieces. The explosives and the fuse were

given to him by an anonymous friend in a Munich cafe.'

Himmler was equally unsuccessful. He admitted to Hitler that there was 'no possibility of any connection between Elser and Best and Stevens. I don't deny that British Intelligence may be connected with Elser through other channels,' the Reichsfuehrer went on. 'Elser admits he was connected with two unknown men, but whether he was in touch with any political group we just don't know...They may have been Communists, agents of the British Secret Service or members of the Black Front (a German dissident movement led by the refugee former Nazi Otto Strasser). There is only one other clue: our technical men are practically certain that the explosives and the fuses used in the bomb were made abroad.'

The Fuehrer was unconvinced. 'I want you to use every possible means to induce this criminal to talk,' he told Reinhardt Heydrich, the head of the Reich Main Security Office. 'Use hypnosis, give him drugs—everything that modern science had developed in this direction. I've got to know who the instigators are, who stands behind this thing.' Heydrich faithfully carried out his orders. Elser was injected with massive doses of Pervitin, the

latest truth drug, and hypnotised by four of the best hypnotists in Germany. He still stuck stubbornly to his original tale.

DEATH AT DACHAU

Eventually, even the Gestapo was forced to admit failure. Elser was despatched to Sachsenhausen concentration camp, where he was held in solitary confinement until the last month of the war. He was then transferred to Dachau, where he was executed. Coincidentally, Best and Stevens were imprisoned in the same camp. They survived to be liberated by the Allies.

The identity of the two men who apparently aided Elser has never been discovered. After the war, it was even alleged by Georg Thomas, a former Wehrmacht general giving evidence at the Nuremberg War Crimes Trial, that the Nazis had stage-managed the bombing themselves to give the regime the excuse for a savage clamp-down on dissidents in high places who were opposed to the war. The truth, however, almost certainly will never be fully known.

Above: *US troops on guard at the gates of Dachau concentration camp shortly after the German capitulation in 1945. It was here that Elser, after years of imprisonment in solitary confinement at Sachsenhausen, was finally executed in April 1945.*

The Phantom Spy of Scapa Flow

When Kapitan-Leutnant Gunther Prien, commander of the German submarine U-47, penetrated Scapa Flow, Britain's vast naval base in the Orkneys, on the night of 12 October 1939 and sank the battleship Royal Oak, there was rejoicing in Berlin and consternation in the Admiralty. The sinking left the British with crucial questions to answer. How had a single U-boat managed to break through Scapa Flow's supposedly impregnable defences? Was it down to British naval incompetence or had there been a spy at work?

Above: *The remains of the Balfour battery, built at Hoxa Head during World War I, was one of 19 coastal batteries intended to cover the approaches to Scapa Flow and Kirkwall Bay, so protecting the fleet from surface attack. It never saw action.*

Left: *The* Royal Oak, *one of Britain's Resolution-class battleships, first saw action at the battle of Jutland in 1916. With a maximum speed of less than 20 knots, she was obsolete before the war broke out in 1939. When she was sunk by U-47 at anchor in Scapa Flow on 21 October, 833 out of her 1,234-strong crew were killed or died of wounds.*

William Shirer, an American journalist based in Berlin, summed up the general feeling on both sides when the news of the sinking broke. 'The place where the German U-boat sank the British battleship *Royal Oak* was none other than Scapa Flow, Britain's greatest naval base,' he wrote in his diary. 'It sounds incredible. A World War submarine commander told me last night that the Germans tried twice to get a U-boat into Scapa Flow during the last war, but both attempts failed and the submarines were lost.'

Shirer went on to describe Prien's unexpected appearance at a hastily-convened press conference. 'Captain Prien, commander of the submarine, came tripping into our afternoon press conference at the Propaganda Ministry this afternoon, followed by his crew—boys of 18, 19 and 20,' he recorded. 'Prien is 30, clean-cut, cocky, a fanatical Nazi, and obviously capable. Introduced by Hitler's press chief, Dr Dietrich, who kept cursing the English and calling Churchill a liar, Prien told us little of how he did it. He said he had no trouble getting past the boom protecting the bay. I got the impression, though he said nothing to justify it, that he must have followed a British craft, perhaps a minesweeper, into the base. British negligence,' Shirer concluded, 'must have been something terrific.'

BRITISH BUNGLING

Shirer was closer to the truth than he knew at the time. Far from being impregnable, Scapa Flow's defences were decrepit. The old steel underwater netting guarding its main points of entry had rotted, rusted or broken up. Warned that these points were 'not properly netted', Winston Churchill, who had returned to the Admiralty as First Lord on the outbreak of war, issued an urgent order authorising new nets and booms to be installed and more blockships to be sunk. By the middle of October, however, nothing had been done. Work on the improved anti-submarine defences Churchill had ordered to be constructed only began after the sinking of *Royal Oak* and then took two years to complete.

There was even more to it than this. In 1938, a maritime survey had revealed that Kirk Sound, part of Holm Sound and one of the key access points to the base, had a deep channel some 300 feet to 400 feet wide running clear through it. The following March, the Admiralty ordered an old merchant vessel to be sunk in it as a blockship. Just two months later, however, a further survey revealed that the channel was still navigable. Admiral Sir William French, commanding

Orkney and Shetland, confirmed this, warning that a submarine or destroyer could make it through the channel easily at slack water. At the time, the Admiralty dismissed his fears. Indeed, after the *Royal Oak* was sunk, it did its best to cover up the survey's findings and French's report.

DOENITZ PREPARES

What the Admiralty may have been counting on was German ignorance of the state of Scapa Flow's defences and the fact that there was an open channel leading right into the heart of the base. Unfortunately for the British, the Germans were not. On 1 October, Commodore Karl Doenitz, then the commander of Hitler's U-boat fleet, summoned Prien to see him on board a depot ship moored in Kiel harbour. Doenitz knew Prien as a skilful and daring submarine commander. He had decided to entrust him with the execution of Special Operation P, one of the most daring naval missions of the entire war.

Doenitz had been planning the venture for some time. He handed over all the documentation for Prien to study. Aerial reconnaissance photographs, taken by the Luftwaffe as early as 6 September,

Above: *Scapa Flow, seen from one of the Churchill Barriers, built to block the small channels to the east of the anchorage.*

Opposite: *The corvette* Camellia *was credited with the sinking of U-48 while on escort duty southeast of Iceland.*

showed the entire British Home Fleet at anchor with anti-submarine booms and blockships notionally blocking the bay's seven entrances. Or were they? In Kirk Sound, the three blockships the British had sunk there lay just far enough apart for a U-boat to zigzag through between them in the still water just after high tide. It would require skilful seamanship, though. A U-boat Doenitz had sent to scout the inlets had faced powerful ten-knot rip tides. Even in daylight let

alone at night, navigation would be tricky at best. Nevertheless, the Grand Admiral concluded that 'a penetration at this point (Kirk Sound) on the surface at the turn of the tide would be possible without further ceremony.'

Prien assessed the wealth of information Doenitz had provided at home that evening. 'I worked through the whole thing like a mathematical problem,' he later wrote. The next day, he reported to Doenitz again. The Commodore was sitting at his desk. 'He did not acknowledge my salute,' Prien recalled. 'It seemed he hadn't noticed it. He was looking at me fixedly and asked me "Yes or no?"'

Prien answered simply 'Yes, sir.' Doenitz rose to shake his hand. 'Very well,' he said. 'Get your boat ready.' U-47 sailed from Kiel on 8 October.

'TORPEDO LOS!'

Having successfully negotiated a northern course around the blockships that had been sunk in Kirk Sound to make the passage supposedly impassable, Prien slipped into Scapa Flow shortly after midnight on 14 October. Still on the surface, he headed west across the flow towards the main fleet anchorage. Much to his surprise, he found this empty. He turned his U-boat about and made for the northeastern corner of the flow. Here, he struck lucky. He spotted two targets, one of which was *Royal Oak* lying peacefully at anchor. The other Prien thought looked like the battle-cruiser *Repulse*; in fact it was a seaplane carrier.

Prien fired his first torpedo salvo at the silent battleship, scoring a single hit. His second salvo missed. He then manoeuvred to fire a third. This was the fatal blow. All three torpedoes struck

home. There was a tremendous explosion and the mortally-wounded *Royal Oak* started to sink immediately. With the help of a Ministry of Propaganda ghost writer after the event, Prien vividly recalled what he himself saw. 'A wall of fire shot up towards the sky. It was as if the sea suddenly stood up on end. Loud explosions came one after another like drumfire in a battle and coalesced into one mightily ear-splitting crash. Flames shot skyward, blue…yellow…red. Behind this hellish firework display, the sky disappeared entirely. Like huge birds, black shadows soared through the flames and fell hissing and splashing into the water. Fountains yards high sprang up where they had fallen, huge fragments of the mast and funnels. We must have hit the munition magazine and the deadly cargo had torn the body of its own ship apart. It was as if the gates of hell had suddenly been torn open and I was looking into the flaming furnace.'

Prien decided to run for home. Back in Kirk Sound, he took the gap to the south of the blockships. With the tide now falling, U-47 had to battle against a fierce 10-knot current, but eventually she reached the comparative safety of the open sea. Prien and his crew

reached Wilhelmshaven and safety on the morning of 17 October. They were immediately flown to Kiel to be greeted by Doenitz, now promoted to the rank of Rear Admiral, and Grand Admiral Erich Raeder, the commander-in-chief of the Kriegsmarine. From Kiel, they were flown to Berlin to be decorated by the Fuehrer himself.

SEARCH FOR SCAPEGOATS

No sooner had the news of the sinking been released by the Admiralty than the search for scapegoats began. Why, for instance, had the crew of *Royal Oak* apparently failed to realise that they were under enemy attack as soon as Prien's first torpedo hit their ship? It appeared that many of the crew were sure that the explosion had been an internal one—probably of inflammable materials in the paint store—and that the ship's fire crew could be trusted to deal with it. Many of the ship's portholes, which had been left open, were never closed with the result that seawater was free to pour through them when *Royal Oak* began to list. No one ordered

Right: *Karl Doenitz, head of the U-boat arm of the Kriegsmarine, personally planned the operation that led to the successful torpedoing of* Royal Oak.

the watertight doors to be closed. Above all, no formal order was ever given to abandon ship. Out of *Royal Oak*'s 1,146-strong crew, 833 of them perished with her. 120 were boy sailors aged between 14 and 18; all had been sent to the battleship as their first naval posting.

It was useless trying to blame Rear Admiral Henry Blagrove—he had gone down with his ship. Captain William Benn and the *Royal Oak*'s other officers were exonerated by a Board of Enquiry. Benn went on to become a Rear

Admiral himself. French was less fortunate. The Board of Enquiry blamed him for the poor state of Scapa Flow's defences and, after the sinking, for the slowness to react to the presence of Prien's submarine. He was forcibly retired. MI5, the British counterintelligence service, was also blamed. The Admiralty was convinced that a German secret agent in the Orkneys must have provided the information that enabled Prien and his U-boat to reach their target. MI5 agents were rushed to the islands to flush out the elusive

Above: *Churchill Barrier 1 was belatedly built to block Kirk Sound, which Kapitan-Leutnant Gunther Prien, commander of U-48, used to enter Scapa Flow and sail out of it to safety after torpedoing Royal Oak.*

Opposite: *Prien, like many of his fellow U-boat commanders, preferred to attack his targets on the surface, rather than submerged. Unlike this U-boat, seen here under air attack in the Atlantic, he managed to get in and out of Scapa Flow undetected.*

Nazi spy. Their search failed. Major-General Vernon Kell, the head of MI5, paid the price for failure. The mysterious events surrounding the sinking of *Royal Oak* were seized upon as an excuse to get rid of him. He, too, was forced to resign.

THE SCAPA FLOW SPY

In the spring of 1942, the *Saturday Evening Post*, one of the most popular US magazines of the day, published a sensational article, which supposedly shed new light on the entire Scapa Flow disaster. It claimed to have solved the hitherto unanswered question as to how Doenitz had obtained his knowledge of the state of Scapa Flow's defences by identifying a Captain Alfred Wehring, a World War 1 officer in the Imperial German Navy where he had served under Admiral Wilhelm Canaris, subsequently head of the Abwehr (German Intelligence), as the Scapa Flow master-spy.

According to the *Post*, after World War I, Wehring had left the navy and settled in Switzerland, where, as instructed by German intelligence, he trained to become a jeweller and watchmaker. In 1927, armed with a Swiss passport, he moved to Britain using the name of Albert Oertel, and became a naturalised British citizen four years later. Shortly after that, he opened a small jewellery store in Kirkwall in the Orkneys. His main business, of course, was to spy on British naval activity at nearby Scapa Flow.

It was in the late summer of 1939, said the *Post*, that Wehring brought off his greatest and most audacious coup yet. He signalled detailed information about the state of Scapa Flow's defences to the Abwehr, including the invaluable news that its eastern approaches were not closed off by anti-submarine nets but only by hulks lying relatively far apart. It was this vital intelligence that prompted Doenitz to draw up the plans for Special Operation P and brief Prien to carry out the planned attack.

This was by no means all. Again according to the *Post*—and again as late as 1959 by *Coronet* magazine—Wehring actually boarded U-47 before she entered Scapa Flow and acted as Prien's pilot and right-hand man during the course of the actual attack. The story was repeated by Walter Schellenberg in the memoirs he dictated after the end of the war and shortly before his death. Wehring's achievement, Schellenberg said, amply demonstrated 'how important intelligently planned long-range preparatory work can be—and how rewarding in the end.' Schellenberg concluded: 'The sinking of this battleship took less than 15 minutes, but

Above: *Gunther Prien, the commander of U-48, photographed after his triumphant return to Germany. His sinking of* Royal Oak *made him into a national hero.*

15 years of patient and arduous work by Alfred Wehring had been the necessary foundation for this supremely successful mission.' After his enforced retirement in June 1940, Vernon Kell chimed in as well. 'The Germans,' he opined, 'had been supplied with up-to-date information by a spy.'

FACT OR FANTASY

It was an impressive tale. Unfortunately, it was almost certainly fiction. The writer of the original article, Curt Reiss, a refugee newspaperman who wrote the original *Saturday Evening Post* article, never revealed his sources. Prien perished in March 1941 when his U-boat was sunk by a British destroyer. Wilhelm Canaris, implicated in the July 1944 bomb plot against Hitler, was executed in Flossenburg concentration camp on 9 April 1945. Schellenberg's memoirs were published posthumously. Karl Doenitz rose to the rank of Grand Admiral, succeeded Raeder as commander-in-chief of the Kriegsmarine and, after Hitler's suicide, took over from him as Fuehrer. Sentenced to ten years' imprisonment for war crimes, Doenitz was released in 1956 and lived in retirement until his death in 1980. He made no mention of the Scapa Flow spy in

his autobiography.

Even more to the point, journalists investigating in the Orkneys after the war failed to find anyone who had even known of, much less seen, Wehring during the entire 12 years he was supposed to have lived there. One leading Kirkwall tradesmen testified: 'I certify with the utmost assurance that never at any period has there been a watchmaker in Kirkwall known as Albert Oertel, or any person connected with the trade who could possibly be identified with the mystical "Watchmaker Spy of Kirkwall." I am convinced beyond possibility of doubt that such a person has never existed and is only a journalist's fabrication.' Checks of the archives of the Imperial German Navy, the Kriegsmarine and the Abwehr found no mention of a Captain Alfred Wehring—or, indeed, of an Albert Oertel—either.

If there was no spy living on Orkney, what was the source of the information on the basis of which Doenitz decided on the attack? The answer is that there was a real-life spy involved—a secret agent working for Commander Hermann Menzel, head of the Abwehr's naval intelligence division. In August

1939, Menzel arranged a trip to the Orkneys for one of his most astute operatives. He was Captain Horst Kahle, the skipper of the freighter *Theseus* who doubled up as an Abwehr operative. Kahle returned with a detailed account of the state of Scapa Flow's defences, which he had obtained through his own observations or from what he had heard being talked about in Kirkwall itself.

Added to this was the information brought back by Kapitan-Leutnant Horst Wellner, commander of U-14, who had been despatched to scout the approaches of Scapa Flow almost immediately after the outbreak of war. Wellner discovered that, though the British had blocked Hoxa and Switha Sounds effectively, Kirk Sound was comparatively clear. It was via Kirk Sound that Prien cautiously made his way into Scapa Flow to launch his deadly attack.

If It Hadn't Been Churchill

For Britain, 8 May 1940 was one of the decisive days of World War II. At the end of a two-day debate on the conduct of the war, the government majority in the House of Commons fell from 213 to 81; 33 Conservatives voted with the Opposition and 60 abstained. It was clear that Neville Chamberlain could no longer carry on as Prime Minister. The question was who could – or should – succeed him?

When it came, Chamberlain's downfall was swift. It was also unexpected. In April 1940, he had confidently told a Conservative Party meeting: 'After seven months of war, I feel ten times more confident of victory than I did at the start.' Having explained to his enthusiastic audience just why he was so sure that the Allies would defeat the Nazis, he concluded: 'One thing is certain. Hitler has missed the bus.'

These injudicious words were to come back to haunt the premier. Unknown to him, Hitler's Wehrmacht was poised to invade Denmark and Norway. What US Senator William Borah had christened 'the phoney war'

Above: *Troops from the British Expeditionary Force march through Paris in September 1939.*

Left: *Neville Chamberlain, Prime Minister at the outbreak of war, was forced out of office in May 1940.*

was about to end. Chamberlain's premiership ended with it. On 7 May, with the evacuation of Allied forces from Norway in full swing after a short-lived and disastrous campaign, he faced the House of Commons to debate the government's conduct of the war.

'IN THE NAME OF GOD, GO!'

The House of Commons was packed. Harold Nicolson, an ex-diplomat and now a prominent writer, broadcaster and National Labour MP, described the scene. 'The House is crowded and when Chamberlain comes in, he is greeted with shouts of "Missed the bus!" He makes a very feeble speech and is only applauded by the yes-men. He makes some reference to the complacency of the country, at which the whole

House cheers vociferously and ironically, inducing him to make a little, rather feminine gesture of irritation.'

Nicolson went on to give his view of the rest of the day's debate. 'Attlee (Clement Attlee, the Leader of the Opposition) makes a feeble speech and Archie Sinclair (Sir Archibald Sinclair, leader of the Liberals) a good one. When Archie sits down, many people stand up and the Speaker calls on Page Croft. There is a loud moan from the Labour Party at this and they practically all rise in a body and leave the House. He is followed by Wedgewood, who makes a speech which contains everything he ought not to have said. He gives the impression of being a little off his head. At one moment he suggests the British Navy has gone to Alexandria since they are frightened of being bombed.'

Wedgewood's speech provoked the first dramatic intervention of the two-day debate. 'When Wedgewood sits down', Nicolson chronicled, 'Keyes (Admiral Sir Roger Keyes) gets up and begins his speech by referring to Wedgewood's remark and calling it a "damned insult." The Speaker does not call him to order for his unparliamentary language and the whole House roars with laughter, especially Lloyd George who racks backwards and forwards in boyish delight with his mouth wide open. Keyes then returns to his manuscript and makes an absolutely devastating attack upon the naval conduct of the Narvik episode and the Naval General Staff...It was by far the most dramatic speech I have ever heard and when Keyes sits down there is thunderous applause.'

Leo Amery's speech later in the evening was even more powerful.

A former cabinet minister and now one of the most prominent Conservative backbenchers, he attacked not only the mishandling of the Norwegian campaign, but also the government's complacency as a whole. 'We cannot go on as we are,' he said grimly, 'there must be a change.' He finished as dramatically as he had begun. 'This is what Cromwell said to the Long Parliament when he thought it was no longer fit to conduct the affairs of the nation,' he concluded. "'You have sat here too long, for any good you have been doing. Depart, I say, and let us have done with you. In the name of God, go!'"

THE FATEFUL DIVISION

The battle had been joined. It was to be fought to a bitter conclusion when the debate continued the following day. Herbert Morrison, the deputy leader of the Labour opposition, began by announcing that his party would demand a vote on the motion of adjourn the House. This was tantamount to a vote of censure and Morrison's closing remarks made it clear this was exactly what he had in mind. 'If these men remain in office,' he asserted, 'we run grave risk of losing this war.'

No sooner had Morrison sat

down than Chamberlain sprang to his feet to answer him. The Prime Minister was visibly incensed. 'I do not seek to evade criticism,' he exclaimed, 'but I say this to my friends in the House—and I have friends in the House. No government can prosecute a war effectively unless it has public and parliamentary support. I accept the challenge. I welcome it indeed. At least we shall see who is with us and who is against us and I call upon my friends to support us in the lobby tonight.'

The appeal backfired. Many MPs felt that the issue was one upon which the outcome of the war might depend and that it was no time for a personal appeal to friendship. Alfred Duff Cooper, who had resigned from Chamberlain's Cabinet as First Lord of the Admiralty in protest against the Munich Agreement, said as much when he spoke. He told the premier that he, for one, would be voting against the government. David Lloyd George, the veteran Liberal politician who had led Britain to victory in World War I, was even more vitriolic. He and Chamberlain had disliked each other for years and it was now Lloyd George's chance to take his revenge on the beleaguered premier.

Chamberlain, Lloyd George said, had 'met this formidable foe of ours in peace and in war. He has always been worsted. He is not in a position to appeal on the grounds of friendship, he has appealed for sacrifice. The nation is prepared for every sacrifice so long as it has leadership, so long as the government show clearly what they are aiming at and so long as the nation is confident that those who are leading it are doing their best. I say solemnly that the Prime Minister should give an example of sacrifice, because there is nothing which can contribute more to victory in this war than that he should sacrifice the seals of office.'

The vote, when it came, was as dramatic as anything that had gone before it. When the division was called, MPs filed out of the chamber and into the respective lobbies. Chamberlain's supporters catcalled 'Quislings' and 'Rats' at the Conservative rebels as they made for the 'noes' lobby. The latter replied with the taunt of 'yes-men.' Some were highly emotional. Duff Cooper saw 'a young officer in uniform, who had been for long a fervent admirer of Chamberlain,

walking through the Opposition lobby with the tears streaming down his face.' He and Amery were joined by two other former ministers—Lord Winterton and Leslie Hoare-Belisha—in voting against the government.

'RULE BRITANNIA!'

Shortly after 11.00pm, the tellers returned to the chamber to give the Speaker the result of the vote. Captain David Margesson, the Conservative Chief Whip, stood to the right, indicating that the

government had won. The crucial question was the size of the majority. First Margesson and then the Speaker slowly read out the result: 'Ayes to the right 281, noes to the left 200.'

There was an audible gasp. Then pandemonium broke out. The government's normal majority of well over 200 had been slashed to just 81. The Opposition chorused 'Resign' while the loyal government supporters sat shocked and silent as if in a trance on their benches. 41 Conservative

MPs had voted against their leader and another 88 had either deliberately abstained or failed to vote for some reason or another. It was clear that a fifth of the government's backbenchers were in revolt. Nicolson noted: 'The figures are greeted with a terrific demonstration during which Joss Wedgewood starts singing 'Rule Britannia' (joined in uneasy chorus by Harold Macmillan from the Conservative benches), 'which is drowned in shouts of "Go, go, go, go!"' Henry 'Chips' Channon, a loyal Chamberlain supporter who had spent the debate sitting directly behind his leader, hoping to 'surround him with an aura of affection,' noted in his diary that the Prime Minister 'appeared bowled over by the ominous figures.' A sympathetic parliamentary correspondent wrote 'he (Chamberlain) left the chamber with the pathetic look of a surprised and sorely stricken man.'

SEARCH FOR A SUCCESSOR

Shortly after the result of the vote was announced, Margesson and his fellow Whips conferred in anxious conclave. Was it the end of the road for the Prime Minister? How solid was the backbench opposition to him continuing in office? The Whips tried to buy off some of the leading rebels, assuring them that Chamberlain would agree to sacrifice Sir Samuel Hoare and Sir John Simon, his two most unpopular ministers. Others were also plotting and scheming to try to ensure Chamberlain's survival. Prominent among them were Channon, Lord Dunglass, the Prime Minister's Parliamentary Private Secretary, and R.A. Butler, universally known as Rab, who was Under-Secretary of State at the Foreign Office. Chamberlain's position was ambivalent. At first, it looked as if he was going to resign. Then on 10 May, when Hitler's armies struck in the West, it seemed as though he had changed his mind. Everyone from King George VI downwards waited to see what the Prime Minister would decide to do.

There were two possible successors waiting in the wings – Lord Halifax, the Foreign Secretary, and Winston Churchill, whom Chamberlain had called back from years in the political wilderness to be First Lord of the Admiralty at the beginning of the war. Halifax started off as the clear favourite. He had the backing of the king, much of his party, most of the press and Chamberlain himself. The premier summoned both men to see him. When he asked Churchill if he knew any reason why a peer should not be Prime Minister, the First Lord looked out of the window and did not reply. The ensuing silence was broken by Halifax. He said that, as a member of the House of Lords, he would be 'more or less honorary Prime Minister, living in a kind of twilight just outside the things that really mattered.' Churchill, Halifax went on, had 'qualities preferable to his own at this particular juncture.' For this reason, he would not accept the premiership.

It was decided to wait until the Labour leaders, who were consulting their party at its conference in Bournemouth, made up their minds as to whether they would serve in a new government. Late on the afternoon of 10 May, Clement Attlee telephoned through their decision. He confirmed that his party was prepared to enter a coalition – but only under another Prime Minister. Within an hour, Chamberlain had resigned. On the outgoing premier's recommendation, the king sent for Churchill.

FROM SUFFERANCE TO ACCEPTANCE

In his post-war recollections, Churchill wrote vividly of his personal reaction to being appointed premier. He went to bed at nearly 3.00am the next morning, he recorded, 'conscious of a profound sense of relief' he had at last the 'authority to give directions over the whole scene.' He continued: 'I felt as if I were walking with destiny, and that all my past life had been but a preparation for this hour and for this trial.'

In fact, Churchill became Prime Minister by default. He had reached the top of the greasy pole only because Halifax had declined the office. Many Conservative MPs distrusted him and resented his appointment. Even while he was still at Buckingham Palace kissing hands with the king, Channon, Dunglass, Butler and Jock Colville, Chamberlain's junior Civil Service secretary, gathered at the Foreign Office to open a bottle of champagne and drink the health of the 'King over the Water.' Channon recorded in his diary how, on 'perhaps the darkest day in English history... we were all sad and angry and felt cheated and outwitted.' Butler

was particularly vehement. 'He believed,' Channon wrote, 'this sudden coup of Winston and his rabble was a serious disaster and an unnecessary one: the "pass had been sold" by Mr C., Lord Halifax and Oliver Stanley (the Secretary of State for War). They had weakly surrendered to a half-breed American whose main support was that of inefficient but talkative people of a similar type.'

Such feelings were by no means unique. When Churchill entered the House of Commons to speak as Prime Minister for the first time on 13 May, his reception from the Conservative backbenches was no more than tepid. On the other hand, Chamberlain received a standing ovation. According to Sir Alexander Erskine-Hill, the chairman of the powerful 1922 Committee, three-quarters of Conservative MPs would have welcomed the former premier back as Prime Minister.

Churchill recognised his weakness. As soon as he returned from Buckingham Palace, he wrote to Chamberlain telling him 'how grateful I am to you for promising to stand by me and to aid the country at this extremely grievous and formidable moment.' He asked him to become Lord President of the Council with a seat in the War Cabinet. It was there the new premier faced his first open challenge. As the military situation in France went from bad to disastrous, Halifax – still Foreign Secretary – argued for making concessions to Mussolini to try to stop Italy from entering the war.

The unspoken thought was that, if this move was successful, it would be worth finding out via the Duce if Hitler would offer acceptable peace terms. Halifax told Churchill that, if 'reasonable terms could be obtained', he 'would think it right to accept an offer which would save the country from avoidable disaster.' Churchill, who was determined to fight on at all costs, opposed the notion. He appealed to the ministers outside the War Cabinet for backing. They gave him their unquestioning support. So, too, did Chamberlain.

The premier, however, faced continuing difficulties in the House of Commons, The turning point came on 4 July, when he told Parliament why and how, following France's surrender, he had ordered the navy to bombard the French fleet at Oran. According to an observer in the gallery, 'the Chief Whip, Margesson, rose to his feet. Turning towards the Tory backbenchers, he waved his Order Papers in a gesture clearly conveying that they too should rise. At his signal, all the

Conservatives...rose to a man and burst into enthusiastic cheering at the tops of their voices.'

Churchill appeared taken aback. It was the first unanimous display of support he had received from the parliamentary Conservative party. He slumped in his seat with tears pouring down his cheeks. At last, the Conservatives were mirroring popular sentiment. By August, a Gallup poll showed that the premier's personal approval rating had reached an unprecedented 88 per cent. Churchill was finally secure.

Opposite: *George VI inspects an RAF base 'somewhere in France.' The Allied air forces were completely outclassed by the Luftwaffe, which quickly won total air superiority over the battlefield.*

Above: *Winston Churchill, as portrayed by Ambrose McEvoy early on in his career. After years in the political wilderness, his appointment to the War Cabinet in 1939 was unexpected.*

The 'Miracle' of Dunkirk

After the surprise German breakthrough at Sedan in May 1940, the British Expeditionary Force soon found itself fighting for its life as the French and Belgian armies collapsed around it. Its evacuation back across the English Channel from the port of Dunkirk has passed into British historical folklore as a 'miracle'. Was this really the case, or was the evacuation the inevitable outcome of a military catastrophe that could well have been prevented?

The news that the great German offensive in the West had finally begun was greeted by the Allied High Command with near complacency. Having issued his orders for the cream of his armies to advance into Belgium to meet the advancing German thrust head-on, General Maurice Gamelin, the Allied generalissimo, was seen by a staff captain 'pacing up and down the corridor of the barracks, humming audibly with a martial air.' The Secretary-General of the French War Ministry remarked: 'If you had seen, as I have done this morning, the broad smile of General Gamelin when he told me the direction of the enemy attack, you would feel no uneasiness. The Germans have presented him with just the opportunity which he was awaiting.'

In London, General Sir Edmund Ironside, the Chief of the Imperial General Staff, was almost as sanguine. 'On the whole, the advantage is with us,' he confided to his diary. *The Times* was even more confident: 'This time at least there has been no strategic surprise,' it declared. 'It may be taken as certain that every detail has been prepared for an instant strategic reply. The Grand Alliance of our time for the destruction of the forces of treachery and oppression is being steadily marshalled.'

THE TRAP IS SPRUNG

Gamelin's orders were followed to the letter, despite the misgivings of General Georges, the overall commander of the crucial northeastern section of the Allied front. The BEF, commanded by General Lord Gort, together with the French 1st and 7th armies, set off across the Franco-Belgian border. Units of the BEF and the 1st Army headed for the River Dyle, the 7th Army made for Breda, where the plan was for it to link up with the Dutch, whom Hitler had also attacked.

Left: *Admiral Sir Bertram Ramsey was responsible for organising and overseeing the evacuation from Dunkirk.*

Right: *Exhausted but heartened troops jammed into vessels for the voyage back across the English Channel to safety.*

Top: *An RAF signals unit heads for Dunkirk. British and French troops both bitterly complained of lack of air cover. The common cry was 'Why don't our planes protect us?'*

Above: *A stray dog, picked up wandering on the Dunkirk beaches, was an unlikely evacuee. He, too, reached safety in Britain, where he was promptly popped into quarantine against rabies.*

The British were welcomed enthusiastically. Captain R. J. Hastings, second-in-command of D Company, the Royal Norfolk Regiment, recorded how he and his men were greeted by the Belgian civilians as they advanced. 'In towns and villages, they lined our route,' he wrote, 'and little children ran along with the trucks, throwing flowers to the troops... people in motor cars drove up and down the convoy, distributing cigarettes and chocolate, and whenever we stopped the women came out of houses with hot coffee...No expressions of a nation's goodwill could have been more complete.'

The whole thing went smoothly – too smoothly, according to some observers. The Luftwaffe was noticeably absent from the Belgian skies. 'We all expected to be bombed on the way,' Hastings noted. 'Actually we saw no enemy aircraft all day.' Kim Philby, working for *The Times* as a war correspondent, was apprehensive. 'It went too damn well,' he remarked to an American fellow-correspondent. 'With all that air power, why didn't he bother us? What is he up to?'

The Allies were soon to find out. The move into Belgium could not have suited Hitler better than

Above: *British tanks hastily being loaded onto railway flat cars on May 25, 1940. They arrived on the battlefield too late to make a difference.*

Above: *General Maxime Weygand was hastily recalled from Syria to succeed the disgraced Gamelin as Allied generalissimo. He, too, failed to halt the German advance.*

Opposite: *Trucks form an improvised jetty into the sea at Dunkirk. When the evacuation started, many believed that only a relatively few men would be lifted from the beaches.*

The German plan worked to perfection. As they had intended, the Allies were mesmerised by the thrust in the north. Meanwhile, Army Group A – 45 divisions strong, headed by seven out of the ten panzer divisions Hitler had available – was boring its weight unnoticed through the Ardennes. The aim was to cross the River Meuse between Dinant and Sedan. In a two-day battle, starting on 12 May, the panzers forced the crossing of the river and drove relentlessly forward to open up an 80km (50 mile) gap in the Allied line. With the Luftwaffe's dive bombers acting as their flying artillery, the panzers powered through the gap as French resistance started to collapse.

'OU EST LA MASSE DE MANOEUVRE?'

It would have taken inspired leadership to take the necessary steps to halt the Germans as they thrust forward. Neither Gamelin nor any of his subordinate generals seemed capable of getting a grip on the situation and providing it. Indeed, it was not until the evening of 15 May that the Allied generalissimo was forced to admit the extent of the crisis. He had spent the afternoon reassuring the French War Cabinet that he had

if he had dictated the orders for it himself. Far from staging a re-run of the Schlieffen Plan, with which the Germans had gone to war in 1914, what they were intending was a kind of Schlieffen-in-reverse. Just enough of the Wehrmacht had been concentrated to ensure a quick breakthrough into Belgium and Holland – a matador's red cape acting to attract the Allied

bull. The *Schwerpunkt* (main thrust) of the attack was to be further south through the hilly and heavily forested Ardennes. Gamelin and the rest of the French high command considered the region impassable for tanks. Nevertheless, this was where the bulk of Hitler's panzer divisions, backed by the cream of the Luftwaffe's dive bombers, were concentrated.

the situation well in hand. Later, however, he telephoned Edouard Daladier, the Minister of National Defence, with very different news.

William Bullitt, the US Ambassador to France, was closeted with the minister when the call came through. According to Bullitt, Daladier exclaimed as Gamelin revealed the extent of the catastrophe: 'No, what you tell me is not possible! You are mistaken; it's not possible.' Daladier then shouted down the 'phone: 'We must attack soon.' Gamelin replied: 'Attack! With what? I have no more reserves.' He gave much the same answer to Churchill, when, in response to a desperate telephone call from the French premier Paul Reynaud, the new British Prime Minister flew to Paris the following day. After listening to Gamelin outline the military situation, Churchill immediately 'asked: "Where is the strategic reserve?" and, breaking into French, which I used indifferently in every sense, "Ou est la masse de manoeuvre?" General Gamelin turned to me and, with a shake of his head, said; "Aucune (there are no longer any)."'

Churchill was dumbfounded. Daladier interjected: 'The mistake, the unpardonable mistake, was to send so many men into Belgium.' Churchill seized on the point. Why, he asked, were the Allied armies falling back in northern Belgium, abandoning Brussels and Louvain to the enemy? Surely they should be counter-attacking the northern flank of the sinister and ever-growing bulge the Germans had driven into the Allied line? Turning to Gamelin, Churchill demanded point-blank: 'When and where are you going to counter-attack the flanks of the bulge? From the north or from the south?' Gamelin's reply confirmed the bankruptcy of his military thinking. All he could mutter was: 'Inferiority of numbers, inferiority of equipment, inferiority of method.' He shrugged his shoulders hopelessly. It was the last time Churchill was to meet him. On 19 May, Gamelin was sacked. General Maxime Weygand, who had been called back hastily from Syria, replaced him.

THE BEF FALLS BACK

It was true that the BEF was falling back together with its French and Belgian allies. Starved of information from the French high command, its generals, from Gort downwards, failed to appreciate the true nature of the French predicament. They also complained from the highest level downwards about the absence of any clear instructions from London.

Lieutenant-General Henry Pownall, Gort's Chief of Staff, wrote bitterly: 'Nobody minds going down fighting, but the long and many days of indigence and recently the entire lack of higher direction...have been terribly wearing on the nerves of all of us.' When orders did arrive from Churchill for a counter-attack southeastwards by the whole of the BEF, Pownall was even more indignant: 'Can nobody prevent him from trying to conduct operations himself as a super commander-in-chief? How does he think we are to collect eight divisions and attack as he suggests? Have we no front to hold? He can have no conception of our situation and condition...The man's mad.'

Churchill was determined that the BEF should carry out the attack. Ironside himself was despatched to Gort's headquarters to order him to 'force his way through all opposition in order to join up with the French in the south.' Gort received the order with obvious consternation. He and his staff had already started on working out a contingency plan for a retreat to the Channel coast and, after some thought, said he could not agree to the attack. He told Ironside that everything he had seen of the French forces and their leaders in recent days increasingly led him to doubt whether they could stage 'an organised counter-offensive on a large scale.' What he would agree to was to launch a limited attack southwards from Arras.

Armed with Gort's reluctant agreement, Ironside set off to tackle Generals Billotte and Blanchard, commanders of the French First Army Group and the 1st Army respectively. Both seemed totally demoralised. Though Ironside finally bullied them into agreeing to strike northwards, Gort, on his return, told him he was certain that 'they would never attack.' His foreboding was correct. The British attacked at Arras, but the French did nothing.

Weygand, in the meantime, had been planning a pincer movement of his own to sever the corridor the Germans were carving through France as the panzers headed for the Channel. Gort, however, was convinced by this time that the only hope of saving anything of the BEF was to fall back on Dunkirk. He ordered his troops to withdraw from Arras and start moving westwards back towards the port. Weygand abandoned his plan.

THE PANZERS HALT

As Gort's troops retired, Operation Dynamo, the codename for the intended evacuation, was hastily set in motion. The first troops were evacuated on 26 May. 'And so here we are back on the shores of France on which we landed with such high hearts over eight months ago,' Pownall lamented. 'I

think we were a gallant band who little deserves this ignominious end to our efforts.' Ironside had already penned his own comment. 'God help the BEF,' he wrote in his diary. 'Brought to this state by the incompetence of the French Command.' In private, he reckoned that the British would be lucky to evacuate 30,000 men. Gort was as pessimistic. 'I must not conceal from you,' he signalled the War Office, 'that a great part of the BEF and its equipment will inevitably be lost even in best circumstance.' Churchill, too, prepared for the worst. On 28 May, he warned the House of Commons to 'prepare itself for hard and heavy tidings.'

Two days later, Pownall arrived in London to brief the Cabinet's Defence Committee on Gort's plans for holding the Dunkirk perimeter. 'No one in the room,'

Above: *Though hundreds of small civilian crafts – the famous 'little ships' – sailed for Dunkirk to rescue the BEF, the navy had the dominant role. Here, the river gunboat* Locust *is pictured sailing for the port.*

Above: *By no means did all the 'little ships' make it back across the Channel safely. Here the Isle of Man ferry Mona's Queen is sinking off Dunkirk having been hit by a German bomb.*

wrote Ian Jacob, a member of the War Cabinet secretariat, 'imagined that they could be successful if the German armoured divisions, supported by the Luftwaffe, pressed their attack.' Had the panzers pressed home their advantage, Dunkirk undoubtedly would have fallen and the evacuation would have been stifled at birth. They did not. It was one of the most controversial decisions the German high command made during the entire war.

After the war, the German generals roundly blamed Hitler for single-handedly insisting on halting the panzers in their tracks. In fact, it was Field Marshal Gerd von Rundstedt, commander of Army Group B, who ordered them not to cross the Aa Canal and press home their advantage. He was concerned that 50 per cent of the panzers were temporarily out of action and that he needed to conserve those which were operational for the next phase of the battle against the French south of the River Somme. In addition, he considered the muddy Flanders terrain ill-suited to tank warfare. Hitler concurred with the decision. Rounding up the 'remnants' of the BEF would wait. Dunkirk was to be 'left to the Luftwaffe' to subdue.

This was the true 'miracle' of Dunkirk. Gort gained three invaluable days to set the port's defences in order before Hitler was persuaded to rescind his orders and allow the panzers to resume their attack. In his post-war memoirs, General Heinz Guderian, Hitler's most successful panzer commander who had led the drive from Sedan to the Channel, commented: 'What the future course of the war would have been if we had succeeded at the time in taking the British Expeditionary Force prisoner at Dunkirk, it is now impossible to guess.' He was being diplomatic. Had the BEF been compelled to surrender, there is little doubt that Britain would have found it militarily impossible to carry on with the war.

THE EVACUATION

Slowly but surely, the evacuation got underway. The Luftwaffe did its best to put a stop to it, but its attempts were hampered by fog and poor visibility, while Fighter Command threw in every single plane it could muster to protect the bridgehead. Over the course of the action, its pilots flew a total of 2,739 sorties, sometimes flying as many as four a day. Though by the evening of 27 May, only 7,669 men had been evacuated successfully, the next day's figure shot up to 17,804 and the day after that to 47,310. A peak of 68,014 was reached on 31 May, the day a reluctant Gort himself sailed for home, leaving General Sir Harold Alexander in command. By the time the last ship left the port at dawn on 4 June, 337,000 men, of whom 110,000 were French, had been snatched to safety.

Not everything went smoothly. Though the Royal Navy did the lion's share of the work, its task would have been impossible without the assistance of a plethora of small boats despatched across the Channel with their volunteer civilian crews to help to rescue the BEF from the beaches. Some were not impressed by the apparent chaos they found. 'It seems to me incredible that the organisation of the beach work should have been so bad,' wrote Lieutenant Robert Hitchens of the minesweeper *Niger*. 'We were told that there would be lots of boats and that the embarkation of the troops would all be organised,' he wrote. 'That was what all the little shore boats were being brought over from England for...One can only come to the conclusion that the civilians and small boats packed up and went home with a few chaps instead of staying there to ferry to the big ships which was their proper job. As for the shore organisation, it simply did not exist...a more disgraceful muddle... I have never seen.'

Be that as it may, Dunkirk was a success of sorts. However, it was not a victory by any stretch of the imagination – as Churchill told the House of Commons, 'wars are not won by evacuations.' It was, in fact, an unmitigated defeat. It was little wonder, therefore, that, at midnight on the day the port fell, Hitler ordered that church and civic bells be tolled for three days throughout the Reich to celebrate the end of the 'greatest battle in world history.'

The Windsor Kidnapping

After the Duke of Windsor – Edward VIII until his abdication from the British throne in 1936 – and his American Duchess fled from France to neutral Portugal as France fell in June 1940, Churchill was presented with a dilemma. Was the Duke a pro-Nazi or a loyal patriot? Would he even connive at his own kidnapping in return for Hitler's pledge to restore him to the throne? It is still one of World War II's greatest controversies.

Churchill, a long-time friend of the Duke of Windsor who had supported him resolutely through the crisis caused by Edward's determination to marry Wallis Simpson, a twice-divorced American, in 1936, was always convinced that the Duke 'never wavered in his loyalty to the British cause.' Even he could not deny, however, that before, during and after his short reign, the Duke, at times, had displayed pronounced pro-German sympathies.

1936 – the year of Edward's abdication – was also the year that Hitler moved into the Rhineland, which had been demilitarised ever since the signing of the Treaty of Versailles in 1919. The move provoked a European crisis and was the Fuehrer's first and greatest gamble. Had Britain and France stood up to him, he undoubtedly would have been forced to pull back his troops and might well have fallen from power as a result. 'If the French had marched into the Rhineland,' he told Paul Schmidt, his personal interpreter, 'we would have had to withdraw with our tails between our legs.'

In the event, Britain and France confined themselves to muted protests. The French refused to move without British backing and the British refused to move at all.

Left: *The Duke of Windsor is photographed in naval uniform during his days as Prince of Wales. As prince and king, he was hugely popular.*

Opposite: *The Duke of Windsor looks on as Hitler warmly greets the Duchess during the couple's ill-timed visit to Germany in October 1937. British Intelligence suspected her and the Duke of harboring Nazi sympathies.*

Lord Lothian, a prominent British political figure, spoke for many of his fellow-countrymen when he declared that 'the Germans are only going into their own back garden.' According to Leopold von Hoesch, the German Ambassador in London, Edward himself intervened during the crisis. He telephoned Hoesch personally to offer him reassurance. 'I sent for the Prime Minister (Stanley Baldwin) and gave him a piece of my mind,' Hoesch claimed Edward had said to him. 'I told the old so-and-so that I would abdicate if he made war. There was a frightful

scene, but you needn't worry. There won't be a war.'

For her part, Wallis Simpson appears to have been even more pro-German than Edward. According to an FBI report, specially compiled during a visit by the Duke and Duchess to the USA on the personal orders of J. Edgar Hoover in April 1941, she had become the mistress of Joachim von Ribbentrop soon after his appointment to succeed Hoesch as German Ambassador in London. The report stated that the FBI's informant (believed to be the former Duke of Württemberg 'knew

Above: *The Duke reviews an S.S guard of honor during his 1937 German visit. Public opinion at home was scandalised when it was rumored that he had greeted his hosts with a Nazi salute.*

Opposite: *Stanley Baldwin, Prime Minister at the time of the Abdication, told Edward that he and his cabinet would resign if the king dared to try to marry the twice-divorced Mrs. Simpson.*

definitely that von Ribbentrop, while in England, sent the then Wallis Simpson 17 carnations every day. The 17 apparently represented the number of times they had slept together.' Ribbentrop kept in close touch with her even after he had returned to Germany to become Foreign Minister. If the informant was telling the truth, it was little wonder that, embittered at her social ostracism by the British establishment after Edward's abdication, the Duchess did absolutely nothing to hold her husband back.

VISITING THE FUEHRER

In October 1937, shortly after their marriage in France, the Duke and Duchess accepted an invitation to visit Germany as Hitler's personal guests. The Duke announced that the purpose of the visit was to study the ways in which Germany had tackled its unemployment problems, but the trip was soon mired in controversy. The Duchess later wrote somewhat naively that 'it never occurred to David (the family name for Edward) that this purely private trip could become a cause for public concern,' but she was wrong. The Nazis did their best to turn it into a fully-fledged state visit.

The couple were feted wherever they went, the Duke responding to the cheers with the raised-arm Hitler salute on several occasions. They met privately with Hitler at his Bavarian holiday retreat and dined with Rudolf Hess, then the Deputy Fuehrer. Robert Ley, head of the Labour Front, was officially in charge of the visitors until, visibly drunk, he drove the Duke and Duchess straight through a set of locked factory gates in his Mercedes. On Hitler's orders, he was hurriedly replaced by Herman Goering for the rest of the visit.

What exactly the Duke and the Nazi leaders talked about remains unknown, but there is no doubt that Hitler and the other top Nazis were impressed by what they heard. Edward was unstinting in his praise of German industrial developments and social progress. He certainly was all for appeasing the new Germany; he also believed that the Nazi regime would be an invaluable bulwark against the possible spread of Communism, which he loathed. Propaganda Minister Joseph Goebbels summed up the Nazi view: 'It's a shame he is no longer

king. With him we would have entered into an alliance.'

Hitler concurred. Later, he told Albert Speer, his personal architect: 'I am certain that through him permanent friendly relations could have been achieved.' As for the Duchess, the Fuehrer apparently won her heart by telling her that she 'would make a good queen.' She recorded her impressions of the Fuehrer as follows: 'At close

quarters, he gave one a feeling of great inner force...his eyes were truly extraordinary – intense, unblinking, magnetic, burning with the same peculiar fire I had earlier seen in the eyes of Kemal Ataturk.'

In fairness, the Duke and Duchess were by no means the only high-ups from Britain to be impressed by the Nazis and their Fuehrer. A month after their trip to Germany, David Lloyd George, the veteran Liberal politician who, as Prime Minister, had led the British to victory in World War I, also visited the Fuehrer. After his return home, the 'Welsh wizard' described what a deep impression Hitler had made on him in an article he wrote for the *Daily Express*. Having paid tribute to the Fuehrer for 'the marvellous transformation' he had brought about in 'the spirit of the people,' Lloyd George continued: 'One man has accomplished this miracle. He is a born leader of men. He mixes a magnetic, dynamic personality with a single-minded purpose, a resolute will and a dauntless heart. Lloyd George concluded: "He is the George Washington of Germany – the man who won for his country independence from all her oppressors.' In his conversation with Hitler, Lloyd George had gone even further. When Hitler told him that during the war it had been he who had 'galvanised the people of Britain into the will for victory,' Lloyd George replied that he was glad to receive this compliment from 'the greatest German of the age.'

LOOSE CANNON

The British government heartily disapproved of the Duke's and Duchess's visit. It was equally disconcerted when, in May 1939, the Duke unilaterally decided to broadcast an appeal for 'a peaceful solution to the world's problems' to the USA from the World War I battlefield at Verdun. The broadcast, whether deliberately or not, coincided with George VI's and Queen Elizabeth's state visit to the USA. There was no stopping Edward, however. On 27 August, as the German Wehrmacht prepared to strike at the Poles, he cabled Hitler directly 'as a citizen of the world' pleading with the Fuehrer to use his best efforts to preserve peace.

The telegram read: 'Remembering your courtesy and our meeting two years ago, I address to you my entirely personal, simple though very earnest appeal for your utmost influence towards a peaceful solution of the present problem.' The Fuehrer did not reply. So matters rested until the fall of France in June 1940. The Duke and Duchess fled their adopted country – Edward had been serving as a liaison officer between the BEF and the French Army – for safety.

It was after the Duke and Duchess arrived in neutral Portugal after a tortuous journey via Biarritz and then Spain that Hitler received a report that gave him cause to think. Apparently, the Duke had openly expressed his dislike and distrust of his family because of the way they had persistently snubbed the Duchess, and criticised Churchill equally severely for his unnecessary prolongation of the war. According to the report, Edward had gone on to predict that 'protracted heavy air bombardment would make Britain ready for peace.'

The Fuehrer was intrigued by the Duke's apparent loathing of Churchill and his dislike of the war. He came round to the belief, rightly or wrongly, that Edward would be more than willing to return to the throne, albeit as a puppet king, following a British surrender and the conclusion of an armistice. Ribbentrop, Foreign Minister since 1937, concurred. He cabled Eberhard von Stohrer, the German Ambassador in Madrid, telling him to assure Edward that, if he wished it, Germany was willing to smooth the path for 'the Duke and Duchess to occupy the British throne.'

Edward, who had now taken up residence in Lisbon, where he and the Duchess were the guests of Ricardo do Espirito Santo Silva, a banker who was

Above: *Joachim von Ribbentrop, German Ambassador in London in 1936 and later Hitler's Foreign Minister, was rumored to have been one of Mrs. Simpson's lovers.*

Left: *Walter Schellenberg, the rising star of S.S Intelligence, was put in charge of the Nazi attempt to persuade the Duke to leave Portugal for pro-Nazi Spain in the summer of 1940.*

thought to be a Nazi sympathiser, received the message with some consternation. He told the Spanish grandee who was acting as Ribbentrop's intermediary, that the British constitution made it impossible for a monarch who had once abdicated to return to the throne. When the emissary then suggested that events might bring about changes even in the British constitution, the Duchess, in particular, became 'very thoughtful.'

OPERATION WILLI

Ribbentrop was determined not to let matters rest there. He summoned Walter Schellenberg, the rising star of SS Intelligence, into consultation. Ribbentrop started by explaining the Duke's current position – at least as

far as he understood it. 'We've had word,' he told the cynical Schellenberg, 'that he (the Duke) has even spoken about living in Spain and that if he did go there he'd be ready to be friends with Germany again as he was before.' The Foreign Minister continued: 'The Fuehrer thinks this attitude is extremely important and we thought that you with your Western outlook might be the most suitable person to make some sort of exploratory contact with the Duke – as representative, of course, of the Head of the German State.'

Ribbentrop had not finished. 'The Fuehrer feels that if the atmosphere seemed propitious you might perhaps make the Duke some material offer,' he went on. 'Now, we should

be prepared to deposit in Switzerland for his own use a sum of 50 million Swiss francs, if he were ready to make some official gesture dissociating himself from the manoeuvres of the British Royal family. The Fuehrer, of course, would prefer him to live in Switzerland, though any other neutral country would do so long as it's not outside the economic or the political or military influence of the German Reich.'

'If the British Secret Service should try to frustrate the Duke in some such arrangement,' Ribbentrop went on, 'then the Fuehrer orders that you are to circumvent the British plans, even at the risk of your life and, if need be, by the use of force. Whatever happens, the Duke of Windsor must be brought safely

to the country of his choice. Hitler attaches the greatest importance to this operation and he has come to the conclusion after serious consideration that if the Duke should prove hesitant, he himself would have no objection to your helping the Duke to reach the right decision by coercion – even by threats or force if the circumstances make it advisable.'

Schellenberg sat stunned. He rose and was about to leave when Ribbentrop got Hitler on the telephone. The Fuehrer confirmed that the plan was to go ahead. He added that Schellenberg 'should particularly bear in mind the importance of the Duchess's attitude and try as hard as possible to get her support. She has great influence over the Duke.' After this, Schellenberg was finally able to make his getaway. He immediately began planning what he christened Operation Willi. The next day, he left for Madrid.

PLOT AND COUNTER-PLOT

On his arrival, Schellenberg went straight to the German embassy to meet Stohrer. The ambassador told him that it was his contacts in the Spanish aristocracy who had alerted him to the Duke's apparent discontent. They had invited him to hunt with them on an estate near the Portuguese border and he had accepted the invitation, though no date for the hunt had yet been set. The hunt would give Schellenberg the chance to speak to the Duke personally and, if the Duke fell in with the plan, to spirit him across the border into Spain.

Schellenberg decided to play a waiting game. The more he thought about it, the more likely it seemed to him that the Duke's remarks – if, indeed, he had ever made them – were being taken far too seriously. He decided to go to Lisbon to assess the situation. Within a few days, he had reached a conclusion. The Duke no longer intended to accept the hunting invitation. Though he disliked the fact that he was being shadowed by the British Secret Service and did not like the prospect of being sent as Governor to Bermuda, which was Churchill's current intention, he equally

Above: *German troops inspect an abandoned British tank in France. The Duke abandoned his post as a liaison officer with the French Army, fleeing with the Duchess first to Spain and then to Portugal.*

Right: *While the British prepared to fight to the last man in the event of a German invasion, the Duke let it be known that he was in favor of a negotiated peace with Germany.*

had no intention of going to live voluntarily in a neutral or hostile country. The most he had ever said, according to his Portuguese friends, was that he would rather live in any European country than go to Bermuda.

Churchill, for his part, was determined that the Duke and Duchess should leave Europe as soon as possible. An injudicious interview the Duke gave to the press, which Churchill regarded as defeatist, was probably the final straw. The Prime Minister despatched Sir Walter Monckton, previously one of the Duke's closest advisers, to Lisbon to warn Edward to prepare to leave for Bermuda immediately or face the possibility of court-martial. The Duke and Duchess reluctantly obeyed.

Schellenberg, in the meantime, was coming under increasing pressure from Berlin to end his apparent inactivity. About a fortnight after his arrival in the Portuguese capital, he received a peremptory telegram from Ribbentrop. It read baldly: '[The Fuehrer] orders that the abduction is to be organised at once.' Schellenberg decided to get around the order by arranging through his contacts with Portuguese officials for extra police to be drafted in to guard the Duke and the Duchess. With the British Secret Service already on high alert, Schellenberg had the pretext he needed to abandon any kidnap attempt. The day after Edward and Wallis finally sailed, he left for Berlin.

Even Hitler accepted that Schellenberg had acted for the best. 'The Fuehrer has studied your last telegram carefully,' a dispirited Ribbentrop told him, 'and asks me to tell you that in spite of his disappointment at the outcome of the whole affair, he agrees with your decisions and expresses his approval of the manner in which you proceeded. 'As Schellenberg wrote in his post-war memoirs, 'the chapter was closed.'

Europe's Looted Treasures

History demonstrates that conquerors are rarely respecters of property; after the Nazis stormed through most of Western Europe, they proved to be no exception. With many of the great European cultural centres firmly in their clutches, the Nazi leaders – chief amongst them Hitler himself, followed by Hermann Goering – embarked on a systematic looting spree on a scale unmatched since the barbarians swarmed into the Roman Empire.

Above: *Soldiers from the Hermann Goering Division pose outside the Palazzo Venezia in Rome with a looted landscape by the 18th-century artist Giovanni Paolo Pannini. The photograph was taken in 1944 before the Germans evacuated the city.*

Nazi determination to secure the cream of European art for the Reich was clearly in evidence even before the outbreak of war in 1939. On 26 June that year, Adolf Hitler engaged the services of Hans Posse, an art historian and museum director in Dresden, and put him in charge of amassing the art collections that would be needed to fill the grandiose galleries and museums the Fuehrer planned to have built in Berlin and Linz, his birthplace.

Posse and, from 1942, Herman Voss, Posse's successor after his death from cancer, quickly set to work. By 1945, they had gathered together more than 8,000 works of art for their Fuehrer. The collection included 12 Rembrandts, 23 Breughels, two Vermeers and 15 Canalettos, plus paintings by Titian, Leonardo da Vinci, Botticelli, Holbein, Cranach, Rubens and many others. Many of them were simply expropriated from their owners, or acquired at knock-down prices that did not come anywhere near reflecting their true value.

Jewish art dealers and collectors were particularly at risk. After the French surrender in 1940, Hitler ordered all their possessions in France to be confiscated. The property of 15 major Jewish art dealers was promptly seized, together with the fabulous art collections painstakingly built up over the years by Jewish art connoisseurs – most notably the Rothschilds. Vermeer's *The Astronomer* was one of the masterpieces expropriated for Hitler himself. The Fuehrer intended it to form a focal point of his Linz museum. In Holland, a team of Nazi art experts tracked down collections that had been taken to Holland by German-Jewish owners fleeing persecution before the war, confiscated them and had them sent back to the Reich. A classic 1669 self-portrait of Rembrandt was just one of the masterpieces among their number.

France was by no means the first country the Nazis plundered during the course of the war. The looting started in Warsaw, where a grand total of 13,512 paintings and 1,379 sculptures were seized and confiscated after Poland's surrender in 1939. The plundered works of art included Raphael's *A Portrait of a Young Man,* which subsequently vanished from sight. Many were simply destroyed. Countless rare books and manuscripts went up in flames, for example, when the Nazis set fire to the Krasinski Library in the Polish capital.

THE AVARICIOUS REICHSMARSCHAL

Other top Nazis quickly followed the Fuehrer's example. The most avaricious of them all was Luftwaffe commander-in-chief and economics overlord Hermann Goering. By the time the ebullient Reichsmarschal started collecting on a truly massive scale, he already owned ten houses, castles and hunting lodges scattered around the Reich, all provided by taxpayers and maintained at their expense. In all of them – most notably Carinhall, his vast and ever-expanding principal hunting lodge which he had named in memory of his deceased first wife – he was determined to display artworks, tapestries, paintings, sculptures and much else besides to confirm his status as the second most important figure in the Reich.

Like the Fuehrer, Goering employed an art agent – Walter Andreas Hofer – to track down the masterpieces he coveted. He also took the lead in building up his collection. A 1940 visit to Amsterdam triggered off an orgy of competitive acquisition between him and the other Nazi bigwigs; during a two-day visit to Paris that same year, he personally selected 27 works by Rembrandt, Van Dyke and others for his

delectation. As a result of the visit, he ended up with more than 600 paintings, pieces of furniture and other items, which he had valued at low prices if he intended to display them at Carinhall or at much higher ones if his intention was to sell them. Highlights of his collection included Lucas Cranach's *Venus and Cupid* and Rembrandt's *Two Philosophers* as well as several Vermeers, though, after the war, the latter were discovered to be fakes. Goering and his supposed art experts had been taken in by Han van Meegeren, a Dutch artist and art dealer, who had skilfully forged the Vermeers himself.

It is still uncertain exactly how many looted works of art Goering acquired—the latest estimate is around 2,000, over 700 more than had been previously thought. What we do know is what happened to many of them. With the Soviet armies closing in on Berlin as the war neared its conclusion, Goering ordered Carinhall to be evacuated before being blown up by Luftwaffe troops. The majority of the art

Above: *Hermann Goering, seen here seated front row far right in the dock at the 1946 Nuremberg Trial, was the Third Reich's champion art looter. His collection included 10 Van Dycks, nine Rembrandts, and hundreds of other masterpieces.*

collection was loaded onto a fleet of trucks and then private trains, transporting it deep into Bavaria and then towards the Austrian border. The trains were intercepted by American forces and diverted to Munich, where their content was inventoried prior to its eventual return to its rightful owners. As for the

Right: *The reconstructed Amber Room is seen in its full glory. Looted from St Petersburg and transported to Germany, the original is one of the most significant art treasures never to have been recovered.*

Reichsmarschal himself, he, too, fell into Allied hands. He was found guilty of crimes against humanity and sentenced to death at the 1946 Nuremberg Trials, though he managed to kill himself before having to face the hangman.

THE AMBER ROOM

By no means were all the works of art looted by Hitler, Goering and the other Nazi leaders recovered. The whereabouts of the celebrated Amber Room, for instance, still remains something of a mystery. Dubbed 'the eighth wonder of the world' after its creation, its story started in 1701, when Andreas Schulter, a German sculptor, and Gottfried Wolfram, a Danish amber artist, began work on its design and construction for Friedrich I of Prussia. Originally installed in the Charlottenburg Palace, Friedrich William I presented it as a gift to Peter the Great of Russia after the latter expressed his admiration for it during a state visit he paid to Berlin to cement a Russo-Prussian alliance.

The Amber Room was dismantled, crated up and shipped to St Petersburg, where it was reassembled in the Winter House. In 1755, Tsarina Elizabeth ordered it to be disassembled again and moved to the Catherine Palace in Pushkin. The Italian designer Bartolomeo Francesco Rastrelli redesigned it to fit into its new, larger home, shipping the extra amber he needed from Berlin to Russia. After this and other 18th-century renovations, the room was around 180 square feet in size, its amber panels, backed with gold leaf, glowing with six tons of amber and other semi-precious stones. Historians have estimated that the room at that time was worth $142 million in modern dollars.

Above: *General Tomoyuki Yamashita, the so-called 'Tiger of Malaya' who became the Military Governor of the Philippines from October 1944 until the islands' liberation, was thought to have superintended the looting of millions of dollars worth of gold, though whether this was shipped from mainland southeast Asia to the Philippines is considered unlikely.*

LOOTED BY THE NAZIS

It was little wonder that the Amber Room, made by Germans for Germans, became one of Hitler's prime artistic targets as his armies swept into the Soviet Union after their surprise attack caught the Russians off guard in June 1941. As Nazi forces approached Pushkin, where the Amber Room was still housed, attempts were made first to dismantle it and then to hide it – the Russians resorted to pasting wallpaper over its amber panels to conceal them from sight. The attempts were in vain. The Germans quickly found the room. Within three days, they had torn it down and packed the pieces up in crates, which were shipped to Konigsberg (Kaliningrad) on the Baltic coast. There, the Amber Room was installed in the castle museum.

The Amber Room stayed on display for the next two years until late 1943, when Alfred Pohde, the museum's curator, was ordered to take it apart again and crate it away for safety. In August the following year, RAF bombers blitzed the city, destroying most of its historic buildings including the castle. From that point in time onwards, the Amber Room vanished from history.

It seems hard to credit that the crates containing the room could have simply disappeared without leaving any trace, and numerous efforts have been made to solve the mystery. Some say that the crates were destroyed in the bombing; others argue that they are still concealed somewhere in or around Konigsberg. Another theory holds that, in 1945, as the Russians closed in on the city, they were loaded onto a refugee ship, which a Soviet submarine promptly torpedoed, sending it to the bottom of the Baltic.

The search went on and on. Stasi intelligence agents in East Germany spent millions of marks in a fruitless quest that lasted for decades. Then, in 1998, two rival research teams – one in Germany and the other in Lithuania – claimed to have located the missing crates. The Germans said they had been buried in a silver mine south of Berlin, while the Lithuanians claimed that they were concealed at the bottom of a murky lagoon, close to the town of Neringa. Both teams failed to locate the treasure. The same thing happened in 2008, when treasure-hunters were sure they had located the Amber Room's hiding place in a manmade underground cavern near a village on the German border with the Czech Republic. Three years later, yet another group of researchers claimed that the room's amber panels were hidden

Above: *Joseph Goebbels, the Nazi Minister of Propaganda, visits the Exhibition of Degenerate Art held in Munich in 1937. It was designed to showcase the 'deviant and decadent' art that the Nazis dismissed as the work of 'Jews and Bolsheviks' – all of whom were out to destroy European culture.*

Opposite: *Hitler, Gerdy Troost, widow of architect Paul Troost, Adolf Ziegler, and Joseph Goebbels at the opening of the House of German Art in Munich in May 1937. The works of art on display were chosen to celebrate 'two thousand years of German culture'.*

somewhere in an underground bunker they had discovered in the woods outside Auerswalde, a small town near Chemnitz. Further investigation failed to find any trace of the lost room.

LOST OR DESTROYED?

The Nazis did not simply loot art on an unprecedented scale. They also destroyed it. In 1937, they turned out en masse for the opening of the so-called Exhibition of Degenerate Art in Munich. The aim of the exhibition was simple. It was to hold

up contemporary art to ridicule.

It was Hitler's chance to take his revenge on the artistic establishment of the day, which, years before while he was a penniless art student in Vienna, had dismissed his painstakingly realistic paintings of buildings and landscapes as the work of a talentless amateur. That summer, he pledged that 'works of art which cannot be understood in themselves but need some pretentious instruction book to justify their existence will never again find their way to the German people.'

Works by 112 artists were featured in the exhibition. They included paintings by some of the greatest international names in abstract and expressionist art – Marc Chagall, Paul Klee, Oskar Kokoschka, Gustav Klimt, Pablo Picasso and Henri Matisse among them – as well as celebrated German modernists, such as Max Beckmann, Otto Dix, Georg Grosz, Ernst Ludwig Kirchner and Emil Nolde. The overall purpose of the exhibition, the catalogue explained, was 'to reveal the philosophical, political, racial and moral goals behind this movement, and the driving forces of corruption which follow them.'

Entartete Kunst (degenerate art), the Nazis roundly declared, was deviant and decadent. Its practitioners were all part of a conspiracy, the aim of which was to destroy European culture. They were 'Jews and Bolsheviks' to a man. The way the exhibits were displayed visually reinforced the contempt the Nazis had for them and the artists who had created them. Pictures were deliberately hung askew. There was graffiti on the walls, which insulted both the works on display and their creators. The aim was to make it all seem outlandish and downright ridiculous into the bargain.

The paintings were distributed between various rooms according to category. The derogatory labels spoke for themselves. There was art that was blasphemous, art by Jewish or Communist artists, art that criticised German soldiers and art that offended the purity of German womanhood. One room, devoted entirely to abstract art, was labelled simply 'the insanity room.' The catalogue had this to say about

it and its contents: 'In the paintings and drawings of this chamber of horrors, there is no telling what was in the sick brains of those who wielded the brush or the pencil.'

THE MUNICH DISCOVERY

The message was clear – or so it seemed. All degenerate art should be got rid of. Much was thought to have been physically destroyed. In 2012, however, an accidental discovery in a Munich apartment turned the accepted view of the twisted relationship between the Nazis and modern art almost completely on its head.

Ever since the 1937 exhibition, it had been generally assumed that all the so-called degenerate art the Nazis could lay their hands on had either been destroyed or sold abroad to raise hard currency for the regime. Now, while raiding the home of Cornelius Gurlitt, an 80-year-old recluse, customs officials, who were looking for evidence of money-laundering, instead unearthed a hoard of more than 1,500 long-lost modern masterpieces. These included paintings by Cézanne, Picasso, Matisse, Munch, Renoir, Klee, Nolde, Marc, Dix and Kokoschka. The discovery was kept secret for some months; it was not until late 2013 that news of it was made public.

Gurlitt turned out to be the son of Hildebrand Gurlitt, a Hamburg art dealer who, despite being half-Jewish, had been recruited by the Nazis as a useful expert when it came to organising their mass confiscations of degenerate art. Rather than destroying or selling it, Gurlitt secretly hoarded much of it, carefully hiding it away in the chaos that overtook the Third Reich as it headed inexorably towards final surrender. Though the Americans discovered some of it shortly after the capitulation, he was able to convince them that he had acquired the paintings and drawings they found legitimately and they eventually handed them back over to him. The rest of his collection, he said, had been destroyed in the firestorm that followed the RAF bombing of Dresden in February 1945, just over two months before the end of the war.

The unanswered question is whether there were any more hoarders like Gurlitt and, if there were, what lost masterpieces might they have quietly appropriated for themselves? What, for instance, really happened to Klimt's three *University Murals* and *Schubert at the Piano*? The former, created by Klimt to decorate the Great Hall of University of Vienna, have long

been regarded as among the most radical and controversial of his artistic works. Together with *Schubert at the Piano* and nine other Klimts, they were supposed to have been destroyed in 1945, when, on 7 May – the day that Germany unconditionally surrendered to the Allies – a group of SS troopers blew up Schloss Immendorf, a castle in lower Austria where they had been stored since 1943, to prevent the castle falling into Russian hands.

Another masterpiece whose fate is considered uncertain is Van Gogh's *Painter on His Way to Work* (otherwise known as *Painter on the Road to Tarascon*). In the painting, Van Gogh depicted himself as a travelling painter – complete with straw hat, painting equipment and walking stick – accompanied by his prominent shadow. Van Gogh was high on Hitler's blacklist of degenerate artists and this painting was quickly seized and taken off display. Previously thought to have been destroyed in an Allied air raid, it is now one of the 100,000 masterpieces that, according to the US National Archives, are listed as missing. The jury remains out as to whether, in the light of the sensational Munich discovery, any of these, too, will be found.

Top: Portrait of Wally *by Austrian painter Egon Schiele. Wally, Schiele's favorite model became his mistress.*

Left: Pferde im Landschaft *by Franz Mark was one of the paintings rediscovered in the apartment of Cornelius Gurlitt in Munich in 2012.*

The Strange Case of Rudolf Hess

It was an extraordinary event that astounded the world. On 10 May 1941, Rudolf Hess, Hitler's deputy, parachuted into Scotland. His mission, so he told his captors, was to seek an immediate end to the war, though he admitted he had flown to Britain without the knowledge or approval of the Fuehrer. Hitler's response was immediate. He denounced Hess as being insane, a verdict with which his British captors eventually concurred.

Exactly what prompted Hess to fly to Britain on his peace mission remains something of a mystery. Though he always denied that Hitler knew anything about his intentions in advance, some still speculate that, in fact, the Fuehrer was aware of what Hess planned. Persuading the British to come to terms and make peace meant that Germany would not have to fight a war on two fronts when she turned east against the Soviet Union. Indeed, Hess even may have hoped that the British eventually might agree to join in the attack.

There is at least one piece of hard evidence to support this claim. In 2011, a German historian discovered a 28-page handwritten document in the Russian state archives. It was written by Karl-Heinz Pintsch, Hess's former adjutant, while he was a Soviet prisoner. It said that Hitler indeed had approved of Hess's flight as a way of kick-starting peace talks between Berlin and London. According to Pintsch, Hess was to 'use all means at his disposal to achieve at least the neutralisation of England.' Though the Soviets may well have coerced Pintsch into making his assertions, it equally might have been the case that he believed – or knew – them to be true.

Others postulate that Hess may have been the victim of a 'sting' by the British Secret Intelligence Service. According to the theory, MI6 deliberately leaked false stories that prominent personalities in Britain were plotting to topple Churchill and then open negotiations to agree

Above: *Rudolf Hess, Hitler's deputy, flew to Britain in May 1941 in a misguided attempt to persuade the British to make peace and join Germany in attacking the USSR.*

Opposite: *The wreckage of Hess's Messerschmitt Me 110 is seen under British guard. Goering had assured Hitler that Hess could never reach Scotland, but instead would crash in the North Sea.*

Above: *A Messerschmitt Me 110 in flight. Having taken off from Augsburg, Hess flew across Germany and the North Sea to reach Scotland, bailing out of his plane just outside Glasgow.*

Opposite: *Rudolf Hess is seen in the center background of this group photograph, taken in March 1941. At the time he was losing out in a battle for power with the Führer's secretary Martin Bormann.*

a compromise peace. Hess, the theorists hold, was lured into the British trap. Another possibility is that, despite officially still being the third most important figure in the Third Reich after Hitler and Goering, Hess was now finding himself more and more sidelined and his position in the party increasingly under threat. It may

be that he thought by fulfilling his self-appointed mission he would re-establish himself as one of the Fuehrer's closest and most-trusted confidants.

'AS THOUGH OVERCOME BY A VISION'

Like Hitler, Hess fought as an infantryman during World War I.

Unlike the Fuehrer, though, he gained rapid promotion. After recovering from a serious wound he received while fighting in Romania, he transferred to the Imperial Air Service, completing his flying training as a pilot in time to fight in the last aerial battles over the Western Front. In common with many young Germans of his generation, the 1918 surrender left him angry, bitter and disillusioned.

Following the armistice, Hess, now a student at the University of Munich, soon became embroiled in extreme right-wing activities.

He joined the Thule Society, a secret anti-Semitic movement dedicated to asserting Nordic racial superiority, and served in the Freikorps, a group of ex-soldiers involved in putting down Communist uprisings. In July 1920, having heard Hitler speak in a small Munich beer hall, Hess joined the embryonic Nazi Party. He was its 16th member.

Hess never forgot that first meeting with Hitler and the impact the future Fuehrer had on him. He felt, he said, 'as though overcome by a vision.' Hitler, Hess believed, was the only person

who could recreate German self-belief and restore the nation's national pride. From that time on, he attached himself to Hitler body and soul, carving out a niche for himself as his most faithful adjutant.

The two men were incarcerated together in Landsburg Prison after the failure of the Beer Hall Putsch in 1923, during which time Hess helped Hitler to write *Mein Kampf*, the definitive statement of the would-be Fuehrer's political beliefs. When Hitler finally took office as Chancellor ten years later, he

promptly made Hess the deputy leader of the Nazi Party as a reward for his years of faithful service. The newly-appointed Deputy Fuehrer was doggedly loyal and blindly obedient. 'With pride, we see that one man remains beyond all criticism and that is the Fuehrer,' he told a party rally after the Nazis finally came to power. 'This is because everybody feels and knows he is always right and he will be always right. The National Socialism of all of us is anchored in uncritical loyalty, in the surrender to the Fuehrer that does not ask for the why in individual cases, in the silent execution of his orders. We believe that the Fuehrer is obeying a higher call to fashion German history. There can be no criticism of this belief.'

Hess and Hitler, though, were very different in character. Away from the speaker's platform, Hess was shy and insecure, while Hitler brimmed with self-confidence. According to Wilhelm Bohle, head of the organisation representing Germans abroad, he was 'the biggest idealist we have had in Germany, a man of a very soft nature.' One of Hess's adjutants concurred. His master, he said, possessed 'almost feminine sensitivities.' He shared none of Hitler's destructive ruthlessness. He was also a great admirer of the British – he spoke English fluently. Perhaps this admiration played a part in spurring him on to plan his mission to Britain. It was an unquestionably sincere, though perhaps naive, attempt to bring the war between his beloved homeland and the nation he admired so greatly to an end.

THE FLIGHT TO SCOTLAND

Hess started planning his peace mission after the fall of France in June 1940. That August, he asked Albrecht Haushofer, his principal adviser on British affairs,

TO BUSBY

HESS LANDED HERE

FLOORS FARM

AIRCRAFT LANDED HERE

ein ständiger Strom von Waffen und Kriegsgerät aller Art.

Die alliierte Kriegsproduktion übertrifft diejenige Deutschlands und seiner Verbündeten heute bereits um mehr als das Dreifache. Nächstes Jahr wird sie sie um mehr als das Vierfache überflügelt haben.

Daran können auch die U-Boote nichts ändern. In den drei Monaten Mai, Juni und Juli wurden über 90 deutsche U-Boote versenkt. Im August wurden mehr U-Boote als alliierte Handelsschiffe vernichtet. Auch jetzt vergeht kein Tag, an dem nicht mindestens ein deutsches U-Boot versenkt wird. Anderseits wurde in den vier Monaten von Mitte Mai bis Mitte September kein einziges alliiertes Schiff im Nordatlantik versenkt. Der Neubau alliierter Schiffe übersteigt die Verluste allein für die ersten neun Monate dieses Jahres um **mehr als sechs Millionen Tonnen.** Unter diesen Umständen werden sämtliche Schiffsverluste der Vereinten Nationen seit Kriegsbeginn bald wieder wettgemacht sein.

Die U-Boot-Waffe hat wie im letzten, so auch in diesem Weltkrieg versagt.

$\star$ $\star$ $\star$

Das ist die Lage von heute. Und wenn es noch einen Deutschen gibt, der dennoch Hoffnungen auf einen Verhandlungsfrieden hegt, so braucht er sich nur zu fragen: Welchen Grund hätten die Alliierten, heute einen Verhandlungsfrieden mit derselben Clique auzustreben, der England trotz seiner bedrängten Lage schon im Mai 1941 die Antwort gab: Keine Verhandlungen mit Hitler oder seiner Regierung!

Hitler weiss dies genau so gut wie wir. Er weiss, dass er den Krieg unwiderruflich verloren hat. Trotzdem lässt er das deutsche Volk weiterbluten, weil er weiss, dass das Kriegsende sein eigenes Ende bedeutet. Um sein eigenes Ende hinauszuschieben, opfert er euch und Deutschland.

Ihr kämpft, um Zeit zu gewinnen: Zeit für Hitler und Zeit zur Zerstörung Deutschlands.

ZUM FALL HESS

England vom Kontinent vertrieben

Luftwaffe bedroht britische Städte mit völliger Vernichtung

Täglich neue Erfolge der U-Boote

Grossbritanniens Verbindungen mit dem überseeischen Weltreich ernstlich bedroht

10. Mai 1941: Rudolf Hess, Stellvertreter des Führers, fliegt nach England

KÜRZLICH hat die englische Regierung ihre erste ausführliche Schilderung der Ankunft von Rudolf Hess in Grossbritannien gegeben.

Hess legte den Flug in einer Me 110 zurück und landete am Abend des 10. Mai 1941 mittels Fallschirms in Schottland. Hess, der die Uniform eines Hauptmannes der Luftwaffe trug, nannte sich Alfred Horn und verlangte, „in besonderem Auftrag" den Herzog von Hamilton zu sprechen.

Am folgenden Morgen, Sonntag den 11. Mai um zehn Uhr morgens, wurde Rudolf Hess am Orte seiner einstweiligen Internierung dem Oberstleutnant der *Royal Air Force*, Herzog von Hamilton, vorgeführt. Hess, der behauptete, den Herzog von den Olympischen Spielen her zu kennen — woran der Herzog sich allerdings nicht erinnern konnte — erklärte, sein Besuch sei seiner Sorge um das Schicksal der Menschheit entsprungen. Hitler wisse mit Bestimmtheit, er werde früher oder später siegen; Hess aber wolle unnötiges Blutvergiessen vermeiden.

Der Herzog von Hamilton erstattete Bericht über diese Unterhaltung. Darauf flog ein Beamter des Britischen

G.81

to start thinking of ways by which he could get into contact with those in high places in Britain who favoured negotiating a compromise peace. Prominent pre-war appeasers, such as the Duke of Westminster, Lord Londonderry, the Duke of Buccleuch, Lord Tavistock, who succeeded as Duke of Bedford in 1940, and Lord Redesdale, father of the notorious Unity and Diana Mitford, were all possible targets, but in the end the choice fell on the Duke of Hamilton, a member of the Anglo-German Fellowship before the war.

Haushofer had met Hamilton at the 1936 Berlin Olympics and was aware of his liking for Germany. He also knew that Hamilton recently had been

Above: *The British left it to the Germans to announce Hess's flight, but soon started making propaganda out of the affair. This leaflet was one of hundreds of thousands dropped by the RAF over Germany.*

Opposite: *This annotated aerial view shows where Hess landed after parachuting from his plane and where his Messerschmitt crashed. His only injury was a badly twisted ankle.*

appointed Lord Steward of the king's household, a position that gave him direct access to George VI. What Haushofer seems to have been completely unaware of was that, whatever his sympathies may have been before the war, the Duke was a patriot through and through and was now serving in the RAF as a Wing Commander.

Hess asked Haushofer to write to Hamilton suggesting a meeting between the two men, either in Lisbon or in neutral Switzerland. However, the letter was intercepted by the British Security Service and the Duke never received it. All that happened was that MI5 began probing into Hamilton's loyalty. In the meantime, Hess started honing his flying skills in case he had to fly to Scotland to meet Hamilton at

Dungavel House, the Duke's home near Glasgow. He had asked his friend Willy Messerschmitt for the use of an Me 110 fighter-bomber and began making training flights in it under the supervision of Willi Stoer, one of Messerschmitt's top test pilots. As Hess's request, the Me 110 was specially adapted for long-distance flying; it was fitted with two huge 900-litre drop tanks and a special radio compass. He also started having weather conditions in the North Sea specially monitored.

The weather on 10 May 1941 was perfect for Hess's purpose. He arrived at the Messerschmitt airfield at Augsburg in the late afternoon and immediately began getting ready for take-off. As he prepared to climb into the cockpit of his plane, he handed four letters

to Karl-Heinz Pintsch, who had gone with him to the airfield. One was addressed to Hitler, the others to Hess's wife, Willy Messerschmitt and Helmut Kaden, a pilot whose flying suit Hess had appropriated. Telling air traffic control his destination was Norway, he took off at 5.45pm that evening.

'A MISSION OF HUMANITY'

Just after 10.00pm, a radar station on the northeast coast of England detected an unidentified aircraft approaching British airspace. As it approached the coast, it dived to pick up speed, crossed the Scottish border and headed almost due west flying at low level – so low, in fact, that three Spitfires scrambled to intercept the plane missed their target completely.

The aircraft was Hess's Messerschmitt. Having made his landfall, Hess flew on but, despite a full moon, failed to locate his target. He flew out over the Firth of Clyde before turning back inland. By now his fuel tanks were running dry and he had no alternative other than to bail out of his aircraft or make an emergency forced landing. Hess settled for the former. He parachuted gently down onto a moonlit field barely 12 miles from the Duke's estate, overcome, as he later wrote, with 'an indescribable sense of elation and triumph.' His plane crashed a short distance away, breaking up into pieces upon impact.

The first person to approach the wreckage was David McLean, a local ploughman who had heard the Messerschmitt flying overhead. He found Hess lying on the ground with a sprained ankle. Introducing himself as Captain Alfred Horn, Hess asked to be taken to Dungavel House, saying that he had 'a secret and urgent' message for the Duke of Hamilton. Instead, McLean escorted him to his nearby cottage, where his wife offered Hess a cup of tea. The Deputy Fuehrer politely declined the offer, saying that he would rather have a glass of water.

The police and Home Guard were soon at the scene. Hess repeated his request to be taken to the Duke, but he was hauled off to the local Home Guard headquarters and then to a military hospital in Glasgow. In the meantime, Hamilton had been contacted at RAF Turnhouse. He said he had never heard of anyone called Horn, but nevertheless would drive over to the hospital the following morning. Hess immediately revealed his true identity to the bemused Duke. He told him he had flown to Scotland on 'a mission of

humanity' to stop the unnecessary slaughter that would ensue should fighting between Britain and Germany continue. Hamilton listened patiently to what Hess had to say and then left to report to his superiors. That afternoon, he flew south to personally inform Churchill of Hess's unexpected arrival.

Churchill was as taken aback as Hamilton had been, but knew exactly what to do. Any hope of peace talks was out of the question. Instead of being welcomed as a negotiator, Hess

Above: *Hess reading in his cell in Spandau Prison. Mystery still surrounds his death in 1987. The official verdict was suicide, but his family claimed he was murdered.*

Opposite: *A section of the fuselage of Hess's Messerschmitt on display in a local museum.*

would be treated as a prisoner of war. The Prime Minister ordered Ivone Kirkpatrick, a high-ranking Foreign Office official and expert on German affairs, to fly north to interrogate him. Kirkpatrick concluded that Hess's obsession

with his mission was bordering on monomania. Once he had finished his task, Hess was shifted south. After being housed in the Tower of London for a few days, he was handed over to MI6 and held in close confinement in a country house near London for the rest of the war.

WAS HESS INSANE?

Churchill ordered the news of Hess's arrival to be kept top secret. Hitler reacted differently. After he had read the letter Hess had asked Pintsch to give him, his immediate response was one of blind fury. Goering, who

was hastily summoned to the Berghof, the Fuehrer's Bavarian retreat, tried to reassure him that it was highly unlikely Hess had made a successful landfall. In all probability, the portly Reichsmarschal said, he and his plane would have crashed into the North Sea.

Hitler was taking no chances. He decided to act on a suggestion that Hess had made himself. According to Isle Hess, his letter to Hitler ended: 'Should, my Fuehrer, my mission end in failure, you can always distance yourself from me and declare me mad.' That was exactly what Hitler proceeded to

do. A special radio communiqué broadcast on 10 May announced that the Deputy Fuehrer had taken off on an unauthorised flight from which he had not returned. 'A letter which he left behind,' the communiqué continued, 'unfortunately shows traces of mental disturbance which justifies the fear that Hess was the victim of hallucinations.' Though it did not say so directly, the broadcast gave the clear impression that Hess was a fantasist, who was now over the edge of lunacy.

This was the same conclusion the British medical experts monitoring Hess reached as the

Left: *Churchill, Roosevelt, and Stalin confer at Yalta in 1945. At the time of Hess's flight, Stalin believed that he had been negotiating directly with Churchill to persuade the latter to join Hitler in attacking the Soviet Union. In fact, Churchill never met Hess.*

Right: *Hess in the dock at Nuremberg. At first, he was considered unfit to plead, but then he told the judges he had been faking his amnesia.*

war progressed. At first, no one questioned his mental balance. One doctor described him as being 'surprisingly ordinary...quite sane, certainly not a drug-taker, a little concerned about his health and rather faddy about his diet.' As time passed, however, Hess's behaviour became more irrational. He alleged that his food was poisoned or contained drugs and then claimed to have lost his memory completely. After trying to commit suicide by throwing himself down a stairwell, a psychiatrist concluded that he had 'definitely passed over the border that lies between mental instability and insanity.'

FROM NUREMBERG TO SPANDAU

Hess had still one more surprise in store. Before the Nuremberg Trial opened in 1946, ten psychiatrists concluded that, though Hess was not insane, he was not fully competent to stand trial. As the

court was about to rule on the issue, Hess asked for permission to speak. He told the judges that he had been shamming amnesia. 'It was only his 'ability to concentrate', he said, that was 'somewhat reduced.' He took his place with the other defendants.

Over the next months, Hess cut an increasingly remote figure in the dock, at times scarcely seeming to be following the proceedings at all. It was not until the time came for him to make his final statement that he spoke again. He had been privileged, he said, 'to work for many years of my life under the greatest son whom my people had brought forth in its thousand-year history. Even if I could, I would not want to erase this period of time from my existence. I am happy to know that I have done my duty to my people, my duty as a German, as a National

Socialist, as a loyal follower of my Fuehrer. I do not regret anything.' The court sentenced him to life imprisonment.

Hess spent the last 46 years of his life in Spandau Prison, Berlin, guarded by rotating contingents of troops from the four Allied powers. He was known to his guards only as Prisoner 7 – it was forbidden to speak his name. The other war criminals held in Spandau gradually became eligible for release. The last to leave were Albert Speer and Baldur von Schirach in 1966, leaving Hess as Spandau's sole remaining inmate. The Soviets steadfastly refused to consider granting him parole.

On 17 August 1987, the 93-year-old Hess supposedly committed suicide by hanging himself from a window latch in a summerhouse in the prison garden. Even this last act was controversial. Many, including Hess's son, believed that Hess was not physically strong enough to have killed himself. Instead, they claim that he was secretly murdered to stop him from revealing any embarrassing wartime secrets. The trigger for the killing, it was alleged, was the announcement that the Russians were finally ready to consent to Hess's release.

Forewarned But Not Forearmed

When Nazi Foreign Minister Joachim von Ribbentrop flew to Moscow in late August 1939 to conclude a Non-Aggression Pact with Joseph Stalin, the world was taken completely by surprise. However, when Hitler's armies stormed into the Soviet Union on 22 June 1941, the only man surprised was apparently Stalin himself. Why did the Soviet dictator ignore the numerous warnings he had been given of an imminent German attack?

Hitler's lightning decision to come to terms with Stalin came down to one word. It was expediency. In less than two weeks time, he planned to invade Poland and, with both Britain and France guaranteeing Polish independence, he needed to ensure that the Soviet Union would not side with the West should it come to war.

For weeks, the British and French themselves had been negotiating half-heartedly with Moscow, but to little or no avail. The talks were bungled from start to finish, perhaps not that surprisingly since Neville Chamberlain, the British premier, never really wanted to embark on them in the first place. Hitler had no such inhibitions. Though Nazi Germany and Soviet Russia had been at loggerheads for years, he realised that reaching an agreement with Stalin was a tactical necessity even if the Nazi and Communist political ideologies were diametrically opposed. There was no questioning the fact that, should Stalin decide to side with Poland and the West, he could put substantial military forces into the field.

The public terms of the pact Ribbentrop and Vyacheslav Molotov, the Soviet Foreign Minister, agreed were innocuous

Above: *Russian prisoners being herded into captivity in 1941. Hitler's attack on the Soviet Union took Stalin completely by surprise.*

Opposite: *Molotov and Ribbentrop meet in Berlin in October 1940. The year before the two men had negotiated the Nazi-Soviet Non-Aggression Pact.*

enough on the surface. The two countries pledged themselves not to go to war with each other or support any country at war with the other for a period of not less than ten years. They also agreed to increase their mutual trade. The sting was in the secret clauses. These gave each country 'spheres of influence' – in other words, future control – over distinct areas of Eastern Europe. Stalin demanded – and was granted – control of all the territories that had been ruled by Tsarist Russia and lost in World War I. As for Poland, the country was to be partitioned, the Germans occupying the territories to the west of the River

Vistula and the Russians those to the east of the river.

Ribbentrop and Molotov signed the pact on 24 September. Six days later, the Germans swept into Poland from the west, their Blitzkrieg immediately shifting into top gear. On 17 September, more than 600,000 Soviet troops invaded Poland from the east and headed rapidly for the agreed-on demarcation line. Within days, the Red Army had occupied its half of the country.

At the same time, Stalin moved into the Baltic states of Lithuania, Estonia and Latvia, his intention being to shift the Soviet frontier westwards and create a buffer

Left: *A German Panzer IV rolls forwards into the attack.*

Top Right: *A Soviet playing-card shows an idealised cavalryman triumphing over a battered Hitler.*

Bottom Right: *The German advance slowed to a halt as 'General Winter' came to the Russians' aid.*

zone to shield himself against any possible future Nazi attack. He also tried to bully Finland into conceding a swathe of its territory so that he could create a protective salient around Leningrad (now St Petersburg), but the Finns refused point-blank. In late November, Stalin ordered the Red Army to attack, expecting a swift and easy victory. The so-called 'Winter War' that followed was a disaster. It dragged on for months and cost the Russians thousands of their best troops. Though the Finns were finally overwhelmed by sheer weight of numbers, the apparent inadequacy of Soviet military leadership was exposed for the world to see.

THE PACT'S IMPACT

Relationships with the Western powers took a dramatic turn for the worse following the pact's conclusion. In France, the government ordered the dissolution of the French Communist Party on 27 September; 35 Communist Party deputies were thrown into prison and Maurice Thorez, the party's lead who had deserted from the army to escape arrest and fled to neutral Belgium, was deprived of his citizenship. From his exile, Thorez, in accordance with Stalin's dictates, defiantly proclaimed his party's new policy – all-out resistance to the continuance of the 'imperialist war'.

Undercover Communist agitators stirred up dissent in the French Army at the front, while saboteurs set to work to undermine armaments manufacture at home. The sorely-needed Renault B1 heavy tank was a favourite target. A report itemised the damage saboteurs inflicted on its production: 'nuts, bolts, various bits of old iron put in the gear-boxes and transmissions...filings and emery-dust in the crank-cases, saw-stroked producing incipient ruptures of the oil and petrol ducts, intended to make them fall to pieces after several hours' running.'

More positive action directly against the Soviet Union was also mooted. At the highest levels of government in both Britain and France, it was agreed to allow military supplies to be shipped to Finland. Only that country's eventual surrender prevented the despatch of an actual Allied expeditionary force to aid the Finns. The Allies also planned to bomb Baku, Batum and Grozny in an attempt to halt the shipment of Soviet oil to the Third Reich. Luckily, Operation Pike, as it was codenamed, was stillborn.

Hitler, in contrast, was getting on well with his new ally. As early as the end of September 1939, Stalin had pledged to Ribbentrop that the Soviet Union would not stand by and see Germany defeated. Though the Russian dictator later denied ever making such a promise, recently declassified Russian archives reveal exactly what he said. 'If, against all expectation, Germany finds itself in a difficult situation,' Stalin declared, 'then she can be sure that the Soviet people will come to Germany's aid and will not allow Germany to be strangled. The Soviet Union wants to see a strong Germany and we will not allow Germany to be thrown to the ground.'

Whether Stalin meant what he had said is open to question. Certainly at the time Hitler

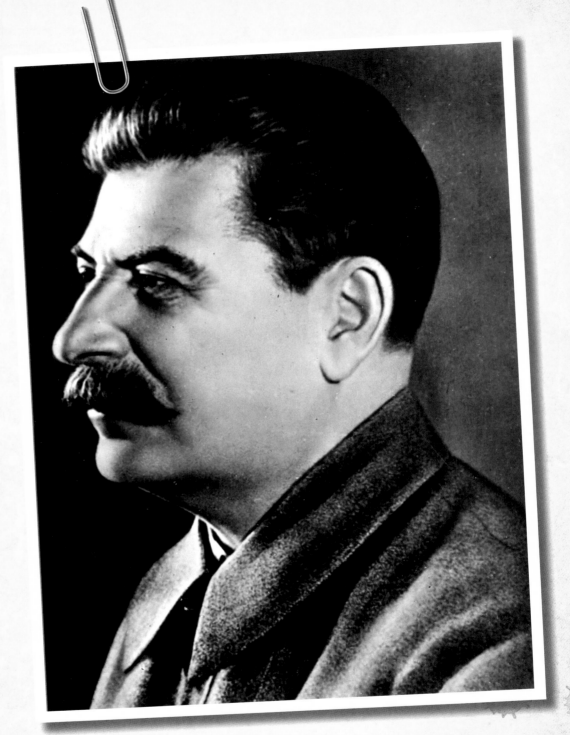

Above: *Stalin believed that Hitler would not be foolish enough to attack Russia before defeating Britain.*

seems to have believed him. On 1 October Propaganda Minister Joseph Goebbels wrote in his diary: 'Conference with the Fuehrer in private. He is convinced of Russia's loyalty.'

THE TURNING-POINT

Events soon pressured Stalin into playing a dangerous double-game. The triumphant Blitzkrieg Hitler launched against France in May 1940 was the catalyst. Though he congratulated the Fuehrer publicly on the Wehrmacht's 'splendid success,' Stalin was completely taken aback by the rapidity and the scale of the Nazi victory. What he had been counting on was a long, mutually destructive war, which would leave both sides so weakened that, regardless of which of them won it, they would not be in a position to threaten the Soviet Union. The young Nikita Khrushchev, then one of Stalin's closest acolytes, recalled his master 'racing around, cursing like a cab driver. He cursed the French. He cursed the English. How could they allow Hitler to defeat them, to crush them?'

Though Stalin, believing Britain to be beaten, rejected British attempts at a rapprochement, Hitler now became convinced that he could not trust the Russians after all. He was infuriated by the Soviet decision to unilaterally annex the Romanian province of Bukovina, a region that had not been assigned to Russia by the terms of the Non-Aggression Pact. Britain's stubborn refusal to consider entering peace negotiations convinced the ever-suspicious Fuehrer that Churchill and Stalin were up to something behind his back. On 31 July, he told his generals that he had decided to attack the Soviet Union if the British continued to refuse to come to terms with him. 'Russia is the factor on which Britain is relying the most,' he concluded. 'Something must have happened in London. The British were completely down, but now they have perked up again. With Russia smashed, Britain's last hope would be shattered. The sooner Russia is crushed the better. If we start in May 1941, we would have five months to finish the job.'

APPEASING THE FUEHRER

Stalin, for his part, knew that he had to avoid war for as long as he could. As the 'Winter War' against the Finns had demonstrated, the Red Army was in no fit state to face the Wehrmacht. Early that December, after Molotov had paid an inconclusive visit to Berlin, the Soviet dictator told his generals: 'We know that Hitler is intoxicated with his victories and believed that the Red Army will need at least four years to prepare for war. Obviously, four years would be more than enough for us. But we must be ready much earlier. We will try to delay the war for another two years.'

To buy the time his country needed, Stalin decided to appease the Fuehrer. On 10 January 1941, the Soviet Union ratified a new trade agreement with Germany that doubled the amount of grain being shipped from the Ukraine to the Third Reich. More trade concessions followed. The Soviet Union was now supplying nearly three-quarters of the phosphates Germany needed, more than two-thirds of its imported asbestos, a little less of its imported nickel and, even more crucially, more than a third of its imported crude oil. Nothing, however, could deter Hitler from preparing to attack. 'The Russians are inferior,' he assured Field Marshal Walter von Brauchitsch and General Franz Halder, the commander-in-chief of the army and the chief of the army general staff. 'Their army is leaderless.' Crushing the Soviet Union, he continued, would be 'child's play'

Above: *Junkers JU 87 Stuka dive-bombers fly into the attack. The Luftwaffe caught most of the Soviet air force in western Russia on the ground and destroyed it.*

Opposite: *This Soviet propaganda poster carries the blunt message 'Death to the German occupiers'.*

compared to what it had taken to invade and defeat France.

As the winter snows in Poland melted and the ground started to thaw, a massive build-up of men and equipment began in the east. Eventually, more than three million German soldiers with another half a million troops from Romania, Finland and other allied countries, would be poised to strike at the Soviet Union along a front stretching more than a thousand miles from the Finnish border and the Baltic to the Black Sea hinterland far to the south. They would be equipped with 3,600 tanks, 600,000 motor vehicles and 700,000 artillery pieces. More than half the Luftwaffe would provide air support.

Many in the Soviet high command were worried that such a build-up signalled a German attack was imminent, but Stalin dismissed all such fears. Though he told a group of graduates from the Red Army Academy that 'war with Germany is inevitable,' he was convinced that Hitler was simply playing hard-ball with him to try to secure even more economic concessions. He failed to grasp that the Fuehrer, rather than waiting until he had defeated or secured peace with Britain, had decided to strike in the east first. 'We must be under no illusions,' Stalin warned the members of

Above: *Soviet T-34 tanks pour off the production lines. Their debut took the Germans by surprise; antitank shells simply bounced off their thick frontal armour.*

the Politburo, 'Fascist Germany is clearly preparing for an attack on the Soviet Union.' Then he uttered a fatal caveat. 'Why should Hitler want to make an agreement with England,' he asked? 'Because,' he continued, 'he wants to avoid a war on two fronts.'

Even when General Georgi Zhukov, his newly-appointed Chief of Staff, and General Semyon Timoshenko urged that 'considering the complicated military-political situation, it was

necessary to take urgent measures in time to remedy shortcomings in the Western Front,' Stalin refused to listen. Instead he warned the worried generals against the implementation of 'wild unrealistic plans for which Russia lacks the means.' His information, he told them, was that the German troops massing in Poland were there simply for training exercises.

CHURCHILL'S WARNING
If Stalin ignored the advice of his own senior generals, he was hardly likely to respond to a warning from Churchill. Nevertheless, despite all the rebuffs Britain had

received from Moscow so far, Churchill decided to try again. In April 1941, he wrote to the Soviet leader to tell him that 'a trusted agent' – in fact, the source was decoded Enigma messages – had forewarned the British about an imminent German attack on the Soviet Union.

Stalin dismissed the approach out of hand. Then, the following month, news of Rudolf Hess's self-appointed peace mission to Britain reached Moscow. According to Sergio Beria, the son of Stalin's feared intelligence chief, Kim Philby, the Soviet spy at the heart of the British Secret

Intelligence Service, was passing the latest information through to his Russian controllers even before Churchill received it himself. On its receipt, Stalin jumped to a conclusion that was to have disastrous consequences.

Stalin had suspected Churchill's motives from the start. Now it all seemed crystal-clear. Churchill's message and the intelligence reports he was receiving were all part of a sinister conspiracy, designed to trick him into launching a pre-emptive attack on the Third Reich. He told the Central Party Committee: 'On the one hand, Churchill sends us a personal message in which he warns us about Hitler's aggressive intentions. On the other hand, the British meet with Hess, who is undoubtedly Hitler's confidant, and conduct negotiations with Germany through him.'

According to Stalin, there was only one possible conclusion. 'Apparently, when Churchill sent us his personal warning, he believed that we would "activate" our military mechanism. Then Hitler would have a direct and fair reason to launch a pre-emptive crusade against the Soviet Union.' Stalin continued: 'We must not supply Hitler with reasons to attack us...Let's not complicate our relations with him.'

COUNTDOWN TO WAR

For the next weeks, Stalin stubbornly stuck to this conclusion, dismissing warning after warning of imminent German attack. He ordered that nothing should be done that would provoke a Nazi response. 'We must carefully fulfil our obligations under the Soviet-German treaty,' he reiterated repeatedly, 'so that Germany will be unable to find any violations of the treaty on our part.' Colonel Hans Krebs, the German Military Attaché in Moscow, reported to Hitler that 'Russia will do anything to avoid war.'

On 12 June, Stalin told his generals: 'I am certain that Hitler will not create a second front by attacking the Soviet Union. Hitler is not such an idiot.' Two days later, Tass, the official Soviet news agency, issued a statement hot from the Kremlin. 'In the opinion of Soviet circles,' it began, 'rumours of Germany's intention to break the pact and open an attack on the USSR are devoid of all foundations. The USSR, consistent with its policy of peace, has observed and intends to observe the provisions of the Soviet-German Non-Aggression Pact and therefore rumours that the USSR is preparing for war with Germany are lies and provocations.'

Angrily, Stalin now turned on his generals, who were urging him to authorise at least partial mobilisation. 'Have you come to scare us with war, or do you want a war because you're not sufficiently decorated or your rank isn't high enough?' he bellowed at Zhukov and the other members of the Soviet General Staff. 'You have to realise that Germany will never fight Russia on her own. You must understand this.' He stormed out of the meeting, only to return a minute or so later. 'If you're going to provoke the Germans on the frontier by moving troops there without our permission, then heads will roll,' he said.

On the evening of 21 June, Stalin left the Kremlin to spend the weekend at his country *dacha,* west of the capital. After a gruelling Politburo meeting, he retired to bed and within minutes he was asleep. Just two hours later, at 3.30am, the telephone rang insistently. 'Who's calling?' the NKVD security officer on duty asked. 'Zhukov, Chief of Staff,' was the reply. 'Please connect me to Comrade Stalin. It's urgent.' On the same date that Napoleon had invaded Russia, Hitler had followed in his footsteps. What the Russian eventually christened the 'Great Patriotic War' had begun.

Pacific Mysteries

When US Lightning P-38 fighters shot down the aeroplane carrying Admiral Isoruku Yamamoto, supreme commander of the Japanese fleet, on 18 April 1943, they killed the man who had made history as the architect of Japan's surprise air strike on the US Pacific Fleet at Pearl Harbor. But was the planning of the attack all his own work, or did he utilise ideas put forward by unsung American and British naval experts years before the outbreak of war?

Yamamoto was a military genius. He was also less insular and far more open-minded than the bulk of the Japanese officer class. In 1919, he went to the USA to study at Harvard University; seven years later, he returned to the USA for a two-year stint as the Japanese naval attaché in Washington. Consequently, he spoke and read English fluently. During that time, he naturally took advantage of the chance to study books and papers on naval strategy written by Western experts.

One such paper was an extraordinary document entitled *Sea-Power in the Pacific*, written by Hector Bywater, a British author who specialised in naval affairs. A crucial part of it dealt with the pattern a future war in the Pacific might follow. It was first published in London in 1925 and subsequently appeared in translation in several languages, including Japanese. Shortly after its first appearance, Bywater expanded the paper – or at least

Left: *The battleship* West Virginia *is pictured sinking and in flames after the Japanese surprise attack on the US naval base at Pearl Harbor. It was, said Roosevelt, a 'day of infamy'.*

the part of it dealing directly a future Pacific war between the USA and Japan – into a full-length novel, which he titled *The Great Pacific War*. Both texts rapidly became recommended reading in the naval staff colleges of all the major powers.

Bywater had a fascinating career. Welsh by birth, he moved as a teenager with his family to the USA from Britain in 1901. After becoming a newspaper reporter, he was appointed a correspondent by the *New York Herald*, which sent him back to Europe after he had made a name for himself through his coverage of the Russo-Japanese War. There, he combined journalism with spying for the British Admiralty, reporting on the progress of the German naval building programme. He returned to the USA in 1915, where he helped to thwart German sabotage efforts on the New York waterfront.

It was after the Washington Naval Conference of 1921 – where he scooped the world by revealing the eventual terms agreed on by the great powers before they were officially released – that Bywater started writing about the possibility of a naval war in the Pacific between Japan and the USA. *Sea-Power in the Pacific* and

The Great Pacific War followed. Bywater became something of a celebrity as a result, though his fame was relatively short-lived. During that time, it is possible he even met Yamamoto himself.

PREDICTING THE FUTURE

Later events proved many of Bywater's prophesies to be extraordinarily accurate – though he did not predict that his Pacific war would begin with a surprise Japanese assault on Pearl Harbor. Instead, his war started with a major battle between the Japanese and American fleets off the Philippines. However, he did predict that carrier-born aircraft would play a major part in such a battle. This, in itself, was not that extraordinary, because by the mid-1920s, the British, American and Japanese navies all possessed embryonic carrier forces. An effective demonstration of what aircraft could do to warships had already been conducted in summer 1921, when a combined force of US Navy and Army Air Service bombers attacked several German naval vessels that had been handed over to the USA after the end of World War I. They included the battleship *Ostfriesland*.

The sinking of the *Ostfriesland* was the climax of a series of bombing tests carried out by the aircraft commanded by Lieutenant-General William 'Billy' Mitchell, the most prominent – and controversial – advocate of air power in the USA during the 1920s. He led the operation personally in his De Havilland DH-4. As well as the *Ostfriesland*, the bombers attacked a German U-boat, the old US battleship *Iowa*, which had been converted into a radio-controlled fleet target ship, a destroyer and a light cruiser. It was the *Ostfriesland*, however, that was the icing on the cake. The tests proved, Mitchell reported, 'that seacraft of all kinds, up to and including the most modern battleships, can be destroyed easily by bombs dropped from aircraft and further that the most effective means of destruction are bombs.'

Whether Bywater was aware of Mitchell's experiment is unclear. What was really remarkable was the accuracy of his account of subsequent Japanese attacks on Guam and the Philippines. Guam, he wrote, would be subjected to an intensive aerial and naval bombardment, after which Japanese forces would land in a pincer movement on the east and west sides of the island. American forces would be unable to counter the attack and would soon be compelled to surrender.

This was almost exactly what happened when the Japanese struck in the Pacific in December 1941. The similarity between Bywater's account of their invasion of the Philippines and what actually happened is also astonishing. He predicted that the assault would begin with massive air attacks mounted by aircraft launched from a carrier task force cruising to the west of the islands, which it did. This would be followed by a three-pronged invasion, with Japanese forces landing at Lingayen Gulf and Lamon Bay on Luzon and at Sindangan Bay on Mindanao.

The Luzon landings took place exactly as Bywater had predicted, the Japanese advancing inland to attack Manila from two sides. Only the Sindangan Bay prediction was wide of the mark; instead of landing there, on the western side of Mindanao, the Japanese went ashore at Davao Gulf at the southeastern tip of the island.

This was by no means all that Bywater predicted. He foresaw how the Americans would eventually reconquer the Pacific with the aid of powerful naval forces moving relentlessly towards the Japanese Home Islands in a series of carefully-planned island-hopping operations. He also envisaged how the Japanese, faced with defeat, would throw every single available resource into the battle – including suicide planes.

The decisive naval engagement that would finally shatter Japan's dreams of Pacific victory, Bywater wrote, would take place where the war had begun – off the Philippines. Strangely, he failed to appreciate the role that air power would play in the battle. When it actually happened in late 1944, the opposing forces traded blows by means of their carrier air groups. The surface fleets seldom came within sight of one another.

LEARNING FROM TARANTO

All in all, it seems that the predictions made by Bywater and the strategy adopted by Yamamoto in the opening stages of his Pacific campaign are too closely parallel to be a coincidence. Bywater also predicted that torpedo bombers would be the main type of aircraft employed in naval warfare – and in this, too, he was absolutely correct.

If Yamamoto, who had been in favour of developing naval aviation for years previously,

Above: *Admiral Isoruku Yamamoto was the architect of the Pearl Harbor attack. Personally, he had been opposed to war with the US.*

Above: *A Japanese Mitsubishi 'Betty' bomber, painted with green crosses as a sign of surrender, flies towards an Allied airfield in 1945. Yamamoto was shot down and killed when flying in such a plane; the Americans had found out his intended route by cracking the Japanese naval code.*

Opposite: *The former German battleship* Ostfriesland *being bombed from the air by General William 'Billy' Mitchell's bombers in 1921. Mitchell was determined to prove that capital ships were vulnerable to aerial attack.*

needed any further confirmation of his theories, the British supplied it. In November 1940, a little over a year before the Japanese attack on Pearl Harbor, torpedo- and bomb-carrying Swordfish on the Royal Navy struck at the Italian fleet in harbour at Taranto, In a brilliantly-executed night attack, the Swordfish crippled three of Italy's most modern battleships and two heavy cruisers. It took six months to make two of the battleships and one of the cruisers seaworthy; *Conte di Cavour* and the other cruiser had to be scrapped.

The attack was the brainchild of Admiral Sir Andrew Cunningham, the commander-in-chief of the Mediterranean Fleet. As the Italians refused to sail out to meet him and fight a surface action, he decided that his best course of action was to launch an aerial attack. The plan was a bold one. The Swordfish torpedo-bombers Cunningham was relying on to carry out the attack were ungainly, slow and cumbersome – a sitting target for modern fighters and easy prey for efficiently-operated anti-aircraft guns. Cunningham could muster a maximum of 21 Swordfish to make the attack.

On 11 November, *Illustrious*, Cunningham's sole carrier – *Eagle* had been damaged in action and was undergoing repairs – launched two waves of Swordfish, flying about an hour apart. Two planes in each wave flew high and dropped flares to distract the Italian defences. The others skimmed almost at sea level across the harbour to launch their torpedoes at the anchored Italian ships. *Conte di Cavour* was hit towards her bow and her forecastle erupted in flames. She sank at her moorings. *Littorio* was torpedoed twice. The second wave hit the *Caio Duilio* and damaged *Littorio* again. The attack cost Cunningham two Swordfish. More than half the Italian battlefleet was put out of action.

DISPUTES IN TOKYO

The lessons of Taranto were not lost on Yamamoto. As far as he was concerned, Cunningham's triumph finally settled the argument as to whether or not capital ships were vulnerable to aerial attack. Nor were the ones he derived from the widely-publicised US naval manoeuvres held off Hawaii in 1932, when the Americans themselves demonstrated how it would be possible for a carrier force to approach Pearl Harbor undetected and launch a devastating surprise attack on the base at dawn.

Right: Arizona's *forward magazine explodes after the battleship was hit four times by Japanese bombers during the Pearl Harbor attack.*

Opposite: Battleship Row before *the Japanese attack. Of the seven US battleships anchored there,* Arizona, California, Oklahoma *and* West Virginia *were sunk.* Nevada *was badly damaged.*

Yamamoto, too, probably looked back to 1927, when, as a young captain, he had taken part in war games held at the Japanese Naval War College, which included an examination of a possible Pearl Harbor carrier strike.

In December 1940, Yamamoto began preparatory planning for the attack. His hardest task, it seems, was to persuade the Japanese Naval General Staff that the operation was viable. Its chief concern was that such an attack was simply too risky to mount. It was not until the following August that it was agreed the war games scheduled to begin on 11 September should include an examination of the Pearl Harbor plan. On 24 September, Yamamoto was told that it had been rejected. Even his fellow admirals in the Combined Fleet doubted its feasibility. All bar one of them also opposed the attack.

Yamamoto was not to be deterred. He told the doubting admirals bluntly that he was the commander-in-chief and, for as long as he was in charge, planning for the attack would go ahead. Telling Koshiro Oikawa, who was Navy Minister from September 1940 to October 1941, that 'we should do our very best to decide the fate of the war on the very first day,' he gave him an ultimatum. Unless the plan to blitz Pearl Harbor was approved, he and the entire staff of the Combined Fleet would resign. The Naval General Staff gave in. Leading figures within it from Admiral Nagano Osami, the Chief of Staff, downwards had already reached the conclusion that war with the USA was rapidly becoming inevitable. Yamamoto was officially authorised to go ahead with his preparations.

WHAT REALLY TOOK PLACE?

The carrier task force sailed from Japanese home waters on 26 November. Yamamoto had put Vice-Admiral Chuichi Nagumo in command. It consisted of Japan's six crack fleet carriers, escorted by two battleships, two heavy cruisers, a light cruiser, nine destroyers and three forward reconnaissance submarines. Seven oil tankers accompanied the task force, since mid-ocean refuelling would be necessary to give the task force the range to sail to Hawaii and back again.

Each carrier could deploy around 70 aircraft – a mix of Nakajima high-level and torpedo bombers, Aichi dive bombers and Mitsubishi Zero fighters. Deliberately choosing to take the longer northern route to Hawaii to lessen the possibility of being spotted by US reconnaissance patrols, the blacked-out fleet maintained strict radio silence as it ploughed its way across the stormy ocean. It was only when it reached its launch position approximately 200 miles north of Hawaii that it received a terse signal from Tokyo. It read simply 'Climb Mount Fujiyama.' It was the signal to launch the attack.

The first wave of Japanese aircraft started to take off from their carriers at around 6.00am on 7 December. The second wave followed 70 minutes later. Flying time to their target was approximately one hour 50 minutes, the pilots tuning into Honolulu radio to get a fix on their positions. The first attack began at precisely 7.49am. Four minutes later, as the bombs and torpedoes started to rain down, Lieutenant-

Commander Mitsuo Fuchida, the attack's commander, signalled Tora, Tora, Tora (Tiger, Tiger, Tiger) to the waiting carriers. It was confirmation that complete tactical surprise had been achieved.

By 10.00am, all the Japanese planes had completed their mission. Fuchida's was the last aircraft to leave the scene. He had remained on station to observe both waves' attacks and assess the extent of the damage

they caused. It was certainly impressive. Out of the eight great capital ships lying peacefully at anchor in Battleship Row when the Japanese struck, *Arizona*, *California* and *West Virginia* were sunk. *Oklahoma* capsized. *Maryland*, *Nevada*, *Tennessee* and *Pennsylvania* were heavily damaged, as were three cruisers and three destroyers. Some ships had to be totally rebuilt before they could put to sea again. The Japanese hammered the US air bases as well. 92 Navy planes and 71 Army Air Corps aircraft were destroyed on the ground and 31 and 128 damaged.

ABANDONING THE PLAN

So far, everything had gone according to Yamamoto's plan – indeed, the attack had succeeded beyond his wildest expectations. Now, however, things started to go wrong. Fuchida and Commander Minoru Genda, the man who had been responsible for the detailed planning of the aerial assault, urged Nagumo to launch a third strike just as Yamamoto had originally intended. The cautious Nagumo, supported by Rear-Admiral Ruyunosuke Kusaka, his Chief of Staff who had been opposed to the operation in the first place, decided against proceeding with it.

Above: *US troops island-hopped across the Pacific as part of the master plan to take the war to Japan.*

Genda pleaded with the two admirals in vain. He pointed out that, despite the Japanese success, major targets – most notably the harbour's vast oil bunkers – remained intact. At least, he argued, the Japanese carriers should hold their position until the US Pacific Fleet's two aircraft carriers, which had been at sea delivering fighter reinforcements to Wake Island and now were heading back towards Pearl Harbor, had been located and attacked. Nagumo would not change his mind. He had no idea where the American carriers were and feared they might locate him and strike first. He ordered the task force to turn for home.

ADVANCED KNOWLEDGE

By deciding to rest on his laurels rather than hunt the US carriers down, Nagumo committed a major strategic blunder. Its consequences, though, were not immediately apparent. As their Pacific offensive proceeded southwards, going from strength to strength, what became clear was that the Japanese possessed an almost uncanny knowledge of the whereabouts of American naval forces and air bases.

How the Japanese had obtained this information remained a mystery until after the war. It was then discovered that a special naval air force unit, initially based on Formosa, had been making clandestine reconnaissance flights over US bases ever since April 1941. Among the places its planes photographed were Legaspi, on the southeast tip of Luzon in the Philippines, Jolo Island, Mindanao, Rabaul and Guam. Then, after one of their aircraft had been detected by the Americans – though they had no idea it was a reconnaissance flight – the Japanese brought the missions to an end. They had all the aerial intelligence they needed to proceed with planning their actual attack.

Above: *A Japanese propaganda poster celebrates the Pearl Harbor Attack. Note the flags of Japan's two Axis allies in the background next to the billowing Rising Sun.*

The 'Battle' of Los Angeles

Just over two months after Pearl Harbor, Los Angeles and much of southern California was thrown into a state of panic. At precisely 2.00am on the morning of 25 February 1942, the city's air-raid sirens began to wail, searchlights flickered across the sky and the anti-aircraft batteries of the 37th Coastal Artillery Brigade opened fire. Thousands of citizens took to the streets, believing that their city faced a surprise Japanese air attack.

It was early in the morning of 25 February when diners at the fashionable Trocadero Club in Hollywood were startled and shocked into silence. Suddenly, the lights winked out and air-raid sirens started to wail throughout greater Los Angeles. As searchlights scanned the skies, the anti-aircraft guns protecting the city's vital aircraft factories and shipyards went into action. Was Los Angeles coming under enemy air attack? Or had the Japanese landed on California's long stretches of hospitable beaches?

Author Ralph Blum, who was nine years old at the time, had no doubts. 'I thought the Japanese were bombing Beverley Hills,' he later recollected. 'There were sirens, searchlights and anti-aircraft guns blazing away into the skies over Los Angeles. My father had been a balloon observation man in World War I and he knew big guns when he heard them. He ordered my mother to take my baby sisters to the underground projection room – our house was heavily supplied

with Hollywood paraphernalia – while he and I went out onto the upstairs balcony.' Blum and his father both looked upwards in amazement as subsequent events unfolded. 'What a scene!' he wrote. 'It was after three in the morning. Searchlights probed the western sky. Tracers streamed upward. The racket was terrific.'

Peter Jenkins, a staff editor on the *Los Angeles Herald-Examiner*, was another eyewitness as was Long Beach Police Chief J. H. McClelland. 'I could clearly see the V formation of about 25 silvery planes overhead moving slowly across the sky towards Long Beach,' Jenkins reported. McClelland 'watched what was described as the second wave of planes from atop the seven-storey Long Beach City Hall. I did not see any planes, but the younger men with me said that they could. An experienced Navy observer with powerful Carl Zeiss binoculars said he counted nine planes in the cone of the searchlights. He said they were sliver in colour.'

McClelland continued: 'The group passed along from one battery of searchlights to another and, under the fire of the anti-aircraft guns, flew from the direction of Redona Beach and Inglewood on the land side of Fort

MacArthur and continued towards Santa Ana and Huntingdon Beach. The anti-aircraft fire was so heavy,' he concluded, 'we could not hear the motors of the planes.' According to the *Glendale News Press*, some observers claimed to have counted as many as 200 planes over the area.

THE MORNING AFTER

The 'battle' lasted for little more than 20 minutes. At 2.21am, Lieutenant-General John L. DeWitt ordered his anti-aircraft gunners to stop firing. As soon as dawn broke, hundreds and thousands of inquisitive Californians took to the streets to see if anything untoward had occurred. 'When daylight and the all-clear signal came,' the *Glendale News Press* reported, Long Beach took on the appearance of a huge Easter egg-hunt. Kiddies and even grown-ups scrambled through the streets and vacant lots, picking up and proudly comparing chunks of shrapnel fragments as if they were the most prized items they owned.'

Californian commuters, for their part, were confronted by giant traffic snarl-ups caused as a result of the black-out. Thousands of them were an hour or more late for work. Most of them were unconcerned. It had all been 'a

Left: *A storm of anti-aircraft fire lights up the sky above Los Angeles, when, early in the morning on February 25 1942, the city was believed to be threatened by a Japanese bombing attack.*

great show' and 'well worth losing a few hours' sleep.'

There were a handful of casualties. A State Guardsman died of an apparent heart attack while driving an ammunition truck, as did an air-raid warden. A woman was killed when a car and a truck collided in Arcadia and a Long Beach police sergeant died in a traffic crash on his way to an air-raid post.

There were other incidents as well. Three Japanese-Americans – two men and a woman – were arrested in Venice on suspicion of signalling out to sea with a torch near the beach's pier. John Y. Harado, a 25-year-old Japanese-American vegetable man, was detained and charged with violating the black-out. Apparently, Harada was stopped while driving a load

of cauliflowers to market and arrested when he refused to dim the lights of his truck.

OFFSHORE BOMBARDMENT

Almost immediately after the all-clear sounded, the controversy started about whether Los Angeles had been the victim of a Japanese aerial attack, or, indeed, whether there had been any aircraft anywhere near the city at the time at all. Speaking from the calm of Washington D.C., Frank Knox, the Secretary of the Navy, was quick to pooh-pooh the entire affair. 'There were no planes over Los Angeles last night,' he asserted confidently at a press conference. 'None have been found and a very wide reconnaissance has been carried on.' He stated categorically: 'It was just a false alarm.'

'Reports of enemy air activity in the Pacific coastal region,' Knox concluded, 'might be due largely to "jittery nerves".' The *Los Angeles Times* was quick to respond. It noted that the army's Western Defence Command was still insisting that the sudden black-out and anti-aircraft action definitely followed the sighting of unidentified aircraft over the city, though it was admitted that no bombs had been dropped and no bombers shot down. The newspaper asked rhetorically: 'Whose nerves, Mr Knox? The public's or the army's?'

It was not surprising that tension on the west coast was running high. On 23 February, two days before the alleged air raid on Los Angeles took place, the Japanese submarine I-17, captained by Commander Nishimo Kozu, surfaced half an hour after sunset about a half a

Above: *A Japanese I-class submarine noses its way out to sea. It was a submarine of this class that briefly bombarded the Ellwood oil fields on the Californian coast north of Santa Barbara.*

Opposite: *A Los Angeles searchlight battery combs the skies in a fruitless search for Japanese bombers. Why so many people believed that the city was under attack is a complete mystery.*

mile offshore near the town of Goleta, 12 miles north of Santa Barbara. Five minutes after surfacing, its deck gun began firing at the Ellwood oil fields, close to the town. The submarine's gun crew fired between 16 and 26 shells in total before discontinuing their bombardment. Kozu then submerged and made for the open sea.

Three shells hit the Bankline oil refinery, which was the apparent target of the attack. An oil well around half a mile inland, together with rigging and pumping components, was also reported as being hit, though the oil storage tanks next to and close

by the well escaped unscathed. Two more shells dropped onto two nearby ranches. One exploded, but the second did not. It simply dug a five-foot-deep crater in the ground. The other shells fell short and dropped harmlessly into the Pacific.

SUBMARINES AND SEAPLANES

It was the first time the American mainland had been directly attacked by enemy armed forces since the War of 1812. That June and September, the Japanese struck again.

On 21 June, the Japanese long-range submarine I-25, having cleverly dodged an American

Above: *Secretary of the Navy Frank Knox dismissed the entire Japanese air attack on Los Angeles as nothing more than a false alarm.*

Right: *A submarine-borne Yokosuka E14Y seaplane became the only Japanese aircraft to comb the US mainland successfully. It dropped several incendiary bombs on an Oregon forest in September 1942.*

minefield by following in the tracks of a fleet of fishing boats near the mouth of the Columbia River in Oregon, surfaced to fire a total of 17 shells at Battery Russell, part of Fort Stevens, from around ten miles offshore. The shells did little or no damage – the only thing hit was the backstop of the fort's baseball diamond, while some power and telephone lines were slightly damaged by shell fragments. Perhaps, it was not that surprising that the attack was unsuccessful. Commander Mejii Tagami, the I-25's captain, later recalled that 'in shooting at the land, I did not use any gun-sight at all – I just shot.' Tagami thought he was shelling a US submarine base; the battery's gunners were ordered not to try to return the I-25's fire as this would give away their position.

I-25 returned to the attack just under three months later. On 9 September, it catapulted the tiny fold-up Mitsubishi seaplane with which it was equipped into the air off Oregon's coast. Nobuo Fujita, the plane's pilot, was under orders to drop his bomb-load

– this consisted of a couple of incendiary bombs – on the thick forests and woods around Mount Emily. The idea was to trigger a massive forest fire.

It was a dank, foggy day and Fujita's plane went undetected. Fortunately, the fog lifted and the smoke from the fire was spotted by a Forest Ranger before it could take hold. Once it had been extinguished, the fire-fighting party found a crater in its centre. They also recovered fragments of metal casings and thermite pellets scattered around the scene. The casings had Japanese markings on them. The next day, Fujita tried again, but with the same lack of success.

PROJECT FU-GO

Like their German allies, Japan's leaders prepared to produce new reprisal weapons as the tide of war turned inexorably against them.

Unlike the German V1 and V2, the weapon they hit on was not technologically advanced or costly. Instead, the Japanese developed a weapon that was relatively inexpensive and simple to build.

Project Fu-Go, as it was named, was the brainchild of Major-General Sueyoshi Kusaha, head of the Japanese 9th Army's Number Nine Research Laboratory. The plan was to launch thousands of unmanned fire balloons against the American mainland, taking advantage of the high-altitude jet stream to carry them across the Pacific, over the Californian coast and deep into the American heartlands. They were capable of carrying two incendiaries and one high-explosive bomb.

The balloons were assembled by hand before being partially inflated with hydrogen, usually by schoolgirls working after their classes. Some 33 feet in diameter,

they were made of paper made from mulberry bushes, further toughened with vegetable starch to make them leak-proof. An aluminium ring, was suspended by cables from the envelope to provide support for the control equipment, ballast and bombs.

The intention was to launch the balloons from sites on the east coast of Honshu, the largest Japanese Home Island. As the balloons rose to their cruising height of around 30,000 feet, the hydrogen their envelopes contained would expand and the balloons would become spherical in shape. As night fell and the gas began to cool, the envelopes would contract and the balloons start to fall. To get over this problem, barometric altimeters were set to trigger small electrical charges once the balloons dropped to a predetermined height. The charges triggered the release of two bags of ballast, so that the lightened balloons would start to rise back into the jet stream. The cycle was repeated

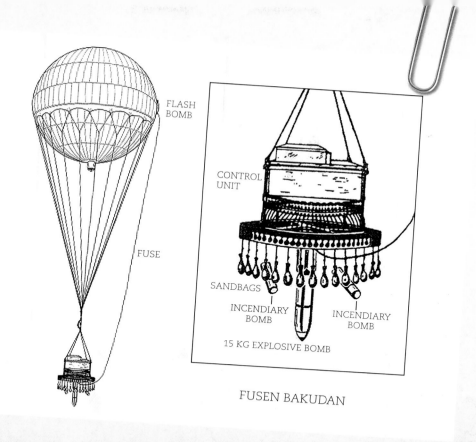

FLASH
BOMB

FUSE

CONTROL
UNIT

SANDBAGS

INCENDIARY
BOMB

INCENDIARY
BOMB

15 KG EXPLOSIVE BOMB

FUSEN BAKUDAN

throughout the balloons' long journey. If they shot up to an excessive altitude, the altimeters released a spring-loaded valve to vent a puff of hydrogen.

The Japanese estimated that it would take their balloons approximately three days to drift across the Pacific and reach their target areas. If all went according to plan, blow-out plugs would fire and the balloon's bombs would be over enemy territory. Flash bombs attached to the balloons would then incinerate them, so adding to the mystery of where the incendiaries had come from and how they got to their destinations in the first place.

FUN-GO IS ACTIVATED
The first balloons took to the skies on 3 November 1944, the Japanese Emperor's birthday. By the end of the month, 700 had been launched with another 1,200 following in December. In January 1945, the figure went up to 2,000 and then to 2,500 in February and March. In early April, however, the total dropped to just 400. Later that month, the campaign was abandoned. The Japanese were disappointed by the small amount of damage their balloons had done. They never managed to start the giant conflagrations that had been confidently expected. The hydrogen the balloons needed in order to fly was running short as well, thanks to the great US fire bombing campaign

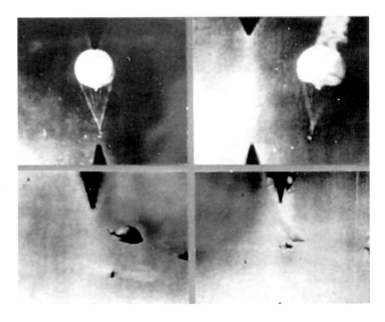

Right: *This sequence of photographs, shot by a camera-gun fitted to a US fighter, shows a Japanese balloon bomb being intercepted and shot down before it could reach its target.*

Opposite: *Curtiss P-40s were the US's home-based air defence fighters for much of the war. They also served in the Royal Canadian Air Force, whose pilots shot down several balloon bombs in early 1945.*

General Curtis LeMay had launched against Japan's most important industrial centres.

Quite a few of the balloons came down over the Pacific and never got near their intended targets. US records, however, indicate that some got as far as Alaska in the north, California's border with Mexico in the south and as far east as the Great Lakes. The authorities hushed the attacks up as much as possible. Their greatest fear was the type of weapon the balloons might be carrying. In the second week of December 1944, after fragments of balloons had been found near the towns of Thermopolis in Wyoming and Kalispell in Montana, Colonel Murray Sanders, a top bacteriologist from Fort Patrick in Maryland, was hastily called into consultation.

Sanders' task was to examine the accumulated debris the Americans had amassed – more was found in Alaska and Saskatchewan – for any evidence that the Japanese were employing biological warfare. 'The balloons were brought in,' he later recalled, 'and we all stood around them in a circle. We examined them and then we went away to make our individual reports. Mine scared them (the authorities) stiff. I told them that, if we found Japanese B-encephalitis on any of the balloons, we were in real trouble. Our population had no defence against B-encephalitis...four out of five people who contracted it would have died, in my view.'

The bacteriologist perturbed the authorities even more with his next speculation. 'Anthrax is a tough bug,' he opined. 'The Japanese had used it in China. They could have splattered the west and southwest of Canada and the USA with it. They could have contaminated the pastures and forests and killed all the cows, sheep, horses, pigs and deer – plus a considerable number of human beings.'

'The hysteria,' Sanders concluded, 'would have been terrible. One of the strengths of biological warfare as a weapon is that you can't see it, but it kills.'

OPERATION STORM

In fact, the Japanese did not deploy biological weapons

against the USA, though they certainly had the means to do so. It is likely that they feared the retaliation that would ensue. Fun-Go was a flop. So, too, was their plan to bomb New York and Washington D.C. with Aichi NGA1 seaplanes, launched from top-secret giant 1-400 submarines. These underwater juggernauts were by far the largest submarines produced by either side during the war. Each carried three Aichis, folded up to fit into their 115-foot watertight deck hangars. All three aircraft could be assembled, armed and catapulted into the skies in 45 minutes. The submarines themselves could travel one-and-a-half times around the world without refuelling.

The Japanese left it too late. Only three I-400s were ever completed and none of them saw action before the war ended with Japan's unconditional surrender. The plans to bomb New York and Washington had long been abandoned, as was a daring scheme to destroy the locks of the Panama Canal. This operation was cancelled in June 1945, when the I-400s were diverted to attack the 15 US aircraft carriers massed at Ulithi atoll, preparing to launch their planes against the Japanese Home Islands. Japan surrendered before the I-400s could attack. One of them was sunk on its way to its battle-station; US submariners captured the other two.

Who Torched the *Normandie*?

The crack trans-Atlantic liner Normandie *was the pride of France until she was laid up in New York harbour at the start of World War II. Two years later, while being converted into a giant troopship for the US government, she caught fire and capsized at her moorings. The great ship was a total loss. Had the mysterious fire that brought about her destruction started accidentally? Or had Nazi saboteurs been to blame?*

Above: Normandie *on fire alongside Pier 88 and starting to list to port. She eventually capsized.*

As 1941 drew towards a tumultuous close, *Normandie* was berthed at Pier 88 in the Hudson River, just a stone's throw from bustling 42nd Street. She had been mothballed there ever since shortly after the outbreak of war, when she had steamed into the harbour seeking sanctuary. The US government interned her.

Much had happened since then. France had been knocked out of the war by Hitler's Wehrmacht. The RAF had won the Battle of Britain and the Blitz was in full swing. As far as the *Normandie* was concerned, her future was uncertain. It was costing the French Line berthing charges of 1,000 dollars a day to keep her in port. Consequently, most of the seamen who sailed her had been paid off. Only a skeleton crew commanded by Captain Herve Lehude remained on board. In May 1941, they were joined by around 150 US Coastguards, who had been ordered by the Treasury Department to secure the ship and Pier 88 to 'insure *Normandie*'s safety and guard against sabotage.'

So matters stood on 7 December when the Japanese attack on Pear Harbor precipitated the USA into World War II. Four days later, Hitler announced to a cheering Reichstag that he 'had

arranged to have the American charge d'affaires handed his passports.' Ever since the 1920s, it had been the Fuehrer's belief that at some point his country would have to fight the USA. That moment had now arrived. Benito Mussolini, Italy's bombastic Duce and Germany's long-time ally, followed Hitler's example. The whole world was now at war.

FROM NORMANDIE TO LAFAYETTE

Tension between the USA and the Third Reich had been intensifying for months, even though the USA had been still officially neutral. New York City and New Jersey were honeycombed with nests of Nazi spies and sympathisers, many holding down labouring jobs along the Manhattan, New Jersey and Brooklyn waterfronts. Some were more upmarket—Lily Stein, a model who claimed to be an Austrian refugee, ran a smart dress store in fashionable Manhattan. The store was a post-box for the German intelligence service, the Abwehr.

Waldemar Othmer was a typical Nazi agent. He had emigrated from Germany to the USA in 1919 and in 1935 took out naturalisation papers. He married a New York girl and settled down to

raise a family. No one dreamt that this likeable, affable character was in reality a sleeper agent for the Abwehr. Even his membership of the German-American Bund did not arouse suspicion. He became the leader of its Trenton, New Jersey, branch while at the same time working in the Brooklyn Navy Yard. He moved from there to Camp Pendleton in Norfolk, Virginia. It was not until 1944 that his spying was finally detected.

In any event, the Abwehr and its commander, the wily Admiral Wilhelm Canaris, had long been keeping a beady eye on *Normandie*. Only a fortnight after the fall of France, Canaris had ordered his spy network in the USA to 'observe' the ship. The German High Command's fear was that, if the Third Reich and the Americans went to war, the ship would be commandeered and converted into a giant troop transport to ferry US forces to Europe. It was estimated that *Normandie* would be easily capable of carrying 10,000 or more US soldiers in a single Atlantic crossing.

This was exactly what happened. On 12 December 1941, five days after Pearl Harbor and the day after Hitler had declared war on the USA, the

Coast Guard took over the entire ship. Lehude and his skeleton crew were ushered ashore. Normandie was to be stripped of all her luxurious trappings to be converted into a troopship, just as the Nazis had feared. Even her name was changed. She was now to be rechristened *Lafayette*, in honour of the 18th-century French nobleman who had fought on the American side in the War of Independence against Britain.

MUDDLE AND CONFUSION

Because there was no dry dock in New York harbour big enough to accommodate *Normandie*, it was decided she should be converted to her new role at her mooring alongside Pier 88. Soon, hundreds of civilian contractors were swarming all over the great ship. They were up against a tight deadline. The US Navy, who, after some debate with the US Army as to which of them would eventually operate the ship, insisted that she should be ready to sail by 14 February. Her initial port of call was to be Boston, where she would take on board her first cargo of troops for transportation across the Atlantic – probably to Northern Ireland, where the US Army was planning to set up its first European bases and training camps.

The work ran late. When Captain Robert S. Coman, the vessel's designated commander, arrived in New York, it was clear that it would not be finished by 31 January as had originally been planned. Coman had another problem to worry about into the bargain. He had been assigned just 458 men as his crew – 'less than half the number,' he complained, 'required for the efficient operation of the vessel at sea.' He and Captain

Above: Normandie *at sea. The crack trans-Atlantic liner was one of the most luxurious vessels of her day.*

Right: *Admiral Wilhelm Canaris, head of the Abwehr, was in charge of German intelligence efforts in the US.*

Clayton M. Simmers, the 3rd Naval District Material Officer who had already advised the Bureau of Ships that the conversion could not be completed in time to meet the Navy's deadline, both urged Washington to postpone the sailing date. At first, the Navy Department agreed. Then it changed its mind. *Normandie*, it insisted, must sail on schedule.

On *Normandie*, gangs of workmen ploughed on in a desperate race to beat the ominously-ticking clock. The extra pressure caused by the Navy Department's refusal to countenance a further extension of the deadline it had imposed only served to deepen the chaos and confusion that already existed on board. Frank Knox, the Secretary of the Navy, later admitted: 'The enormity of the expansion of ship construction and conversion resulted in the placing of an extremely heavy burden upon the shoulders of those engaged in readying ships for military service. As a result, corners had to be cut and responsibility delegated to personnel less experienced and capable than would be the case in normal times.' Coman and Simmers continued to complain. On the afternoon of 8 February, both men were summoned to a top-level meeting to decide once and for all when exactly *Normandie* would be fit to sail.

The meeting never took place. At 2.30pm, fire broke out on board *Normandie*. Charles T. Collins, a 19-year-old workman, recalled what happed. 'I was working on a chain gang,' he recorded. 'We had chains around some pillars and eased them down when they were cut through. Two men were operating an acetylene torch. About 30 or 40 men were working in the room and there were bales and bales of mattresses. A spark hit one of the bales, and the fire began. We yelled for the fire watch and Leroy Rose, who was in our chain, and I tried to beat out the fire with our hands. Rose's clothes caught fire and I carried him out. The smoke and heat were terrific.'

FROM BLAZE TO CONFLAGRATION

Collins was wrong in two particulars. It was a pile of kapok life jackets that had been stored temporarily in the main salon that the sparks – not a single spark – from the torch welder Clement Derrick was operating set ablaze. Though prompt action might have extinguished the fire quickly, this was singularly lacking. There was no fire watch on duty and no one could locate the fire alarms, which in any case were disconnected. Though someone managed to turn on a fire hose, it ran dry almost at once.

Vain attempts continued to beat the fire out, using coats, pieces of carpet and anything else that came to hand. The efforts were in vain. The blaze, variously described as a 'racing fire', a 'surging fire on the surface of the bales' and a 'grass fire', grew and spread inexorably, fanned by a strong northwesterly wind blowing over the ship's port quarter, which swept the fire forwards. Eventually, it engulfed the three upper decks of the vessel.

Above: *The side elevation of* Normandie. *Had the New York Fire Department had access to such plans, it might have been able to save the ship.*

It took 12 minutes for the New York City Fire Brigade to be summoned and a further 15 for the first fire trucks to reach Pier 88. The firemen had to force their way through panicking crowds of workmen, Coast Guards and navy sailors before they could get into action. Eventually thousands of gallons of water were being pumped over, onto and into *Normandie* from the fire trucks on the pier and the fire boats clustered along the liner's port side – all part of the desperate effort to get the conflagration under control and save the stricken ship.

Dark black plumes of smoke spread across the Manhattan skyline as thousands of New Yorkers took to the streets to try to find out what was going on. Up to 30,000 of them massed in 12th Avenue to watch the spectacle. Hundreds more people gathered along the waterfront, while skyscraper windows all over Manhattan were thrown open as people attempted to catch a glimpse of the action.

Fiorello La Guardia, the Mayor of New York, was quickly on the scene. He had been in the middle of a radio address, assuring New Yorkers that he had no intention of raising the nickel subway fare, when news of the disaster reached him. He cut short his speech, quit the studio and raced to Pier 88. Later, having been assured that the fire was finally 'under control' and 'mopping-up' operations were proceeding, he and Rear-Admiral Adolphus Andrews, in command of the 3rd Naval District, decided to try and board *Normandie*. As they approached a gangplank, the sorely-wounded liner suddenly lurched several feet to port. It was the beginning of the end.

NORMANDIE CAPSIZES

It was not the fire that now presented the greatest threat to *Normandie*. It was the 6,000 gallons of water that the fire-fighters had pumped into her in their desperate efforts to save her. The water flowed inexorably downwards into the ship's lower decks; as it did so, *Normandie* listed more and more to port. Around midnight, all attempts to right her having failed, Andrews ordered the liner to be abandoned. At 2.45am, she finally capsized, coming to rest on her port side at an angle of around 80 degrees. Her stern slid under Pier 88, while her bows skewered towards Pier 90.

The one man who might have been able to save *Normandie* stood helplessly on the pier side as the list became more and more pronounced. He was Vladimir Yourkevitch, who had actually designed her. Rushing to Pier 88 when he heard of the disaster, he wanted to volunteer to go on board, make this way through the maze of corridors and passageways down into the bowels of the ship and open the sea-cocks to counter-flood her. If he had succeeded, *Normandie* would have settled on an even keel in the Hudson mud, rather than keeling over completely. Yourkevitch, however, was stopped from approaching the vessel at a police line set up to keep rubberneckers away from the pier. The police did not realise who he was and, thanks to his thick French accent, did not understand what he was desperately trying to tell them. All he could do was watch as the ship listed more and more until the inevitable happened.

ACCIDENT OR ARSON?

Immediately after *Normandie* capsized, rumours began to spread concerning what had triggered the disaster. Had the fire been a tragic accident or

Above: Normandie *arrives in New York harbor to be taken in tow by the waiting tugs. The Statue of Liberty can be seen in the background.*

Right: Normandie *anchored at the New York quayside. She held the record for being the biggest ship in the world for five years.*

had it been started deliberately by Nazi or even Vichy French saboteurs? Why had it proved so difficult to get the fire under control? Had someone slit the fire hoses? How did the fire manage to spread so fast? The nation demanded answers.

Spies were certainly active along the waterfront. Only a month before in a Brooklyn courtroom, 30 German agents had been found guilty of espionage and sentenced to serve a total of more than 300 years in prison. The spy ring had been uncovered thanks to William Sebold, a 42-year-old German-American who was working as a counterespionage agent for the FBI. J. Edgar Hoover's men had set him up in a 42nd Street office, where they could observe his meetings with the unsuspecting spies through a two-way mirror and bug their conversations. Was this just the tip of the iceberg? How many more Nazi agents and Axis sympathisers might be at work?

Demands for a full-scale enquiry escalated rapidly. An editorial in the New York Times thundered: 'The investigation should be relentless. It is not alone a ship that has been damaged. Men may have to die on the other side of some ocean because help did not get to them in time.' Even President Roosevelt himself got in on the act. Immediately after the fire, his first thought was to ask Secretary of the Navy Knox if enemy agents or pro-Nazi Fifth Columnists had been allowed to work on the ship.

THE MAFIA CONNECTION

Nazi saboteurs were the obvious candidate to blame. Much later, however, there was talk of Mafia involvement. The finger was pointed at Charles 'Lucky' Luciano, the uncrowned king of the New York underworld, who, so it was alleged, had ordered his henchmen to sabotage Normandie as part of a scheme to secure his release from jail.

Luciano had been held in prison in upstate New York since 1936, having been sentenced to a term of between 30 to 50 years for trafficking in prostitution. Now, he hatched a plot with fellow crime bosses Frank Costello, Mayer Lansky and Moe Polakoff to blackmail the US government into granting him parole. Alberto Anastasia and his brother 'Tough' Tony – the latter was a prominent figure in the International Longshoremen's Association – were also involved.

According to Luciano's memoirs, published 16 years after his death in 1962, the plan was as follows. Torching Normandie would force US Naval Intelligence to turn to Luciano to help to protect the New York docks against further acts of sabotage. It would be easy enough for Luciano to enforce his dictates as he and his fellow racketeers controlled most of the waterfront.

Whether the allegation was true or not, no one still can say. Certainly, there were meetings between mob bosses and representatives from US Naval Intelligence after the Normandie fire. It was also the case that, after the war, Luciano was released prematurely and deported to Italy. He never made it back to the USA.

The official verdict, however, ruled out all talk of sabotage. A Congressional investigation concluded that the disaster was the result of 'carelessness in how the burning operations were carried out,' compounded by an 'absence of proper coordination between the various units on board, divided authority and lack of a unified command' and 'undue haste, indecision and lack of careful planning in connection with the conversion.' In short, it had been a bungle. Normandie paid the price.

'Project Amerika'

To avenge the Allied bombing of the Third Reich, Hitler wanted nothing more than to blitz the USA's greatest homeland city to destruction. He failed, but how near did the Nazis come to fulfilling the Fuehrer's dream of reducing New York to ruins? How far did they get towards developing a super-bomber with the range to get to New York and back? Or did they plan to unleash a devastating missile attack?

Above: *A Blohm & Voss BV222 'Wiking' flying boat seen in flight. Only 14 of these massive aircraft were built; they had a range of some 3,790 miles and could be refuelled at sea by tanker U-boats.*

Surprisingly enough for a man whom *Time* magazine chose to feature on its cover as its Man of the Year as late as 1938, Adolf Hitler always detested the USA and everything it stood for. It was understandable, therefore, that, as the tide of war swung increasingly against the Third Reich, the Fuehrer's lust for revenge focused more and more obsessively on the USA as his favourite potential target for aerial revenge attacks.

'I never saw him so completely beside himself as towards the end of the war, when, in his delirium, he envisaged to himself the destruction of New York in firestorms,' Albert Speer wrote in his *Spandau Diaries*. 'He described how the skyscrapers would be transformed into gigantic burning torches; how they would collapse onto one another and how the glow of the burning city would brighten the night sky.' It was part of Speer's job, as Minister for Armaments, to try to turn his Fuehrer's fantasies into grim reality.

PLANNING TO STRIKE

Until 1972, little was known about specific German long-range bombing plans. Indeed, many military historians and researchers doubted whether any such plans had ever been devised. Those who thought otherwise assumed that the plans had been lost or destroyed as the war came to its end. Then German military historian Olaf Groehler made a momentous discovery while researching in the military archives in Potsdam in what was then East Germany. It was a copy of the actual plan the Luftwaffe had drawn up for a major transoceanic aerial bombing offensive.

Luftwaffe experts completed work on the plan on 27 April 1942. They handed it over to Reichsmarschal Hermann Goering on 12 May. The final version they submitted was 33 pages long. Attached to it was a map of the world with various potential targets and flight patterns indicated on it. There were also notes of which types of long-range aircraft could be used to carry out the attacks.

The man responsible for putting the plan together was Dietrich Schwenke, a highly-respected Luftwaffe colonel reporting directly to Field Marshal Erhard Milch, Goering's sometime deputy and the Luftwaffe's air armaments chief. As far as the eastern seaboard of the USA was concerned, Schwenke and his team reported as follows. 'On the coast of the USA,' he wrote, 'there are aluminium works, aircraft-engine works, propeller works and arms factories. These can be attacked only by Messerschmitt 264s with DB613 motors carrying 5.5 tons of bombs and starting from Brest. If the Azores could be used as a transit airfield, it would be possible to reach these targets with He 177s (refuelled) with 2 tons, BV 222s (refuelled) with 4.5 tons, Ju 290s with 5 tons and Me 264s with 6.5 tons.

Persuading neutral Portugal to allow the Azores to be used as a forward air base had already been discussed. A naval briefing document dated 14 November 1940, stated that Hitler was planning to 'attack America in case of war' from the islands. On 24 March 1941, the Fuehrer confirmed this was his intention. He confided to one of his adjutants that aerial attacks on the US east coast were necessary 'to teach the Jews a lesson.'

Among the specific targets Schwenke itemised were the Pratt & Whitney aeroengine plant at East Hertford, Connecticut, the Sperry Gyroscope factory in Brooklyn and the Curtiss Wright works at Caldwell, New Jersey. However, he added a caveat. 'The Panama Canal cannot be attacked with the planes mentioned unless there can be a refuelling at sea (BV 222).' Colonel Victor von Lossberg, a Luftwaffe bomber expert, had come to the same conclusion. In early August, he proposed that a BV 222 should fly across the Atlantic, rendezvous with a U-boat stationed around 800 miles from New York, refuel and top up its bomb-load to eight tons and then fly on to bomb its target. The operation would be repeated the following night after which the BV 222 would fly back to Europe.

Lossberg volunteered to pilot the plane himself. He proposed bombing New York primarily with incendiaries – he calculated that a BV 222 could drop about 4,000 of them on the city each time it attacked. The bombing would target what Lossberg termed 'the Jewish quarter' or the dockyards. He had high hopes that such an attack would reduce New Yorkers to a state of panic. 'The 22-kilo magnesium bomb,' he told Milch, 'has an explosive segment which detonates after four to ten minutes...if they (the bombs) could be laid in a swathe across New York and the bombs kept exploding round the ears of the fire-fighters like hand grenades, it would have a terrific effect.' The Kriegsmarine and Blohm & Voss,

the BV 222's manufacturer, both supported the plan. However, General Hans Jeschonnek, the Luftwaffe's Chief of Staff, turned it down as impractical.

THE 'AMERIKA BOMBER'

Jeschonnek may well have been right in this instance. Employing a flying boat to bomb New York was probably too risky. In order to strike effectively at such a target, the Germans needed more than plans. They needed suitable planes. What the Luftwaffe lacked was a long-range bomber capable of reaching the North American continent from Europe in one non-

Left: *Heinkel's He177 was the only German heavy bomber to enter service. Its coupled engines frequently caught fire in flight and the whole aircraft was unreliable. Hitler inelegantly described it as 'junk'.*

Above: *Eugen Sanger planned to build a rocket-powered orbital aircraft that could easily reach and bomb New York. The project, which was years ahead of its time, was cancelled in 1941. The so-called Silverbird never got off the ground.*

stop hop, dropping its bombs and then flying back again safely.

With the exception of the Heinkel He 1777 and the BV 222, the aircraft Schwenke had listed only existed on the drawing board or, at best, were nearing the prototype stage. The BV 222, however, had been deemed unsuitable by the Luftwaffe high command. As for the He 117, it was unreliable and plagued by structural flaws in its airframe and other major mechanical problems. In flight, its wings tended to buckle

under stress, while its engines, coupled together in tandem, were all too prone to catch fire in mid-air. An exasperated Hitler later described the plane as a 'rattletrap' and dismissed it scornfully as 'obviously the worst junk ever to have been manufactured.'

Even before the war, Goering had recognised that the absence of such a bomber meant that there was a gaping hole in the Luftwaffe's armament. He told a gathering of Germany's leading aircraft manufacturers:

'I completely lack the bombers capable of round-trip flights to New York with a five-ton bomb-load. I would be extremely happy to possess such a bomber which would finally muzzle some of the arrogance coming from over there.'

Willy Messerschmitt was the first to take up Goering's challenge. In 1937, he had started work on designing the long-range Messerschmitt Me 261 at Hitler's personal behest. Popularly known as the 'Adolfine', the plane was intended to carry the Olympic flame from Berlin to Tokyo to inaugurate the 1940 Olympic Games. According to high-level rumour, Hitler intended to be a passenger on the flight himself.

It was obviously logical for Messerschmitt to develop a long-range bomber in parallel with the 'Adolfine'. Initial work on what he christened Project 1061 started in late 1937, though, thanks to more pressing demands on the Messerschmitt design department's time, it did not really get underway until mid-1940. Despite Messerschmitt's personal assurances to the Fuehrer that the project was on time – he told Hitler that 'the aircraft can be used

for special purposes even before testing is completed' – he was promising the impossible. He even showed Hitler what the Fuehrer took to be a finished plane – in fact, it was simply a mock-up.

The first prototype of what was now designated the Messerschmitt Me 264 did not fly until December 1942, a full year behind schedule. The intention had been to allow Messerschmitt to build an initial 28 and try them out in action against New York and other US targets. The long delays led to the plan being aborted. Messerschmitt was permitted to

build just three prototypes. They were all destroyed in an Allied air raid in July 1944.

THE LUFTWAFFE OVER NEW YORK

Where Messerschmitt had failed, it looked like Junkers might succeed. Their other rivals – Focke-Wulf with the Ta 400 and Heinkel with the He 277 – never got further than wind-tunnel models before the Luftwaffe ordered them to stop work. The monstrous six-engined Ju 390 took advantage of the tried-and-tested Ju 90 and Ju 290 airframes. According to Junkers'

records, the prototype made its first test-flight on 20 October 1943. Just over a month later, it was flown to Insterburg, not far from the Fuehrer's headquarters in East Prussia, for Hitler to inspect. Junkers nicknamed it the 'New York bomber', probably to distinguish it from the rival Me 264.

The Luftwaffe immediately ordered 26 of the planes, but only a second prototype was ever built. In June 1944, the contract was cancelled. The prototypes, it is believed, were destroyed by the Germans in late April 1945 to stop them falling into US hands

Above left: *The prototype of the Me264, Willy Messerschmitt's 'Amerika bomber', first flew in December 1942. In October 1943, all work on the aircraft was stopped and Messerschmitt told to concentrate on his Me262 jet fighter-bomber.*

Above right: *The Me264 looked elegant enough on the ground, but is performance was inferior to that of its rivals. It had a slow rate of climb, was hard to maneuver and lacked in-flight stability.*

as American forces neared the Dessau factory where they had been built.

The plane was more than capable of doing its job – that is, if various claims that the first prototype actually managed to fly to New York and back are to be believed. The earliest of these claims was made in letters published in *RAF Flying Review* in 1955 and 1956. According to the second of these letters, the flight had taken place in the latter part of 1944, when the Junkers had got to within 12 miles of the US east coast just north of New York before turning back to its base in France. Though many experts dismissed the tale as unlikely, it soon passed into aviation folklore.

The second claim dates from 2011, when an article in *Veterans Today* stated that, in August 1943, a Ju 390, apparently flying from an airfield outside Bergen in Occupied Norway and refuelling in mid-air over Iceland, had crossed the Atlantic to photograph industrial plants in Michigan and then flown over New York before heading back to land at a Luftwaffe base near Paris, having refuelled again over the Azores on the way. The author of the article also claimed that the Ju 290's co-pilot was a woman – Anna

Kriesling, the so-called 'White Wolf of the Luftwaffe'. She got the soubriquet, the article said, because of her 'frost blonde hair and icy blue eyes'.

World War II aviation authorities were quick to denounce the article's claims. How, they asked, could the Junkers have flown the Atlantic two months before its first officially documented test-flight? Why was there no apparent mention of the flight in either the Junkers or Luftwaffe archives? Others said that the story was true, but the article got the date wrong. The flight, they opine, actually took place in January 1944.

No one knows the truth. If such a flight did indeed take place, it was more than likely to have been carried out by KG 200, a mysterious Luftwaffe unit whose records are still classified, lost or destroyed.

HITLER'S STEALTH BOMBER

Paradoxically, as the military situation deteriorated and the Luftwaffe faced the imminent threat of being driven out of the skies, prominent Nazis still clung to the dream of bombing New York, even though Germany's leading aircraft manufacturers were no longer directly involved. They were

desperately churning out fighters rather than bombers, despite the fact that fuel and pilot shortages meant that the Luftwaffe could not get many of the planes they were producing so feverishly off the ground and into the air.

Accordingly, the Germans turned to aviation mavericks to devise revolutionary new aircraft for the task. Chief amongst them were Reimar and Walter Horton, who devised an ingenious 'flying wing' jet aircraft design, variants of which could fly as day fighters or long-range bombers. The Horton Ho 229 bomber was the result.

Still in their 30s, the brothers broke completely with convention. They had had the notion for a 'flying wing' aircraft years before, but it was only now that they were given the chance to put their theories to the test. Work on the construction of an unpowered prototype began in Gottingen in early 1944. The first of them flew – or, rather, glided – successfully later that year. A second powered day fighter prototype followed in early 1945.

Carrying a 4,400lb bomb-load and flying at a maximum height of just over 49,000 feet at a top speed of 620 miles per hour, the Ho 229 was designed to fly to New York and back without the

Top: *A Heinkel 177 rear gunner in his turret. The Luftwaffe ordered hundreds of the planes – only a few ever flew.*

Above: *The revolutionary 'flying wing' Horton Ho 229 first flew in early 1945, but the jet-powered prototype crashed after a few test flights.*

Right: *Werner Baumbach commanded the Luftwaffe special duties squadron KG200. His men would probably have flown the Amerika bombers had they been built.*

need for refuelling. It was to be a pure jet aircraft, powered by either BMW 003A or Junkers Jumo 004B turbojet engines. As if this was not revolutionary enough, Reimar Horton came up with the idea of coating the plane with a mixture of charcoal dust and wood glue. This, he believed, combined with the Ho 222's unusual sculpted shape, would make it practically impossible for enemy radar to detect the aircraft. In short, the Ho 229 would be the world's first stealth bomber. It was 40 years ahead of its time.

The first unpowered prototype survived the war, to be captured by the Americans along with the blueprints for all the projected variants. The powered prototype crashed trying to make an emergency landing during a test flight after one of its Junkers Jumo engines caught fire in the air. Time ran out for the bomber prototype. Though work on it started in March 1945, it was never completed.

SPACE PLANES AND MISSILES

Austrian engineer Eugen Sanger was another maverick, who came up with an even more extraordinary notion. His plan, first mooted in the mid-1930s, was to attack New York with a rocket-

Right: *Pratt & Whitney's Connecticut aircraft engine plant.*

Left: *A German poster warns of the danger of falling flak splinters.*

power bomber that would drop a single, TV-guided 8,800lb bomb on the city from near space.

Sanger's suborbital 'Silver Bird' was to be catapulted into the air from a rocket sledge, after the latter had powered down a two-mile long monorail track. At 5,500 feet, the plane's own rocket engine would ignite and push the 'Silver Bird' upwards to a height of around 90 miles above the Earth to the edge of space. It would then literally bounce off the denser atmospheric layer below it – rather like a stone skipping across a pond – to reach its target. Having dropped its bomb, the 'Silver Bird' would fly across the USA and on over the Pacific to land in Japanese-controlled territory.

Though, by 1941, facilities for full-scale rocket engine tests were under construction, the German

Air Ministry decided to halt development of the project later the same year. Sanger tried again in 1944 to win official support, but it was too late. The 'Silver Bird' never flew.

Other ideas, such as engineer Bodo Lafferentz's idea to tow giant floating containers by U-boat to within 100 miles of the US eastern coast and fire V2 rockets from them, also failed to get off the ground. Though construction of three prototype containers started in early 1945, Soviet troops occupied the shipyard in which they were being built before they could be completed. The plan to build a multi-stage A10/A9 New York rocket suggested by Wernher von Braun and his fellow-rocketeers at Peenemünde also never took concrete form, though, given time, such a project might well have succeeded.

The Mystery of the Murdered Redhead

For two hectic years at the height of World War II, beautiful redheaded socialite Jane Horney was the uncrowned queen of Swedish high society. The dominant figure in Stockholm's hectic social life, she partied hard and had a host of influential friends. Was she simply an adventuress on the make? Was she an Allied agent, a Nazi spy or working for both sides? Like her probable murder, the riddle remains unsolved.

In the European theatre of war during World War II, there were two neutral capitals where the diplomatic and other representatives of the warring powers came into frequent contact with one another. One was Lisbon in Portugal. The other was Stockholm in Sweden.

For both the Allies and Nazi Germany, it was vital to keep in close daily touch with the Swedes, since Swedish industry was trading with both sides. There were many personal negotiations and much secret mail; Stockholm was awash with spies. In addition, the capital was a transit point for mail en route to prisoner-of-war camps in the Third Reich. USAAF and RAF aircrews, too, came down

in Sweden – some deliberately sought sanctuary there – while others managed to find their way there after evading capture after having been shot down or having escaped from prison camps within Hitler's Germany.

Many Norwegians seeking to flee from their Nazi-occupied country used Sweden as an alternative escape route to reach Britain, rather than risking the obvious perils and dangers of a small-boat North Sea crossing. High-ranking Allied personages helped the Norwegian effort. In March 1942, President Roosevelt himself actively supported the Royal Norwegian Air Force centre in London in its attempt to obtain two Lockheed Lodestar airliners

Above: *Food lines were a common feature of daily life in the Scandinavian countries during the war — even in neutral Sweden.*

Left: *Jane Horney photographed at the wheel of her car. An attractive adventuress, she may have been a spy for both sides during her short-lived career.*

to transport 50 of their fellow-Norwegians a week from Sweden to Scotland. Some of them had been waiting 18 months for the chance to fight with the Allies.

A BATTLE FOR SUPPLIES

Even more crucially, Britain was obtaining special engineering products from Sweden, such as ball-bearings, special steels for machine tools, fine springs and

in the British Ministry of Supply advised that it was 'of the greatest importance to obtain as many bearings as possible from Sweden with the minimum of delay.' After the US 8th Army Air Force's raid on Germany's most important ball-bearing factories at Schweinfurt, two top British government officials were flown to Sweden by Mosquito, each Mosquito specially modified to carry one passenger each in their bomb bays. The officials' task was to try and corner all Sweden's ball-bearing exports to stop the Germans getting hold of them. In this, they were partially successful. Interestingly, the German subsidiary of the giant Swedish industrial combine SKF controlled the most important of the Schweinfurt factories.

Above: *Jane Horney married Herje Granberg in 1937. He was the Berlin correspondent for a pro-Nazi Swedish newspaper at the time. The marriage ended in divorce two years later.*

Right: *So fast that they were practically immune to German attempts at interception, RAF Mosquitoes in civilian BOAC colours ferried priority passengers to and from Sweden.*

electrical resistors. The Germans were doing the same. Ball-bearings, in particular, were an indispensable part of both the Allied and Nazi war machines. In 1942, the Swedes supplied 59 per cent of the Third Reich's ball-bearing requirements and 31 per cent of British needs.

Ensuring a continued supply of ball-bearings was considered essential by both powers. In 1943, the Controller of Bearings

HOTBED OF INTRIGUE

In that year, Stockholm – the only city in northern Europe where the lights still blazed every night – was a hotbed of intrigue. With the war entering a crucial phase, secret plots and counter-plots were being constantly hatched in the city's most exclusive night-clubs and restaurants. It was a glittering scene, where partying and pleasure went hand-in-hand with intrigue and treachery.

In the early months of 1943, a beautiful redhead in her mid-twenties called Jane Horney arrived in the Swedish capital and swept like a whirlwind onto the Stockholm social scene. Her reign as the uncrowned queen of Swedish high society lasted for only two years, but during that time she broke the hearts of diplomats from half the world. And when she vanished abruptly in January 1945, she left behind a mystery that still remains unsolved today.

WHO WAS JANE HORNEY?

Jane Horney, or Ebba Charlotta Horney to give her proper full name, was a Swedish citizen, probably born in Stockholm in 1918 though some say she was actually born illegitimately in Scotland and later adopted by her Swedish foster father and Danish mother. The truth is that no one knows the exact facts about her origins. What is known is that she was always something of an adventurer. Tall, handsome and outgoing, she liked people – especially men.

In 1939, Jane married journalist Herje Granberg, whom she had met on a trip to Greenland. Two years later, the couple moved to Berlin, where Granberg had been appointed correspondent for the pro-Nazi Swedish newspaper *Aftonbladet*. Two years later, they divorced and Jane moved back to Scandinavia – first to Copenhagen, where she had relatives, and then to Stockholm. She was attractive, young and fancy-free. In a matter of weeks, she became one of the leading lights of Stockholm's party

Above: *Alexandra Kollontai was Soviet Ambassadress to Sweden during the war. She was one of the few people Stalin trusted unreservedly.*

Opposite: *Before the Mosquito came on the scene, US Lockheed Lodestars flew between Britain and Sweden. To avoid being shot down by the Luftwaffe, they were forced to fly only at night or in bad weather.*

scene – and her escorts were almost always senior diplomats or known secret service operatives from half a dozen countries.

SPY OR DOUBLE AGENT?

Whatever game Jane was playing, it was a dark, deep and dangerous one. Before long, the British had become convinced that she was a German agent. So had the Danes, many of whom had taken refuge in Sweden when their country was overrun by the Wehrmacht in April 1940. Rumours began to circulate that she had helped the Germans to track down and arrest some of the key figures in the Danish resistance movement.

What neither the British nor the Danes realised was that the Germans suspected Jane of being a British spy – or at least that she was a double agent. Her contacts certainly included Ronald Turnbull, a serving officer in Britain's Special Operations Executive, and Otto Danielsson and Martin Lundqvist, both members of Swedish Military Intelligence. Danielsson noted that she had 'no moral scruples' when it came to trading sex for secret information. Jane was also linked with the NKVD, the Soviet espionage service. It was thought that she sometimes acted as a courier for Alexander Pavlov, the

TASS news agency correspondent in Stockholm who doubled as an NKVD agent.

In all probability, the exact truth will never be established. What we do know is that Jorgen Winkel, a prominent Danish textile manufacturer and member of the Danish Resistance, became one of Jane's lovers and that, to try to get him out of prison, she embarked on an affair with Karl Heinz Hoffman, head of the Gestapo in Denmark. Her other high-level German friends included SS Obersturmbannfuehrer Hermann Seibold, in charge of Germany's Scandinavian counterintelligence operations.

We also know that, in summer 1943, she took up with another new boyfriend. He was 54-year-old Horst Gilbert, a German living in Copenhagen where he ostensibly ran the Scandinavian Telegraph Bureau. This was simply a cover. In actuality, he was an important Abwehr military intelligence officer, who, possibly under direct orders from Admiral Wilhelm Canaris, was playing a double game. Like Canaris, Gilbert was a secret anti-Nazi, who, long before the war while he was serving in Russia as an unofficial adviser to the Red Army, had become friendly with Alexandra Kollontai, now Soviet Ambassador to

Sweden. Gilbert, using Jane as a go-between, contacted Kollontai again to try to establish whether there was a chance of the Russians agreeing to open negotiations for a separate peace with Germany.

Gilbert managed to survive until 14 October 1844, when he was shot down in his office in central Copenhagen by Ella von Cappeln, a one-time nun, and other members of the cell she ran in the Danish Resistance. He died of his wounds a month later. The previous autumn, Jane often went from Stockholm to Copenhagen to visit him. The curious thing was that she travelled not by conventional

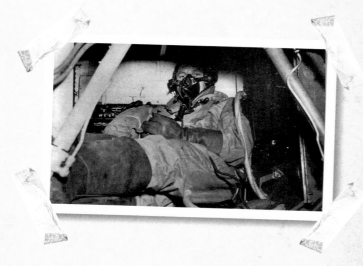

Top: *Mosquitoes in flight. From 1943 until the end of the war, they flew regularly between Leuchars air base in the north of Scotland and Stockholm.*

Above: *Mosquitoes could carry one person at a time, crammed into their bomb bays. The Danish physicist Niels Bohr was one of the first passengers.*

Opposite: *Per Albin Hansson, neutral Sweden's Prime Minister, had to tread a tricky tightrope between the demands of the Allies and those of Nazi Germany.*

means, but by a secret shuttle service set up by the Danish Resistance to ship weapons and ferry refugees across the Kattegat and Skagerrak.

PLOT AND COUNTER-PLOT

Just what Jane thought she was up to trying to play one side off against the other is anybody's guess. Early in 1944, for instance, equipped with a special pass that allowed her to cross the frontiers of the occupied countries without hindrance, she went to Germany several times. Why is unclear. To complicate the story even further, she passed on information about the Nazi intelligence set-up in Scandinavia to her Swedish intelligence contacts on her return to Sweden.

In March 1944, Jane's latest boyfriend was a major in British Intelligence attached to Britain's embassy in Stockholm. No one knows whether this anonymous figure was sent to Stockholm with specific orders to become friendly with her, but he certainly did so. Jane apparently fell head over heels in love with him. For several months, they were inseparable and then the major suddenly broke off the affair. It may be that he had discovered everything there was to know about her and was ordered to terminate the liaison.

In any event, Jane was heartbroken by the break-up. She vanished from the Stockholm scene for some weeks. When she returned, she seemed to pay more attention to the Germans than ever before – whether this was because of the unhappy outcome of her love affair with the British officer will never be known for certain. In any event, the Danish Resistance was certainly becoming more and more suspicious of her. Its agents shadowed her everywhere, photographing her and the people she met. That autumn, acting on information supplied by the Danes, the Swedish Secret Service arrested her and took her in for interrogation.

The Swedes questioned Jane for three weeks. Eventually, on 13 October, they set her free. They told the Danes who had denounced her that she had been completely cleared of all suspicion and the Danes outwardly expressed their satisfaction with the Swedish conclusions. Secretly, however, their top agents were still convinced that Jane was a dangerous spy in the pay of the Nazis.

A COLD-BLOODED MURDER

The Danes had plotted to murder Jane before, but aborted the attempt. Now, they decided to proceed. Sven Aage Geisler and Asbjorn Lyhne, both members of the Danish Resistance, were sent to Stockholm with instructions to win Jane's confidence and then persuade her to return with them to Denmark to clear herself of the espionage allegations once and for all. Jane, taken in by Geisler's charm, eventually fell in with the plan.

For the lovely redhead who had captivated Stockholm society for so long, the clock was ticking and time was fast running out. On 16 January 1945, Geisler, Lyhne, Jane and Bodil Frederickson, a girlfriend of hers who was also a member of the Danish Resistance, boarded the evening train to Malmo from Stockholm's Central Station. Having arrived in Malmo, the party checked in at the Grand Hotel, where rooms had been reserved for them. They were joined there by Hjalmar Ravnbo, a young student going under the name of 'Jens' who was also a member of the Danish Resistance.

Jane was completely unaware that she was in any danger. Indeed, when Geisler and Lyhne told her that they were not making the ferry-crossing to Denmark with her, she insisted on hosting a dinner party at the Savoy Hotel the following night to say goodbye to them. At 10.00pm, she left the hotel with Bodil Frederickson and Ravnbo to travel by taxi to Hoganas, outside Helsingborg, where she was to board the Danish ferry.

It was a stormy night, but the ferry still sailed punctually on time. Halfway through its crossing, however, it hove-to and Jane, together with two or three other men, was transferred to *Taman*, a Danish fishing boat, which pulled alongside. Several of the ferry's crew saw the transfer happen, but took no particular notice of it. Such secret exchanges were commonplace. It was only after they were later questioned by the police that they realised that something sinister had been afoot.

What happened next remains conjecture. Somewhere out in the darkness after the ferry continued on its way, Jane was cold-bloodedly murdered. The likelihood is that she was shot twice, her lifeless corpse wrapped in heavy iron chains and dumped overboard into the freezing water. It sank without a trace.

CONTINUING CONTROVERSY

Jane's disappearance, however, was only the start of a continuing mystery, rather than its conclusion. After the war, her father pressured the Swedish police to investigate her disappearance and supposed death. The investigators ran up against a wall of silence. The Swedish Secret Service closed their files on her, as did the Danes. The British claimed never to have heard of her, while former Abwehr, Gestapo and SS officers who had known her stubbornly held their tongues.

In 1947, there was an apparent breakthrough, when Asbjorn Lyhne, who was serving a short sentence in a Swedish prison for forging documents, unexpectedly confessed to having participated in Jane's murder. Later, though, he withdrew his confession, leaving the Swedes with no alternative but to release him in the absence of any corroborative evidence. Geisler, too, was investigated but cleared.

As the years passed, the rumours escalated. Some claimed that Jane had not been killed at all. The person who had been murdered was Bodil Frederickson, who, for some unknown reason, had been persuaded to change places with her. Certainly, the two women looked remarkably alike. Staff at the Grand Hotel confirmed to the police that two striking redheads had stayed there in adjoining rooms. One of the two was later seen at Malmo station, boarding the Stockholm train. Was it Bodil or was it Jane? No one will ever know for certain.

Others argue equally confidently that, though Bodil indeed did change clothes with Jane and assume her identity for a time, this was just part of the Danish master plan to get the real Jane secretly out of Sweden. Another theory holds that Jane's death was staged so that she could be spirited to Britain to spy for MI6 against the Russians. No concrete evidence has ever been produced to prove conclusively that this was the case. Many hold the entire thing is a hoax, perpetrated by a former schoolteacher and current multimedia artiste on the two Danish writers who put the theory into general circulation. An even more extraordinary theory claims that Jane's supposed death was engineered so that she could smuggle Princess Margrethe and another member of the Danish Royal Family to safety in Sweden.

The controversy continues. In Denmark, Jane's career was even dramatised as a TV mini-series. The jury is still out as to whether she really was a top-ranking secret agent or even a double agent. Or there might be an even more intriguing and tragic explanation – that Jane was an adventuress, a girl-about-town who lived life to the full at the expense of the secret service men who tried to use her and who outwitted them. Put at its simplest, she was murdered because she knew too much, particularly about alleged corruption inside the Danish Resistance. If she had ever talked about what she knew, she all too easily could become a source of political embarrassment.

Right: *The voluptuous Jane Horney captured in a pensive mood. Her lovers were legion.*

The Lost Liberator

It failed to return from a bombing raid over Italy in April 1943. Its remains were discovered virtually intact deep in the torrid wastelands of the Libyan Desert 450 miles south of Benghazi more than 16 years later. The radio still worked. The coffee in the crew's vacuum flasks was still drinkable. But what had happened to the men who flew the B-24 Liberator they had christened 'Lady Be Good'?

Deep in the vast featureless wasteland that makes up the Libyan Desert, there lies the wreck of a wartime bomber. It is a Consolidated B-24 Liberator. On its nose it bears the number 64 and the sun-faded name 'Lady Be Good'.

At 1.30pm in the afternoon of 4 April 1943, 'Lady Be Good' had taken off from the airfield at Soluk, on the coastal strip south of Benghazi, in company with 24 other Liberators from the USAAF 376th Bomb Group, to attack enemy airfields around Naples, some 750 miles across the Mediterranean to the north. The attack had been planned to ensure that the bombers got to their targets around dusk and made their return flight at night. The darkness, it was thought, would help them to elude any pursuing Luftwaffe or Regia Aeronautica fighters. The records show that 11 of the B-24s bombed their primary target, the remainder hitting the secondary ones.

Although some of the Liberators were damaged by hostile anti-aircraft fire and others suffered from engine trouble, all bar one of them made it back to Soluk safely by midnight. The exception was 'Lady Be Good'. Then, shortly after midnight, the

control tower at Benina received a radio transmission from the overdue plane. First Lieutenant William J. Hutton, its pilot and commander, told the controller that he was unable to locate his home airfield because of the dense cloud that was now blanketing the entire North African coast and that his Liberator was running low on fuel. He asked for a radio fix so that he could home in on Benina and make an emergency landing there.

The Benina tower gave the fix as requested, but 'Lady Be Good' never arrived. An air-sea rescue search the next day failed to find

Above: *The crew of 'Lady Be Good' pose for a group photograph. They arrived in Libya just a week before their first operational flight was scheduled.*

Opposite: *The nose and cockpit of 'Lady Be Good'. The crashed section was remarkably well-preserved – even its machine guns were still in place.*

any trace of the missing bomber or its crew. They were assumed to have crashed and drowned in the Mediterranean.

DISCOVERING THE WRECK

The incident in itself was not unusual. It was Hutton's and his crew's first combat mission and

Above: *The crash site of 'Lady Be Good' viewed from the air. This picture was taken shortly after the wreck's discovery by oil prospectors in 1959.*

Below: *Inside the plane, everything was surprisingly intact. Even the radio still worked, while the coffee in the crews' Thermos flasks had not evaporated.*

so they were at far greater risk of being shot down or failing to make it home than other, more experienced aircrews. It was what happened after that return flight that made the story of 'Lady Be Good' unique.

In 1959, more than 16 years later, British geologists surveying for oil deep in the Libyan Desert by air advised the US Air Force's Wheelus Field airbase that they had spotted the wreckage of a large World War II aircraft some 440 miles south of Benghazi. A C-47 transport plane with a search crew on board was promptly despatched to investigate.

The C-47 touched down safely on the gravelly ground close to the wreckage and the investigators disembarked into the blistering heat. They quickly identified the crashed aircraft as a Liberator, but, as they walked towards the wreckage an amazing sight met their eyes. There was no trace of corrosion on the bomber's metalwork. The dry, furnace-like heat of the desiccated desert air had preserved it perfectly. It was almost as if the Liberator had been deposited in the desert only the day before.

INVESTIGATING THE INTERIOR

'Lady Be Good' lay spread-eagled on its belly, its right wing

Above: *B-24 Liberators returning home to their airfields in Italy after raiding enemy territory. All too many did not make it back to base unscathed.*

raised slightly with the left wing crumpled in the sand. The rear of the fuselage and the tail unit had broken away and was lying off to one side at an angle. One of its Pratt & Whitney R-1830 Twin Wasp radial engines had been torn away. The starboard landing gear had dropped from its well. Amazingly, its tyre was still inflated.

Scattered debris lay littered around the aircraft. There were oxygen bottles, steel helmets, first-aid boxes, belts of ammunition and items of flying clothing. Cautiously, the investigators peered inside the fuselage. There

were no human remains to be seen. The interior was completely deserted. Sweltering in the blistering heat, they clambered inside to investigate further. They tested the radio and found that it was still in working order. They also discovered some vacuum flasks with coffee inside them. The coffee was still drinkable.

The Liberator's fuel tanks turned out to be practically dry. It also became clear that three of the plane's four engines must have stopped in flight because their propeller blades were feathered – that is, turned edge-on to the

airflow in order to cut down drag. The fourth engine appeared to have still been in action at the time of the crash. The rear escape hatch and the bomb-bay doors of the aircraft were open and there were no parachutes or Mae West life-preservers to be found.

It was clear that the crew had bailed out of 'Lady Be Good' deliberately shortly before the plane crashed. Evidently, they had not panicked when their aircraft ran into difficulties. It was well-known that Liberators were notoriously difficult to ditch or belly-land successfully. They had

Above: *Another group of B-24s in flight. More Liberators were produced than any other American aircraft in World War 2. The RAF ordered them as well.*

Opposite: *The wrecked tail section of 'Lady Be Good' through which the crew would have parachuted. The crash investigators' C-30 is seen in the background.*

also been dubbed 'flying coffins' by some of their more disgruntled aircrews. The nickname came about because the only way in and out of the bomber was at its rear. This meant that the crew on the flight deck – pilot, co-pilot, navigator, wireless operator, flight engineer, bombardier and nose gunner – had to scramble right back through the aircraft, battling against time and hampered by their bulky parachutes.

In this instance, 'Lady Be Good' was almost certainly flying on automatic pilot as it approached its last moments. Presumably, Hutton had switched over from manual control in order to keep the aircraft flying straight, level and steady while the crew abandoned ship. It also gave him the opportunity to get clear of the cockpit and so escape the crash.

TWO CRITICAL QUESTIONS

By now, two questions were uppermost in everyone's minds. The Liberator showed no signs of having suffered any battle damage. The crew had obviously abandoned it as it ran out of fuel. But what was it doing in the desert, hundreds of miles from where it ought to have been? And what had become of the members of its crew?

After their return to Wheelus Field, the investigators completed their report on what they had found at the crash site and forwarded it to Washington. From wartime USAAF records, details of the bomber and its crew – and of their last flight – were unearthed. Only when the investigators pieced together the story of what had happened on the night of 4 April did the truth come to light. What was revealed was a tragic chain of circumstances.

When Hutton requested the radio fix, the Benina control tower assumed that 'Lady Be Good' was flying northwest of its home base and still out over the Mediterranean. What Hutton had to do was to compensate for his own speed, wind velocity and other navigational factors and correct his course accordingly. This would have brought him safely over the Benina base. Then 'Lady Be Good' could have been 'talked down' through the thick cloud cover to make a safe landing on the airfield's runway. In fact, the Liberator was already a long way to the southeast of Benina and heading steadily into the wastes of the Libyan Desert.

Circumstances conspired to throw Hutton off-course. The first was a sudden change in the weather. Unknown to the Liberator's crew, the wind had veered direction to the northeast and increased in velocity into the bargain. An aircraft's speed over the ground depends on the direction and speed of the winds it encounters. With an unexpectedly powerful tail wind behind it, Hutton's aircraft was flying much faster southwards than he realised.

The second problem seems to have been the radio fix. When Hutton radioed asking for assistance from the HF/DF station at Benina, he received a directional reading of 330 degrees. What probably happened then was that the Liberator's navigator took a reciprocal reading, which seemed to indicate that the plane

Above: *A Liberator is captured banking over the Ploiesti oil refineries in Romania, having dropped its bomb load successfully. In total, 53 planes were shot down in the attack.*

Right: *Odd pieces of equipment lay scattered all around the crash site. 'Lady Be Good' also lost one of her four engines.*

was on course. Hutton therefore believed that he was still over the Mediterranean and on his way to the safety of Benina. He was not. Instead, he was mistakenly flying further and further south deep into the barren desert.

SEARCHING FOR THE BODIES

It took many searches to discover what had become of Hutton and his crew. The first, which lasted from May to August 1959, was unsuccessful, though the searchers did find some clues to suggest that at least some of the Liberator's crew had managed to survive.

The first clue was discovered in a shallow depression about 19 miles from the crash site. It was a pair of flying boots arranged with their toes pointing to the north. As the searchers moved further on, they found a succession of improvised arrowheads, consisting of parachutes weighted down with rocks. Presumably, the survivors had hoped that these markers would help an air-sea mission to locate them.

The markers stopped at the edge of a vast, shifting sand sea. Despite months of further

searching, nothing more was found. Captain Myron C. Tiller decided to end the search. 'The search was abandoned,' he reported, 'when equipment began to deteriorate and fail and the probability of the airmen being completely covered by shifting sand made the danger of further search impractical.'

A REVEALING DIARY

In February 1960, British Petroleum surveyors searching for oil discovered the remains of five of the crew on a plateau inside the sand sea. What was left of their corpses was close together, surrounded by a litter of abandoned canteens, torches, torn pieces of parachutes, flight jackets, other items of equipment and personal effects. Among the latter was a diary belonging to Lieutenant Robert Toner, the

Liberator's co-pilot. The hastily-scribbled jottings, covering the nine days from 4 to 12 April 1943, tell the poignant story of the airmen's courageous battle for survival.

Sunday, Apr. 4, 1943

Naples – 28 places – things pretty well mixed up – got lost returning, out of gas, jumped, landed in desert at 2:00 in morning. No one badly hurt, can't find John, all others present.

Monday 5

Start walking N.W., still no John. A few rations, 1/2 canteen of water, 1 cap full per day. Sun fairly warm. Good breeze from N.W. Nite very cold. No sleep. Rested & walked.

Tuesday 6

Rested at 11:30, sun very warm. No breeze, spent P.M. in hell, no

B-24G of the 376th BG at its Italian Base (USAF via NARA)

Top: *B-24s in characteristic box formation cruise apparently unscathed through a fierce barrage of German anti-aircraft fire. It was intercepting Luftwaffe fighters that were the real killers.*

Above: *A B-24's Flight Engineer checks on the progress of the ground crew maintaining his plane. This is a B-24G variant, fitted with a ball turret and extra machine-guns in the nose.*

planes, etc. rested until 5:00 P.M. Walked & rested all nite. 15 min on, 5 off.

Wednesday, Apr. 7, 1943

Same routine, everyone getting weak, can't get very far, prayers all the time, again P.M. very warm, hell. Can't sleep. Everyone sore from ground.

Thursday 8

Hit Sand Dunes, very miserable, good wind but continuous blowing of sand, every [one] now very weak, thought Sam & Moore were all done. La Motte eyes are gone, everyone else's eyes are bad. Still going N.W.

Friday 9

Shelly, Rip, Moore separate & try to go for help, rest of us all very weak, eyes bad, not any travel, all want to die. Still very little water. Nites are about 35, good in wind, no shelter, 1 parachute left.

Saturday, Apr. 10, 1943

Still having prayer meetings for help. No sign of anything, a couple of birds; good wind from N. --Really weak now, can't walk. Pains all over, still all want to die. Nites very cold. No sleep.

Sunday 11

Still waiting for help, still praying. Eyes bad, lost all our wgt. Aching all over, could make it if we had water; just enough left to put our tongues to, have hope for help very soon, no rest, still same place.

Monday 12

No help yet, very cold nite.

The story was clear. The crew of 'Lady Be Good' bailed out of their aircraft at 2.00am on 5 April. Lieutenant John S. Woravika, the bombardier, was the first casualty – his parachute failed to open – though the rest of the crew were unaware of the fatality. The eight remaining survivors trekked 85 miles north across the desert to the point at which the remains were found. Five of them – Hutton, Toner himself, Second Lieutenant D. P. Hayes, the navigator, and Sergeants Samuel Adams, one of the aircraft's gunners, and Robert E. La Motte, the radio operator – were too weak to continue. Sergeants Guy E. Shelley, Vernon L Moore and Harold J. Ripslinger – the other gunners and the radio operator – continued to struggle on through the desert in search of help.

OPERATION CLIMAX

After the discovery of the remains of the five crewmen, the US Army and US Air Force launched a final, more extensive effort to find the other missing members of the crew. Operation Climax, as it was called, started with high altitude fighters flying extensive photographic reconnaissance missions over the area. The ground party flew into the desert on a C-130 cargo plane. They had helicopter back-up with them.

It was another British Petroleum surveying team, however, which made the initial discovery. On 12 May 1960, geologists came across Shelley's remains at a spot 21 miles northwest of the place where the first five crewmembers perished. Five days later, a search helicopter carrying out an air sweep over the area spotted Ripslinger's remains on the eastern slope of a high sand dune 26 miles north of where Shelley had been found.

The whereabouts of the last two airmen remained a mystery until 1 August, when British Petroleum geologists found Woravika's body about 12 miles northeast of where 'Lady Be Good' had crashed. He was still wearing his high altitude flying suit with his parachute still attached.

Less than half a mile away to the southwest, they discovered discarded parachute harnesses and more high altitude clothing. This obviously had been where the rest of the crew rallied after their bail-out. Moore's corpse has never been located.

The tragedy was all the more acute because it may well have been avoidable. It stemmed from the mistaken decision to head northwards rather than southeast. Had the crew of 'Lady Be Good' chosen the latter course, they would have been able to retrieve the food and water in the crashed aircraft and use its radio to signal for help. At the very least, it would have increased their chances of survival.

Good fortune, however, did not favour 'Lady Be Good' and her crew on its one and only battle mission. The recovered remains were returned to the USA for burial. As for 'Lady Be Good', she became the victim of scavengers and souvenir hunters. What little was left of her eventually was removed from the Libyan Desert by an oil company in 1995. When last seen, she apparently was stored in the backyard of a police compound in Tobruk.

The Leslie Howard Enigma

On 1 June 1943, eight Luftwaffe Junkers 88s shot down a Douglas DC-3 airliner over the Bay of Biscay on its way from Lisbon to Britain. Everyone on board perished, including the celebrated film actor Leslie Howard and his friend and business adviser Alfred Chenhalls, who looked remarkably like Winston Churchill. Did the Germans believe that Churchill himself was on board the plane? Was Howard the target? Or was it all a tragic mistake?

CONFIDENTIAL

TOP SECRET

CLASSIFIED

Right: *The ubiquitous Junkers Ju88. This captured night-fighter variant is being evaluated by the RAF – hence the markings.*

Left: *Leslie Howard was one of Britain's best-known and most popular actors. Some say that he was also a British spy.*

The radio message that came through to the wireless room at the airfield at Whitchurch, near Bristol, at 12.54pm on the afternoon of 1 June 1943 was stark in its simplicity. It read: 'From G-AGBB to GKH. Am being attacked by enemy aircraft.' Then, an ominous silence fell. There was no more word from the stricken plane.

The message had been transmitted from a BOAC Douglas Dakota DC-3 airliner being flown by a Dutch crew from KLM, the Netherland's national air line. There were four of them on board – pilot, co-pilot, radio operator and flight engineer. There were also 13 passengers. In addition to Howard and Chenhalls, they

were Reuters correspondent Kenneth Stonehouse and his wife, Mrs Rotha Hutcheon, and her young daughters, Petra, aged 11, and Carolina, her 18-month-old sister; Mrs Cecelia Paton; Tyrrell Shervington, an oil company director Ivan Sharp, from the United Kingdom Commercial Corporation Wilfrid B. Israel, a prominent British-Jewish activist Francis Cowlrick; and Gordon Thompson MacLean.

The DC-3 had taken off from Portela, the airport of Lisbon, the capital of neutral Portugal, at 9.35am Double British Summer Time on that June morning, bound for BOAC's base at Whitchurch. There was nothing particularly unusual

about the flight; civilian DC-3s flew between Britain, Portugal and Gibraltar on an almost daily basis. The trips, though, always contained an element of risk as they involved flying across the Bay of Biscay, uncomfortably close to the Luftwaffe's airfields around Bordeaux.

For added safety, the airliners were painted pale blue overall, with red, white and blue identification stripes on their wings. Their civilian registration markings were also painted on them in clear visible letters. Sometimes, the airliners were shadowed by German interceptors, but the latter usually broke away when the enemy pilots identified the DC-3s as unarmed civilian aircraft. 1 June, however, was to prove an exception.

WHY FLIGHT 777?

Why did the journey of G-AGBB – Flight 777, the airliner bearing the name 'Ibis' on its nose – end in sudden, unexpected tragedy over the Bay of Biscay? There had been no one among the passengers from whose death the enemy might have profited? Or had there been?

There had been last-minute changes to the passenger list. Originally, there had been 14 names on it, assigned seats in order of priority. At the head of the list came government officials or VIPs, whose seats were allocated by the British Embassy in Lisbon, followed by passengers who had reached the top of a usually lengthy waiting list. Out of these, women travelling with children or children travelling on their own had priority. .

On this occasion, a young boy called Derek Partridge and his nanny, Dora Rowe, were bumped from the passenger list at literally the last minute. They actually had boarded the aircraft and taken their seats in its cabin when a harassed BOAC official asked them to return to the terminal. Howard and Chenhalls took their places.

Another scheduled passenger, Father A. A. Holmes, a Roman Catholic priest, missed the flight after being summoned back to Lisbon by an urgent telephone call summoning him to the British Embassy.

Howard was a much-loved and admired star of stage and screen. Slight, fair-haired and somewhat vague in manner, he was the epitome of an English gentleman, though in fact he came from a Hungarian Jewish family that had migrated to Britain in the late 19th century. At the peak of his movie success – he had starred in box office hits like *The Scarlet Pimpernel,* where he played Sir Percy Blakeney, George Bernard Shaw's *Pygmalion*, as Professor Henry Higgins, and *Gone With The Wind*, where he had been cast as Ashley Wilkes—he had bought himself out of his Hollywood contract and returned to Britain at the outbreak of war to do his bit for the war effort. He broadcast talks to the USA and made short propaganda films for the Ministry of Information.

The two full-length movies Howard directed and starred in after his return home particularly infuriated Joseph Goebbels and other high-ups in the Nazi leadership. These were *Pimpernel*

Smith and *The First of the Few*. In *Pimpernel Smith*, Howard played an eccentric Cambridge professor, who, under the cover of leading an archaeological dig in pre-war Germany, conspired with his accompanying students to smuggle victims of Nazi persecution out of the Reich in the face of the Gestapo. *The First of the Few* was a biopic of the career of R. J. Mitchell, the designer of the Spitfire fighter who died of cancer at the age of only 42. It was to be Howard's last film.

THE NAZI BLACKLIST

Howard was high on the Nazi blacklist. So, too, were Wilfrid Israel and mining expert Ivan Sharp. Israel, who originally hailed from Berlin, was a leading anti-Nazi activist who helped thousands of his fellow Jews to escape the Holocaust. His family had owned Kaufhaus N. Israel, one of the largest department stores in Europe situated next to the City Hall on Berlin's Alexanderplatz, until its forced expropriation by the Nazis in 1939. Israel then went into exile, taking up residence in London, where he set up the Jewish Refugee Mission. He was the mastermind behind the so-called Kindertransport of Jewish children to Britain. Some 10,000

Above: *A British propaganda poster warns against the danger of loose talk. Howard's name, however, was prominently on his plane's passenger list, of which the Germans obtained a copy.*

of them arrived there before the outbreak of war.

At the request of the Jewish Agency, Israel flew to Portugal to help as many as possible of the Jewish refugees who were living there and in Spain to escape to Palestine. The Germans, according to some theorists, believed that he was looking in particular for scientists with special knowledge of rocketry and nuclear physics with the aim of getting them to work for the Allies. This may well have been true. Certainly, some of the people who worked on the Manhattan Project – the Allied effort to build the atomic bomb – were recruited by him.

Sharp was another passenger the Nazis had reason to wish dead. He had been tasked by the British government with the purchase of as much tungsten as he could buy, even if this meant paying vastly inflated prices. The intention was to try to starve the Nazi war machine of this indispensable mineral. Sharp's mission had been successful. He had agreed to pay £5,000 per tonne for the tungsten he had purchased – about 50 times what it is worth today. The payments were not all made in hard currency. According to Sharp's grandson, his great-aunt once 'saw a small bag on the kitchen table. She felt some hard things inside it and thought that they were marbles, but, when she opened it, she saw that they were uncut diamonds. We think that he used them to pay for the tungsten.'

MISTAKEN IDENTITY?

There was another possible explanation for the unprovoked attack. For years, Alfred Chenhalls had been chaffed by his friends because of his close resemblance to Winston Churchill. He had the same portly figure and pink, cherubic face. He wore black Homburg hats, just like the premier. He also smoked six-and-a-half-inch long double Corona cigars.

Like the capital itself, Lisbon's airport was a constant hotbed of intrigue. Abwehr agents were constantly on the watch, noting who might be flying to and from Britain. The British were equally active in observing who was travelling on Luft Hansa planes. Early on the morning Flight 777

Right: *In* Spitfire, *as* The First of the Few *was retitled in the US, Leslie Howard starred as R. J. Mitchell, the designer of the Spitfire. He also directed the movie.*

Opposite: *A BOAC DC-3 stands waiting on the tarmac at Gibraltar. The airline ran a regular service to neutral Lisbon to connect with the Pan American flying-boat flights to New York.*

was scheduled to depart, two Abwehr agents managed to sneak a look at its passenger list. They saw the name Chenhalls on it – not so unlike Churchill to the Germans' prying eyes. They also spotted a somewhat corpulent figure preparing to board the DC-3, dressed in a belted blue Molton overcoat, wearing a black Homburg and smoking a long cigar.

To the Nazis, the well set-up cigar-puffer looked very much like the Prime Minister. Could it

really be him? They knew Churchill was on his way back to Britain following the conclusion of a conference in North Africa. Had it been decided that he should fly on Flight 777?

What the Germans overlooked was that the smiling figure on the tarmac was younger and taller than Britain's wartime leader. In any event, they and their superiors were taking no chances. An urgent message was flashed through to the German High Command.

Above: *KLM DC-3s, leased to BOAC, photographed at their home base near Bristol. The DC-3 Howard boarded was a KLM place with an all-Dutch crew.*

THE FATAL FLIGHT

A few minutes after Flight 777 took to the air, eight Junkers Ju 88 C-6 long-range heavy fighters took off from the Luftwaffe airfield at Kerlin, to the west of Bordeaux. The planes belonged to the 5th Staffel (Squadron) of Kampfgeschwader 40, or V/KG 40 in its abbreviated form. The unit had been formed in September 1942, its primary task being to provide air cover for U-boats in the Bay of Biscay, which were coming under increasingly effective attack on their way to and from their North Atlantic

hunting-grounds by Mosquitoes, Beaufighters, Liberators and Sunderlands from the Coastal Command of the RAF.

According to Luftwaffe sources, Flight 777 was not targeted intentionally. Rather, the Junkers had been despatched to locate two U-boats in the Bay of Biscay and escort them to safety. Due to bad weather, the search for the U-boats was called off and instead the Junkers initiated a general search of the area.

At 12.45pm, the Junkers spotted Flight 777 heading north. Approximately five minutes later, they swept in to attack the aircraft. Oberleutnant Hans Hintze, one of the pilots involved, recalled what happened. 'A grey silhouette of a plane was spotted from 2,000 to 3,000 metres,' he told an interviewer decades later. 'No markings could be made out, but by the shape and construction of the plane it was obviously enemy.'

Oberleutnant Albrecht Bellstedt, leading the attack, radioed 'Indians at 11 o'clock AA,' Luftwaffe shorthand for enemy aircraft ahead, slightly to the left, attack, attack. Immediately, he and the pilot of another Junkers dived to strafe the DC-3 from above and below, setting the port engine and wing on fire. At that point, Hintze, at the head of the other Junkers, caught up with the airliner. Recognising that it was a civilian plane, he immediately ordered the attack to be aborted. It was too late. The mortally-wounded DC-3 crashed into the sea where it floated for a few minutes and then sank. There were no survivors.

Hintze's version of events was corroborated by Ben Rosevink, the son of Enghertus Rosevink, the Flight Engineer of the stricken DC-3 who perished with the rest of the plane's crew and its passengers. In the 1980s, Rosevink patiently tracked down the three surviving Luftwaffe pilots who had taken part in the attack and persuaded them to talk. He interviewed all three of them independently. None were aware that the others were even still alive.

'They said the plane came straight towards them and they attacked straight away because they knew Mosquitoes were patrolling the area,' Rosevink reported. 'They were a lot slower than Mosquitoes so it was either a case of getting in first or they got you. Once they realised it was a civilian plane, there was nothing they could do because it was already going down.'

Rosevink concluded: 'I sat with the commander of the group that took the planes out and he said there was no point in lying after all these years. He said if he was told to go and do it, he would say so – there was no reason not to. He said they came across it and that was that.'

HOW MUCH DID CHURCHILL KNOW?

That appeared to be that, but it still left some crucial questions unanswered. Why had Luftwaffe command not warned the Junkers pilots that a civilian airliner was in the vicinity and then told them not to attack it? Churchill, for one, had no doubts about who was responsible. In *The Hinge of Fate*, the fourth volume of his war memoirs, he wrote: 'As my presence in North Africa had been fully reported, the Germans were exceptionally vigilant, and this led to a tragedy which most distressed me.

'The regular commercial aircraft was about to start from the Lisbon airfield when a thickset man smoking a cigar walked up and was thought to be a passenger upon it. The German agents therefore signalled that I was on board. Although these passenger planes had plied unmolested for many months between Portugal and England, a German war plane was instantly ordered out, and the defenceless aircraft was ruthlessly shot down. Thirteen passengers perished, among them the well-known British actor Leslie Howard, whose grace and gifts are still preserved for us by the records of the many delightful films in which he took part.'

'The brutality of the Germans was only matched by the stupidity of their agents,' Churchill concluded. 'It is difficult to understand how anyone could imagine that with all the resources of Great Britain at my disposal I should have booked a passage in an unarmed and unescorted plane from Lisbon and flown home in broad daylight. We of course made a wide loop out by night from Gibraltar into the ocean and arrived home without incident.'

Churchill might have known more than he was telling. Although he was almost certainly unaware of them, there were rumours that British Intelligence had itself circulated the story that the Prime Minister might be flying back to Britain on the Lisbon plane. If true, this would have been a classic example of intelligence 'disinformation'. The premier almost certainly did know that Howard, with whom he was personally acquainted, was reluctant to go ahead with the Spanish part of the lecture tour, which was the ostensible reason for his trip. He had to be persuaded to do so by Antony Eden himself.

Howard, it appears, was depressed when he left Britain.

Violette Cunningham, his long-time mistress, had died six months previously from meningitis. Apparently, it was Chenhalls, who himself had to fly to Lisbon on business for the British Treasury, who suggested to Howard that a trip to sunny Iberia would do him good. The actor soon seems to have shaken off his depression. Despite being warned that she was a German spy, he started a headlong affair with a certain Baroness von Podewils, who was in charge of the beauty salon at his Madrid hotel.

Through the actress Conchita Montenegro, herself one of Howard's former mistresses, he apparently made contact with General Franco himself. According to Montenegro in an interview she gave shortly before her death in 2008, Howard had been tasked with trying to persuade the Spanish dictator to remain neutral and stay out of the war. If what Montenegro said was true and Howard was doubling up as a British spy, it would certainly have given the Germans sufficient cause to remove him from the scene. Whether they finally decided that shooting down Flight 777 was the best way of achieving this remains open to question.

Right & below: *Even equipped with drop tanks, the Spitfire did not have the range to escort inward-bound DC-3s over the Bay of Biscay. Luftwaffe Junkers Ju88s regularly patrolled the area, but there was a tacit understanding between the two sides that civilian aircraft were not to be attacked. Why Howard's plane was singled out remains a mystery.*

The Man Who Never Was

In spring 1943, the Western Allies debated what their next objective would be after their victory over the Axis armies in North Africa. The problem was, as Winston Churchill famously put it, 'everyone but a bloody fool would know it was Sicily.' Two backroom British Intelligence officers came up with a cunning plan to deceive Hitler into believing the attack would fall elsewhere. Operation Mincemeat, as it was christened, was the result.

Above: *Together with his colleague Charles Cholmondeley, Lieutenant-Commander Montagu fooled the Germans. Into believing the Allies were not planning to invade Sicily.*

At around 9.30am on the morning of 30 April 1943, a fisherman out trawling for sardines off a beach in Spain came across a waterlogged corpse drifting in the sea. He hauled the body onto his boat, headed for the beach and brought it ashore. The dead man was dressed in uniform, was wearing a life jacket and had a briefcase securely chained to his body. From his personal effects, he was identified by the Spanish authorities in nearby Huelva as William Martin, an acting major in the Royal Marines. The immediate supposition was that he was a British military courier who had drowned after an aircraft flying him to Gibraltar had crashed into the sea.

News of the body's discovery was reported to the British Embassy in Madrid, but not before Adolf Clauss, the local Abwehr agent, had been informed. He quickly passed on the information to his own superiors. In the meantime, because of the heat and the state of the body, which was starting to show the effects of decomposition, the Spanish organised a hasty medical examination. It was concluded that Martin had indeed drowned. Two days later, he was buried in the city cemetery. The briefcase and Martin's personal effects were sent for safe-keeping to naval headquarters in the Spanish capital. The navy passed them on to the Spanish General Staff.

The plot then thickened. The British pressed for the immediate return of the briefcase. The Spanish eventually obliged, but, in the meantime, the Abwehr had got its hands on the briefcase's contents and hastily photographed them. It also examined the personal effects. Once the photographs had been taken, the documents the briefcase contained were carefully reinserted in their original envelopes, re-sealed and the briefcase returned to the

Spanish to hand back to the British apparently untouched.

The contents included two highly-important letters – one from General Sir Archibald Nye, Deputy Chief of the Imperial General Staff to General Sir Harold Alexander, the commander-in-chief of British forces in North Africa, and another from Lord Louis Mountbatten, head of Combined Operations, to Admiral Sir Andrew Cunningham, commander-in-chief of the Mediterranean Fleet. They exposed a vital military secret. The Allies intended to strike in Greece and simultaneously capture the island of Sardinia. They had no plans to invade Sicily at all. Any attack there would be simply a decoy or feint.

'HOOK, LINE AND SINKER'
The German Embassy in Madrid radioed the contents of the letters to Berlin and rushed the photographs to OKW headquarters, where they were examined by Admiral Wilhelm Canaris, the head of the Abwehr, Hitler's top military commanders and by the Fuehrer himself. Initially, at least, he questioned whether Martin's corpse might be an Allied plant, but was soon convinced that he had been a genuine courier. It followed logically that the information in the letters in the

briefcase must also be correct.

Hitler acted immediately. On 12 May, he reorganised German defensive priorities throughout the Mediterranean. 'Measures regarding Sardinia and the Peloponnese,' he ordered, 'take precedence over everything else'. Three panzer divisions – one from France and two from the Eastern Front – were rushed to Greece and Rommel despatched to take over command of German forces in the region. Mussolini's protests that Sicily remained the obvious Allied target were dismissed out of hand. General Alfred Jodl, the Wehrmacht's head of operations, was overheard bellowing down the telephone to the German military attaché in Rome 'You can forget about Sicily. We know it is Greece.' More and more troops and military equipment were hastily shifted to be ready to meet and beat the Allied invading forces when they attempted to land.

The British, for their part, were carefully examining the briefcase and its contents to see if they had been tampered with. Despite all the precautions the Abwehr had taken, they soon discovered that this, indeed, had been the case. Instead of being thrown into a state of panic, the opposite was the case. The whole

Left: *The submarine Seraph transported the dead body of 'The Man Who Never Was' secretly to the Spanish coast, where he and his vital briefcase were carefully dumped undetected in the water.*

thing had been an elaborate fake. Hitler had reacted just as British Intelligence had hoped. Churchill, who had been in on the plan, was immediately signalled: 'Mincemeat (the codename for the operation) swallowed hook, line and sinker.' He, too, was overjoyed. Planning for the invasion of Sicily went full steam ahead. As for the supposed Major Martin, he had never existed. He was truly 'the man who never was.'

MINCEMEAT'S GENESIS

Who in British Intelligence had the idea for the great deception is still uncertain. Some say that Ian Fleming, then serving in Naval Intelligence and later to win literary fame as the creator of James Bond, had the inspiration, but this seems unlikely. The real credit for what military historian Professor Michael Howard later labelled 'the most successful

strategic deception in the history of warfare' was down to two men – Lieutenant-Commander Ewen Montagu, a peacetime barrister now turned Naval Intelligence officer, and Flight Lieutenant Charles Cholmondeley, a bespectacled 25-year-old RAF officer attached to MI5.

The story started in late 1942, when Cholmondeley, backed by Montagu, put up a scheme to plant a corpse carrying false documentation somewhere on neutral territory to mislead the Germans as to future Allied plans in the Mediterranean theatre of war. Spain, riddled with pro-Nazi sympathisers, seemed the natural choice. The idea, indeed, might have been sparked by an incident that had taken place there some time before. That September, a few weeks before Operation Torch, the Allied invasion of French North

Africa, was launched, a British Catalina flying boat crashed into the sea off Cadiz. The body of a passenger killed in the accident and carrying a letter giving the date for the projected landings was recovered by the Spanish authorities. They passed the information on to the Germans, who for whatever reason chose to ignore it. If a fake accident could be staged, Cholmondeley and Montagu argued, the enemy this time would be far more likely to act on such information.

Cholmondeley and Montagu called the plan Operation Trojan Horse; it was rechristened Operation Mincemeat at a later date, by which time Montagu had taken over the detailed planning. At the end of March 1943, he had been given the official go-ahead and was ready to proceed. The operational order he drew up read as follows:

OPERATION MINCEMEAT

1. OBJECT

To cause a briefcase containing documents to drift ashore as near as possible to HUELVA in Spain in such circumstances that it will be thought to have been washed ashore from an aircraft which crashed at sea when the case was being taken by an officer from the UK to Allied Forces HQ in North Africa.

2. METHOD

A dead body dressed in the battle-dress uniform of a Major, Royal Marines, and wearing a 'Mae West', will be taken out in a submarine, together with the briefcase and a rubber dingy.

  The body will be packed fully clothed and ready (and wrapped in a blanket to prevent friction) in a tubular airtight container (which will be labelled as 'Optical Instruments').
The container is just under 6 feet 6 inches long and just under two feet in diameter and has no excrescences of any kind on the sides. The end which opens has a flush-fitting lid which is held tightly in position by a number of nuts and has fitted on its exterior in clips a box-spanner with a permanent Tommy-bar which is chained to the lid.

  Both ends are fitted with handles which fold down flat. It will be possible to lift the container by using both handles or even by using the handle in the lid alone, but it would be better not to take the whole weight on the handle at the other end, as the steel of which the container is made is of light gauge to keep the weight as low as possible. The approximate weight when the container is full will be 400lb.
When the container is closed the body will be packed round with a certain amount of dry ice. The container should therefore be opened on deck, as the dry ice will give off carbon dioxide.

3. POSITION

The body should be put into the water as close to the shore as prudently possible and as near to HUELVA as possible, preferably to the northwest of the river mouth.

  According to the Hydrographical Department, the tides in that area run mainly up and down the coast, and every effort should therefore be made to choose a period with an onshore wind. Southwesterly winds are, in fact, the prevailing winds in that area at this time of year.

The latest information about the tidal streams in that area, as obtained from the Superintendent of Tides, is attached.

4. DELIVERY OF THE PACKAGE

The package will be brought up to the port of departure by road on whatever day is desired, preferably as close to the sailing day as possible. The briefcase will be handed over at the same time to the Captain of the submarine. The rubber dingy will also be a separate parcel.

5. DISPOSAL OF THE BODY

When the body is removed from the container all that will be necessary will be to fasten the chain attached to the briefcase through the belt of the trench coat, which will be the outer garment on the body. The chain is of the type worn under the coat, round the chest and out through the sleeve. At the end is a 'dog-lead' type of clip for attaching to the handle of the briefcase and a similar clip for forming the loop round the chest. It is this loop that should be made through the belt of the trench coat as if the officer had slipped the chain off for comfort in the aircraft, but has nevertheless kept it attached to him so that the bag should not either be forgotten or slide away from him in aircraft.

The body should then be deposited in the water, as should also be the rubber dingy. As this should drift at a different speed from the body, the exact position at which it is released is unimportant, but it should be near the body, but not too near if that is possible.

6. THOSE IN THE KNOW IN GIBRALTAR

Steps have been taken to inform F.O.I.C.1 Gibraltar and his S.O. (I).2. No one else there will be in the picture.

7. SIGNALS

If the operation is successfully carried out, a signal should be made 'MINCEMEAT completed'. If that is made from Gibraltar the S.O. (I). should be asked to send it addressed to D.N.I.3 (PERSONAL). If it can be made earlier it should be made in accordance with order from F.O.S.4.

8. CANCELLATION

If the operation has to be cancelled a signal will be made 'Cancel MINCEMEAT'. In that case the body and container should be sunk in deep water. As the container may have buoyancy, it may either have to be weighted or water may have to be allowed to enter. In the latter case care must be taken that the body does not escape. The briefcase should be handed to the S.O. (I) at Gibraltar, with instructions to burn the contents unopened, if there is no possibility of taking that course earlier. The rubber dingy should be handed to the S.O. (I) for disposal.

1. Flag Officer in Charge
2. Staff Officer, Intelligence
3. Director of Naval Intelligence
4. Flag Officer, Submarines (Admiral Barry)

9. ABANDONMENT

If the operation has to be abandoned, a signal should be made 'MINCEMEAT abandoned' as soon as possible (see Para 7 above).

10. COVER

This is a matter for consideration. Until the operation actually takes place, it is thought that the labelling of the container 'Optical Instruments' will provide sufficient cover. It is suggested that the cover after the operation has been completed should be that it is hoped to trap a very active German agent in this neighbourhood, and it is hoped that sufficient evidence can be obtained by this means to get the Spaniards to eject him. The importance of dealing with this man should be impressed on the crew, together with the fact that any leakage that may *ever* take place will compromise our power to get the Spaniards to act in such cases; also that they will never learn whether we were successful in this objective, as the whole matter will have to be conducted in secrecy with the Spaniards or we won't be able to get them to act.

It is in fact most important that the Germans and Spaniards should accept these papers in accordance with Para I. If they should suspect that the papers are a 'plant', it might have far-reaching consequences of great magnitude.

(Signed) *E.E.S. Montagu*
Lt.-Cdr., R.N.V.R.
31.3.43.

WHOSE BODY?

Faking the documentation and giving the corpse an identity was easy enough. General Nye himself wrote the final draft of the key letter in the briefcase, while British Intelligence gathered together an imposing assortment of personal effects to bring Major William Martin – the name chosen for 'the man who never was' – to life. As well as a Marine identity card, these included four other letters – one from Martin's father, two from his fiancée and the fourth from the family solicitor – a snapshot of his fiancée (the picture was actually of a female clerk in MI5), a bill from a leading London jeweller for an engagement ring and another

from his club, two theatre ticket stubs and a used bus ticket. There was even a demand from Martin's bank manager for the repayment of his overdraft.

It was left to Montagu to find a suitable body. He started by consulting Sir Bernard Spilsbury, the most celebrated forensic pathologist of the day. Spilsbury assured him that, because people perished in air crashes for many reasons, it was not essential to find a corpse that had died by drowning. Montagu then turned to William Bentley Purchase, the coroner for the St Pancras district of London, to help him in his macabre quest. Albeit somewhat reluctantly,

EINSATZ
DER DEUTSCHEN KRIEGSMARINE

Left: *Hitler and Franco meet. Montagu chose pro-Nazi Spain as the best place to plant his dead body. He counted on the Spanish giving the Germans access to the documents in the corpse's briefcase.*

Below: *A German Panzer Mk IV prowls the streets of Athens. Operation Mincemeat worked like a charm. When the Allies landed in Sicily, they took the island's defenders totally by surprise.*

Right: *This Abwehr radio operator is busy receiving a message from Spain to Berlin. Just as Montagu had hoped, the warning that Greece, not Sicily, was to be the Allies' target was forwarded directly to the Führer.*

Purchase produced a suitable body – or so Montagu said.

For the rest of his life – he died in 1985 – Montagu kept the true identity of the corpse he obtained a secret. Speculation as to who it really was has continued to the present day. In 2003, former police officer Colin Gibbon claimed that William Martin was in fact Tom Martin, a sailor on the escort carrier *Dasher* who perished as a result of a massive internal explosion on the ship just off the coast of Scotland in March 1943. Montagu, so it was alleged, abstracted the body of the other Martin before it could

be buried in a mass grave with the other victims of the explosion. The following year, John Melville, one of Tom Martin's fellow sailors, was publicly named by a Royal Navy officer as 'the man who never was'.

In 2011, Professor Denis Smyth, a Toronto University historian, came up with fresh evidence that seemed to confirm Montagu's body was indeed procured for him by the St Pancras coroner. It was, said Smyth, definitely that of Glyndwr Michael, a 34-year-old alcoholic Welsh vagrant who committed suicide in London in January 1943. Smyth had

unearthed a hitherto overlooked secret memorandum written by Montagu in which he stated that the rat poison Michael had swallowed would be undetectable in a post-mortem and that therefore the Spanish – and the Germans – would never establish the real cause of death.

Supporters of the *Dasher* theory remain unconvinced. They argue that the body of an alcoholic could never have passed as that of a smart Royal Marine officer. Only Montagu knew the real truth – and he took it with him to his grave.

Disaster in Bombay

On April 14, 1944, the city of Bombay was rocked by two massive explosions. They were triggered by a fire, which had been raging unchecked for several hours, on a cargo ship in its bustling harbor. Next day, Japanese-controled Radio Saigon broadcast a full account of the disaster, while, in India, the censorship tried to keep the whole matter under wraps. Was the disaster caused by sabotage? Or was it an avoidable accident?

Left: *A RAF Dakota drops supplies to troops in the jungle. Air drops like this helped the besieged garrisons at Imphal and Kohima hold out against the Japanese.*

Opposite: *A Hawker Hurricane strafes Japanese troops in Burma. The one thing 14th Army could count on was air superiority.*

Early in 1944, though the tide of war had begun to turn decisively against the Japanese in the Pacific, their forces still remained in control of the whole of Burma. They were now planning a major push forward that would take them across the Burmese frontier and on into India. If they succeeded, there would be little to stop them from advancing swiftly across the fertile plains of Bengal, with the port of Calcutta as the ultimate prize.

The offensive began in March 1944, its initial targets being Imphal and Kohima, two defensive strongpoints in the foothills of Assam. The defenders were soon cut off and surrounded. The Japanese had calculated

that the onset of the monsoon would effectively put an end to Allied attempts at counter-attack, but General William Slim, the commander of the 14th Army, threw reinforcements into battle to relieve the hard-pressed garrisons. British and Indian troops finally broke through to Kohima on 18 April. Imphal, which had come under siege on 5 April, was relieved in mid-May. The Japanese fell back in confusion. Their attempt to thrust into India was over.

FIRE IN THE HARBOUR
During these crucial battles, the British relied heavily on a continuing flow of supplies though the vital port of Bombay

(present-day Mumbai) on the west coast of India. Military stores of all kinds would be unloaded from merchant ships there, and then shipped across India by rail or air.

On 14 April 1944, the port was jam-packed with merchant vessels of every description. Among them was the SS *Fort Stikine*, a 7,142-ton freighter. She had sailed from Birkenhead on 24 February and had steamed via Gibraltar, Port Said, the Suez Canal and Karachi to berth at her final destination two days earlier. For reasons of wartime security, she docked without flying the customary red flag to indicate there were high explosives on board. There were 1,395 tons of them, including 300 tons of TNT, together with 12

Above left: *A shipment of railway locomotives bound for India, where they were vital for hauling supplies across the subcontinent.*

Above right: *Troops board a Dakota to reinforce the garrison at Imphal, which held out stubbornly against the Japanese until the 14th Army could relieve it.*

crated-up Spitfires, timber, scrap iron and $4,293,500 worth of gold bullion. At Karachi, she had taken on in addition 87,000 bales of cotton and a thousand drums of lubricating oil. Some of the latter appeared to be leaky, James Naismith, the ship's captain, vainly protested about being forced to carry such a mixed cargo. It contained 'just about everything that will either burn or blow up,' he complained. His complaints were ignored.

At about 12.30pm that Friday afternoon, the stevedores who been labouring through the night to unload the ship's cargo, came back to resume work after breaking for lunch. As they boarded Fort Stikine, again someone – most probably Mohamed Tagi, the foreman in charge of the stevedores working in No. 2 hold – spotted smoke rising from it on the side nearest the quay and raised the alarm. As swarms of dock workers poured off the stricken vessel, Alex Gow, the ship's Chief Engineer, started its fire pump and the deck crew ran out hoses to the spot where

smoke could now be clearly seen rising from the ship's ventilators. They began to pump water into the hold, joined by the crew from the fire engine stationed on the quay alongside the ship.

Thanks to a breakdown in communication, it took another hour to alert Fire Brigade headquarters to the exact location of the outbreak. Nor were the fire-fighters warned that Fort Stikine had high explosives on board. Complacency may also have contributed to the scale and slowness of the reaction.

Fires were not uncommon in the Bombay docks – 60 of them had broken out between 1939 and 1944. Consequently, only two more fire engines and 60 firemen were despatched to fight the blaze. No general alarm was raised and the docks were not evacuated. Instead, the stevedores were ordered back to work to continue with the unloading of the ship.

STENCH AND SMOKE
Among the cargo carried by Fort Stikine were considerable quantities of fish manure. For

some reason, possibly because it had begun to stink appallingly as the heat of the fire grew in intensity, the stevedores were ordered to unload this part of the cargo first. For the time being, the potentially lethal high explosives were left untouched.

By this time, the fire-fighters had discovered where the fire had begun. The blaze had started among the bales of highly combustible cotton which the ship had taken on board at Karachi. Crates of shells and small-arms ammunition were stacked

directly below the bales, while masses of timber lay on top of them. The upper part of the hold also contained the rest of the high explosives. Belatedly, Fire Brigade headquarters were now advised of their presence.

Immediately, all available pumps were rushed to the scene, but, by this time, the fire was in danger of getting out of control. Captain Brinley Thomas Oberst, an army ordnance officer who had been summoned to the dockside while finishing his lunch in his Colaha apartment, went below to check on the high explosives. He returned grim-faced to report to Naismith. He told the captain that Fort Stikine ought to be scuttled at once.

There was an immediate problem. There was just four feet of water between the keel of the berthed ship and the bed of the harbour. Even if her crew did try to scuttle her, she would not take on enough water to flood even the lower part of the affected hold. The only other option was to take her out to sea and scuttle her there. Because engineers were already at work repairing a valve on the main engine, Fort Stikine was immovable except by tug. It would have taken quite some time to get tugs into position to tow her out of the harbour – and time, of course, was something the fire-fighters did not have on their side.

THE FIRST EXPLOSION

There followed nearly an hour of indecision, muddle and confusion.

More and more fire engines and their crews arrived on the scene as the unequal battle continued against the heat, smoke and flames. They were joined by Norman Combs, the head of the Bombay Fire Brigade. The rattle of exploding small-arms ammunition was heard on board and the water the firemen were standing in started to boil.

The battle to save Fort Stikine was lost. As Combs shouted to his firemen to 'get clear', Naismith ordered his crew to abandon ship. Some of the firemen jumped onto the jetty, while others, including Combs himself, leapt overboard into the water. On Belray, a Norwegian freighter anchored close by Fort Stikine, Roy Hayward, a young Able Seaman,

Left: *A Dakota drops much needed supplies of food and ammunition to the troops on the ground. The Japanese had no such aerial back-up.*

saw the rising flames suddenly turn yellowish-brown. Hayward had fought fires before in the London Blitz. He knew what the change in colour meant. It was caused by burning explosives. He shouted a warning, although it is doubtful whether anyone heard him, and threw himself down flat on the deck.

Moments later, a pillar of fire soared upwards from Fort Stikine and a terrific explosion echoed throughout the docks and the city. It was precisely 4.06pm. The force of the blast was channelled horizontally through the ship's side, sweeping across the quay to obliterate the sheds and warehouses to landward. Jagged metal fragments scythed outwards like a blast from a huge shotgun, cutting down anything and everything in their path.

Just before the explosion, Naismith had returned to his ship to check that everyone had got off her safely. He retraced his steps down the gangplank and started to walk along the quayside to where his First Mate and a marine surveyor from the Bombay office of Lloyds were standing. Then the explosives detonated. The surveyor was blown yards down the quay and rendered unconscious. When he came round, he found that every stitch of clothing had been stripped from his body to leave him totally naked. Miraculously, he was otherwise unharmed. No trace of Naismith or the First Mate was ever found.

Oberst, too, was flung up into the air by the force of the blast, landing in a pile of dunnage. As he surveyed the scene, he could see bodies lying all around him, most with their skin burnt off. 66 of them were firemen who had been killed out rightly; 83 more were badly injured.

A BIGGER BLAST
Derek P. Ings, the Assistant Purser of *Chantilly*, which was moored in a nearby dock, recalled his own experiences some years later.

'I remember going ashore during the afternoon for a haircut. On the return to the ship at about 4.15pm, I was walking along a road just inside Alexandra Dock from Green Gate when I became conscious that smoke and flames were shooting high into the sky in the distance immediately in front of me. Before I could fully realise what was happening the ground around was shaken by a tremendous explosion which made me step back a pace or two and raise my hands as though to protect myself.

'My next recollection is of the surrounding confusion as the people in the dock area took to their heels in no uncertain manner. I made my way to *Chantilly*, which was lying on the outer wall of Alexandra Dock. I expected that a nearby tanker had exploded, but, as I neared the berth, I could see that the explosion had taken place further away than I had thought, and in fact it was in Victoria Dock.

'All the while there were minor explosions but at approximately 4.45pm there was another explosion as violent, if not more so, than the first. By this time I was back on board and the whole ship shook as though hit by a torpedo. A number of windows, window frames and door locks were shattered and shrapnel from the explosion, about three-quarters of a mile away, fell on and around the ship.'

The second explosion was indeed bigger and even more destructive than the first. A huge column of flame and smoke tore through the shattered remains of Fort Stikine and shot up to a height of several thousand feet, flinging tons of metal – including some of the gold bullion Fort Stikine had been carrying – into the harbour area and the adjacent town. Flaming cotton, sulphur and resin cascaded into warehouses and residential homes over a radius of more than half a mile, setting them a flame so that the docks were ringed by fire. Ings continued his story:

'I had to return ashore shortly afterwards and, passing through the dock area, found abandoned vehicles and dhows at many points, some of the dhows in the stream with their cargoes of cotton ablaze. My journey took me through Green Gate and along Ballard Road to St George's Hospital where I intended visiting a shipmate. It was now an hour after the first explosion and all the shops, stalls and eating places had closed. Many of the windows of offices and shops had been blown out and glass and roof tiles were strewn everywhere.

'I reached the hospital at about 5.30 p.m.; passing a dead gharry horse lying at the entrance. My friend had been put out of his bed to make room for the injured that were arriving by ambulance in a very dirty and bedraggled condition. Mattresses were being put down all over the ground floor to treat the casualties.

'On my way back to the ship I could see Royal Indian Navy sailors being sent by lorry to fight the fire at Victoria Dock, the pall of smoke from which hung like a cloud over the whole of the city. The police had now closed Red Gate and I had to walk round to Green Gate to get back into the docks. On the way and only a few yards from Mackinnons' office, I came upon a piece of twisted steel plate about 12 inches by six inches which had been blown over a mile by the explosion to land harmlessly in the road.

'As I neared the ship I saw some of the crew leaving hurriedly and found that another explosion (of 1,200 cylinders of H.P. gas) was expected at any time and we were warned to keep off the decks. The earlier explosions had flung incendiary bombs over a wide area and small fires were burning everywhere. There were now 30 burning dhows in the stream and, as they sank, their cargoes of cotton still smouldered on the surface. The ships on the harbour wall, including ourselves and Mantola, put down boats to rescue the dhow crews.

'Darkness fell and the night sky reflected the blazing parts of the city. I watched from the monkey island and could hear the hiss of the cylinders as they ignited one by one. I turned in at 11.00pm to the sound of the occasional explosion of gas cylinders and with a burning dhow outside my porthole.'

Left: Chantilly *was one of the other merchantmen in Bombay harbour made a casualty when* Fort Stikine *blew up.*

Left: *A fragment of Fort Stikine's propeller is still preserved where it landed after the explosion.*

Right: *General Sir William Slim (later Lord Slim) was commander of the 14th Army in Burma. Because of the lack of press coverage they received, his men referred to themselves as 'the forgotten army'.*

AFTERMATH

In St George's Hospital, 200 victims of the explosions required surgery, while nearly 200 more were treated for less serious injuries. No one was ever able to establish what the final death toll was, as many victims simply disappeared in the blasts. Some sources put it as high as 1,200.

For days, thousands of soldiers and sailors laboured to remove explosives to places from the shattered dock area. They put their own lives at serious risk, for ammunition was constantly exploding in the remains of blazing warehouses. 16 ships, many of them with explosives on board, had to be towed out into the open sea that night and during the following day.

The destruction inside the docks was frightful. No fewer than 27 ships had been sunk, gutted by fire or severely damaged and all the dockyard buildings had been devastated. Three swing bridges at the entrance to the docks had been partly torn from their seatings and leaned at drunken angles. It would take 10,000 British and Indian servicemen and civilians six months to clear away the wreckage and get the harbour in full working order again. In the meantime, the scale of the destruction was kept as secret as possible, thanks in the main to the strict censorship that was imposed.

What caused the fire has never been established. Many at the time suspected it was the result of deliberate sabotage. Certainly, there were a number of pro-Japanese factions active in India at the time and, with the Japanese Army knocking at India's back door, the British authorities were battling with growing civil unrest and active attempts to impede the Allied war effort. Others believed it was caused by something as simple as a carelessly discarded cigarette. The truth remains a mystery that will probably never be solved.

The Death Train

On the night of 3 March 1944, a heavily overloaded freight train stalled inside the Armi tunnel outside the hillside village of Balvano between Salerno and Potenza in southern Italy. Instead of backing the train out of the tunnel to safety, the drivers of the two steam engines hauling it unavailingly tried to force their way forwards. The black clouds of smoke the effort produced were full of deadly carbon monoxide gas. The result was disaster on an epic scale.

Like dozens of other villages scattered throughout the Apennine Mountains of central and southern Italy, Balvano, which lies beside a twisting mountain road between Salerno and Potenza, is picturesque, though otherwise unremarkable. The one odd thing about it is its cemetery, which is larger than most.

Closer inspection, however, reveals a horrifying fact. The cemetery contains three mass graves, the last resting place of some 600 people. All of them died in mysterious circumstances in the same place at the same time – in the early hours of 3 March 1944.

A BLEAK WINTER

Following Italy's capitulation and their landings on the Italian mainland in September 1943, the Allies, after bitter fighting throughout the winter, had succeeded in driving Field Marshal Kesselring's German forces back to new defensive positions halfway up the peninsula. Despite all their efforts, the Allies had not yet managed to break through the so-called Gustav Line; particularly

Above: *An RAF Martin Baltimore bomber attacks enemy rail communications during the battle for Italy. Blocking rail tunnels was a primary objective.*

Opposite: *For the Germans, keeping supply trains like this one running smoothly was vital. They lacked the fuel to rely on motorised transport.*

bitter fighting was in progress at a place called Monte Cassino.

In the south, the Allied occupation forces were trying hard to restore order, rebuild shattered communications and ensure a regular supply of foodstuffs and other essentials to the local

people, many of whom had been forced to live virtually at starvation level during the peculiarly severe winter. The authorities had to content with a flourishing black market centred on Naples, where men, women and even children bargained and bartered with Allied soldiers for cigarettes, chocolate, sweets and chewing gum,. All of these could be swapped in the countryside for eggs, poultry, butter, meat and other dairy products. Consequently, every goods train that ran to and from the city was regularly crammed with hundreds of stowaway black marketers.

Getting on board the trains for free at various places along the tracks presented few problems. The trains, their locomotives fuelled by inferior wartime coal, could only move at walking pace through the mountains, especially when they hit a steep gradient. The black marketers knew exactly where to wait and then jump on board. If they were ejected by military police or Italian carabiniere at a station stop, they simply walked up the tracks and scrambled on board again once the trains were clear of the station.

PRELUDE TO DISASTER

Train No. 8017 crawled out of Salerno just after 6.00pm on the evening of 2 March. Running between the city and Potenza every Thursday night, it was always packed with illicit travellers – a fact that had earned it the nickname of the Black Market Express. Normally, it would have been hauled by an electric locomotive, but, as the overhead power lines of the electrification system had been damaged, a steam locomotive had to be substituted on this occasion.

The train consisted of 47 wagons, about 20 of them open box-cars or flat cars. Although as a freight train it was not supposed to carry passengers, it was common at the time for both soldiers and civilians to hitch rides on any convenient train. As it rattled into the mountains, about halfway into its journey, it had already picked up about 600 illegal passengers as well as between 100 and 200 legitimate ones. High in the mountains, about 30 miles from Potenza, its final destination, it stopped at Romagnano so that

a second locomotive could be attached to help the overloaded train cope with the even stiffer climb that lay ahead.

After some delay, the train left Romagnano, churning its way slowly up a steep gradient. After only four miles, however, it was forced to a halt with half its length inside a long mountain tunnel not far from the village of Balvano. The locomotive of the train ahead of it was suffering from a mechanical fault and was blocking the line.

It was nearly three-quarters of an hour before Train No. 8017 was cleared to move forwards again. Most of its passengers had not noticed the delay – they were asleep. By this time it was just a few minutes before 1.00am.

Balvano rail halt was half a mile beyond the tunnel. The train stopped there so that

the locomotives could take on more water and then struggled laboriously onwards up the ever-steepening gradient. As it left the station, Giuseppe Salonia, the assistant station-master, telegraphed to Bella-Muro, the next station up the line, to signal that it was on the move and then watched it disappear towards the next tunnel, a narrow single-track mile-long cut through the mountains called the Galleria delle Armi. He then went indoors to the warmth of his stove and settled down to read his newspaper in peace. The next train was not scheduled for another hour.

DEATH INSIDE THE TUNNEL

The distance between Balvano and Bella-Muro was less than five

Right: *Two RAF Spitfires on patrol in the Apennines. Italy's rugged mountain ranges made long rail tunnels inevitable. They also provided the Germans with great natural defensive positions.*

Opposite: *British troops tramp through the streets of Salerno. They faced a long, hard slog northwards as the Germans fought for every inch of Italian territory.*

miles – a run of about 20 minutes or at the speed Train No. 8017 was travelling. It never arrived. In fact, it never emerged from the far end of the Galleria della Armi.

At Bella-Muro, the station-master was curious about the non-arrival, but put it down to simple lateness. At Balvano, however, Salonia grew anxious as the time passed. He had not received the customary message from Bella-Muro to say that the train had arrived. The only thing he heard was that it was running late and that he was to hold the next train in the station until he received word that the line was cleared.

When the train arrived at about 2.40am, Salonia ordered its locomotive to be detached so that he could steam up the line to see if he could find out what was going on. Almost immediately after the locomotive had started off, he spotted a man by the side of the track, shouting and swinging a red lantern wildly. As Salonia dropped down off the footplate, the man collapsed. He murmured to Salonia: 'They're all dead.'

Salonia was baffled. The night was still. If there had been a crash or derailment, he would certainly have heard the noised. By now, the man was crying bitterly. Salonia decided to take him back to the

Above: *General Mark Clark commanded the US 5th Army in Italy. A military prima donna, he was determined his troops should be first to reach Rome.*

station and try to coax what had happened out of him.

THE BRAKEMAN'S TALE

The man turned out to be Michele Palo, the brakeman of Train No. 8017. He described how the train had suddenly shuddered to a halt after entering the curving mile-long tunnel. With the exception of his brake van and three freight cars at the rear, the entire train was stuck inside. No whistle sounded from either engine to indicate that there was anything wrong, so Palo assumed they must have stopped at a red signal. He fell into a fitful doze.

Suddenly Palo woke up and popped his head out of the window of his brake van to see if he could tell why the train

was still not on the move. He could see nothing untoward, so he jumped down onto the permanent way and started up the tunnel to investigate further. As soon as he came across some dead bodies, he turned on his heels and hurried back down the line towards Balvano.

Having listened horror-struck to Palo's grisly story, Salonia set off again on the borrowed locomotive. It was nearly 4.00am before he reached the tunnel and Train No. 8017. He climbed down from his locomotive and made his way up the track to the first carriage he could see. He slid one of its doors open and shone his lantern inside. The passengers were sprawled across their seats and on the floor. All were dead. Salonia checked the rest of the train. It was the same story. Dozens of corpses lay beside the track as well. He hastened back to Balvano to raise the alarm.

Police, railway officials and US Army troops soon arrived on the scene. They brought the locomotive into the tunnel and hooked it up to Palo's brake van. Releasing No. 8017's brakes, they towed the stricken train slowly back to the station at Balvano. It was there that the full extent of the horror was revealed.

Above: *US staff officers confer at Salerno. The landings on this beach were relatively unopposed. But it was a different story elsewhere.*

Right: *US troops go ashore. Operation Avalanche got off to a good start, but the Americans soon faced fierce resistance. The 16th Panzers were ordered to drive them back into the sea.*

Left: *The British battleship* Warspite, *flagship of the Mediterranean fleet, readies itself to take part in the preliminary bombardment at Salerno.*

Right: *U.S. transport going ashore. Initially, only three Allied divisions took part in the Salerno invasion, landing on two beaches 10 miles (16 km) apart.*

GRISLY AFTERMATH

The entire train was choked with dead bodies. They appeared to have died quietly, with no signs of struggle. A US Army officer noted: 'The faces of the victims were mostly peaceful. They showed no signs of suffering. Many of them were sitting upright or in positions they might assume when sleeping normally.' There were apparently only five survivors in all. Three of them were rushed to hospital in the military vehicles that had raced to the scene of the disaster from Potenza. They had been fortunate enough to have been in the last three freight cars – the ones closest to the fresh air outside the long tunnel.

Another survivor was an olive-oil salesman, who had left the train for a few minutes to get a breath of fresh air while it was stopped at Balvano. Perhaps because of this, he was one of the few passengers who failed to drop off to sleep. After the train stopped in the tunnel, something made him start to cough violently, so he wrapped his scarf over his mouth. Then he climbed down from the train and began to pick his way unsteadily down the tunnel. He tried to climb into the train again, but collapsed by the side of the tracks. There, he was eventually discovered by two policemen, who assumed, like the rest of the victims, he was dead. He came round in the makeshift mortuary that had been set up in the station at Balvano. A second died as a result of brain damage shortly after his rescue.

WHAT CAUSED THE DISASTER?

Exactly what happened inside the tunnel will never be known since the drivers and footplatemen of both locomotives lost their lives. The survivors – the other three disappeared after being given first aid, probably to avoid police questioning – had little or no recollection of the incident, although either one or two of them thought that the train had started to slide backwards for some little distance before finally coming to a halt.

The likeliest explanation of the catastrophe was that when the locomotives reached the middle of the tunnel, they could no longer develop sufficient power to pull the overloaded train further forward. Instead, they began to lose traction, causing the whole train to start to slip backwards on the already-icy rails. At that moment, conflicting actions by the two drivers effectively sealed the fate of the hundreds of people on board.

When railway accident investigators first climbed onto the two locomotives while they were still in the tunnel, they found an extraordinary thing. Whereas the leading locomotive's controls were set in reverse with its brakes full off, the second one had its brakes full on and its throttle set at full ahead. The two drivers, each with his own idea of how to extricate the train from its predicament and get it on the move again, had acted independently of one another and, in so doing, had succeeded only in rendering it completely immobile.

Smoke and toxic gases – mostly carbon monoxide – pouring back down through the tunnel from the locomotives' smoke stacks had done the rest. Most of the passengers must have died in their sleep, never realising what was happening to them. The lucky ones were, like the olive-oil salesman, in the part of the train in the rearward part of the tunnel, where the air was not yet starved of oxygen. When the fumes reached them, they wakened, coughing and fighting for breath. Just five staggered out into the clean air. The rest perished alongside the train on the track. The final death toll was never precisely established, but stood between 500 and 600.

KEEPING IT QUIET

The really curious aspect of this terrible tragedy was that there does not appear to have been a searching investigation into its cause. The Americans did order a Board of Enquiry, which swiftly reached a conclusion. The five US Army officers who sat on it concluded that the disaster was 'an act of God.' Nor were questions asked as to if anything similar had ever happened before.

In fact, it had, though neither the Italian nor the Allied authorities were aware of it. Exactly three months earlier on 3 January 1944, between 500 and 800

people had died from asphyxiation as a result of the fire that broke out after three trains collided in the Torro tunnel near the village of Torre del Bierzo in Spain. The accident happened when the brakes of the Galicia Express from Madrid to Corunna failed. The runaway collided with the rear of a freight train that was already in the tunnel. Minutes later, an oncoming coal train ploughed into the wreckage. The resulting fire took two days to extinguish.

The incident was hushed up at the time on the orders of General Franco, the Spanish dictator. Details of it began to emerge only years after the war. A similar news black-out was imposed after the Italian train disaster. Both the Italian and Allied authorities

judged that allowing it to be reported fully might severely dent civilian morale. There may also have been another more sinister reason – to protect those who had authorised the purchase of cheaper low-grade coal on the railways in an effort to get around wartime shortages.

After the incident, the Italian railway authorities streamlined the procedure for the movement of trains through the mountain tunnels and established new safeguards to prevent such a disaster ever occurring again. For the bereaved families of the victims, however, it was all too little and too late.

In 1951, 300 lawsuits alleging 'manslaughter through negligence' were filed against the Italian state

railways by relatives of the victims. The decision to allow the use of sub-standard coal was cited in support of the accusation. The claimants demanded more than a billion lire in compensation. The lawyers for the railways successfully argued that the relatives were not entitled to claim compensation because none of the dead had paid for their tickets. Magnanimously, it was agreed to compensate the families of the dead train crews.

Above: *Spitfires on patrol over Sicily. Forced to fly from bases on the mainland, the Luftwaffe was conspicuously absent for much of the campaign.*

Above: *General Sir Bernard Montgomery commanded the 8th Army in Sicily and Italy until he was transferred to command the ground forces in the D-Day landings.*

The Submarine that Sank Itself

*On 24 October 1944, USS **Tang** was nearing the end of her fifth wartime patrol. To date, she had sunk 31 Japanese vessels – a total of roughly 227,800 tons of enemy shipping. She had sent two more tankers to the bottom, badly damaged a troop transport and sunk a destroyer early that morning. Now, with just two torpedoes left, she manoeuvred for the kill. The first torpedo struck the wounded transport. Then something totally unexpected occurred.*

The USS *Tang* was a naval phenomenon. A Balao class fleet submarine launched in 1943, she had sunk 20 Japanese vessels on her first four Pacific war patrols. On her fifth, which began on 24 September 1944, she had already added nine more to her score. Now, as dawn broke on 25 October, she began to close in on yet another Japanese convoy in the Formosa Strait, a 100-mile-wide stretch of water that separated the Island of Formosa (present-day Taiwan) from the Chinese mainland.

INTO ACTION

Commander Richard H. O'Kane, *Tang's* skipper, was confident of yet another success. In his first encounter with the enemy on the evening of 10 October, he had torpedoed and sank two heavily laden freighters. The next convoy he attacked was larger – it consisted of five freighters and five escort vessels. O'Kane skilfully manoeuvred *Tang* past the escorts without being detected. Then he fired nine torpedoes at point-blank range, sinking three out of the five freighters.

A ferocious free-for-all followed. With freighters exploding right and left and escorts steaming flat-out in all directions attempting

to locate the attacker, *Tang* dodged and weaved, trying to avoid contact with the enemy. Looming out of the smoke, a troop transport bore down on *Tang* and attempted to ram her. O'Kane managed to dodge the collision. Now, he faced the escorting Japanese destroyers. Instead of submerging, O'Kane swung his submarine around to attack his attackers. Though his torpedo tubes were not yet reloaded, O'Kane aimed *Tang's* bow straight at the nearest destroyer and charged the Japanese ship at full speed. The bluff worked. Unwilling to risk a possible torpedo hit, the destroyer swung away, and *Tang* made good her escape.

Late in the evening of 24 October, *Tang* made radar contact with yet another convoy. O'Kane

Above: *A Japanese destroyer, seen through the periscope of the attacking US submarine, goes down after a torpedo hit.*

Opposite: *Tang sunk 33 Japanese ships on its five operational patrols before being sunk by its own malfunctioning torpedo.*

shadowed it patiently through the night, before readying the submarine for a daybreak surface attack. This time, as *Tang* closed in on the Japanese, she was detected by the convoy's escorts. They immediately opened fire. The undaunted O'Kane boldly remained on the surface and calmly manoeuvred into position for his attack. .

At a range of 1,000 yards, O'Kane fired six torpedoes: two at a transport, two at a second transport and two at a tanker. All the torpedoes hit their targets. As

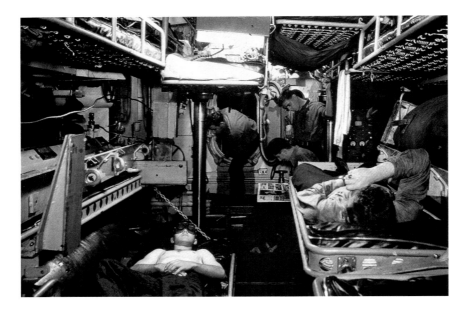

Left: *US submariners relax in their crowded quarters. In an emergency, they all had to know what to do instantly.*

Top right: *A US submarine commander scans the horizon through his periscope for targets.*

Bottom right: *The rogue torpedo that hit and sank* Tang *was fired from the forward torpedo room.*

O'Kane manoeuvred *Tang* to strike again, three Japanese destroyers charged at the submarine, steaming flat-out at 30 knots. Also at full speed, *Tang* counter-charged her attackers. This time, there was no bluff involved. The submarine's bow torpedo tubes were fully loaded. As he closed the range, O'Kane quickly fired three torpedoes to clear his way. The first torpedo struck the tanker; the second hit the transport and stopped it dead in the water; and the third struck one of the destroyers. *Tang* dashed through the resulting gap.

THE ROGUE TORPEDO

Tang had just two torpedoes left. O'Kane decided he would use them to try to finish off the transport he had crippled during his earlier attack. He brought *Tang* onto a new heading, settled down behind the torpedo sight on the bridge and passed the deflection angle to the bow torpedo compartment below. Once he received word that the torpedo crew was ready, O'Kane gave the order to fire.

The two torpedoes streaked out of the bow tubes. The first ran straight and true towards its intended target. The other did not. Suddenly, one of the eight other men on the bridge with O'Kane, shouted in alarm and pointed out to sea. Several pairs of eyes picked out the phosphorescent wake of

a torpedo heading straight for the submarine. It was still some distance away off the port bow.

Preoccupied as he was, O'Kane still found time to wonder where the attack had come from. There were no Japanese warships within range apart from the one he had recently attacked and was now clearly out of action. Constant sonar sweeps had not detected the presence of an enemy submarine. *Tang* was fitted with the most up-to-date detection equipment. It was inconceivable that she could have been taken by surprise.

Yet the torpedo was still powering its way towards her. O'Kane was confident that it

Right: *US submarine deck gunners at exercise with their weapon. Like many U-boat commanders, O'Kane favored attacking on the surface whenever possible.*

would miss. He had ordered the necessary evasive action to be taken in plenty of time. Then came the shock. The incoming torpedo was not running on a straight track. It appeared to be moving around *Tang* in a big circle – but one that was getting gradually smaller in diameter. The submarine was trapped.

In his book, *Clear the Bridge!*, which he wrote some 30 years later, O'Kane vividly described what happened next:

"'All ahead emergency! Right full rudder!' initiated a fishtail manoeuvre in a desperate attempt to move our ship outside of the speeding torpedo's turning circle. On our bow, and now coming abeam, the torpedo continued

to porpoise as it heeled in the turn, causing the jammed vertical rudder to become momentarily horizontal. In less than ten seconds it had reached its maximum distance abeam, about 20 yards. It was now coming in. We had only seconds to get out of its way.

"'Left full rudder" to swing our stern clear of the warhead was our only chance. The luminous wake

from our screws, the black exhaust from four overloaded diesels, each told that our engineers were doing their damnedest. The problem was akin to moving a ship longer than a football field and proceeding at harbour speed clear of a suddenly careening speedboat. It would be close.'

TANG IS TORPEDOED

O'Kane continued his dramatic account:

'The torpedo hit abreast the after torpedo room, close to the manoeuvring room bulkhead. The detonation was devastating, our stern going under before the topside watch could recover. One glance aft told me that there would be insufficient time to clear the bridge. My order, "Close the hatch," was automatic, and my heart went out to those below and to the young men topside who must now face the sea.

'Our ship sank by the stern in seconds, the way a pendulum might swing down in a viscous liquid. The seas rolled in from aft, washing us from the bridge and shears, and of small consolation now was the detonation of the

23rd torpedo as it hit home in the transport.

'*Tang's* bow hung at a sharp angle above the surface, moving about in the current as does a buoy in a seaway. She appeared to be struggling like a great wounded animal, a leviathan, as indeed she was. I found myself orally cheering encouragement and striking out impulsively to reach her. Closing *Tang* against the current was painfully slow and interrupted momentarily by a depth-charging patrol. Now, close ahead, *Tang's* bow suddenly plunged down to Davy Jones' locker, and the lonely seas seemed to share in my total grief.'

A BATTLE FOR SURVIVAL

The men in the various compartments of *Tang* were unaware of the unfolding drama.

The first they knew of it was when the submarine whipped round violently – 'like a giant fish grabbed by the tail,' recalled Motor Machinist Mate Second Class Jesse DaSilva – and then shook as a terrific explosion echoed through its hull from somewhere near the stern. The immediate thought of those who survived the impact was that *Tang* must have struck a mine. The men in the three stern compartments never stood a chance. Mercifully, many of them would have been rendered unconscious by concussion before the water poured in to drown them.

On the bridge, O'Kane just had time to shout an order to close the conning-tower hatch before the torpedo struck. Then the force of the explosion threw him and the eight others into the sea. Some of them were injured and unable to help themselves; no one had been wearing a life-jacket. Within seconds, there were only four survivors in the water – O'Kane, Bill Leibold, the Chief Boatswain's Mate, Lieutenant Larry Savadkin, the Engineering Officer, and a radar specialist named Floyd Caverly, who seconds before the torpedo struck, had come topside to report the failure of some of his equipment.

Tang went down stern first at terrifying speed. There was another shock as her stern struck the bottom at a depth of 180 feet t. O'Kane's split-second action in ordering the closing of the conning-tower hatch had undoubtedly saved many lives, but the plight of the crew trapped inside the submarine was still desperate. Several were seriously injured In addition, an electrical fire had broken out in the forward battery compartment. It was quickly extinguished, but the interior of the boat continued to fill with smoke and fumes from the smouldering cables.

One of the men trapped in the boat was a seaman mechanic named Clayton Oliver. When he recovered his senses, he found himself next to the venting valve for a main ballast tank. He knew

that, for the survivors to have a chance of using their Momsen Lungs – a primitive form of underwater escape apparatus – the submarine needed to be more or less on an even keel. He vented the tank and Tang began to settle. He and some of the other survivors then destroyed the top secret documents filed in the control room before making their way to the forward torpedo compartment and its escape chamber.

The attempt had to be delayed for four hours. Japanese destroyers had started dropping depth charges in random patterns in the vicinity of what remained of the convoy Tang had savaged so severely. Though none of the depth charges exploded near enough to damage the submarine further, the continual concussions were nightmarish. Some of the 30 or so survivors lapsed into unconsciousness. The rest waited patiently for the Japanese to give up their attacks. They knew that, should they proceed with their escape while the attack was still in progress, the underwater shock waves could and would kill them.

ESCAPING TO THE SURFACE

Eventually, the depth charging came to an end and the survivors, directed by Lieutenant Jim

Flanagan, the Tang's Torpedo Officer, set about preparing to abandon the submarine. Flanagan got the first four men into the escape chamber. An inflatable rubber dinghy was passed to them before the chamber was flooded. It was drained and opened 30 minutes later. Three of the four men were still inside it, half-drowned and barely conscious. Only one had managed to get through the escape hatch, and, as Flanagan later discovered, he did not manage to make it to the surface.

Flanagan tried again. This time, five men were squeezed into the chamber and the flooding-up and draining-down process took 45 minutes to complete. When it was over, Flanagan found that only three men had managed to make their escape. The other two were still inside.

By this time, Flanagan was exhausted. Ensign Basil Pearce Jr took over from him. Four more men entered the chamber. Although all of them cleared the escape hatch safely, only one survived to reach the surface. Pearce then persuaded Flanagan to leave with the fourth group. As he laboriously hauled himself up the cable that led from the escape chamber to the surface, where it was attached to a float,

Above & left: *Lieutenant-Commander Richard O'Kane, captain of* Tang, *portrayed by artist Albert K. Murray and photographed, survived the sinking and subsequent Japanese imprisonment. He was awarded the Congressional Medal of Honor for the heroism he displayed on board his submarine.*

he felt a series of concussions below. Before his departure, he had noticed that the fire in the battery compartment had flared up again. It was now so fierce that the paint on the inside of the bulkhead separating the forward torpedo room from the compartment had started to bubble and blister. Worse still, the rubber gasket sealing the watertight door had begun to smoulder in the intense heat. It must have given way. There was now no hope of escape for those still trapped in the wreck. They were all asphyxiated by smoke from the fire and deadly chlorine gas leaking from the battery compartment.

THE SURVIVORS

Of the 87 officers and ratings that had made up *Tang's* crew, only 15 survived. They were plucked from out of the Pacific by a Japanese destroyer, one of four which were already searching for Japanese troops and naval personnel from the ships the US submarine had torpedoed. The survivors were promptly set upon and beaten. O'Kane commented dryly: 'When we realised that our clubbings and kickings were being administered by the burned, mutilated survivors of our own handiwork, we found we could take it with less prejudice.'

For the survivors, the ordeal was just beginning. They were taken to Formosa, put on a train to the other end of the island and thrown into a prison camp there. Two days later, they were separated and sent on two ships to Japan. After arriving at a naval training centre, they were again put on a train – this time, bound for Ofuma, not far from Tokyo. It was wet and cold when they reached the town to be force-marched to their new prison camp.

'The only thing I had on was a pair of dungarees,' DaSilva recalled. 'I had lost one of my sandals after we were torpedoed and I kicked the other one off before I escaped, so my feet were very sore and numb from the cold.' Pete Narowanski still wore the pair of Hawaiian shorts he had on when he escaped. Both men were issued with a dry shirt, trousers, and a pair of tennis shoes 'about three sizes too small.' According to DaSilva, that was all the clothing they received for the ten months they were prisoners.

Food was in equally short supply. 'We mostly talked about food, food, food,' DaSilva said, 'as our rations were getting smaller.' Things grew even worse when they were moved to Omori, in the vicinity of Yokohama. There, the survivors' rations consisted of a mixture of barley and rice and a small bowl of soup three times a day. Sometimes, they were given a few small pieces of fish. They were never fed meat.

It was a starvation diet. When the prison camp was finally liberated by American troops on 29 August 1945, they found only nine of the original 15 survivors still alive. Commander O'Kane was among them. At the time he was freed, he weighed only 88lb. Savadkin, Flanagan, Caverly, Leibold, DaSilva, Decker, another Torpedoman called Hayes Tucker and Narowanski were the others.

No one was more surprised than the Navy Department that there were any survivors at all. It believed *Tang* had gone down with all hands. It also puzzled over what had caused the submarine to sink. It did not believe she had been destroyed by the Japanese, but how she had really met her end remained a mystery.

It was O'Kane who supplied the answer. *Tang* had sunk itself with its malfunctioning last torpedo. It was a tragic ending to what Vice-Admiral Charles Lockwood, commander of the submarine task force in the Pacific, called 'one of the greatest submarine cruises of all time.'

Above: *The 22 downed US airmen Tang rescued from the sea on her second war patrol pose for the camera on and in front of her coning tower.*

Double Cross: The Story of the D-Day Spies

In 1944, everybody knew that D-Day, when it happened, would decide the outcome of the war. If Hitler could discover where and when the landings would take place, he might well be able to drive the Allies back into the sea. If they could fool him into believing that the landings would take place elsewhere, they would gain vital time to build up their bridgeheads before sweeping forward to victory. The scene was set for an epic battle of wits.

On 6 June 1944, 150,000 Allied troops landed on the beaches of Normandy in northern France. Operation Overlord, the official codename for the D-Day invasion, was finally underway. It had been more than a year in the planning. So, too, had a far more shadowy, but equally vital plan to fool the Germans into believing that the invasion would take place elsewhere.

The overall deception plan was called Operation Bodyguard. The name came from a chance remark made by Winston Churchill to Joseph Stalin during the Tehran Conference in November 1943 when the plans for the proposed invasion were being discussed. The British premier pronounced, 'the truth is so precious that it should always be attended by a bodyguard of lies.' The Soviet dictator riposted: 'This is what we call military cunning.' Thomas Argyll Robertson, universally known as Tar, and John Masterman, two of the leading lights of British counterintelligence, were tasked with devising a foolproof scheme for deceiving the Germans and getting it up and running in the shortest possible time. Their part of the plan was called Operation Fortitude.

Robertson was a counterintelligence professional, who had been persuaded by Vernon Kell, the Director-General of MI5, to abandon his unsatisfactory career in banking to join the Secret Service in 1933. He was now head of Section B1 (a) of MI5. Masterman was a cerebral Oxford history don, who had volunteered to join British counterintelligence when war broke out. He chaired the so-called Twenty Committee, so named because 20 in Roman numerals is a double cross. The two men were

so successful that, by 1942, they had 'turned' every known German spy in the UK into double agents.

WHERE AND WHEN?
The people planning Overlord were faced with an immediate problem. In the words of one of them, it was 'utterly impossible to disguise the fact that the major attack would come somewhere between the Cherbourg Peninsula and Dunkirk.' The most obvious place for the invasion forces to land was in the Pas de Calais in the extreme northeast of France. It was

Below: *An RAF Handley Page Halifax bomber in flight over Normandy. The Allied air forces were the ground troops' flying artillery.*

Opposite: *British airborne troops prepare to board the transports and gliders taking them to their date with destiny in Normandy.*

the region nearest to the British coast. It possessed two large deep-water ports in Calais and Boulogne, at which reinforcements could easily be landed once both places were firmly in Allied hands. Successful landings there would also open up the shortest route to Paris and the German industrial heartland of the Ruhr. There were, however, counterbalancing disadvantages.

The Pas de Calais was where Hitler expected the Allies to strike. 'It is here that the enemy must and will attack, and it is here – unless all the indications are misleading – that the decisive battle against the landing forces will be fought,' he told his generals. It was also one of the most heavily fortified sections of the Fuehrer's much vaunted Atlantic Wall. By July 1943, the Overlord planners had concluded that the coast of Normandy north of Caen was a better bet.

As to when the landings would take place, Stalin had long been agitating for them to be initiated as soon as possible. The Americans were just as enthusiastic. The British, though apparently also in favour of launching the Second Front, prevaricated. Churchill's military advisers were totally opposed to any early landing. Sir Alan Brooke, Chief of the Imperial General Staff, noted in his diary: 'This universal cry to start a Second Front is going to be hard to compete with, and yet what can we do with some ten divisions against the German masses?' They then argued that there was no chance of mounting an invasion because of the shortage of landing craft.

Left: *A VI is hauled to its firing ramp. Double agents fed the Germans false information about its accuracy.*

Above: *US assault troops take shelter on Omaha Beach, which was defended stubbornly by the Germans.*

Right: *A US paratrooper prepares to hump into action. The airborne divisions took heavy casualties.*

Below: *One of the invasion convoys makes its slow way across the English Channel.*

The debate continued well into 1943. Eventually, after much Anglo-American discussion, D-Day was finally scheduled for 1 May 1944 (it was put back to early June because of persistent storms in the English Channel).

FOOLING THE GERMANS

Robertson, Masterman and the intelligence operatives with whom they worked were not concerned with high-level policy making and the intricacies of grand strategy.

Their task was straightforward. Once Normandy finally had been confirmed as the Allied landing site, they were to 'persuade the enemy to dispose his forces in areas where they can cause the least interference with Operations Overlord and Anvil (the invasion of Southern France)' and 'to deceive the enemy as to the strength, timing and objective of Overlord and Anvil.'

Through a long period of careful nurturing, Robertson

and Masterman had built up a team of double agents they believed they could trust. Even more crucially, the Abwehr, the German intelligence service, believed wholeheartedly in the information these agents were feeding back to it. The key figures – in alphabetical order, they were codenamed Bronx, Brutus, Garbo, Treasure and Tricycle – were the motliest collection of individuals that even the Secret Service had ever recruited.

Bronx (real name Elivira de la Fuente Chaudoir) was an attractive 29-year-old Peruvian bi-sexual, who was cutting something of a swathe through wartime London's high society when she was recruited into British Intelligence by Lieutenant-Colonel Claude Dansey, the assistant chief of MI6. He sent her to Vichy France with instructions to contact German Intelligence and offer to spy for them after her return to Britain. Through a Nazi collaborator, she got an introduction to Helmut Bleil, a freelance spy who reported, so he claimed, personally to Hermann Goering. Bleil sent her back to Britain, where she became one of Robertson's star recruits.

If Bronx was a talented amateur, Brutus (real name Roman Czerniawski) was the consummate professional. He lived and breathed spying. Though a qualified pilot, the Polish Air Force had deemed him unfit to fly because he was so small. He was shifted to Polish Air Intelligence in which he was serving when the war broke out. After the fall of Poland, he fled to France. When the French, too, capitulated, he went underground, only to emerge as the brains behind the Interallie. This soon became the most important spy network in Nazi-occupied France.

Then disaster struck. Czerniawski and Mathilde Carre, his fellow-agent and mistress, were betrayed to the Germans and arrested by the Gestapo.

Carre was the first to crack. She betrayed the entire network to the Germans and then volunteered to become a double agent for them. Czerniawski, too, came to terms with the Abwehr. The decision to fake his escape and allow him to get back to Britain to spy for Germany was authorised by Admiral Wilhelm Canaris, the head of the Abwehr, himself. The Pole, however, had no intention of fulfilling his bargain. Six weeks after his return, he offered to turn triple agent. MI5 and the Free Poles both had their doubts about his sincerity. MI5's Christopher Harmer spent weeks interrogating him before deciding he could be trusted. 'With his imagination and with his very original mind,' Harmer reported, 'we might possibly confuse and deceive the Germans to a

Opposite: *US troops wade ashore on Omaha Beach. Even though Hitler had been fooled into holding back his panzer reserves, the landing almost turned into an Allied catastrophe.*

Above: *Some of the many US casualties on Omaha are helped onto the beach. Their troop transport had been sunk before they could disembark from it.*

Above: *Landing craft approach the Normandy shore as smoke emanates from German defensive positions.*

Opposite: *US soldiers examine a knocked-out German self-propelled gun. A dead crewman lies slumped over the barrel.*

remarkable extent. Brutus joined the Double Cross team and began sending false radio messages back to his German controllers. The Germans swallowed whatever he told them hook, line and sinker. No one in the Abwehr ever suspected that he had been 'turned' again.

THE CHICKEN FARMER WHO HATED CHICKENS

Garbo (Juan Pujol) was even more imaginative. A 29-year-old Catalan, he had failed at practically every occupation he had tried, ending up as a poultry farmer outside Barcelona, although he detested chickens. The business went bust. When war broke out, he decided he wanted to spy for Britain.

In January 1941, he went to the British Embassy in Madrid to volunteer his services, but was turned down. He then approached the Germans. His reasoning was that, if he became a German agent, he could show the British just how valuable he could be to them. He did not have to be 'turned'. He was a natural double agent.

Karl Erich Kuhlenthal, Pujol's Abwehr controller in Madrid, dutifully supplied him with invisible ink and a substantial cash advance, and christened him Agent Arabel. He told him to go to Lisbon and make his way from there to Britain. Pujol obeyed the first instruction, but ignored the second. Though, on 19 July 1941, he cabled

Kuhlenthal to confirm his safe arrival in Britain, he never left Lisbon. For the next nine months, relying on newsreels, second-hand books and the Lisbon public library, he made up what he thought his German paymasters would most like to hear.

Soon, the amount of spurious information Pujol was giving the gullible Kuhlenthal, who then forwarded it on to Berlin, was such that he was fooling the British as well as the Germans. They suspected that the latter had managed to get a spy into Britain who was not under MI5's control. Closer examination of the decoded signals, however, revealed that Arabel not only suffered from verbal incontinence but that much of the information being supplied was risibly wrong – a fact that seemed to escape the notice of the Abwehr completely.

MI6 was the first intelligence agency to identify Arabel as Pujol. When MI5 was finally made aware who Arabel was, its comment was short and to the point. It was, they minuted, 'a miracle that he had survived so long'. Pujol was smuggled out of Lisbon to Gibraltar and then flown to Britain. He arrived there on 22 April 1942. Over the next three years he and Tomas 'Tommy' Harris, his MI5 controller, bombarded

the Germans with hundreds of thousands of words contained in 315 letters in secret ink and more than 1,200 wireless messages. Garbo even invented an entire team of sub-agents reporting to him.

A WOMAN AND HER DOG

Treasure (Lily Sergeyev), a 29-year-old Parisian of White Russian descent, was recruited by Major Emile Klieman in Paris to join the Abwehr in October 1941. Once he

had recruited her, however, Klieman seemed not to know what to do with her. It took him well over a year to decide to employ her in the field. Then, she faced months of waiting in Madrid before, in October 1943, she flew to Britain from Gibraltar. She had already told the British she would spy for them, so they were ready and waiting for her when she finally arrived.

There was a fly in the ointment. Treasure owned a dog

called Babs, a white cross between a poodle and a terrier to which she was totally devoted. Forced to leave Babs behind, she was convinced that she had MI5's promise to smuggle the animal into Britain for her in defiance of the strict British quarantine laws. The next she heard, however, was that Babs was dead, accidentally run over by a passing car. Sergeyev refused to believe the story. She was certain that MI5 had

had her dog deliberately killed to rid themselves of a nuisance. On the surface, she seemed to come to terms with her loss. Inwardly, she was plotting her revenge.

It was May 1944 – just before D-Day – that Treasure got her opportunity. Some months before, MI5 had sent her back to Lisbon to contact Klieman to demand that she should be supplied with a radio transmitter. Unbeknownst to the British, Treasure had agreed with him that she should transmit a special radio signal – inserting an extra double dash into a routine message – to indicate she was operating under British control. She now told MI5 what

she had done. What she would not reveal was the nature of the signal or whether she had already transmitted it. Robertson's view was that she was blackmailing the whole Double Cross operation for the sake of a dead dog.

In fact, Treasure never transmitted the signal, but, three days after D-Day, Robertson had his revenge. He sacked her. She was sent back to Paris in disgrace as soon as the French capital had been liberated.

THE SEDUCTIVE SERB

Tricycle (Dusan 'Dusko' Popov) was another Abwehr recruit who secretly changed sides. Next

to Garbo and Brutus, he was probably the most successful of all MI5's double agents. A flamboyant womaniser, he was persuaded by his friend Johnny Jebsen – who himself was to be 'turned' successfully later during the war – to join him in spying for the Abwehr in early 1940. Popov secretly contacted MI6 in Belgrade and offered to work for the British instead. On 20 December, having journeyed first to Lisbon to contact Ludovico von Karsthof, his designated Abwehr controller, he landed at Whitchurch airport, near Bristol. He was immediately chauffeured to London to meet Robertson. His career as a double agent had begun.

Tricycle soon started living up to his codename, shuttling back and forth between Britain and Portugal in the guise of a Yugoslav businessman. The Germans were so pleased with what he told them that, in August 1941, they sent him to the USA to spy on the Americans. MI5 thought this was the perfect opportunity for Popov to create an American equivalent of

Double Cross. Unfortunately, J. Edgar Hoover and the FBI loathed him. The Germans, too, began to doubt his bona fides.

On 4 October 1942, Popov arrived back in Lisbon, primed with fresh information by MI5 to help him rehabilitate himself in German eyes. Von Karsthof put it to him that, while his work in Britain had been 'very good' and in the USA initially 'excellent', it had then become 'medium' and, for the last three months, 'terribly bad'. The self-assured Serb had an immediate answer. It was all the Abwehr's fault, he said, for sending him to the USA 'with no help whatsoever, no contacts,' and 'a few miserable dollars.' Von Karsthof was more than willing to accept the story, especially since he had been creaming off dollars from the money he had been supposed to despatch.

Popov was in the clear. He was sent back to London to resume his spying and was soon being hailed as 'the best man the Abwehr has.' In early 1944, he returned to Lisbon for one last time to pass 'a mass of detailed information' to von Karsthof. The Abwehr man swallowed the deception whole. He told Berlin that 'the landing in Western Europe will not take place until next spring.'

Above: *A Waco CG-4 glider is examined by German troops. The airborne landings caused considerable confusion amongst Normandy's defenders.*

A COMPLETE SUCCESS

As D-Day neared, the volume of false information pouring into German hands reached a crescendo. On the ground, too, major deception schemes were being mounted. An entire phantom US Army Group, supposedly commanded by the redoubtable General George Patton, was reported as being readied for an assault on the Pas de Calais. Any invasion in Normandy would be a ruse, specifically designed to draw off German troops before the main assault. An attack on Norway by the equally fictitious British 4th Army was also a 'strong possibility', according to German Intelligence, while an attack on Denmark was rated a 'certainty'.

It was little wonder that the Germans were painfully slow to react when D-Day dawned. Even after the landings, the crack German 15th Army stayed in its positions in the Pas de Calais waiting for an assault which never came. The decision to impose a stand-still order was largely the result of Garbo's analysis of supposed Allied intentions – the Germans were so convinced by it that it ended up in the hands of Hitler himself. The stand-still lasted for seven weeks. By the time it was finally lifted, the Allied armies had broken out of their bridgeheads and were penetrating deep into German territory. It was a fitting conclusion to what one military historian later called 'the most successful strategic deception of all time.'

The Mysterious Death of Glenn Miller

On the night of 15 December 1944, the legendary US bandleader Glenn Miller – now a 40-year-old Major in the US Army Air Force – boarded a light aircraft to fly the English Channel to SHAEF headquarters outside Paris to prepare for his band's visit to the French capital to give a Christmas concert. The aircraft never reached its destination. No trace of it or its passengers was ever found. The episode remains one of the greatest riddles of the entire war.

Above: *Glenn Miller sacrificed his civilian stardom to enlist in 1942. The new band he founded for the US Army Air Force became world-famous.*

Opposite: *Miller hitched a ride in a Norseman like this to fly to Paris in December 1944. He never arrived. The plane vanished somewhere over the English Channel.*

Glenn Miller became an all-American musical legend. His celebrated orchestra, formed in 1938, rose out of initial obscurity to achieve speedy greatness. In just four years, 70 of the disks Miller and his musicians cut became Top Ten hits; Time magazine noted that 'of the 12 to 24 disks in each of today's 300,000 US jukeboxes, from two to six are usually Glenn Miller's.'

The band, Miller leading as principal trombone, became a household name. Its first hit was the 1939 *Wishing (Will Make It So)*, closely followed by *Moonlight Serenade*. The following year, *In The Mood, Tuxedo Junction* and *Pennsylvania 6-5000* all climbed to the top of the charts. The orchestra was now universally recognised to be the USA's top dance band. It was not for nothing that Miller was dubbed the 'King of Swing.'

A MUSICAL VOLUNTEER

In 1942, with his orchestra at the height of its popularity, Miller amazed Tin Pan Alley by disbanding it. Like hundreds of thousands of his fellow Americans following Pearl Harbor, he abandoned civilian life. He tried to get into the US Navy, but was turned down as being too old to fight. By pulling every string in Washington he could, he managed to get into the Army Specialist Corps in August 1942. He was transferred to the US Army Air Force that October.

Miller, however, did not leave music behind him. What he wanted to deliver to the troops was 'real, live American music'. His aim, so he said, was to 'put a little more spring into the feet of our marching men and a little more

Left: *Miller's records constantly topped the charts. Here he is being presented with the gold disc he won for Chattanooga Choo Choo.*

Right: *A schematic diagram shows the workings of the V1 cruise missile. Miller and his band were almost killed by one shortly after their arrival in Britain.*

sought him out to compliment him: 'Next to a letter from home', he said, 'your orchestra is the greatest morale booster in the European Theatre of Operations.'

TWO BRUSHES WITH DEATH

Miller had been agitating to be allowed to take his band overseas for some time, but the air force had been reluctant to give its consent. It took an appeal from General Dwight D. Eisenhower, the Allied supreme commander in Europe, to General Arnold to get Miller and his musicians shipped across the Atlantic.

Miller and his band were feted everywhere they went. They played on airfields, in aircraft hangars, for the wounded and performed on the American Forces Radio Network and the BBC weekly. Among their most enthusiastic fans were Princesses Elizabeth and Margaret – George VI's young daughters. Their oddest appearance was probably on a programme called *The Wehrmacht*

joy into their hearts.' To do this, he needed to create a new band. On 20 March 1943, the 50-strong 418th Army Air Force Band made its debut playing to an audience of cadets undergoing their military training at Yale University.

Initially, Miller's efforts to introduce swing into marches met with some resistance within the military hierarchy. One senior officer reminded him coldly that John Philip Sousa had been good

enough for the American armed forces during World War I. 'Are you still flying the same planes you flew in the last war?' Miller reposted. Luckily, General Henry 'Hap' Arnold, commander-in-chief of the US Army Air Force, liked Miller and his music. So, too, did Lieutenant-General James 'Jimmy' Doolittle, now commanding the US 8th Army Air Force. After a concert Miller gave at Wycombe Abbey on 31 July 1944, Doolittle

FIG 76

Hour, broadcasting a potent blend of swing – and propaganda – to the troops battling the Allies. Miller himself spoke to his enemy listeners, though, according to reports, he had something of a struggle with his German.

Right at the start of the tour, however, Miller and his band had a close encounter with death. Initially, they were housed at 25 Sloane Court, London. This was situated in the heart of what was nicknamed 'Buzz Bomb Valley' – so-called because it lay immediately beneath the flight path of the deadly VI pilotless missiles with which Hitler was now pitilessly bombarding the capital. Miller immediately decided to move his musicians out of London to Bedford. They left for their new quarters on 2 July. The next day, a VI crashed directly in front of their Sloane Court billet, demolishing the building and killing more than 100 people. When he heard the news, Miller commented laconically to Lieutenant Don Haynes, the band's manager: 'As long as the Miller luck stays with us, we have nothing to worry about.'

Miller and his band had another, even closer brush with a VI. They were playing at an open-air concert in Kent when the characteristic puttering of the missile's ram jet was heard overhead. It suddenly cut out – a sure signal that the missile was about to crash and explode. The audience dived for cover. Miller and his musicians played on regardless even through the

Above: *When he heard a VI had destroyed his London billet, Miller joked that his legendary luck was still holding good.*

explosion. They were given a standing ovation.

THE FATEFUL FLIGHT

The strain of constant performance began to tell as autumn gave way to winter. In one month alone, according to a letter Miller wrote to a friend, 'we played at 35 different bases and, in our "spare time", did 46 broadcasts.'

On average, he and the band were spending 18 hours a day performing or recording.

Miller was becoming somewhat homesick, but nevertheless he was determined to continue with the tour. In particular, he wanted to visit France to perform for the front-line troops. This was deemed impracticable, but a compromise

was agreed. Miller and his musicians would move to Paris, where they could entertain Allied soldiers on leave. The plan was to start with a gala concert on Christmas Day.

On 15 November, Miller's planned visit finally got the official go-ahead. At first, the idea was for Don Haynes to fly to Paris ahead of the musicians to make all the necessary preparations, but, at the last minute, Miller decided to go himself. The problem was the weather. Foggy flying conditions had grounded the SHAEF shuttle on which Miller had been ordered to fly and even when flights resumed, the passenger backlog meant that he was likely to be bumped off the plane. Then, he had what looked like a stroke of luck. The day before he was due to fly, he ran into Lieutenant-Colonel Norman F. Baesell, a friend of Haynes, who was flying to Paris the following day in a general's private plane. There was room for another passenger. Baesell invited Miller along.

As take-off time neared, the C-46 Norseman sat waiting on the tarmac. Its pilot, Flight Officer John Morgan, told his two passengers that, though it was raining heavily and visibility was poor, the word was that the weather was clearing over the Continent. Miller apparently was somewhat dubious. First, he raised doubts about the aircraft – the Norseman was a single-engined light plane. Baesell countered by reminding him that one engine had been enough for Charles Lindbergh, the first man to fly solo across the Atlantic in 1927. Then, as Miller took his seat, he asked 'Hey, where

Left: *An Avro Lancaster bomber in flight. It is possible that a bomb dropped by a Lancaster could have fatally damaged the plane carrying Glenn Miller on his final flight.*

the hell are the parachutes?' Baesell jocularly retorted: 'What's the matter, Miller? Do you want to live forever?'

The Norseman slowly taxied into its take-off position. As Morgan started to accelerate down the runway, Haynes stood waving Miller goodbye. He was the last person to see Miller alive. The Norseman never reached France. No trace of it, its pilot or its two passengers was ever found.

ACCIDENT OR HEART ATTACK

What exactly happened to the Norseman and its passengers has never been fully explained. Indeed, it was not until Haynes himself arrived at SHAEF headquarters in search of Miller on 18 December that it was even realised he had been on board the missing aircraft. A search was hurriedly mounted, but it found nothing. The 8th Air

Force set up a Board of Enquiry. It said that Miller had boarded the wrong plane on the wrong day without the knowledge or approval of his military superiors.

The Norseman, in the Board's opinion, had either crashed in the English Channel as a result of pilot disorientation, or suffered a disastrous engine failure, possibly due to fuel icing inside the carburettor. Poor weather, the Board added, had certainly been a contributing factor. Flying conditions were marginal at best and were deteriorating rapidly. The unspoken conclusion was that the Norseman should not have been in the air at all.

Even before the Board of Enquiry reported, however, rumours about the true nature of the accident – if there was one – were mounting. As late as the 1980s and 1990s, new theories

IN MEMORY
Major A. Glenn Miller
0505273
U.S. Army Air Force- W.W. II
Born- Clarinda, Iowa-
March 1, 1904
Missing in Action-
Europe, Dec. 15, 1944
1943 - 1944
418th A.A.F.T.T.C. Band-
Yale University- New Haven, CT.
I SUSTAIN THE WINGS

Sustineo Alas

Above: *Glenn Miller's memorial in Grove Street Cemetery, New Haven, Connecticut. His music lived on even after his death.*

Opposite: *General Henry 'Hap' Arnold was commander-in-chief of the US Army Air Force. He personally broke the news of Miller's disappearance to the great bandleader's wife.*

were emerging to expose the real reasons for Miller's untimely death. Some of these theories are plausible, at least on the surface. Some are ridiculous. At one time or another, all have come under heavy critical fire.

One of the strangest theories was put forward by German journalist Udo Ulfkotte in 1997. According to *Bild* magazine, Ulfkotte had come across hitherto secret evidence while researching a book he was writing on German intelligence agencies. The evidence stated, so *Bild* claimed, that Miller had never been on board the Norseman at all. In fact, he had arrived safely the day before on 14 December, only to die of a heart attack in the arms of a prostitute in a Paris brothel. The official story was a cover-up.

Later, however, Ulfkotte claimed that *Bild* had misquoted him. He had never told the magazine that he had found evidence to support his claim. The story, he said, had been told to him by wartime German intelligence specialists in an off-the-record conversation.

UNDERCOVER SPY

An even more far-fetched theory was put forward by journalist and retired US Colonel Hunton Downs in his 2007 book *The Glenn Miller Conspiracy*. In it, Downs stated that Miller was an undercover OSS superspy, who died while on a secret mission for General Eisenhower. The mission, so Downs claimed, involved Miller getting into Germany to make contact with a group of dissident German generals and persuading them to turn against Hitler. He was also to get in touch with the Reich's leading rocket and nuclear scientists, including Wernher von Braun, and offer them sanctuary should they come over to the Allies.

Miller, said Downs, was betrayed, captured, tortured and finally beaten to death by Nazi extremists. They smuggled his battered corpse back to Paris, where it was unceremoniously dumped on the doorstep of a

brothel in Rue Pigalle. Miller's body, Downs claimed, was flown back to the USA and buried in Ohio in a secret location. The theory convinced some, but many considered it unbelievable.

FATAL ILLNESS OR FRIENDLY FIRE

Two other theories also gained wide currency. One came from no less a person than Herb Miller, the bandleader's younger brother. He broke a nearly 40-year silence in 1983 to say that 'Glenn Miller did not die in a plane crash over the Channel, but from lung cancer in a hospital.'

Miller, his brother explained, had indeed boarded the Norseman that December afternoon, but only half an hour into the flight he had been taken so ill that the aircraft had to make an emergency landing. He was rushed by ambulance to a military hospital where he died the following day. It was Herb Miller who concocted the story of a mid-Channel air crash as a last service to his brother, who had wanted to die a hero and not 'in a lousy bed'.

Herb produced supporting evidence to back up his claim. To substantiate the story, he cited a letter that the chain-smoking musician had written earlier that summer. 'I am totally emaciated, although I am eating enough,' it read. 'I have trouble breathing. I think I am very ill.'

Other testimony indeed seemed to confirm the fact that Miller was suffering from an undiagnosed illness. He often appeared exhausted and suffered from what he described as repeated sinus attacks. According to Don Haynes, the bandleader had lost a lot of weight. His tailor-made uniforms, Haynes noted, 'didn't fit him well at all. They merely hung on him.' He had lost much of his customary optimism and bounce. George Voutsas, the director of Miller's radio broadcasts, recalled a late-night discussion of post-war plans. 'I don't know why I spend time making plans like this,' Miller apparently sighed: 'You know, George, I have an awful feeling you guys are going home without me.'

It all sounded convincing, but it ran up against a specific fact. Herb Miller's account of his brother's death was never confirmed by the US military authorities. Why, after so long, should it still be kept secret? And why was Miller's body apparently buried anonymously in some military cemetery?

Another equally plausible explanation for Miller's disappearance emerged the

Above: *Lieutenant General Jimmy Doolittle congratulated Miller on his band's morale boosting-performances.*

following year, when Fred Shaw, a former RAF Bomber Command navigator now living in South Africa, succeeded in getting his story about the vanishing Norseman published after years of trying. On the day Miller's plane vanished, Shaw was on board a Lancaster bomber returning from an aborted raid on the railway yards at Steigen. Approaching Britain's south coast, the bomb-aimer dropped the aircraft's bomb-load as it entered the officially designated South Jettison Zone. The bomb-load included a 4,000lb 'cookie' which apparently exploded just before the bomb hit the sea. As Shaw looked out from the cockpit to catch a glimpse of the explosion, he spotted a small plane, which he identified as a Norseman, flying below him. A moment later, the rear gunner

called out over the intercom 'Did you see that kite (RAF slang for plane) go in?' Shaw believed that the shock waves from the explosion had literally knocked the Norseman out of the sky.

Back in Britain, Alan Ross, a member of the Glenn Miller Appreciation Society, contacted the Air Historical Branch of the Ministry of Defence and asked them to investigate Shaw's allegation. The reply was non-committal. The Norseman and the bomber stream, the investigators said, could have crossed in flight. Equally, they could have been miles apart.

Ross had more luck with an advertisement he had placed, asking anyone who could confirm Shaw's story to come forward. Victor Gregory, the Lancaster's pilot, responded. Although he personally had seen nothing, he confirmed that Shaw and the rear gunner, who was now dead, spotted the Norseman and said what they had said.

Gregory never mentioned the incident on his return to base. 'Don't think me unsympathetic or callous,' he said, 'but when I heard of the plane going down, I would have said he shouldn't have been there – forget him.' Forgetting Glenn Miller, however, was something that anyone who had ever heard his band play could never do.

Above: *A Glenn Miller commemorative stamp, issued in 1996. Even today, speculation continues about where and how he disappeared and what possibly caused his death.*

The *Cap Arcona* Tragedy

On 3 May 1945 – four days after Hitler's suicide in his Berlin bunker – the German passenger liner Cap Arcona was sunk in the Baltic by RAF fighter-bombers. The pilots who attacked the ship believed it was carrying fleeing SS troops, but, in fact, it was packed with prisoners from the Neuengamme concentration camp near Hamburg. Out of the 4,500 passengers, only 500 managed to survive. It was one of the greatest disasters in maritime history.

On the morning of 3 May 1945, the skies over northern Germany and the Baltic Sea were bleak, misty and overcast. The Germans welcomed the bad visibility, because it gave them some respite from attacks by the Allied fighter-bombers, which, for days now, had been mercilessly pounding the shipping crammed into the north German ports or clustered around them offshore. The ships were packed with military personnel and equipment of all kinds. Most of them were bound for Norway, where the German High Command was planning to make a desperate last stand.

Most of the shipping attacks were carried out by the RAF's Second Tactical Air Force, although Coastal Command and the US 9th Army Air Force also took part in them. It was the RAF's deadly Hawker Typhoon fighter-bombers that the Germans feared the most. Ever since the Allied landings in Normandy in June 1944, the Typhoons had harried the Germans remorselessly from the air as they fell back into their homeland. Now they were star players in the last act before the curtain finally fell on Hitler's vaunted thousand-year Third Reich.

Armed with four 20mm cannon, the Typhoon could also

Right: *A RAF Mosquito strafes an enemy transport ship. There is a complete absence of enemy anti-aircraft fire, allowing the pilot a clean shot at his target.*

carry up to 1,000lb of bombs or eight rockets, each with a 60lb high-explosive warhead. A full salvo of rockets had the destructive force of a broadside fired from a cruiser. It was more than enough to tear any merchant ship apart.

SHIP-BUSTING IN LUBECK BAY

The weather soon turned in the Allies' favour. On the afternoon of 3 May, the skies cleared. The Second Tactical Air Force could now unleash its Typhoon squadrons against the enemy shipping in Lubeck Bay, where several large vessels already had been spotted by aerial reconnaissance. Four squadrons from 123 Wing were briefed to carry out the mission. The planes from 184, 263 and 198 Squadrons were armed with rockets, while the aircraft from 197 Squadron carried bombs. The pilots were certainly keyed up for the attack. 'No quarter was

asked for or given in the air today,' that evening's Air Intelligence Survey reported, 'and operations proceeded at full blast.'

It was four Typhoons from 197 Squadron that carried out the first attack on what the pilots described as a 'two-funnel cargo liner of 10,000 tons with steam up in Lubeck Bay.' She was, in fact, the 21,046-ton passenger liner *Deutschland*, which was in the process of being converted into a hospital ship. The Typhoon pilots had no means of knowing this, however. Only a single small Red Cross had been painted on the side of one of her funnels, both of which had been painted white.

When the Typhoons struck, *Deutschland* had only an 80-strong skeleton crew on board, plus a 26-strong medical team. The ship was hit by four bombs, one of which failed to explode. Another started a small fire, which was quickly extinguished. No one was

hurt in the attack. After it, the medical team went ashore, while the vessel's captain ordered white sheets to be draped over the *Deutschland* and all her lifeboats to be swung out in their davits, ready for a speedy launch if or when the RAF returned.

STRIKE TWO, STRIKE THREE

The second attack, some three hours later, was delivered by nine Typhoons from 198 Squadron. They were led by Group Captain Johnny Baldwin, who also commanded 123 Wing. This time, the Typhoons attacked two vessels – a large three-funnel liner and a smaller ship moored nearby. It was devastatingly successful. 40 rockets out of the 62 that were fired struck the bigger vessel, their warheads smashing through her hull to explode deep inside her. She was soon ablaze from stem to stern. 30 more rockets ships hit the smaller ship. She began to list heavily and then to sink, continuously belching thick black smoke into the sky.

There were few survivors from the second vessel. Bogdan Suchowiak, a 38-year-old Polish prisoner from Posen, was one of them. 'It was clear to me that if we did not jump overboard immediately,' he recalled, 'we would all be drawn down into the deep by the suction of the sinking ship. I undressed to my shorts and let myself down slowly by a rope. The water was damned cold. I clung to a wooden plank. It must have been around 3.30pm in the afternoon, the sun was shining, but then there were passing clouds and rain showers. The sea was relatively calm with small waves. It was about five kilometres to the shore.'

Somehow, Suchowiak managed to stay afloat for a couple of hours. Then he spotted a minesweeper looking for survivors and swam as fast as he could towards it. When he got close, he could hear a young officer shouting at the crew through a loudhailer. 'Don't pick up any prisoners,' he was directing them, 'only SS personnel and sailors.' Luckily for Suchowiak, he spoke fluent German and so was able to talk his way on board.

The third attack, made by 263 Squadron, was again directed against *Deutschland*. As the Typhoons darted in, her crew scrambled into the lifeboats and made for the shore unharmed. Deutschland, though, was set on fire and was sunk a few minutes later by bombs dropped by 197 Squadron's Typhoons.

Top: *RAF armorers load a Typhoon with air-to ground rockets – a totally lethal combination.*

Middle: *A Hawker Typhoon fighter-bomber ready for take-off on yet another mission.*

Bottom: *The* Cap Arcona *in happier peacetime days sailing from Hamburg for South America.*

Opposite: *Lubeck Bay looks tranquil enough here. In 1945 it was a different story.*

Left: *Bomb damage in Hamburg. The city never really recovered from the great fire storm raised by Allied bombers in 1943.*

Right: *Wesel in northern Germany – or what was left of it – photographed in May 1945 after the Germans surrendered.*

THE GRIM REALITY

The Typhoon pilots headed back to their bases along the River Elbe. The next day, British ground forces entered the port of Lubeck – and the full horror of what had happened was revealed. The second two ships indeed had been packed to capacity, but not with German troops being evacuated to Norway. They had been filled with thousands of concentration camp inmates.

As the war in Europe approached its inevitable conclusion, Reichsfuehrer Heinrich Himmler, the head of the SS, had ordered that no concentration camp inmates should be allowed to fall into Allied hands. Those who could still walk were to be force-marched back, away from the Allied line of advance. The remainder were to be killed.

At Neuengamme, near Hamburg, where half the prisoners were either Russians or Poles, 1,000 of the camp's inmates were murdered immediately. Many of the 20,000 others were quickly dispersed across northern Germany, but, during the last days of April, several thousand more were herded into Lubeck. Around 2,300 of them were forced to board the 1,936-ton freighter *Athen*, which ferried them to the three-funnel liner. This was the 27,561-ton *Cap Arcona*. Before the war, this luxury liner had been known as 'the Queen of the South Atlantic, plying the seas between Hamburg and Rio de Janeiro. Now, she was to become a prison ship.

Heinrich Bertram, the liner's captain who had taken over command on only 27 February, did not like the idea. After the war, he reported to the ship's owners, telling them at first he had refused to allow the prisoners on board. The SS, however, were not taking no for an answer.

Betram continued: 'On Thursday 26 April 1945, SS Sturmbanfuehrer Gehrig, who was in charge of transport, appeared, accompanied by an advisory merchant marine captain and an executive Kommando, consisting of soldiers armed with machine-guns. Gehrig had brought a written order for my attention. It called for me to be shot at once if I further refused to take the prisoners on board. At this point, it became clear to me that even my death would not prevent the boarding of the prisoners and so I informed the SS officer that I categorically renounced any responsibility for my ship.'

The captain concluded: 'Gehrig proceeded to order the transfer of the prisoners from the *Athen* to *Cap Arcona*. Additional transports arrived from Lubeck, so that on 28 April I had a total of about 6,500 prisoners on board in spite of the statement of the merchant marine officer that the ship was capable of holding a limit of 2,500.' The luckless Bertram had to find room to accommodate 500 SS guards into the bargain.

Below: *Despite being designed as a high-altitude interceptor, the Hawker Typhoon really excelled in low-level ground attacks.*

Left: *Shellfire damage in an unknown German town. As the war drew to a close, many towns were quick to capitulate.*

Right: *Luftwaffe Field Marshal Erhard Milch (centre) together with Arms Minister Albert Speer to his left. Both men struggled to keep weapons production going in the face of Allied bombing.*

Meanwhile, 3,000 more prisoners had been loaded onto another vessel, the 2,815 freighter *Thielbeck*. On both vessels, the prisoners were battened down below for days in darkness and stinking squalor, many half-dead already from starvation. In addition, two large barges were filled with several hundred men, women and children from another concentration camp at Stutthof.

DISASTER IN THE BAY

Events proceeded inexorably to their tragic conclusion. On 2 May, a transfer of prisoners took place between *Cap Arcona*, *Thielbeck* and *Athen*. This left 4,150 prisoners on the liner and 2,750 on the freighter. Another 2,000 were on board

Athen, whose captain decided to put back to port. The SS guards on board protested, but, according to some accounts, were disarmed by the crew.

The vessel put into Neustadt. Mikelis Mezmalietis, one of the prisoners on board, recalled what happened. 'On the morning of 3 May,' he wrote, 'there was a terrible explosion. After a short time, one of the stronger prisoners who had been aloft ran down to tell us that the Americans (sic) had bombed *Cap Arcona* and sunk it. Everyone who could move got very excited and tried to get to the one exit. In a moment, we felt the ship starting to move fast. Then it stopped.'

'Nobody spoke for an hour,' Mezmalietis went on. 'Then all those who could, but up and ran out, especially the German crew: we had arrived at Neustadt. I was unable to move and was left for dead. After perhaps another hour, I crawled on all fours up to the top deck...

'That afternoon two strong young prisoners boarded the ship to see what they could take. They were not from my ship; they turned out to be French students. They were very surprised to see me; they went searching for other prisoners but found none. Then they carried me from the ship and took me to the barracks at Neustadt, where they washed me and put me to bed in a spare bed in their room.'

SWIMMING FOR SURVIVAL

Meanwhile, on board the stricken, blazing *Cap Arcona*, more than 4,000 prisoners were burning to death or suffocating in the smoke. A few managed to jump into the sea, where they were picked up by some fishermen. Berek Bronek (later Benjamin Jacobs) was one of their number. In his memoirs, *The Dentist of Auschwitz*, he recalled the moments leading up to his rescue.

'I heard people begging to be picked up,' he wrote. 'As a man was pulled from the water, I waved and yelled to get their attention. "We can't take anyone! We have no more room! We are full!" they shouted back to me. But that did not deter me. In a final effort, I lurched, throwing my arms forward to get a bit closer to them. Then I saw how low their boat was in the water, just barely above the waterline. I begged and pleaded with them until I could shout no more. "It's Bronek, the dentist. Let's try to take him," someone yelled. The motor slowed and the boat turned and headed in my direction. A minute later, a few hands pulled me into the boat. I slumped down, barely conscious. My naked comrades and the sunburned fisherman were my archangels. As the little boat slowly ploughed through the water towards the shore, many people were begging to be picked up. "If we take one more, we'll all go down," the fisherman cautioned.

'The small engine pulled the heavily laden boat as the waves rolled it up and down. The fisherman skilfully manoeuvred it to avoid capsizing. I sat still with my head between my pulled-up knees and thought of my brother. I had cheated death once more, but he could not. All hope that *Cap Arcona* would stay afloat was fading.'

More survivors – about 350 in all, many suffering from burns – managed to escape before the liner capsized and swim unaided to the shore, only to be shot and clubbed to death by SS troops and fanatical members of the Hitler Youth. Of the 2,750 prisoners on *Thielbeck*, only around 50 managed to escape. Most of them met the same fate as the survivors of *Cap Arcona*.

As for the hundreds of prisoners on the two barges, there were no survivors. When British troops arrived on the scene, they found the barges stranded on the shore and the beaches littered with corpses. The adults had been shot, the children clubbed to death with rifle butts. Max Pauly, the commandant of Neuengamme concentration camp and the man responsible for the massacre, was later tried as a war criminal in Hamburg and hanged, together with several of his subordinates.

AFTERMATH

That should have been the end of the *Cap Arcona* affair – but it was not. Nearly 40 years later, a series of sensational articles in the West German press claimed that the true facts behind the attacks had been kept secret for decades. One of the claims was that British Intelligence had known that the vessels were packed with concentration camp inmates, but had not warned he RAF this was the case. Another was that the RAF, knowing whom the ships carried, nevertheless had deliberately allowed them to be attacked to give new pilots fresh from Britain some operational experience before the war ended.

Such claims are nonsense. In fact, the British had issued clear warnings that all shipping in the Baltic would be open to air attack, unless the vessels concerned were displaying prominent Red Cross markings. This was not the case. The RAF had no reason to believe that they were carrying anything other but troops – and perhaps even members of the Nazi leadership – to sanctuary in Norway. To turn the argument on its head, it is not impossible that the ships were used as a convenient dumping ground for the unwanted prisoners by the Nazis in the hope that they would be sunk, so completing the Nazis' dirty work for them.

Whatever the truth, one mystery still remains unsolved. Mikelis Mezmalietis recalled how the decks of *Athen* were crammed with tons of sugar, rice, flour and macaroni. *Athen* was to have remained in company with the other two ships, so who were the supplies intended for? The quantities were far greater than would have been needed to meet the needs of the ships' crews and the SS guards. It is just possible that they were intended to keep the prisoners alive while the SS attempted to use them as a bargaining counter with the Allies in order to save themselves – tragic pawns in a last desperate gamble by murderers who had nothing to lose but their lives.

Above: *A colourful recruiting poster calls on Dutch civilians to volunteer for the German Land Army. The grim alternative was to be deported for forced labor.*

Drugs, Doctors and the Fuehrer

In 1941, Adolf Hitler was a relatively healthy man who looked younger than his years. By April 1945, he was 'a shell of a man no longer able to lead Germany,' according to an army doctor summoned to attend him in his Berlin bunker just days before he killed himself. What turned the Fuehrer into a physical and mental wreck? Was his decline caused by an illness his physicians failed to diagnose or could not treat? Or was there another, more sinister reason?

From a relatively young age, Hitler was a hypochondriac – a man obsessed with his health. But, as a future Fuehrer, he knew that he could never afford to be seen to be ill. This was why he kept it quiet when the early symptoms of what was to become his first significant illness appeared in the late 1920s. Doctors today hold that what he was suffering from was almost certainly gallstones, associated with intermittent obstruction of his bile ducts, but, at the time, the condition remained undiagnosed.

MYSTERY PAINS

The first symptoms Hitler suffered from were episodes of sharp cramping pain in the upper right of his abdomen. The pain usually occurred after meals and, when it did, Hitler left the room. Sometimes he came back after the spasm had passed. Sometimes, he did not return at all. According to Albert Speer, Hitler later told him that things became so bad that he was suffering pain after every meal. He also complained of abdominal distension accompanied by duller pain and frequent belching.

From the start, the underlying cause of the pain remained a mystery. It occurred for no obvious reason and usually disappeared

Opposite: *Hitler's doctor was already worried about his health when he addressed the Reichstag in December 1941.*

Right: *Hitler was fit and well when he became Chancellor in 1933.*

after an hour or so. Some attacks were severe enough to incapacitate the Fuehrer, while others were milder – more like a nagging soreness. Sometimes, Hitler was free of pain for several months, but it always came back to haunt him. The condition was chronic. Attacks continued to recur for the rest of the Fuehrer's life.

HITLER TREATS HIMSELF

Any normal person would have consulted a doctor, but Hitler, always reluctant to take the advice of experts, refused to undergo a comprehensive medical examination. Whether this could have helped him much is open to doubt; as what causes abdominal pain is often difficult to diagnose precisely. What he did decide to do was to treat himself.

Sensibly enough, Hitler started by reassessing what he ate and drank. He noted which foods led

to the worst pains and cut them out of his diet. He eschewed rich pastries and meat in favour of vegetables and cereals, though some of the former – notably cabbage and beans – still proved troublesome. Zwieback, honey, mushrooms, curds and yoghurt all became dietary staples with oatmeal soup. Mashed linseed, potatoes baked in linseed oil and muesli were added for variety. Cakes and sweets, which Hitler had greatly enjoyed, were eliminated completely, as was bacon, which, up to 1932, had been a breakfast favourite. Even bread and butter no longer found a place on the Fuehrer's table.

Hitler turned to patent medicines for relief as well. He started by dosing himself liberally with a medicinal oil called Neo-Balestol. Originally, Balestol was a gun-cleaning oil used by soldiers in World War I.

Word got around in the trenches that it was also an effective cure for stomach pains. After the war, an enterprising businessman had concocted a similar oil, which was marketed under the trade-name of Neo-Balestol.

The problem was that one of Neo-Balestol's constituents was fusel oil. This was poisonous. Hitler, however, retained his faith in it, even though he suffered from headaches, double vision, dizziness and ringing in his ears immediately after taking a dose of it. The oil's potential toxicity was such that, according to Professor Ernst-Gunther Schenck, Neo-Balestol was eventually banned by the Reich Health Agency.

The Fuehrer finally settled on a different over-the-counter remedy – Dr Koester's Antigas Pills. The pills' ingredients included strychnine, belladonna or deadly nightshade and gentian. The gentian was harmless enough, but, taken in sufficient amounts, the strychnine and the atropine contained in belladonna would prove poisonous. The pills were safe enough provided Hitler stuck to the recommended dose of no more than two to four pills before each meal. In fact, he was probably swallowing as many as 20 of them on a daily basis.

Above: *Theodore Morell became Hitler's personal physician in 1937. The Fuehrer trusted him, but many thought he was a charlatan.*

Opposite: *Hitler is beginning to show the signs of age on this 1944 postage stamp.*

Hitler also dosed himself with laxatives regularly, wrongly believing that they would help to relieve his stomach pains and also would stop him gaining weight. His standby was a laxative called Mitilax, though later he experimented with other laxatives and enemas. He was terrified of becoming portly. He once commented to one of his aides: 'Imagine the Fuehrer of the Germans with a pot belly!'

HITLER'S PERSONAL DOCTOR

Diet and self-medication did nothing to relieve the underlying condition from which Hitler was suffering. The various doctors he reluctantly consulted could do nothing to help him. The Fuehrer became convinced that he was going to die in the not-too-distant future – probably of cancer like his mother.

Hitler confided his fears to Speer. 'I shall not live much longer,' he told him. 'I always counted on having time to realise my plans. I must carry out my aims as long as I can hold up, for my health is getting worse all the time.' Back in 1935, Hitler had anxiously asked Professor Carl von Eicken, a noted ear, nose and throat specialist called in to excise a tiny polyp on his vocal cords which was

affecting his voice, whether the growth was malignant. Von Eicken reassured him. The polyp turned out to be benign.

The abdominal pains continued to recur. Hitler grew weaker and thinner. Then he developed eczema. 'I had it on both legs,' he recalled. 'It was so bad that I was covered in bandages and couldn't even get my boots on.' Then, during Christmas 1936, he was introduced to a new doctor.

Theodor Morell was a fashionable Berlin general practitioner who had successfully treated Heinrich Hoffman, Hitler's close friend and personal photographer. It was Hoffman who introduced Morell to the Fuehrer. Most of Hitler's entourage disliked the obese, balding, venal and sycophantic Morell intensely. The Fuehrer's other doctors –the young surgeon Karl Brandt and the physicians Werner Haase and Hanskarl von Hasselbach – were united in dismissing him as a charlatan.

Hitler, however, took to Morell immediately. When he promised to cure him 'inside one year,' the Fuehrer was delighted. He praised him to the skies. 'Nobody has ever told me so clearly and precisely what is wrong with me,' he said. 'His method of cure is so logical that I have the greatest confidence in him. I shall follow his prescriptions to the letter.' From then on until the Fuehrer finally turned against him, Morell was Hitler's Doktorchen ('little doctor) – his resident court physician.

MUTAFLOR AND OTHER MEDICINES

First, though, Morell had to fulfil his promise. He suspected that abnormal bacteria in the intestinal tract were responsible for Hitler's stomach pains. Fortunately, so he thought, he had a suitable remedy to hand. This was Mutaflor, the trade name for a strain of living bacteria first cultivated by Professor Alfred Nissle in 1917. The healthy bacteria in Mutaflor overgrew the abnormal types and so restored a normal bacterial balance in the gut.

Above: *Hitler gloried in public acclaim until the war went against him. Then he shunned public appearances.*

Hitler liked the sound of Mutaflor. He had an inbuilt sympathy with all doctors who had broken away from standard medical practices, turning to naturalistic treatment with herbs, massage or other unconventional methods instead. He gave Morell the green light to start his Mutaflor course. The Fuehrer's new doctor accordingly began dosing him with Mutaflor capsules – a yellow capsule on the first day, a red one from the second to the fourth days and then two red capsules a day for as long as the treatment lasted.

Nissle advised carrying on with Mutaflor even when the samples of faeces Morell submitted to

him for analysis showed that the bacterial balance had returned to normal. He said it would help 'Patient A' as Morell codenamed Hitler, to cope with his heavy workload since 'one's nervous energy is increased.' Perhaps both men's enthusiasm was not that surprising since Nissle owned the rights to Mutaflor and Morell was a director of the company that manufactured it.

Morell kept administering Mutaflor to Hitler until 1943, though, as time passed, it became less and less effective. To take its place, he started giving the Fuehrer Glyconorm, which had to be injected intramuscularly. So, too, did Euflat, the next gastrointestinal drug he tried. When this, too, failed, he turned to a cocktail of Eukodal, a synthetic narcotic, and Eupaverinum, an anticonvulsant made from poppies. Morell mixed the two together in the same syringe and injected them intravenously.

It was the thin end of the wedge. As time passed, the number of medicines Morell injected into the Fuehrer multiplied. By mid-1943, Hitler was averaging three to five different shots daily. His arms were punctured so often that Morell sometimes could not find

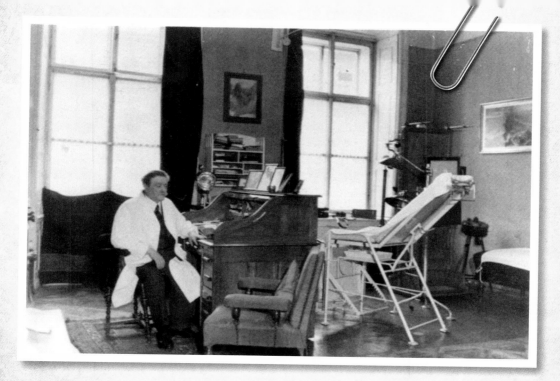

Above: *Edward Bloch was the Hitler's family doctor when the Führer was a boy. He was also Jewish.*

anywhere to insert a needle into the scarred veins. It was not for nothing that Goering sardonically christened Morell the 'Reich Injection Master'.

No one knew precisely what Morell was injecting into Hitler. Dr Erwin Giesing, an ear, nose and throat specialist who, much to Morell's displeasure, was called in to treat Hitler's head traumas after he was wounded in the July 1944 bomb plot, was particularly scathing. 'Morell,' he later wrote, 'converted the largely healthy man that Hitler had earlier been into one constantly plied with injections and fed with tablets which made Hitler more or less dependent on him. He played on Hitler's neuropathic nature by spouting utter rubbish about how Hitler's heavy workload meant that he was burning energy at the same rate as people in the tropics, and that the lost energy had to be replaced by all manner of injections like iodine, vitamins, calcium, heart-and-liver extract and hormones.'

DRUG DEPENDENCE

The doctors were not the only ones to start asking questions. In June 1943, Foreign Minister Joachim von Ribbentrop cross-examined Morell personally about his treatment of the Fuehrer. Was it a good idea for Hitler to be given so many injections, Ribbentrop wanted to know? Was he getting anything other than glucose (Morell injected this regularly to provide the Fuehrer with extra calories)? Was Morell giving him anything else? All Ribbentrop could get out of Morell by way of a reply was the laconic sentence: 'I give him what he needs.'

Many of the drugs Morell employed – most were the

EXTRA **THE STARS AND STRIPES** EXTRA

HITLER DEAD

*Fuehrer Fell at CP, German Radio Says;
Doenitz at Helm, Vows War Will Continue*

Churchill
Hints Peace
Is at Hand

Above: *Just before his death, Hitler sacked Morell. He suspected the doctor of trying to poison him.*

Opposite: *Hitler as he would have wished to be remembered — a poster produced for the 1939 Party Day.*

product of his own Hamma factory – were harmless. Some, like Ultraseptyl, which he liberally dispensed to treat colds, coughs and catarrh, were not. In particular, the Hamma-produced Vitamultin-CA, with which, from late 1941 onwards, Morell injected Hitler nearly every morning before he had even got out of bed, was suspect. It was Morell's practice to add a dose of Strophantin, a

digitalis preparation, to the same syringe. Was anything else added?

Certainly, the injections produced remarkable results. Heinz Linge, Hitler's valet, personally testified to its dramatic effects. Hitler, he said, immediately became 'fresh' – alert, active and ready for the day – even while the needle was still in his arm and before the injection had been completed. Other members of

the Fuehrer's headquarters staff concurred, especially when, as the news from the battlefronts worsened, Morell stepped up the number of injections. Walter Hewell, a Foreign Ministry official, recalled how Hitler became cheerful, talkative and tended to stay awake long into the night. Traudl Junge, one of Hitler's secretaries, said that, after an injection, he became extremely alert and garrulous. Even outsiders noticed the difference.

It is more than probable that Morell was injecting Hitler with some type of stimulant. The likelihood is that it was Pervitin, the trade name for methamphetamine, the German form of amphetamine. Methamphetamine was also present in the Vitamultin-F pills Hitler took to combat tiredness – a major problem for one whose sleeping habits were erratic to say the least. It seems Vitamultin-F was a one-off, prepared personally by Dr Kurt Mulli, Hamma's chief chemist, in his own home laboratory solely for the Fuehrer's use.

Hitler took up to ten Vitamultin-F pills daily. According to Linge, they enabled him 'to work long after his secretaries became too fatigued to work.' In addition to vitamins and methamphetamine, the pills contained caffeine, another stimulant that significantly increased the methamphetamine's effects.

HEART DISEASE AND PARKINSONIANISM

Constant dosing with methamphetamine – though, at times, Morell tried to wean Hitler off the drug – probably contributed to the Fuehrer's developing heart disease. Morell took his first electrocardiogram of Hitler's heart in August 1941; according to Dr Karl Weber, a well-known cardiologist Morell consulted, the tracing showed clear evidence of incipient coronary sclerosis. Subsequent cardiograms showed the condition slowly worsening.

Morell, however, did not reveal Weber's diagnosis to Hitler until December 1942 at the time of the siege of Stalingrad. Then he told the Fuehrer that he was the victim of progressive heart disease, adding that, as the blood vessels of the coronary artery narrowed, he might suffer attacks of angina pectoris as well. It was confirmation of a gradual, but constant physical decline that was to continue until Hitler's suicide at the end of the war.

There were other new symptoms as well. Early in 1943, Morell noticed that Hitler had developed a slight tremor in his left arm and saw that he was perceptibly dragging his left leg. He had dealt with the |Fuehrer's previous illnesses – notably dysentery and jaundice – effectively, but these symptoms were new to him. He initially thought they were hysterical in origin, but, to be on the safe side, he stepped up his intravenous glucose and iodine injections, combing them with intramuscular injections of a male sex hormone called Testoviron. Exactly what he thought this would accomplish is unclear, but it had little or no effect.

Paradoxically, the tremors stopped after Hitler was caught in the July 1944 bomb blast. However, they returned and grew steadily worse. Professor Maximilian de Crinis, a leading neurologist, put them down to Parkinson's disease, though he never personally examined the Fuehrer. Morell disagreed. Nevertheless, starting on 16 April 1945, he began injecting Hitler with Homburg 680, a well-known belladonna-type specific against the condition.

It was the last addition to the exhaustive catalogue of drugs he had prescribed for the Fuehrer. On 21 April, Hitler turned on him and sacked him. Morell fled beleaguered Berlin for the comparative safety of Munich.

The tremors probably indicated that Hitler was suffering from Parkinsonian syndrome, rather than the disease itself. He may also have suffered a minor stroke. Whatever their cause, Hitler was a physical wreck. Traudl Junge described him as being 'hardly able to walk' and 'needing help to sit down or stand upright.' Heinrich Hoffman concurred. His old friend, he said, was 'mentally stunted to the point of derangement and physically exhausted beyond redemption.' He was, Hoffman concluded, 'but a shivering shadow of his former self.' On 30 April, the Fuehrer took the only course of action left open to him. He committed suicide.

The Race for the A Bomb

Despite the commanding lead the Germans had established in nuclear physics before the Second World War, their efforts to build an atomic bomb failed. Was this because of Hitler's rabid anti-Semitism, which meant that their best nuclear physicists, who were Jewish, fled abroad? Was it due to basic flaws in their research? Or was it because their foremost scientists did not want to build a bomb for Hitler at all and sabotaged the process?

The story began in October 1938, when Otto Hahn and Fritz Strassman, two leading German scientists working at the Kaiser Wilhelm Institute in Berlin, discovered that when they bombarded uranium with neutrons they could split the uranium atoms' nuclei into two. Lise Meitner, a brilliant Jewish physicist whom Hahn had helped to flee to safety in Sweden, and Otto Robert Frisch, her young nephew, used the Berlin results to work out the basic mathematics of nuclear fission – the term coined by Frisch to describe what happened as energy and neutrons were released. The following March, French physicist Frederick Joliot, the son-in-law of Marie Curie, the discoverer of radium,

took the next step forward, when he demonstrated that the liberation of extra neutrons during the fission process was the result of a chain reaction. A whole new science had been born.

It was obvious to many physicists around the world that, at least in theory, it was now possible to create a self-perpetuating chain reaction, which would be triggered by the neutrons from one split atom bombarding the atoms surrounding it, splitting them in their turn. If controllable, such a chain reaction could be employed for constructive peaceful purposes. If, on the other hand, it was uncontrolled, the result would be an explosion of incalculable power. The great fear was that the

German physicists would use this newfound knowledge to build a Nazi nuclear bomb.

THE ALLIED PHYSICISTS

It was in Britain, though, that the possibility of creating an atomic bomb was first mooted. Rudolf Peirls, a young physicist who, like many of his Jewish contemporaries, had fled Germany to escape Nazi persecution, was one of the key figures in the process.

Peirls was the first physicist to address in practical terms the question of how much uranium would be needed in order to make an atomic bomb work. His initial conclusion was that the amount would be so massive that it could not possibly be carried by any aeroplane of the day. Soon, however, he changed his mind. In early 1940, he and his friend Otto Frisch began to try to calculate the proportion of U235 – the uranium isotope 235 – to uranium that would be needed to produce the explosive force required in an atomic bomb. As the two men worked on the problem, Peirls realised that his previous assumption had been incorrect. It now seemed as if the critical mass necessary to sustain a chain reaction might well weigh less than a pound.

Through an intermediary, Peirls and his associates communicated their findings to Sir Henry Tizard, the inventor of radar and one of the government's most respected scientific advisers. His backing led to the setting up of a scientific committee to investigate the feasibility of producing an atomic bomb. The conclusion, which the committee reached in December 1940, was short and stark. An atomic bomb, it opined was 'not just feasible; it was inevitable.' The committee's recommendation was that Britain should launch a full-scale effort to make such a bomb.

Progress was being made on the other side of the Atlantic as well. Long before the USA entered the war, physicists there

Above: *Walter Gerlach was another German physicist deeply involved in nuclear research.*

were determined to alert the US government to the risk of the Nazis becoming the first to build an atomic bomb. Many of these physicists – notably Leo Szilard, Enrico Fermi and Edward Teller – were themselves political refugees. Eventually, through Albert Einstein, they managed to alert President Roosevelt to their fears. The President grasped the significance of what he was being told immediately. 'Alex,' he said to Dr Alexander Sachs, who had been tasked with getting Einstein's fateful letter to the White House, 'what you're after is to see that the Nazis don't blow us up.'

What quickly became clear to the Americans and the British was

that, in nuclear physics, there were no shortcuts to success. Creating an atomic bomb inevitably was going to be incredibly costly. Nearly bankrupted by the cost of the war, Britain made a deal with the USA to hand over its latest technology – including the results of its nuclear research – as a quid pro quo for the arms, foodstuffs and other supplies the Americans were providing under the terms of lend-lease. Most of the scientists who had been involved in the project also moved across the Atlantic, where the US programme to develop an atomic bomb – codenamed the Manhattan Project – was getting underway with Robert Oppenheimer, Professor of Physics at Berkeley, California, as its scientific director.

NUCLEAR NAZIS

Almost up to the moment of the German capitulation, Oppenheimer and his fellow physicists lived in fear that the Nazis might pull the cat out of the bag and be the first to produce an atomic bomb. They had a healthy respect for German nuclear physics and its pre-war achievements. They also knew what an effort it had been – at least initially – to persuade the Western democracies to act to get

Right: *Werner Heisenberg, deviser of the theory of quantum mechanics, headed the German nuclear effort.*

Below: *Lieutenant-General Leslie R. Groves, a brilliant organiser, was put in charge of the Manhattan Project in September 1942.*

the nuclear programme up and running. Things must have been so much easier for their German counterparts, they reckoned. In a dictatorship like Hitler's, what the Fuehrer decreed automatically became law.

The physicists were worrying unduly. They were convinced that the Nazi economy was geared up for total war, whereas the opposite, in fact, was the case. Hitler and his fellow Nazis had little time for strategic thinking and long-term planning. Their diplomatic, military and economic efforts revolved around the notion of waging short, sharp wars. Thus, potentially war-winning weapons that would take time to develop were mostly put on the back

burner or simply ignored.

With this kind of attitude, it was hardly surprising that the Nazi nuclear effort was slow to get off the ground. What was christened the 'uranium project' started shortly after the outbreak of war in 1939, when an army research team, headed by physicist Kurt Diebner, began investigating possible military applications of nuclear fission. By the end of the year, Werner Heisenberg, the leading German physicist of the day, had calculated that, in theory, fission chain reactions were achievable. If slowed down and controlled in a so-called 'uranium machine' – what otherwise would be termed a nuclear reactor – these chain

reactions would generate energy. If uncontrolled, the result would be a 'nuclear explosive' many times more powerful than any conventional one.

Whereas only natural uranium was suitable for use in a 'uranium machine', Heisenberg concluded that U235 could be employed as an explosive. In summer 1940, Carl Friedrich von Weizsacker, one of his colleagues, took the speculation further. If, he said, a 'uranium machine' could be made to sustain a chain reaction, some of the more common isotope U238 in the uranium fuelling it would be transmuted into what he called 'Element 94' – in other words, plutonium. This, von Weizsacker postulated, would be far easier to obtain than U235 and would be just as powerful an explosive.

Heisenberg himself summed up what von Weizsacker was hoping to accomplish. In a lecture he gave to high-ranking Nazi bigwigs in early 1942, he said: 'As soon as such a machine is in operation, the question of the production of a new explosive takes a new turn, according to an idea of von Weizsacker. The transformation of uranium in the machine produces, in fact, a new substance, which is most probably, just like U235, an explosive of the same unimaginable effect. This substance can be obtained much more easily from uranium than U235 because it may be separated chemically from the uranium.'

The German physicists were already aware that they could create significant amounts of U235 only by isotope separation. First they tried a chemical process known as thermal diffusion and then, when this proved a failure, turned to building massive centrifuges to literally spin the various uranium isotopes apart. Plutonium looked like an easier bet, but, of course, it required a nuclear reactor capable of achieving a self-sustaining chain reaction to make it. The Germans never accomplished this; the reactor they started to build towards the end of the war never went critical.

Left: *The Norsk Hydro plant was the Germans' sole source of the heavy water they needed as a moderator for their atomic pile. They mistakenly believed graphite would not work.*

Below: *Members of the Allied Alsos team, tasked after the war with ferreting out Nazi Germany's closely guarded nuclear secrets.*

THE NAZIS MISCALCULATE

Two crucial miscalculations contributed to the delay. To produce a controlled reaction, a 'uranium machine' needs what is technically termed a moderator – a substance that slows down the fast neutrons liberated by the chain reaction. The Americans chose graphite, which was relatively easy to obtain. In Germany, however, because the industrial granite he used in his experiments was not pure enough, Professor Walther Rothe mistakenly convinced his colleagues that what is technically termed heavy water would have to be used instead.

The only plant producing heavy water in any quantity was located in Norway. After the Nazi occupation of the country in 1940, production was ordered to be stepped up, though it still fell short of what was needed to satisfy German demands. Then, in 1942 and 1943, British commandos, aided by the Norwegian Resistance, tried to sabotage the plant. The second attempt was successful.

The Germans decided to abandon production In Norway and move all the existing stocks of heavy water to Germany. The ferry carrying the stocks across Lake

Left: *Examining the German nuclear pile after the war. It never went critical.*

Below: *Samples of the deuterium oxide, or heavy water, produced by the Norsk Hydro plant.*

Tinnsjo was sabotaged and sank in deep water. The Nazi nuclear programme never recovered from the loss. The other miscalculation was made by Heisenberg himself. He grossly overestimated the amount of fissile material that would be needed to make an atomic bomb.

What is also clear from the historical record is that, unlike the Manhattan Project, there was no single driving force behind

the Nazi nuclear effort. Certainly, Heisenberg's role was ambivalent to say the least. When it came to organising the attempt to develop an atomic bomb, he seems to have left the competing research teams to squabble amongst themselves. For whatever reason, too, when Heisenberg met with Albert Speer, Hitler's armaments minister, in June 1942, he downplayed what his colleagues had accomplished and was pessimistic about

Above: *The R.A.F. and U.S.A.A.F. tried to bomb the Norsk Hydro plant unsuccessfully several times. The failure forced the Allies to resort to sabotage.*

whether or not a bomb could be produced at all.

When Speer enquired what financial support would be needed in order to speed the programme up – the armaments minister had it in mind to give Heisenberg several hundred million marks immediately – all Heisenberg asked for was a million or so marks to fund further research. Speer immediately concluded that there was no

possibility of producing a German atomic bomb in the foreseeable future. He poured the money he had been thinking of allocating to the nuclear programme into rocket research instead.

After the war, Heisenberg recalled how he and his colleagues 'felt already in the beginning that, if it were possible at all to actually make explosives, it would take such a long time and require such an enormous effort

that there was a very good chance that the war would be over before that could be accomplished... we thought that the probability that this would lead to atomic bombs during the war was nearly zero.' Rudolf Meutzel, the head of German weapons research, not only concurred with Heisenberg, but went further. In July 1943, he reported to Goering. 'Though the work will not lead in a short time towards the practical use of engines (nuclear reactors) or explosives, it gives on the other hand certainty that in this field the enemy cannot have any surprises in store for us.'

WHY THE GERMANS FAILED

Such over-confidence, as much as anything else, was one of the major reasons for the German failure. If they, the best nuclear physicists

in the world, could not produce an atomic bomb, then no one else could possibly achieve the breakthrough. Their self-confidence was demonstrated by the reactions of ten of their number – Heisenberg and Otto Hahn among them – to the news that the Americans had dropped the first atomic bomb on Hiroshima. At the time, they were interned at Farm Hall, a house near Cambridge, following their capture at the end of the war. The house was bugged so that their captors could listen in on their conversations.

Shortly before dinner on 6 August 1945, Otto Hahn was the first of the Germans to be told that an atomic bomb had been dropped successfully on Hiroshima. He promptly broke the news to his fellow internees. The Farm Hall transcripts clearly demonstrate how stunned the German physicists were by the news. They simply could not believe that the Americans had succeeded where they had failed. Heisenberg's immediate reaction was to dismiss the news as nothing more than a gigantic bluff.

After dinner, the Germans crowded around a radio to listen to a full report of the bombing for themselves. They spent the next two days trying to establish

Above: *When Norwegian saboteurs sank this ferry in February 1944, the loss of the heavy water it carried finally put an end to Germany's nuclear research programme.*

Opposite: *Otto Hahn was one of the first to recognise that a uranium atom would split when bombarded by neutrons.*

how the Allies had succeeded in building the atomic bomb and the reasons why they had failed to do so. It was apparent from their conversations that they still did not understand the complex workings of the bomb completely – or, indeed, those of a nuclear reactor – but gradually they began to piece the picture together.

Otto Hahn, who himself was relieved that the Nazis had not succeeded in building a bomb and had had nothing to do with the nuclear research programme, taunted his fellow-scientists with their failure. 'If the Americans have a uranium bomb,' he said, 'then you are all second-rate.' Horst Korsching commented that the news showed 'at any rate that the Americans are capable of real cooperation on a tremendous scale,' adding that this 'would have been impossible in Germany.' Von Weizsacker admitted that 'even if we had got everything we wanted, it is by no means certain whether we would have got as far as the Americans and English have now.' Heisenberg said that he 'was absolutely convinced by the possibility of our making a "uranium engine", but I never thought we would make a bomb.' For his part, he continued, 'at the bottom of my heart, I was really glad that it was to be an engine and not a bomb. I must admit that.'

THE BOMB THAT WASN'T

Up until 2005, the accepted consensus was that the Nazi attempt to build nuclear weapons had been a total failure. Then, in 2005, German historian Rainer Karlsch came forward with a highly-controversial claim. He said he had hard evidence that a second German nuclear research team, led by Kurt Diebner, had managed to develop a primitive fission-fusion bomb. This was tested, Karlsch alleged, three times – first on the Baltic island of Ruegen in autumn 1944 and then in Thuringia in March 1945.

Karlsch's assertions, though, have been dismissed by practically every other serious historian. Germany, they say, never possessed the U235 and plutonium necessary to build any sort of true nuclear device. The most the Germans could possibly have achieved was the construction of a so-called 'dirty bomb' – a conventional weapon laced with enough radioactive material to pollute everything in the area surrounding the explosion – but this, too, is considered highly unlikely.

Above: *The Allies won the race when they dropped two atomic bombs on Hiroshima and Nagasaki in August 1945. Had the German nuclear effort succeeded, mushroom clouds could well have shrouded New York and London.*

Index

Picture Credits

Bundesarchiv, pp.54, 59b, 60, 68, 69, 115, 211, 233, 232, 236, 238

Getty Images, pp.65, 148

Catwalker, Shutterstock.com, p.221

Golovniov, Igor, Shutterstock, p.136

Johnbraid, Shutterstock.com, p.22

Kingsley, Gregory J, p.25

Klebsattel, Rolf, Shutterstock.com, p.224

MrHanson, Shutterstock.com, p.239b

Neftali, Shutterstock.com, p.235

Penfield, Daniel, p.131

Robert Jackson Collection, pp.12, 13, 14, 15, 17, 18, 19, 21, 22, 24, 29, 30, 32, 33, 36, 38, 39, 40, 41, 42, 43, 44t/b, 45, 46, 47, 49, 50, 52, 53, 55, 57t/b, 58, 59t, 62, 66, 67, 72, 73, 74, 75, 77, 80, 82, 83, 84, 85t/b, 88, 89, 90, 92, 96, 98, 99, 100, 101, 102, 104, 105, 106, 107, 108, 109, 110, 111, 118b, 120b, 122, 124, 125, 126, 127, 129, 130, 132, 134, 135, 137, 138, 139, 141, 142, 143, 144t/b, 145, 146, 147, 149, 150t/b, 152, 153, 155, 156, 157, 158, 161t, 162, 164, 165t/b, 169, 170t/b, 171, 172, 173, 174, 175, 176, 177, 179, 180, 181, 182, 183, 184, 185, 186, 187t/b, 188, 189, 190, 191, 192, 193, 194, 195t/b,

196, 197, 198t/b, 199, 202, 203, 204, 208, 212, 213, 214, 219, 220, 222, 223, 225t/c/b, 226tl/tr, 227, 228, 229, 231, 234, 237, 240, 242, 243t/b, 244, 245, 246t/b, 247, 248, 249, 250, 251

Wikipedia, pp.27, 28, 35, 64, 71t/c, 78, 79, 81, 86, 95, 97, 112, 114, 117, 118t, 120t, 133, 161b, 205t/c/b, 206, 207, 209, 210, 215, 216, 218